DRAWN FROM THE SOURCE

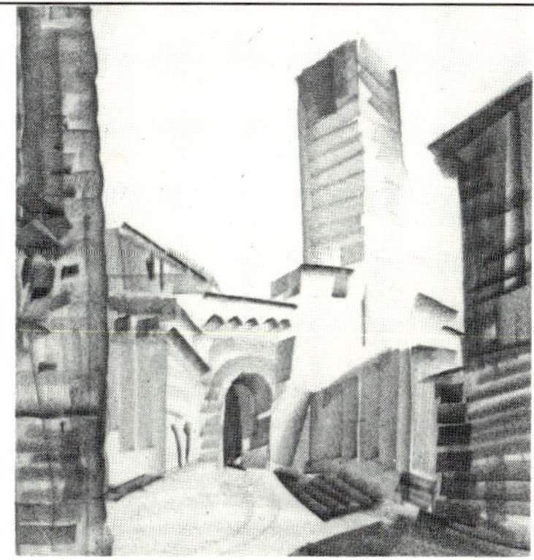

The Travel Sketches of

LOUIS I. KAHN

Eugene J. Johnson

Michael J. Lewis

WITH AN ESSAY AND SITE PHOTOGRAPHS BY

Ralph Lieberman

WILLIAMS COLLEGE MUSEUM OF ART

The MIT Press
Cambridge, Massachusetts
London, England

Library of Congress Cataloguing-in-Publication Data
Johnson, Eugene J., 1937–
Drawn from the source: the travel sketches of Louis I. Kahn / Eugene J. Johnson, Michael J. Lewis; with an essay and site photographs by Ralph Lieberman.
p. cm.
Exhibitions: Williams College Museum of Art, April 6–June 9, 1996; Jewish Museum, New York; Art Institute of Chicago.
Includes bibliographical references.
ISBN 0-913697-20-6 (pbk.)
1. Kahn, Louis I., 1901–1974—Sketchbooks, notebooks, etc.—Exhibitions. 2. Europe—Pictorial works—Exhibitions. 3. Egypt—Pictorial works—Exhibitions. I. Lewis, Michael J., 1957– . II. Lieberman, Ralph. III. Williams College. Museum of Art. IV. Jewish Museum (New York, N.Y.) V. Art Institute of Chicago. VI. Title.
NA2707.K33A4 1996
720' .22'22—dc20 96–4672
CIP

Williams College Museum of Art ISBN 0-913697-20-6
MIT Press ISBN 0-262-60026-9

Distributed by the MIT Press.

This catalogue accompanies the exhibition "Drawn from the Source: The Travel Sketches of Louis I. Kahn," presented at the Williams College Museum of Art from April 6 through June 9, 1996. The exhibition was organized by Eugene J. Johnson, Class of 1955 Professor of Art, and Michael J. Lewis, Assistant Professor of Art, Williams College, with the assistance of Deborah Rothschild, Curator of Exhibitions at the Museum.

COVER

Street and tower, San Gimignano, 1928, graphite on paper, 16.8 x 16.2 cm, Collection of Sue Ann Kahn (cat. no. 12)

EXHIBITION VENUES

Williams College Museum of Art
Williamstown, Massachusetts

The Jewish Museum
New York, New York

The Art Institute of Chicago
Chicago, Illinois

WILLIAMS COLLEGE MUSEUM OF ART
Main Street
Williamstown, Massachusetts

CONTENTS

Director's Foreword and Acknowledgments iv

Lenders to the Exhibition viii

KAHN'S GRAPHIC MODERNISM
Michael J. Lewis 1

Color Plates 25

SKETCHING ABROAD
Eugene J. Johnson 33

IN THE FOOTPRINTS OF THE MASTER:
The Photographic Campaign
Ralph Lieberman 111

Exhibition Checklist 119

Notes 124

Select Bibliography 135

Credits 136

FOREWORD AND ACKNOWLEDGMENTS

Louis I. Kahn made his first trip to Europe in the spring of 1928 and traveled for a year, sketching as he went. Recently the Williams College Museum of Art had the good fortune to acquire one of the drawings from this trip, a luminous watercolor and pencil work on paper, *Towers, San Gimignano, Italy* of 1928. The drawing was brought to our attention by Michael J. Lewis, assistant professor of art here at Williams College. An historian of American art and architecture, Lewis had organized a small exhibition of Kahn's travel drawings in 1993 as part of his duties as historiographer at the Canadian Centre for Architecture in Montreal. There he came to know Sue Ann Kahn, the architect's daughter, and in 1994 he introduced her to the museum at Williams; before long we were talking about an in-depth exhibition of Kahn's travel drawings.

Critical interest in Kahn's travel drawings has been consistent: in addition to being exhibited at the Canadian Centre, they were shown in 1978 at the Pennsylvania Academy of the Fine Arts, and some were featured in 1991–94 in the large traveling exhibition "Louis I. Kahn: In the Realm of Architecture" organized by the Museum of Contemporary Art, Los Angeles; Kahn's two-dimensional work is also the subject of Jan Hochstim's book *The Paintings and Sketches of Louis I. Kahn* (New York: Rizzoli, 1991). However, "Drawn from the Source: The Travel Sketches of Louis I. Kahn," which charts Kahn's travels in North America, Europe, and Africa, is the first exhibition to explore systematically the drawings and their relation to his architecture. While Kahn is recognized today as one of the great architects of our century, this particular body of work is not nearly as well known as his built work. The travel sketches are of particular interest to us precisely because they provide the major evidence for Kahn's early architectural thinking and eloquently foreshadow what he would later accomplish in actual buildings. What we appreciate today—his unparalleled sensitivity to light and his unique articulation of materials, space, and scale—can already be sensed in these drawings.

Professor Lewis enlisted the collaboration of Eugene J. Johnson, architectural historian and the Class of 1955 Professor of Art at Williams College. Professor Johnson has had a long involvement with the college museum, including the organization as guest curator of the Charles Moore exhibition in 1986 celebrating the Moore expansion of the museum. I have found that his unbounded enthusiasm for his subject, his untiring drive to unearth new information, and his ability to communicate all of it to others are precisely the reasons why he is considered such a distinguished teacher and scholar. Working with Professors Lewis and Johnson has been a pleasure, and I would like to thank them for bringing their scholarship, their knowledge, and their love of architecture in general, and Louis Kahn in particular, to the museum.

Key to their concept is an understanding of the sources for these drawings, hence "drawn from the source." Two quite remarkable developments have come to light as a result of this undertaking. For the first time, the precise locations from which Kahn sketched these drawings have been documented; and Kahn's own postcards of some of the sites have very recently been discovered. It is not far-fetched to consider a "source" both a geographical or physical site and its own reproduction; one is as "real" as the other. And clearly they each provided Kahn with what he was looking for.

Ralph Lieberman, noted architectural photographer, is responsible for the documentation of the physical sites. During the summer of 1995 Lieberman followed in Kahn's footsteps and photographed in Greece, Italy, and France. His trip was made possible by grants from the Graham Foundation for Advanced Studies in the Fine Arts, as well as Williams College Division I Research Funds; we are greatly indebted to both the foundation and the college for providing this important support at a crucial early stage of the project.

Mr. Lieberman's contribution to the project has been considerable, and I am most grateful to him for the role he has played in helping to realize this exhibition and publication. I was pleased to learn that this undertaking has provided all three contributors with a genuinely collaborative experience, an occurrence which is often aspired to but only rarely achieved.

On behalf of the guest curators, I would like to extend our sincere appreciation to the many individuals who have aided their research in countless and substantive ways. Michael Lewis would like to acknowledge David B. Brownlee of the University of Pennsylvania, Marian Burley-Motley, Susan Glassman, Thora Jacobson of the Fleischer Art Memorial, Bruce Laverty of the Athenaeum of Philadelphia, Henry Magaziner, H. Barrett Pennell, Jr., and Susan G. Solomon. E. J. Johnson would like to thank James S. Ackerman, Veronique Barthes, Malcolm Bell, Robert Bridges, Antonella Bucci, Charles Dew, Peter F. Dorman, Zirka Filipczak, Rita Freed, Jan Hochstim, William Jordy, Rosemary Lane, William MacDonald, Joan C. Malloy, Miranda Marvin, Vincenzo Palumbo, Franklin Robinson, Robert Russell, Peter Smithson, Anne Griswold Tyng, William Wagner, and Charles Williams. Professor Johnson is especially grateful for his 1995 fellowship at the Francis Christopher Oakley Center for the Humanities and Social Sciences at Williams College, which provided him with the opportunity to pursue his research on Kahn. Both professors have asked me to express their profound gratitude to Julia Moore Converse, director of the Architectural Archives, University of Pennsylvania, whose graciousness and generosity have been truly remarkable. In addition, a number of students have played a crucial part in helping us accomplish all tasks large and small; we would like to thank Mary LaRuffa, Silvina Fernandez-Duque, and especially Isabel Taube, who has been truly indispensable.

No exhibition or publication occurs, however, without the dedication and skills of a committed and talented staff. The staff at the Williams College Museum of Art consistently distinguishes itself and has once again made certain that we can be proud of our efforts. First of all, Deborah Rothschild, the museum's curator of exhibitions, must be thanked for her role as project director; she has overseen and choreographed every phase with her customary enthusiastic involvement and eye for excellence. Brenda Niemand, normally the public relations assistant, has taken on the job of editor for this catalogue and skillfully produced this handsome and informative publication under enormous time constraints; I am deeply grateful to her. I extend my most sincere appreciation to Diane Hart Agee, registrar, and Scott Hayward, preparator; their coordination and management of the packing, shipping, framing, and installing of the actual drawings has been nothing short of spectacular. And finally, to Marion Goethals, assistant director, and Zelda Stern, director of development, go my profound thanks, for the former's always calm administrative insights and the latter's legendary fundraising talents.

We are particularly grateful to Kristina Almquist, the designer of the catalogue, and Amy Reichert, with whom we consulted on the challenging task of designing the exhibition itself. Their respective creative talents are vividly in evidence on the pages and walls of "Drawn from the Source."

All exhibitions like this one rely on the good will and generosity of the lenders; it is a true sacrifice for each of them, whether private collectors or public institutions, to release their drawings for even a short length of time. There is no doubt that the high esteem and deep affection with which Louis Kahn is held contributed significantly toward a universal willingness to lend to this show. There is one lender, sadly, for whom this acknowledgment comes too late: Esther Kahn, who generously lent three of her husband's works, died just before this catalogue went to press.

After its showing at the Williams College Museum of Art, the exhibition will travel to the Jewish Museum in New York City and then to the Art Institute of Chicago. At the Jewish Museum, "Drawn from the Source" will be accompanied by a presentation of Kahn's studies for synagogues. Working with Joan Rosenbaum, director, and Eric Zafran, deputy director for curatorial affairs, has been a pleasure. At the Art Institute of Chicago, Kahn's travel sketches will be presented with the travel drawings from that institution's permanent collection; in some instances viewers will be able to compare other architects' interpretations of the same sites that Kahn sketched. I am grateful for the enthusiastic support of James Wood, director and president of the Art Institute; John Zukowsky, curator of architecture; and Martha Thorne, associate curator of architecture. I am delighted to be able to share this exhibition with these two fine institutions.

Just as the lenders are vital to a successful outcome, so too are the sponsors. I speak for all of us in the arts when I express my most sincere gratitude to the National Endowment for the Arts. The prestige and honor of a grant from the National Endowment for the Arts not only encourage further support but bestow national significance on the museum. A grant from another crucial federal agency, the Institute of Museum Services, provides a portion of this museum's general operating funds. We must do all we can to sustain the federal cultural agencies so that the impact of their important work is not diluted. In addition, funding from the Andrew W. Mellon Foundation enables the museum to initiate and develop projects with Williams College faculty, and this specific project has benefited enormously from the foundation's enlightened support. The Graham Foundation, cited earlier, is recognized as a valuable resource for many architectural history ventures; it provided critical sponsorship at just the right time, and we are very grateful. And finally, Williams College, through the Office of the President, has provided support for the catalogue and the scholarly contributions of Professors Lewis and Johnson. The Williams College Museum of Art is fortunate indeed to have a parent institution that is so encouraging and supportive.

I have saved one individual for last, and that is Sue Ann Kahn. She has been an active participant in every phase of the project, from beginning to end, and it is to her that we all owe our heartfelt thanks. Not only is she lending more than half of the drawings in the exhibition, but her advice and collaboration have been a guiding force for each of us. I am also deeply grateful to her for her willingness to work with the staff of the Jewish Museum to develop the complementary exhibition of her father's synagogue designs. Her acute sensitivity to and love of her father's work have inspired us to produce an exhibition and publication that we hope would have made Louis Kahn himself proud.

Linda Shearer
Director

February 1996

LENDERS TO THE EXHIBITION

Olivia Israeli Abelson and Milton Abelson

The Architectural Archives of the University of Pennsylvania

M. Louis Goodman

Mr. and Mrs. James Gubelmann

Herbert F. Johnson Museum of Art, Cornell University

William S. Huff

Esther I. Kahn

Sue Ann Kahn

Museum of American Art of the Pennsylvania Academy of the Fine Arts

Theodore T. Newbold and Helen Cunningham

Private Collection

Der Scutt, New York

Robert Venturi

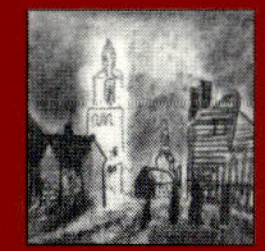

1 • 24

KAHN'S GRAPHIC MODERNISM

Michael J. Lewis

Virtually everything Louis I. Kahn had learned was made irrelevant in October 1929. His architectural training and practice had revolved around several fundamental certainties—that buildings would be composed in plan according to certain classical principles; that their forms would derive ultimately, if distantly, from the monuments of classical antiquity and the Renaissance; that architectural designs would be presented in sumptuous ink renderings prepared with great effort; and that commissions would flow from private patronage. One by one, as the Depression unfolded across America, each of these certainties was cast off, until Kahn had to reassemble his architectural identity almost from scratch. The rest of his career was one prolonged and extraordinary act of catching up.

In the years after 1929, Kahn transformed himself into a modernist of impassioned conviction, taking his impulses from Walter Gropius and Le Corbusier and preoccupied with those cardinal modernist themes of housing, urban form, and technology. Of course, a whole generation was making this transition, some less happily than others, but Kahn was more a man of the Beaux-Arts than were many of his colleagues. For him the realignment must have been particularly traumatic. That staple of Beaux-Arts education, the graded wash drawing, was Kahn's strong suit; now it was held in contempt. And precisely the kind of building at which he was most experienced, the classical civic building, had become a favorite target of modernist abuse. Nonetheless, after the passage of several decades, Kahn's dormant and long suppressed Beaux-Arts lessons would re-emerge to stamp his modernism. In this eventful trajectory—saturation at first in the Beaux-Arts, then conversion to modernism, and at last a distinctive and original synthesis of the two—Kahn's painting and sketching followed a similar but not parallel course, sometimes racing ahead of his architecture, and sometimes turning back to rake over earlier ideas. Only by including Kahn's drawings is it possible to write his architectural biography.

Kahn was the last of the great pupils of Paul Cret (1876–1945), that extraordinary architect and educator who brought the architecture of the French Beaux-Arts to its apogee of development in the United States.[1] Cret had been recruited in 1903 to revitalize the school of architecture of the University of Pennsylvania. This he achieved in one heroic decade of activity, culminating triumphantly when four of his students in a row won the Paris Prize of the American Society of Beaux-Arts Architects, a winning streak that was interrupted only when the First World War intervened.[2] Cret promoted a variant of Beaux-Arts architecture that was strikingly lean and rather cerebral when compared with the swaggering examples of New York or Boston. He initiated Kahn into an architecture of austere planes, tautly drawn masses, and strict axial order. So strong and decisive were these compositional devices, Cret insisted, that they could function without any applied column screens, florid moldings, or sumptuous porticoes.[3]

Kahn studied at Penn from 1920 until 1924, taught by Cret and his stable of young and faithful disciples, including John Harbeson and Harry Sternfeld. Not only did Kahn imbibe the modern classicism of Cret, but he also learned the kinds of

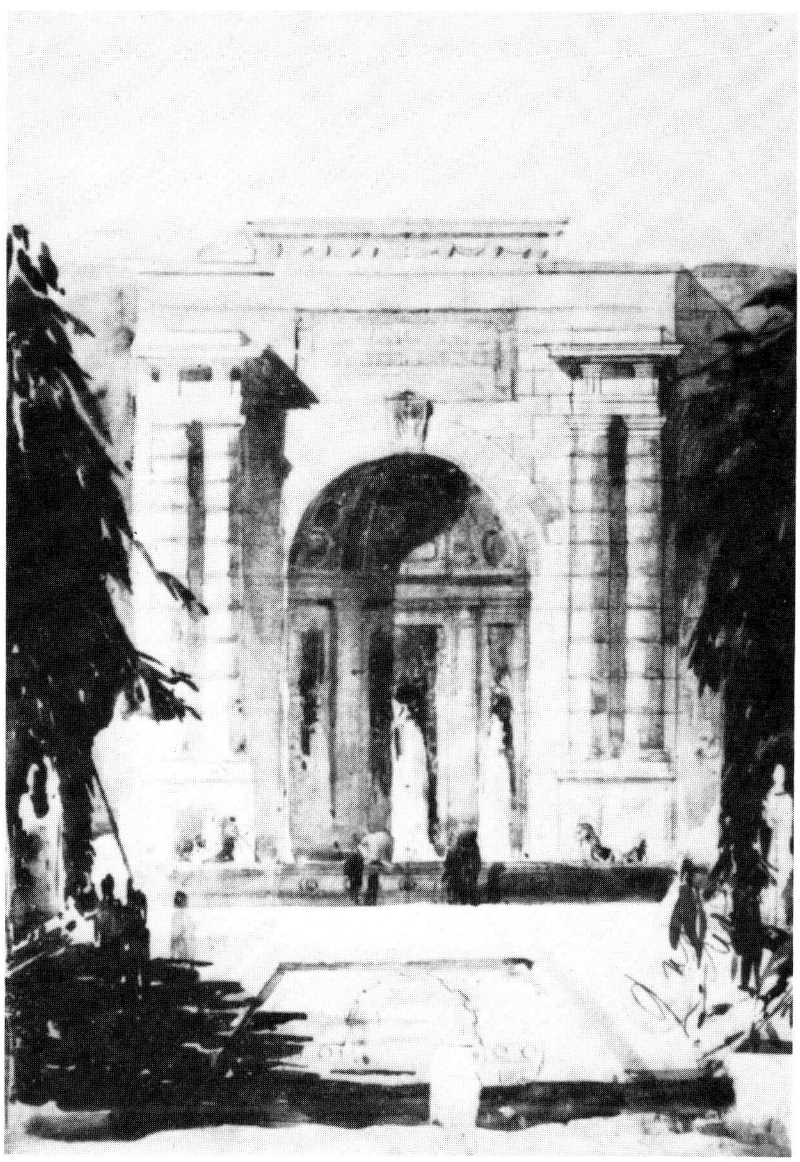

commissions that the Frenchman favored—typically big public buildings like museums, schools, or libraries. For commercial architecture there was little room in Cret's system; here too Kahn followed suit.

Kahn's performance at Penn was not spectacular, nor were his grades, and he came no closer than a ninth place in his try for the Paris Prize. Still, he had a good visual facility.[4] His rendering in watercolor and ink wash was deft, especially during the timed and rather stressful *esquisse.* One of his winning projects in this competition was judged good enough to be included in a rare portfolio of student work published by the school around 1928 and overlooked in the Kahn literature.[5] This was a senior grade *esquisse* showing a monumental fountain, a tersely delineated classical aedicule set within a frame of dense foliage (fig. 1). But unlike the tight draftsmanship of the fountain itself, Kahn's staffage was an impressionist flurry of loose and rapid brush strokes, placed far forward of the plane of the fountain. Here was an early hint of his predilection for layering drawings in depth, superimposing multiple framing planes in front of the more distant spaces of his drawings. Clearly this rapid study was selected to show the ready facility with brush and ink that Penn's School of Architecture

FIGURE 1
A MONUMENTAL FOUNTAIN
(from *University of Pennsylvania, School of Fine Arts, Architecture,* Philadelphia: University of Pennsylvania, no date)

inculcated. For it the architect, still called Louis Isadore Kahn, won a Second Mention.

The 1920s were a heady time to be at Penn. Philadelphia was at the summit of her prosperity, a powerhouse of industry and manufacturing among American cities, and a vast campaign of public and commercial expansion was proceeding apace. Modern art found a cordial welcome here, and the Pennsylvania Academy of the Fine Arts brought Man Ray, Georgia O'Keeffe, John Marin, and others to the public eye.[6] The city's architecture was also the subject of national scrutiny as a splendid array of civic monuments, surely America's finest ensemble of Beaux-Arts urbanism, unfolded along the new Benjamin Franklin Parkway.[7] At the same time, a school of residential architecture had arisen in the works of Edmund Gilchrist, Wilson Eyre, Mellor, Meigs & Howe, and others, which was marked by flawless taste and scrupulous sensitivity to site, materials, and the regional vernacular. Penn's graduates could expect to leap into private practice, or at least into lucrative positions in successful offices.

Kahn, strapped for money, spent his student summers as a junior draftsman in a series of local offices, where he encountered the broad range of buildings rising around the city. In 1921 he worked for Hoffman and Henon, a firm that specialized in engineering and industrial work. The following year he sought out the vigorous, venerable William D. Hewitt, who a half century earlier had taken the young Louis Sullivan under his wing; Hewitt, who had helped teach Sullivan drafting in 1873, was a poignant intersection in the lives of these two American Louises.[8]

Kahn, who had never developed an appetite for the wooing of businessmen, navigated toward civic rather than commercial work. Upon graduation he entered the office of John Molitor, Philadelphia's municipal architect, the man responsible for the city's hospitals, fire houses, park structures, and police stations. From 1924 to 1927 he worked here, his chief achievement being the preparation of drawings for the Sesquicentennial Exhibition. Perhaps America's least-remembered World's Fair, the exhibition commemorated the 150th anniversary of the Declaration of Independence. Its buildings were stripped classical boxes built of temporary materials on steel frames, with little ornament besides the sculptural frieze capping the Fine Arts

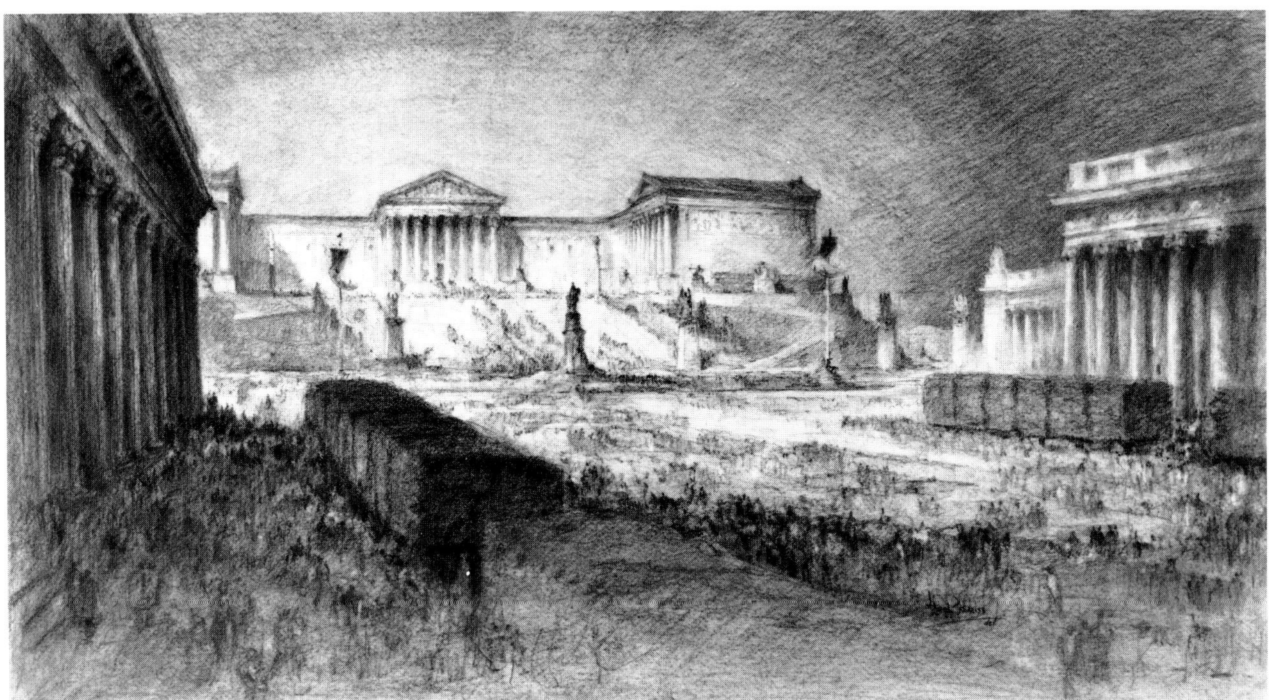

FIGURE 2
Hugh Ferriss, illustrator.
PHILADELPHIA MUSEUM OF ART, 1925; photograph courtesy Philadelphia Museum of Art

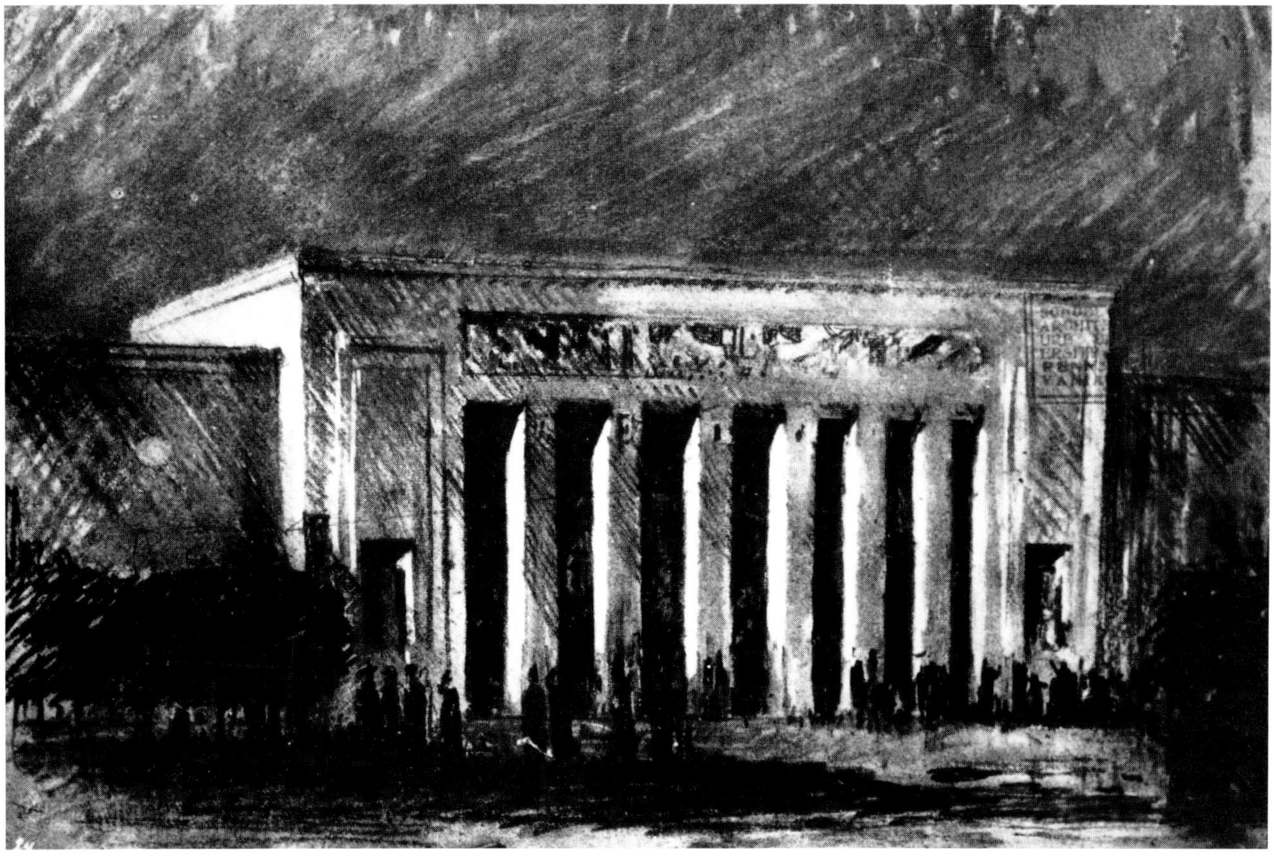

FIGURE 3
Louis I. Kahn, illustrator. *MAIN PORTICO, PALACE OF LIBERAL ARTS, Sesquicentennial International Exhibition, Philadelphia,* 1926 (from *American Architect* vol. 130, November 5, 1926)

Building. Years later, Kahn remembered that he had been chief designer, assisting the city architect who was traditionally more administrator and bureaucrat than artist. In fact, Molitor's principal assistant was W. J. Sutphen, and Kahn was only one of a "corps of assistants" that included twenty other draftsmen.[9]

Kahn prepared some of the renderings, smoky atmospheric studies that derive closely from Hugh Ferriss (1889–1962).[10] Ferriss was America's most celebrated renderer of the day, and there were few draftsman who did not try to match his strong tonal contrasts and loose pencil technique. Typically, Ferriss's buildings emerge from dark streets and skies blazing with the reflected glow of some unseen light source, although it is seldom clear whether this is sunlight, electric lamps, or even moonlight. He did not favor a hard-edged image, working rather with loose, even fuzzy textures, which had their counterpart in the soft-edged photographs of the period.

Ferriss's reputation was made in New York, but in 1925 he was summoned to Philadelphia to prepare a rendering of the city's proposed art museum. This design had just been completed after long deliberation and restudy by the associated architects Borie, Trumbauer, and Zantzinger, and Ferriss now rendered it in crayon, showing it as the heroic culmination of the city's grand new Beaux-Arts axis (fig. 2). To hire a renderer from New York was rather unusual for Philadelphia, which had its own tradition of accomplished renderers. Clearly the new monochrome renderings being published in New York were highly prestigious. Kahn's renderings for the Sesquicentennial buildings, prepared roughly around the time that the art museum drawing was exhibited, were in the distinctive Ferriss mode. The drawing of the Palace of Liberal Arts, surviving only in a poor contemporary illustration, is typical of these.[11] In it, the details of the building melt away and it becomes an assembly of flat planes and piers (fig. 3). The principal focal point, the portico of the palace, is treated with the fewest lines, and as in Ferriss's art museum, it emerges as a light-bathed

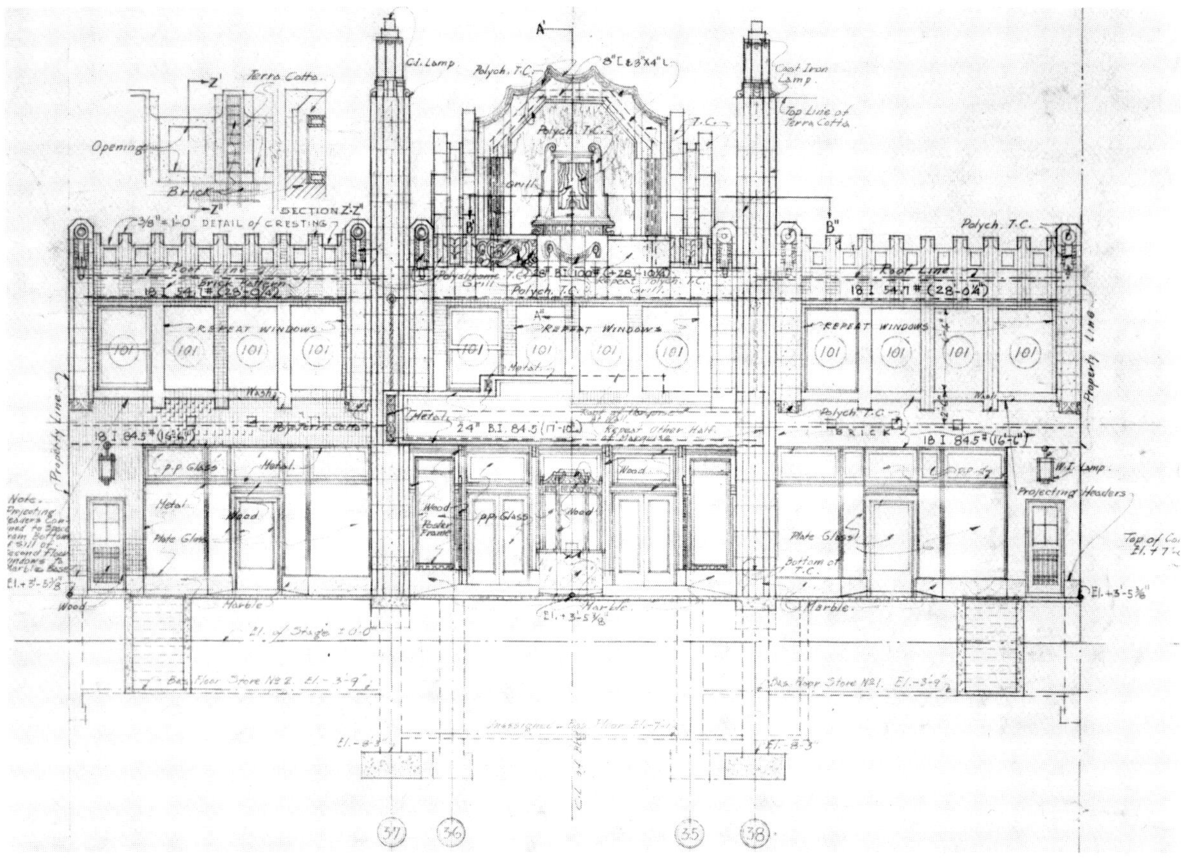

Figure 4
Louis I. Kahn, draftsman.
ELEVATION OF ANTHONY WAYNE THEATER, Wayne, Pennsylvania, William H. Lee, architect, 1927; photograph courtesy Athenaeum of Philadelphia

form from amidst the heavily drawn background. Kahn's lines were less patient, however. The darkness of the sky was drawn in a rough and scratchy scribble, the strokes darting in every direction. Nor was space described with Ferriss's consummate control. Nonetheless, this drawing is vigorous and forceful, and of a much higher caliber than the rendered line drawings that most Philadelphia architects offered. The judicious use of illumination, and an almost photographic overexposure of the central subject, would remain with Kahn, as we shall see.

In Molitor's crowded workshop Kahn accomplished at least one lasting thing: he came into contact with a circle of young draftsmen, many of them Jewish, including Hyman Cunin and Joseph Rovner, whom he would assemble into a workshop in the 1930s. After the work of the exhibition was complete, in 1927, he moved into the office of William H. Lee, an adroit but overworked designer of exotic motion-picture palaces. Here he spent a year serving as a first-rate draftsman, summoned to labor over the cartouches and crestings after lesser hands had traced in the outlines (fig. 4). It is likely that he also produced the presentation drawings.[12]

These jobs as a draftsman paid well, and Kahn patiently saved, but they were not positions leading to an independent career, surely his goal from the beginning. For this he had to find a different trajectory. Here Kahn faced the perennial dilemma of the young architect: to establish a private practice one requires a clientele, but would-be clients need the assurance of seeing completed works. Until there was a tangible record of achievement, the first projects must come from family or friends. And here Kahn was woefully ill-equipped. His range of acquaintances was still largely restricted to the Jewish immigrant circles around his family, not a terribly prosperous group. Philadelphia had a growing number of Jewish architects, such as Gabriel Roth or Clarence Thalheimer, but they struggled along working for Jewish realtors and merchants, their work consisting of apartment house alterations and storefronts. The great institutional patronage of the city was closed to them. The only Jewish architect to escape from this parochial patronage was Louis Magaziner, and he had done so by forming partnerships with socially connected gentiles. But he drew his clients from far more privileged ranks than those in which Kahn moved.[13]

Philadelphia traditionally closed ranks to the outsider. The city's social elite was much smaller than in cosmopolitan New York and less likely to be awed by financial success; inward-looking, it banked, built, and married among its cousins.[14] If men of achievement and wealth such as Peter Widener and Albert Barnes found Philadelphia society impenetrable, how much less welcoming would it be to the immigrant Russian Jew! The architects who dominated the city in the 1920s were typically Quaker or Episcopalian, graduates of Haverford College or Princeton, and members of the Rittenhouse Club, Union League, or the Athenaeum. Against such old, established firms as Mellor, Meigs & Howe or Willing, Sims & Talbutt, Kahn could scarcely hope to compete; he would be lucky to find a berth in the drafting room.

Kahn was hardly the first young architect to be richer in talent than in social affiliation, and like others before him he searched for a way to convert ability into reputation. Reflexively he now turned to his strength, the gift he had cultivated since long before architecture school: his skill with the pencil and the brush. In the spring of 1928 he devised plans for a year-long sketching tour of Europe. Not only would this trip serve as an act of social grooming, but it would also hone his talent as a renderer. Architect-illustrators were a recent phenomenon in the 1920s. There had long been anonymous renderers in architecture, but the explosion of reproduction technology toward the turn of the century created a class of what might be called celebrity renderers, including Hughson Hawley and Jules Guerin.[15] Now a type of architectural success was possible without the necessity of assembling a clientele, but simply through deftness at the drawing board. In 1920 a journal had even been launched to showcase the work of these facile pencils: *Pencil Points*. This was the year Kahn arrived in architectural school, and there is considerable indirect evidence that he scoured its pages monthly. Here were unveiled the renderings of America's greatest architectural artists, including Theodore de Postels, Gerald K. Geerlings, and the ubiquitous Ferriss. In addition, painters such as George Bellows and Louis Lozowick showed recent sketches, invariably accompanied with some professional notes on technique and materials. This was the first and only time in history when an American journal was devoted to the professional architectural renderer.

Leaving Lee's office, Kahn sailed for England in May 1928, returning almost a year later. During his travels he made his way across northern Europe as far as the Baltic states and then down to Italy, where he spent five months, and back through France. Here was a classic Grand Tour, on the eighteenth-century model. However, unlike his eighteenth-century counterpart, Kahn apparently spent little time in the actual study of ancient monuments. After all, these were available in published form and in far more reliable photographs. Instead he concentrated on rendering buildings that were generally of no architectural or historical significance. And even where he confronted a major monument, such as the Cathedral of Assisi, he invariably drew it in a way that provided little technical information. Rather, he worked to develop his own distinctive hand, assured and confident, based on simple and solid masses that are described by strong tonal contrasts. He showed little interest in the clutter of architectural detail on the surface, moldings or cornices, and instead of laboring in good Beaux-Arts fashion over the angles of the cast shadows, he broke his buildings into faceted surfaces whose contrasting tonal values expressed volume. Compare Kahn's drawing of San Gimignano (fig. 31) with the contemporary sketch of Louis Skidmore (fig. 5), whom he came to know during his travels; the one is all outline and edge, the other all tone and volume. This year of drawing clarified much of his thinking about architecture. If Cret had been tightening the envelopes of his buildings,

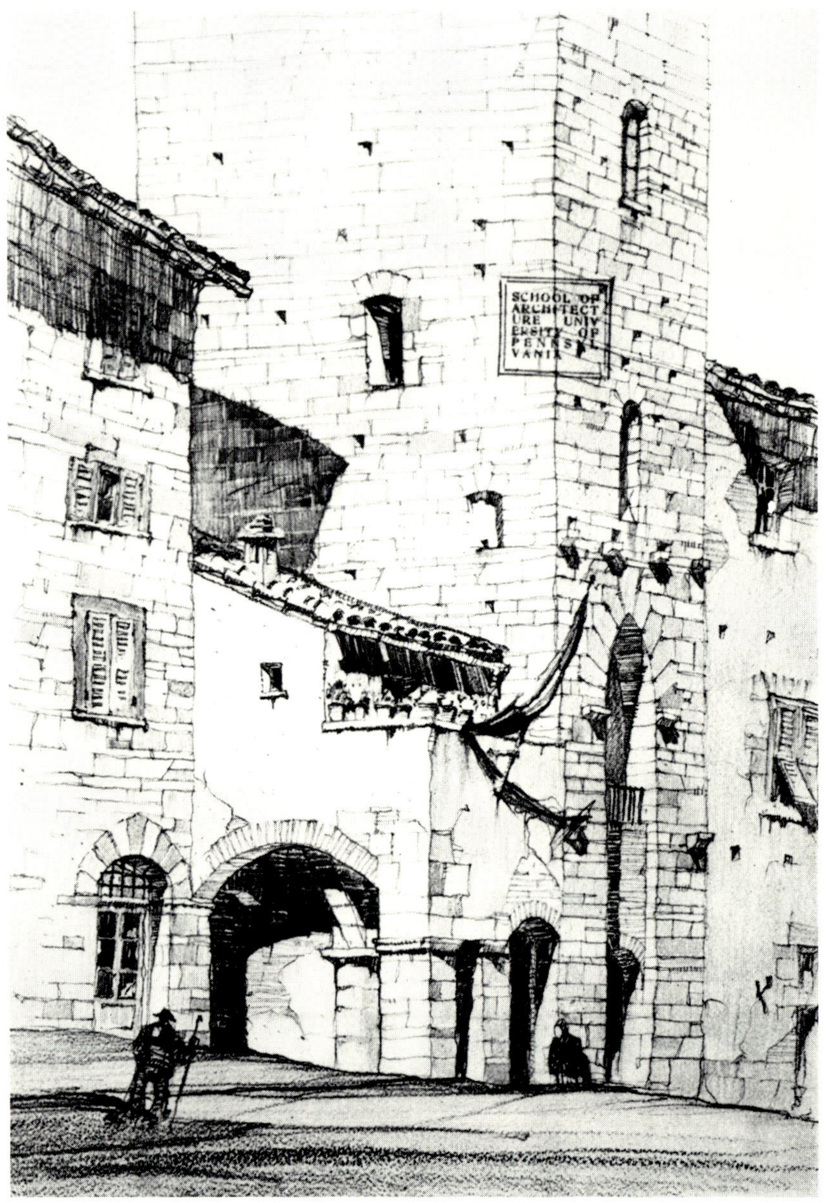

FIGURE 5
Louis Skidmore. *SAN GIMIGNANO* (from *Pencil Points* vol. 10, October 1929)

Kahn pushed the process further in these drawings. Now, on his return, the drawings were ripe for publication or exhibition. With their presentation, the final act of his trip—and his program of social grooming—would be complete.

When Kahn returned to Philadelphia in May 1929, he met with an unpleasant surprise. Before his departure he had discussed plans to go into partnership with another architect, Sydney Carter Jelinek. The two were old friends; classmates at Penn, both had graduated in 1924 and then worked together on the designs for the Sesquicentennial buildings.[16] Jelinek, however, had died unexpectedly during Kahn's absence, leaving him without a job. This misfortune was decisive for Kahn's career. In

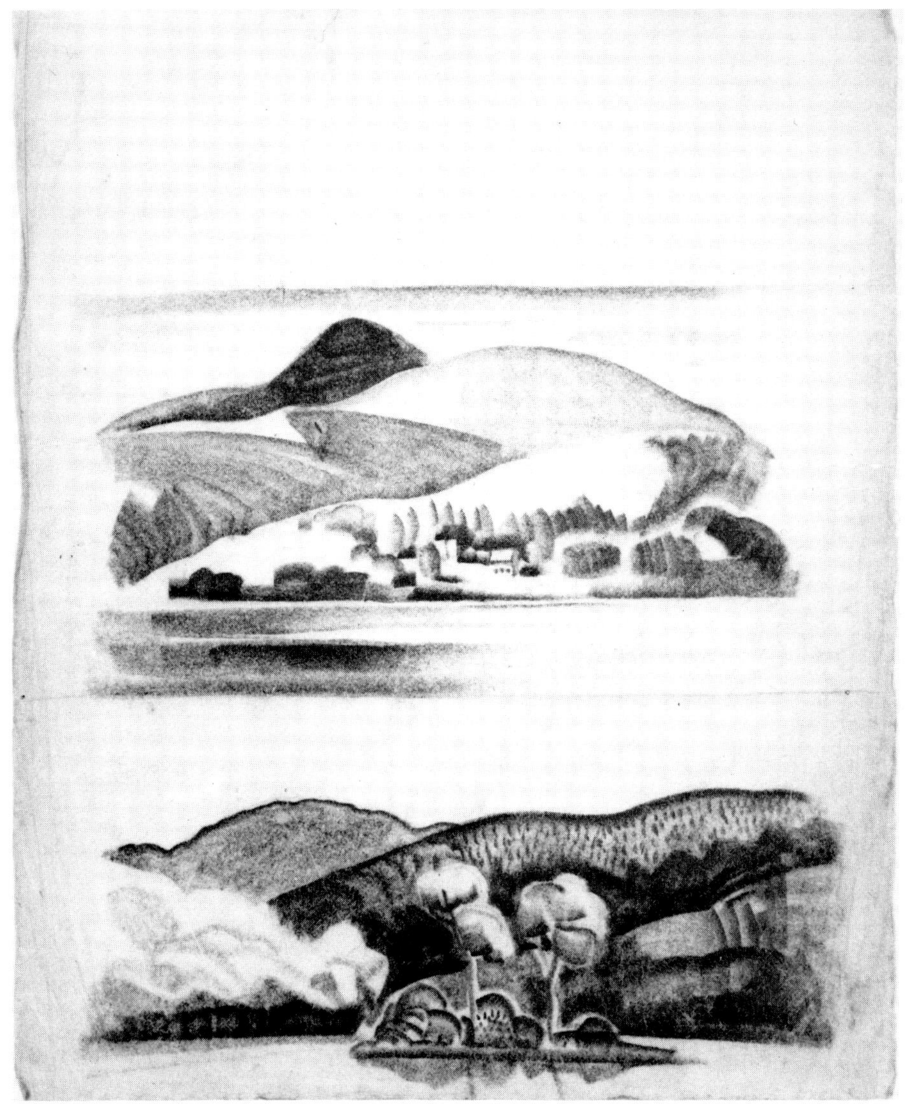

FIGURE 6
PARADOX LAKE, ADIRONDACKS,
1930, graphite on paper
(cat. no. 28)

place of the ill-fated partnership, a position was found for him in the hallowed office of Paul Cret as a paid "designer," no longer the humble draftsman who had ghosted for Molitor and Lee.[17] At last able to work at the summit of the profession, he took his place among the men who had taught him. Cret was building one of his finest works, the handsome and restrained Folger Shakespeare Library (1928–32), that last piece of silver coined in the mint of the Beaux-Arts. One of Kahn's first tasks was to study the circulation of the building.[18] But architecture did not consume him completely, and he remained preoccupied by his year of drawing. For the next three years he devoted a considerable amount of time to drawing, exhibiting, and even writing about sketching. If the sketching tour had been only a means to an end, he might have shifted his energies completely to architecture. This he did not do. Clearly, drawing loomed large in his conception of architecture, and of himself.

Now lucratively employed, Kahn could marry, and after his wedding on 1 August 1930 he and his wife Esther took a honeymoon trip that began in the Adirondacks, crossed into Quebec, and took them back to Philadelphia by way of Atlantic City.[19] This was the first trip he had taken since his return from Europe, and he once again began to sketch avidly, although in a less focused and disciplined way than on his earlier trip. For a time he continued to work with the descriptive graphite contours that he had learned in Italy, as in his drawings of Paradox Lake in the Adirondacks, so much in the style of his European work that they were long thought to portray Switzerland (fig. 6). These drawings, and his portfolio of sketches from Europe, now became the subject of exhibitions. For the next three years he showed in the annual watercolor exhibition of the Pennsylvania Academy of the Fine Arts. Oddly, he chose to show nothing in the city's principal architectural show, that of the T-Square Club. Perhaps Kahn, his position secure in the prestigious Cret firm, felt no need to display his purely architectural work; instead he chose to present himself as an artist. At any rate, the exhibitions of the Academy had been a showplace for Philadelphia architects for a century.

In his first showing, at the 27th Annual Watercolor Exhibition in 1929, Kahn presented seven of his travel sketches.[20] Although this event was nominally a watercolor show, Kahn chose to concentrate on works in graphite. His selection of drawings was not representative of his Grand Tour; it included only Italian subjects, taken from the conclusion of his trip. Although he had dabbled in various techniques during the early weeks of the trip, he was now presenting the single unified style that had emerged as he descended through Italy. Likewise he chose subject matter of rather unified character. Formal architectural studies of monumental buildings, such as he had made during the early months of the trip, were largely absent. Instead he presented himself as an artist of the vernacular scene, showing works such as *Fisherman's house, Conca dei Marini* or *Study of a tree, Borghese Gardens*, in which structures, trees, and mountains all melt into a landscape of expressive curves. The architecture that was depicted was part of an ensemble, not presented in a way descriptive of the building or useful for the architect. Typical of this was his drawing of *Fisherman's house, Conca dei Marini* (fig. 41), based on a postcard view (fig. 40). In it, a stone building rests among beached fishing boats, its odd vaulted roof setting off great curves in the surrounding rocks, as if ripples of some internal force were spreading concentrically outward. Despite the stooped fisherman in the foreground, the whole scene is as desolate and ghostly as any of the enigmatic townscapes of Charles Burchfield.

In the next year's exhibit, in 1930, Kahn again recycled his European trip when he submitted a watercolor entitled *Danube country* (fig. 7).[21] Inspired apparently by recollections of his trip from Germany to Italy, the watercolor shows a village as a ghostly white band on the base of roundly generalized mountains, all pushed up to the surface to emphasize the planarity of the image. Here Kahn is shifting from the angular chiseled forms of 1920s art deco to the undulating curves of 1930s American Scene painters, such as Thomas Hart Benton. The subject matter of *Danube country* was also in the spirit of the American Scene, which featured the landscape of rural America, with its agriculture and wooden farm buildings. But other influences contended as well. Kahn regularly visited the Academy of Fine Arts, where he confronted the recent work of Charles Demuth, Charles Sheeler, John Marin, and other American artists, and traces of those encounters flicker through his variegated canvases of the 1930s. In *Danube country*, for example, the painted frame within the surface, the spare brush strokes, and the white of the paper showing through the colors are all hallmarks of Marin's work. Just as Kahn had learned in the twenties from Ferriss, the best of the architectural renderers, he continued to learn from his contemporaries, adding to the "thick folder" of clippings that served as his artistic reference manual.[22]

Despite the local hubbub over the Academy show, Kahn knew it to be a purely parochial event; his ambition must have run deeper. Now he took steps to present his drawings to a national audience, publishing them in *Architecture* and in the newly formed *T-Square Club Journal*.[23] As at the Academy, he presented a selection of the graphite sketches, repeatedly mining the Positano and San Gimignano material. But the most prestigious venue, and the most logical one, *Pencil Points*, published nothing by Kahn. Perhaps he did not submit; more likely, he did and was rebuffed. His article

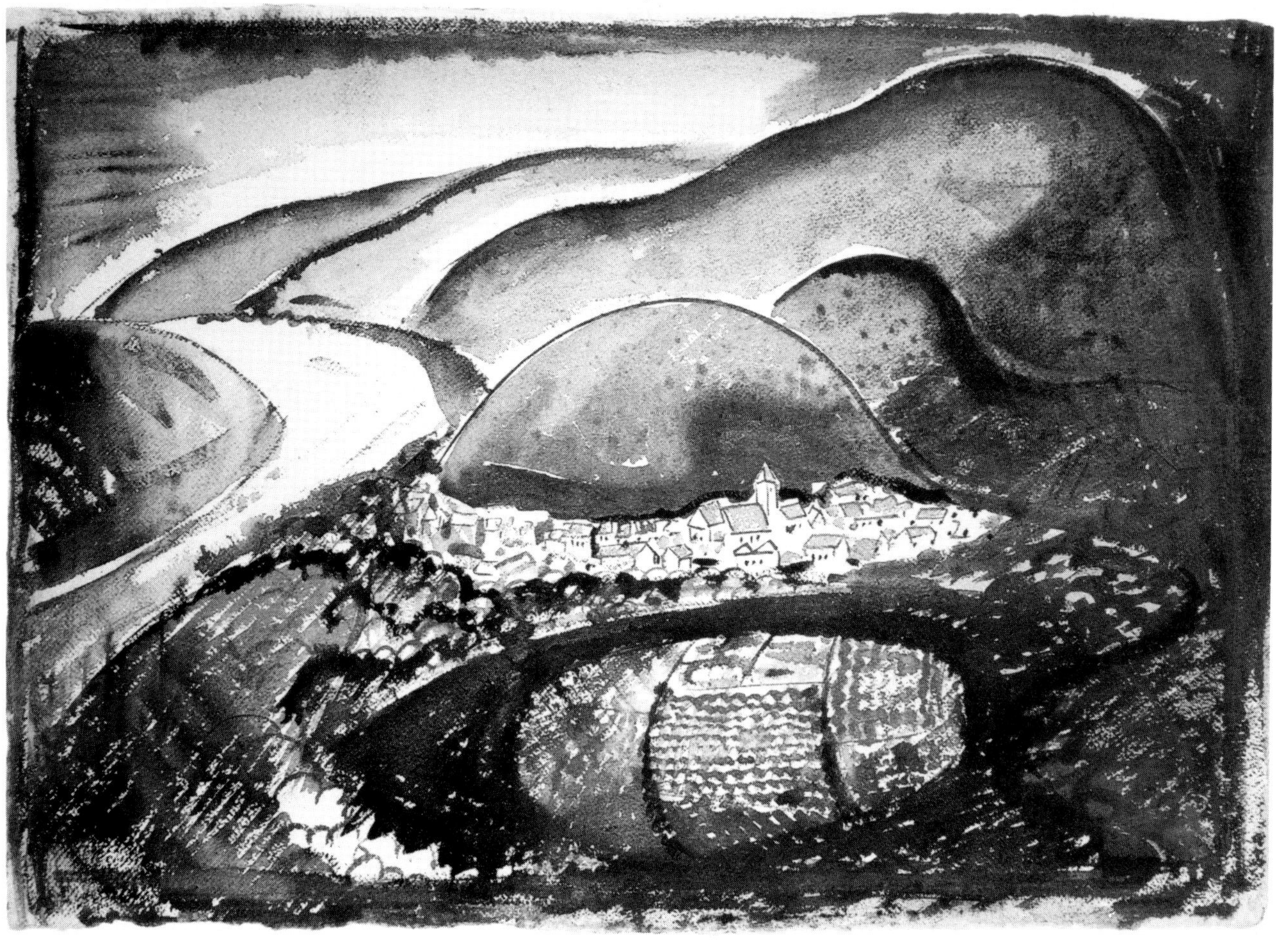

on architectural sketching in the *T-Square Club Journal*, "Value and Aim in Sketching," implies as much.

Writing formally for the first time about architecture, Kahn spoke venomously about "the many cast iron styles of architectural representations" and singled out for abuse two renderers, mentioning them by name: "Why most of the drawings can only be expressions in terms of stylistic Ernest Born, or the shallow Chamberlain, is more than I can understand."[24] Both artists were rising stars in *Pencil Points*, and their sketches filled its pages in the months after Kahn's return. Samuel Chamberlain, a particular favorite of the journal, worked in a meticulous topographic style that represented the best of the picturesque technique popular at the turn of the century. Ernest Born was a more interesting figure. A California-trained architect who had worked with John Galen Howard and the New York office of Gehron & Ross, Born preferred subjects of powerful and simple monumentality, which he turned into abstract, looming icons (fig. 8).[25]

Clearly, Kahn was criticizing the two figures who most reminded him of himself. Close in age to Kahn, they had also recently returned from lengthy sketching tours of Europe. Chamberlain's "shallow" vignettes were not too far from Kahn's drawings of mid-1928, before the great loosening began. And Born's luminous masses, glowing with internal energy, were not unlike Kahn's more expressionist drawings, such as his lovely watercolor of the town of Positano.[26] In many cases these contemporaries had sketched the same buildings, such as those at Assisi or San Gimignano, that Kahn had. It must have been demoralizing to watch them best him at his own game.

FIGURE 7
DANUBE COUNTRY, 1930
[JH128], watercolor on paper; 39 x 55.9 cm; Collection of Sue Ann Kahn

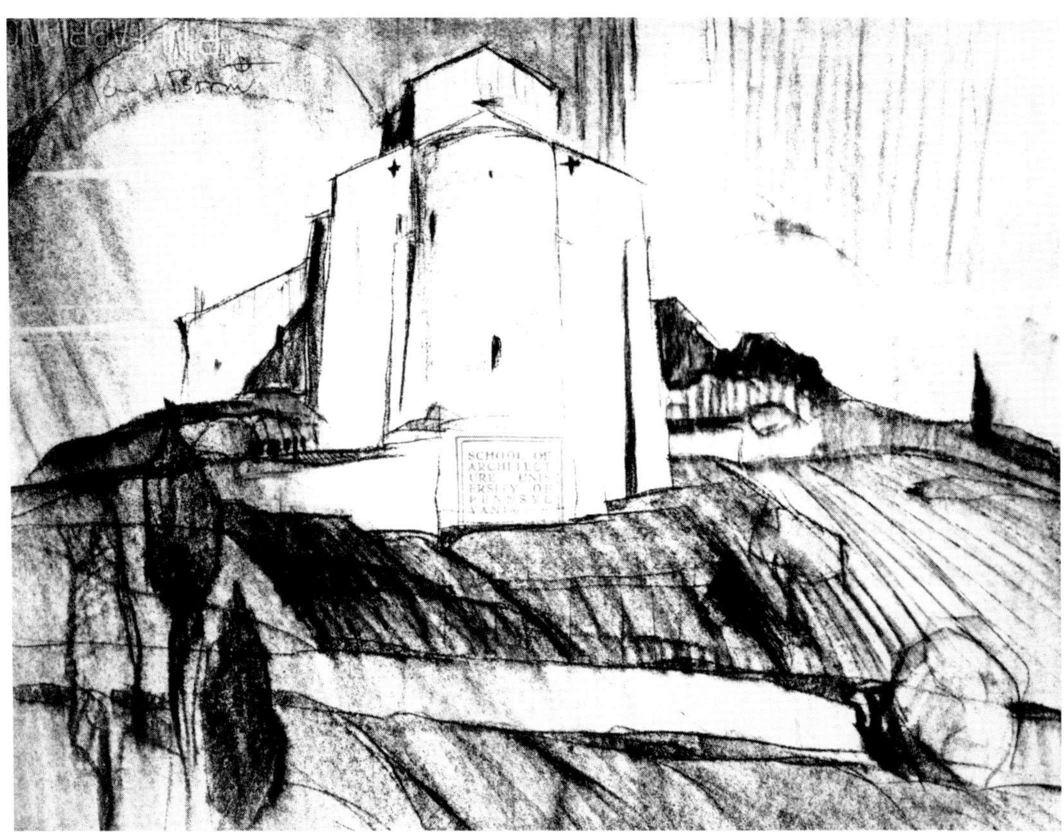

FIGURE 8
Ernest Born. *SAN PIETRO, TOSCANELLA* (from *Pencil Points* vol. 10, November 1929)

"Value and Aim in Sketching" remained Kahn's only published article until 1944, and it reveals much about his early thought on architecture and drawing.[27] In particular, it is a plea for a free and expressive treatment of the subject, rather than a meticulous topographic view. Photographic fidelity as a goal was rejected absolutely:

> *I try in all my sketching not to be entirely subservient to my subject, but I have respect for it, and regard it as something tangible—alive—from which to extract my feelings. I have learned to regard it as no physical impossibility to move mountains and trees, or change cupolas and towers to suit my taste.*[28]

Certainly Kahn did just this, move cupolas and towers at will, as a glance through the pages of this catalogue shows. But these ideas were not unique to Kahn. They were in the air in the twenties, and they show up again and again in the pages of *Pencil Points*. There, for example, the distinguished historian of medieval architecture, Kenneth Conant, argued that the subject should be subjugated to the higher artistic demands of the drawing as a whole:

> *I do not hesitate to draw from two or more points of view . . . if it helps to arrange the picture better, or to make the planes read more easily . . . . If the shadow of a buttress on a tower is prettiest at half-past one and the light effect on a neighboring chapel is handsomest at half-past two, I am not likely to let either effect go, as the camera would have to do.*[29]

Conant's article appeared in Kahn's senior year at Penn, and it seems to have stuck with him. Of course, Kahn's language reveals a much higher degree of personal involvement—"extract my feelings," "suit my taste"—than did Conant's, who was talking of moving shadow lines and wall planes, not, presumably, entire mountains.

Kahn's method differed strikingly from that of Conant. In the early months following his arrival in England, Kahn's drawings appear to have been worked out more or less completely on site. Everywhere there is a cautious fidelity to the objects drawn; everywhere, the evidence of direct observation. Later these fully developed on-site renderings disappear in favor of increasingly abstracted sketches. This evolution culminated as he developed his famous graphite technique of faceted planes, treated in horizontal strokes, with its determined suppression of detail. Kahn, however, made a second kind of outdoor drawing, quite unlike Conant's freely interpreted views. These were preliminary field sketches that were to serve as the basis for a fully worked-up final version. A series of these preliminary drawings would be made (or, occasionally, a postcard would serve the same function), much like the preliminary studies of an architectural program. These studies would then be refined into a solution, a composition that would be completed later, perhaps after the passage of much time, at the drawing table:

> *I try to evolve a composition, and make every sketch count for as much value to me as may be gotten out of a design problem. To make a sketch of this sort requires, of course, the making of many impressions and notes "on the job." You must then get away from it all to work over and crystallize your thoughts in order to develop the picture in the form of a readable design.*[30]

Kahn's *Coming storm*, which dates to the same year as his article, was the product of such an exercise.[31] This work, shown in the 1931 watercolor exhibition of the Academy, was another generalized landscape under a moody sky, a recycling of the theme of his *Danube country*.[32] This time it was a storm over Woodstock, New York, rather than the Danube River. At first a charcoal sketch the size of an index card was dashed off on a sheet of notebook paper (fig. 9). Here again were the hills arranged as broad arcs of circles, fringed with houses and a church composed of flat arrangements of planes. This charcoal preliminary sketch was then worked up into a pair of larger watercolors, one a full-fledged study and the other a spare outline drawing. In all three sketches and the final version the basic components are the same: the rounded hill at center right, the cluster of gabled houses along its slope, the swirls of trees and cultivated fields that frame the village. But in the nearly monochrome line drawing these elements collapse into a flat planar arrangement of parallelograms and swirls (fig. 10). The sense of perspective depth is upset as completely as in a late Cézanne, as the high horizon line lifts the landscape up like so much patterned wallpaper. Only the receding size of the houses acts to push the line back into the plane of the picture. Kahn seemed to relish such ambiguity. "Did not the Chinese painters," he asked, "who succeeded better than any others in representing space, ignore almost completely perspective as we practice it?"[33]

The final version of *Coming storm* was rather different (pl. 6). Marin's mark was still apparent, especially in the bleeding through of the white of the paper, and also in the heavily drawn frame within the picture. And cultivated fields were again contoured with single brush strokes. But now the tonality was dramatically intensified to convey an imminent thunderstorm, captured just at the moment when rolling black clouds coming over a hilltop overwhelm the bright afternoon sun. This rather violent contrast between the storm and the sunlit houses was absent in the earlier sketches. There was nothing of it in his simple contour sketch. Apparently it was the result of what Kahn called "crystallizing" his thoughts about his picture, discovering in the lonely houses on the hillside after repeated drawing—both in line and in tone—a kind of primal encounter of land and sky.

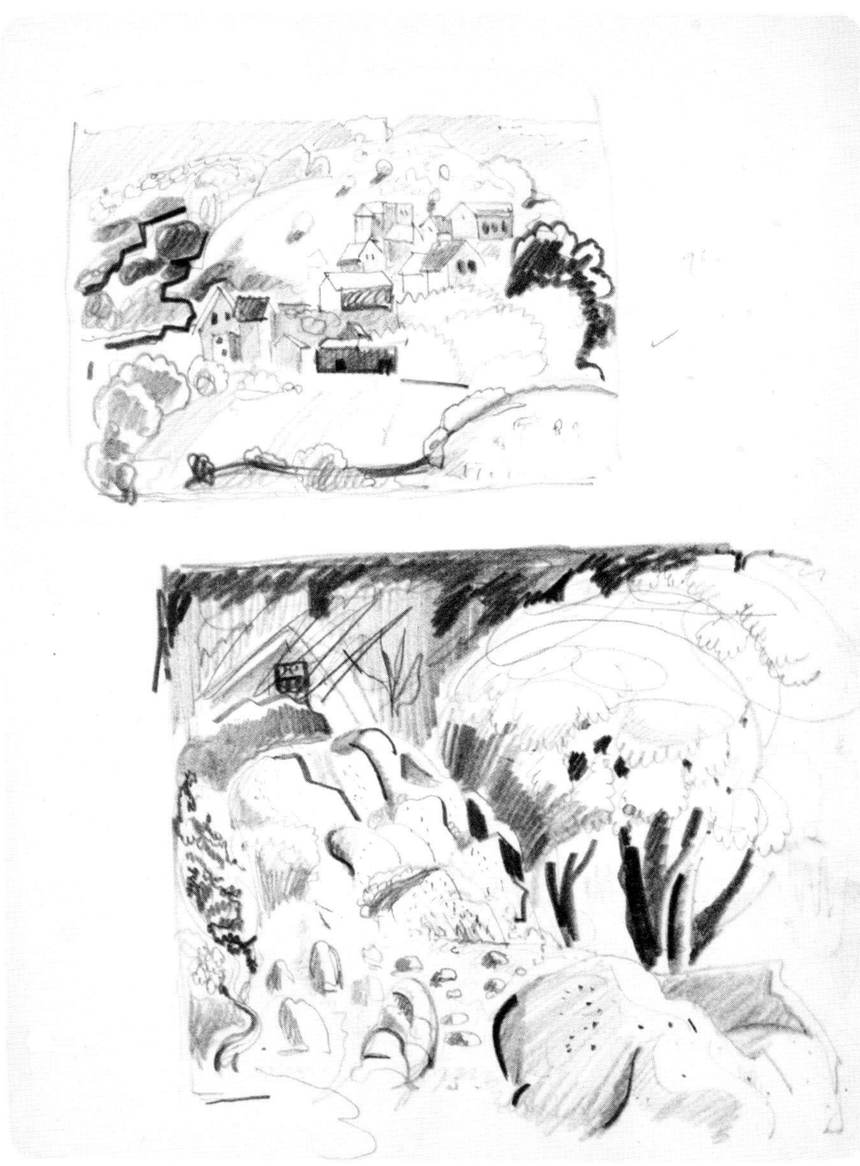

FIGURE 9
Sketches for COMING STORM,
1931, charcoal pencil on bond paper (cat. no. 29)

Although his essay on drawing was his only formal statement on the subject, Kahn seems to have followed his tenets throughout his career. The multiple studies that he described do not survive from his 1928–29 trip (perhaps they were jettisoned to conserve space), but quite a few survive from the 1930s and later. On his 1951 trip to Egypt he redrew and restudied views of pyramids and granite quarries with restless curiosity. All this suggests that Kahn was committed to a notion of finding the underlying formal order, that the drawing was a composition as much as any architectural design, and that the process of refining the composition meant uncovering the underlying forces in the picture. And invariably these forces were big, either geometries or natural forces.

But while Kahn was establishing his credentials as an architect-renderer, the Depression was deepening. In September 1930 he lost his job. He may have been a consummate draftsman, but Cret had several of these, one of whom, William H. Livingston, could draft as lucidly as Kahn. A few months later Cret helped Kahn find a position with Zantzinger, Borie & Medary, the prominent firm who had designed the

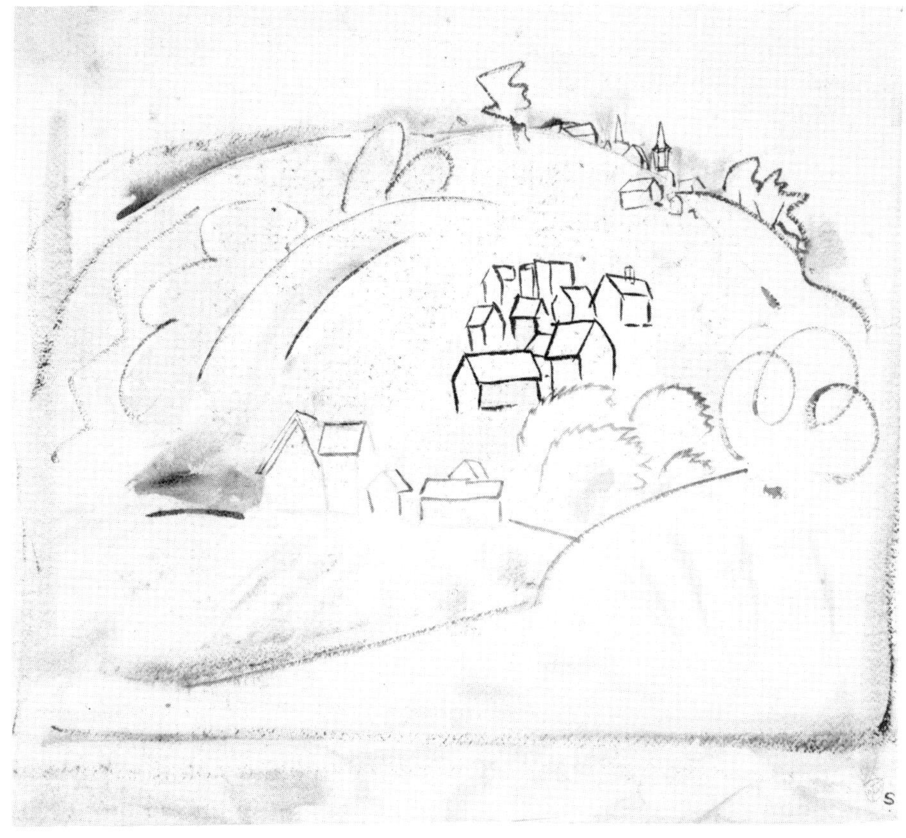

FIGURE 10
Study for COMING STORM, 1931 [JH125], watercolor on paper, 33.9 x 39.4 cm; Collection of Sue Ann Kahn

Philadelphia Museum of Art and who were now designing the Justice Department Building (1931–34) in Washington, D.C. This was an important Beaux-Arts ensemble in the Cret mode, with one of the last great groups of pedimental sculpture in the country (designed by C. Paul Jennewein, author of the execrable pediments of the Philadelphia Museum of Art). Kahn played a large role in the development of the design, living in the Capital and returning to his wife every weekend or so. But the Depression was reaching its climax, and he must have known that his situation was precarious.

In February 1932 Zantzinger reluctantly let him go. For the next three years Kahn was to survive on scraps of work, commissions for tiny alterations, and idea projects that were never built, supported all the while by his wife, who was working as a medical secretary.[34] But Kahn now made a decisive break with architectural tradition. Previously he had been content to follow the accepted career path—the grinding hierarchy that progressed from draftsman to assistant to partner—with its underlying assumption that the goal of all architects was a private practice and a large commercial clientele. According to this model, Kahn should now try to find architectural work as a renderer or draftsman and weather the storm. He did no such thing. Instead, in March, the month following his dismissal, he formed an ad hoc group of unemployed architects and draftsmen that he dubbed the Architectural Research Group. Ultimately two dozen or more young men passed through its ranks, but at the core were ten stalwarts, seven of whom were graduates of the University of Pennsylvania.[35] Many were Jewish but by no means all; one of the exceptions was Howell B. Pennell, the cousin of the celebrated artist Joseph Pennell.[36] A few of them, including Hyman Cunin and Joseph Rovner, had worked on the Sesquicentennial drawings.

Office accommodations were swiftly arranged. One of the men, Willis Humphrey Church, lived in a Victorian row house at 1615 Spruce Street, where rents had fallen to a pittance. Here a pair of second-story rooms was rented by the group, who promptly assembled drawing tables, furniture, and a small library. In the Spruce Street chambers Kahn quickly shed the vestiges of his Beaux-Arts training, as modernism came through from all sides. In April, a month after the group was formed, the celebrated exhibition that coined the term "International Style" traveled from the New York Museum of Modern Art to the Philadelphia Museum of Art. The Architectural Research Group soon became a conventicle of modernism. Working at Kahn's side was a young Alsatian architect, Dominique Berninger, who had emigrated in the 1920s and was the only member with impeccable European modernist credentials. Financially self-sufficient, he was still able to travel overseas and keep the group informed about European modernism. His flat-roofed modernist house at Bryn Athyn became a kind of salon for the group.[37] And Cunin, a childhood friend of Kahn's, was an eager follower of German events; it was he who brought the Bauhaus publications to the group, translating the German for the others.[38]

The Architectural Research Group did not have a single ideological program or focus but diffused its energies broadly. A breathless puff piece published in 1934 in the *Philadelphia Record* called its members "students of sociology and deeply-interested in the human as well as the scientific aspects of their profession."[39] In a kind of muddled modernism, the group dabbled in housing, radical technology, even monuments. Here mixed all the currents of modernism then in circulation—European urbanism and social housing, Buckminster Fuller's model of pure, objective technology, and even the Soviet constructivism of the twenties. But perhaps the most important Soviet contribution was the concept of a cooperative association of architects, engineers, and planners who believed the design problem was not an affair of art but of science, and for whom architecture rested ultimately upon objective truths that could be verified empirically.[40] During the mid-1920s, in the wake of the Bolshevik Revolution, several such cooperatives had sprung up throughout Russia, including the A.R.U. (Union of Architect-Planners) and Asnova (Association of New Architects).[41] Perhaps the crucial figure promoting the doctrine of architectural objectivity was the dashing Nikolai Alexandrovich Ladovsky (1881–1941) of Asnova, who devised an experimental black room in which architectural forms and proportions might be analyzed in terms of the physiological and psychological reactions they induced. The Architectural Research Group, also known by its initials A.R.G., seems to have followed Ladovsky's model. Esther Kahn recalls testing each of its members to see how accurately they could perceive the proportions of the Golden Section.[42]

The group's Soviet orientation is apparent in their most daring project, the plan for a Lenin monument in Leningrad, for which a competition was held in 1933. In this they were surely buoyed by the well-publicized competition for the Palace of the Soviets in Moscow, which proceeded in several publicized stages from 1931 and in which many non-Soviet architects participated, including Gropius, Le Corbusier, and Auguste Perret. Several architects in Philadelphia had competed in this contest, including the German émigrés Alfred Kastner (1900–1975) and Oscar Stonorov (1905–1970). Kastner had won a first prize with his design for a Ukrainian National Theater in Kharkov the year before. Kahn was later associated with both these men; perhaps he heard of the Leningrad competition through them.[43]

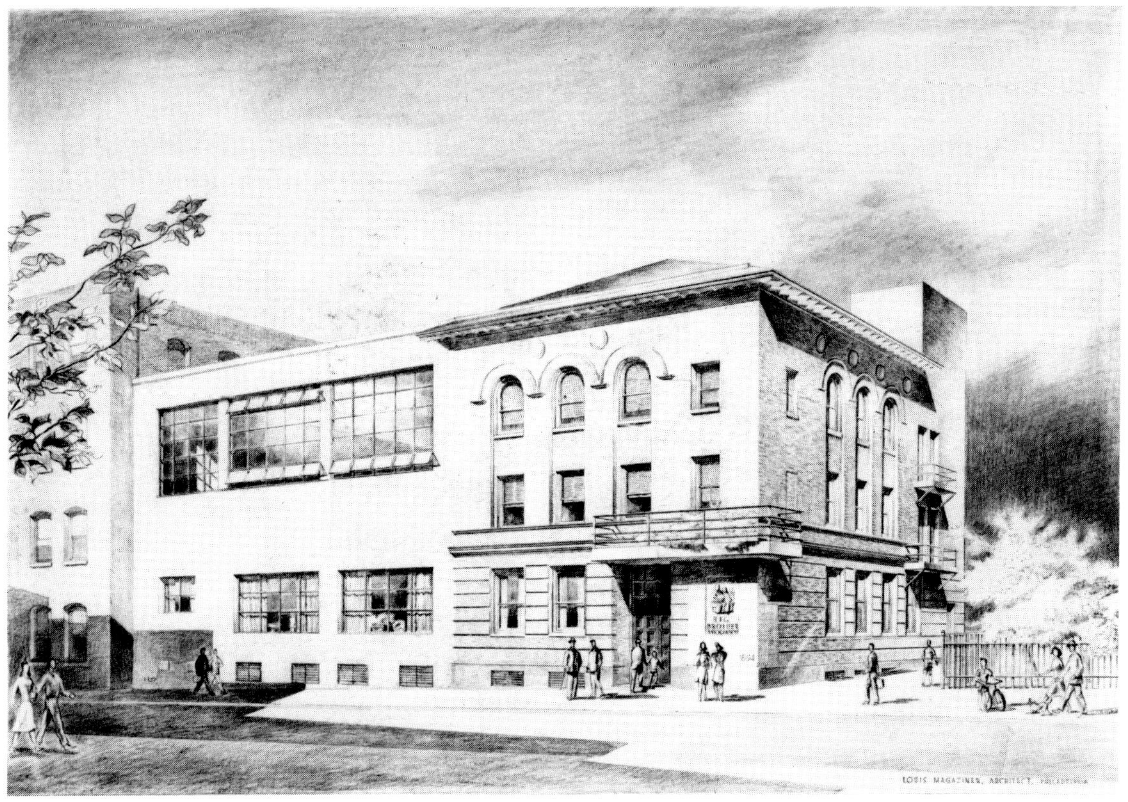

FIGURE 11
Louis I. Kahn, renderer. *BIG BROTHER ASSOCIATION*, Louis Magaziner, architect, c. 1937; photograph courtesy Athenaeum of Philadelphia

A contemporary account describes this project designed by Kahn (whose wife confirms his authorship).[44] The central motif was that of a portal on Leningrad harbor through which one would enter the city of the revolution:

> *They contributed a design to an international competition for a Lenin memorial, which, if accepted and constructed, will make the port of Leningrad the most striking in the world. Through the portals of two towers of red glass rising several hundred feet from the surface of the water the visitor would descend into an enormous circular plaza from which marine spectacles could be viewed. The A.R.G. doesn't do things by half when it gets going—there would be 50,000 square feet of glass brick alone in the two towers.*[45]

Such a daring project, based on the idea of a glittering crystalline monument, recalled the world of Soviet constructivism and entries in the international competitions for the Palace of the Soviets and the Palace of Culture. Many of these were also brilliantly colored, as luminous as Russian folk art, which also seems to have touched Kahn. In 1930, for example, following his trip, he had designed a woodcut of a Christmas card that showed a boatful of Russian fishermen alongside an onion-domed and tower-crested harbor town.[46] And the sentimental gesture of using red for Lenin was a standard device in Russian revolutionary art, most notably in Lissitzky's celebrated *Beat the Whites with the Red Wedge*. But the roots of the Lenin monument also reached back to Kahn's Italian travels and to the traditional urban schemes that he had sketched: the conception of the monument as a picturesque ensemble of towers, the motif of the portal enframing a distant vista, even the sense of vibrantly colored walls that would be activated by light. The idea of towers grouped around a plaza was at least as close to medieval Italy as it was to the modern urbanism of Le Corbusier, which had held little interest for him in 1929.[47] In the end, the Lenin Monument project is the great connective link between Kahn's 1928–29 studies of Italian public spaces and his urban planning schemes for Philadelphia of the 1940s.

Here then was a last flicker of expressionism—a movement, whether of the Soviet or German type, that could be reconciled with historical prototypes—before Kahn embraced the spartan austerity of the Bauhaus, which sanctioned no truck with architectural history. It was perhaps the same impulse that had caused him to sketch a row of skyscrapers marching shoulder to shoulder in his cover for the journal *T-Square,* which suspended publication in 1932 before the drawing could be used.[48] The drawings of the Lenin Monument do not seem to survive in the United States, nor did Kahn ever discuss the project with his biographers. When he achieved celebrity in the late 1950s, there could hardly have been a worse entry on a list of projects for an American architect than a red monument for Lenin. Whatever the reason, this project has remained unknown in the literature until now.

The Lenin project, although it prophesied Kahn's later fascination with monuments, had no immediate consequences for his work of the 1930s. Far more influential were his housing experiments with the A.R.G., who continually championed "the mass-produced home," which they sought to improve through technology as well as planning.[49] Perhaps their oddest innovation was their project for a house whose walls regulated their own temperature with separate thermostats, according to the amount of sunlight and thermal energy on them. The A.R.G.'s interest in social housing quickened after Roosevelt's inauguration in March 1933. In April they proposed a slum clearance scheme for South Philadelphia; then came an ambitious plan for a fifty-four-acre settlement in Northeast Philadelphia.[50] All these projects were saturated in European modernism: flat-roofed buildings with concrete slabs and horizontal strip windows, the buildings grouped in clusters and extended rows about park space. In spirit they were close to Kastner and Stonorov's Carl Mackley Houses (1932–35), which had been initiated under the Hoover administration and represented the best of American social housing in the European mode.

In the Architectural Research Group Kahn pioneered the characteristic role that he would play throughout his life, the inspirational figure at the center of a group of spellbound acolytes—improvising, galvanizing, mesmerizing. But for all their ambition and promise, the members of the group remained in obscurity, and Kahn seems to have overshadowed them all. One by one, the schemes and utopian experiments of the group came to naught, and by May 1934 it was quietly disbanded, two years after Stalin himself had dissolved its Soviet prototypes. Kahn spent the next eighteen months scrambling for small commissions while he cadged modest office space from the firm of Magaziner and Eberhard. Even this successful firm had fallen on rough times, and Kahn offered expertise on social housing, a new and possibly lucrative source of work. Kahn seems to have invested much of this time preparing speculative housing schemes, to which Magaziner and Eberhard were glad to add their names. From time to time he also prepared the odd presentation drawing for the firm. His rendering of the Big Brother Association was one of these rather perfunctory efforts, where only the angular trees betrayed his personal hand (fig. 11).[51] Not until he secured a position with Alfred Kastner at the end of 1935 did Kahn's fortunes begin to pick up.[52]

Kahn was now becoming an architectural but not a pictorial modernist. That is, his architectural development did not at all coincide with his artistic development. The shift to flat-roofed International Style functionalism that he underwent around 1932–34 was heralded by no similar shift in his work on canvas, either in artistic means or ends. And while his architecture evolved radically toward European modernism after 1932, his painting ignored European events—if anything, it became rather more American. There followed a period of intense looking at American

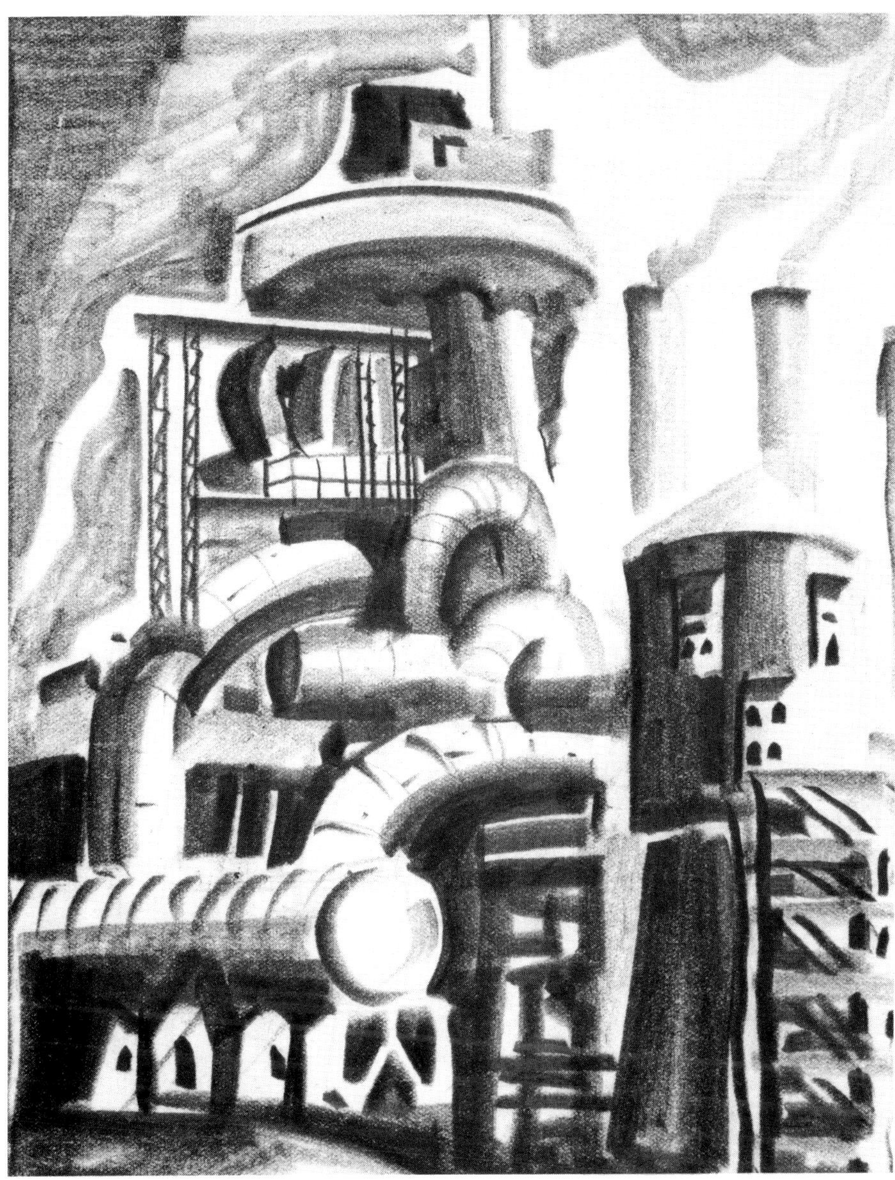

Figure 12
FACTORY, PHILADELPHIA,
c. 1930–35, graphite on paper
(cat. no. 37)

painters and American subjects. In particular Kahn examined the work of that gritty group of urban realists now known as precisionists, many of whom studied at the Pennsylvania Academy of the Fine Arts and imbibed the legacy of Philadelphia realism, of Thomas Eakins, Robert Henri, and their successors. Sheeler and Demuth seem to have been particularly important, but so were Pennell, Louis Lozowick, and even the watercolorist Adolf Dehn. Typical of these was a series of industrial subjects in the Sheeler mode, in which the factory was rendered from very near at hand so that cranes, water towers, and smokestacks would form abstract patterns suggestive of mechanical energy and power without giving much sense of the topography of place (fig 12).[53]

Such industrial vignettes, and his seaside landscapes, were of course far from the utopian internationalism of the housing schemes. Nonetheless, such a turn inward was the central theme of American art during this troubled introspective decade, surely

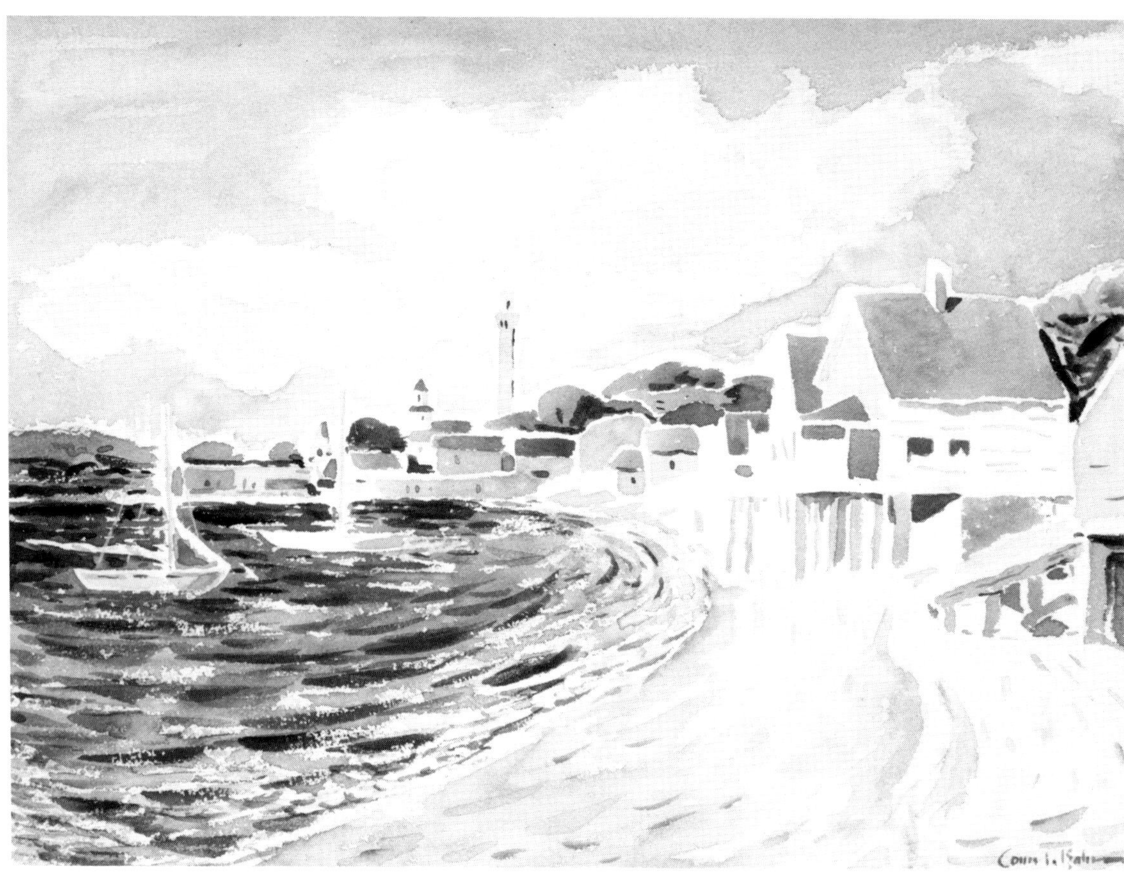

Figure 13
EVENING, PROVINCETOWN,
1934, watercolor on paper
(cat. no. 32)

the greatest period of introspection since the Hudson River school of a century before. And many who had dabbled with experimental modernism in the wake of the Armory show returned to realism in the thirties. After all, the Depression itself was the central experience of modern America, and its artistic exploration—even if conducted by the devices of realism—was fundamentally a modernist endeavor. Not until the latter part of the decade did American artistic sentiment move again in any significant way toward international themes and theoretical modernism. It was no great intellectual fracture for Kahn to design a modern monument to Lenin while painting seascapes like Marin or factories like Sheeler.

Figure 14
VIEW OF ROCKPORT, postcard;
Collection of Esther I. Kahn

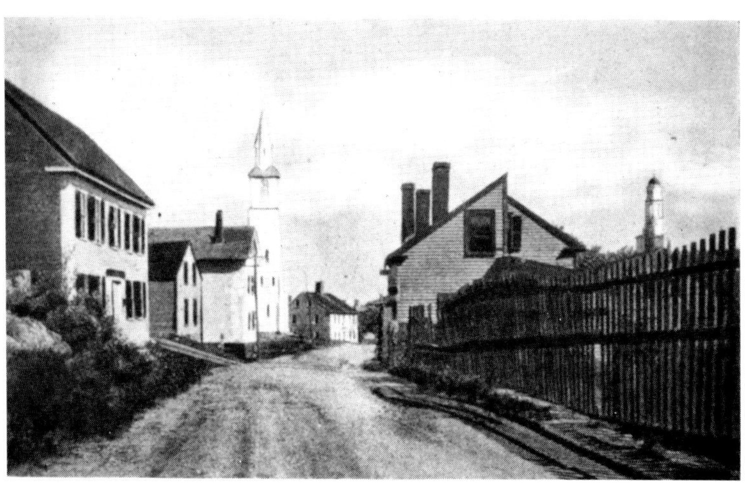

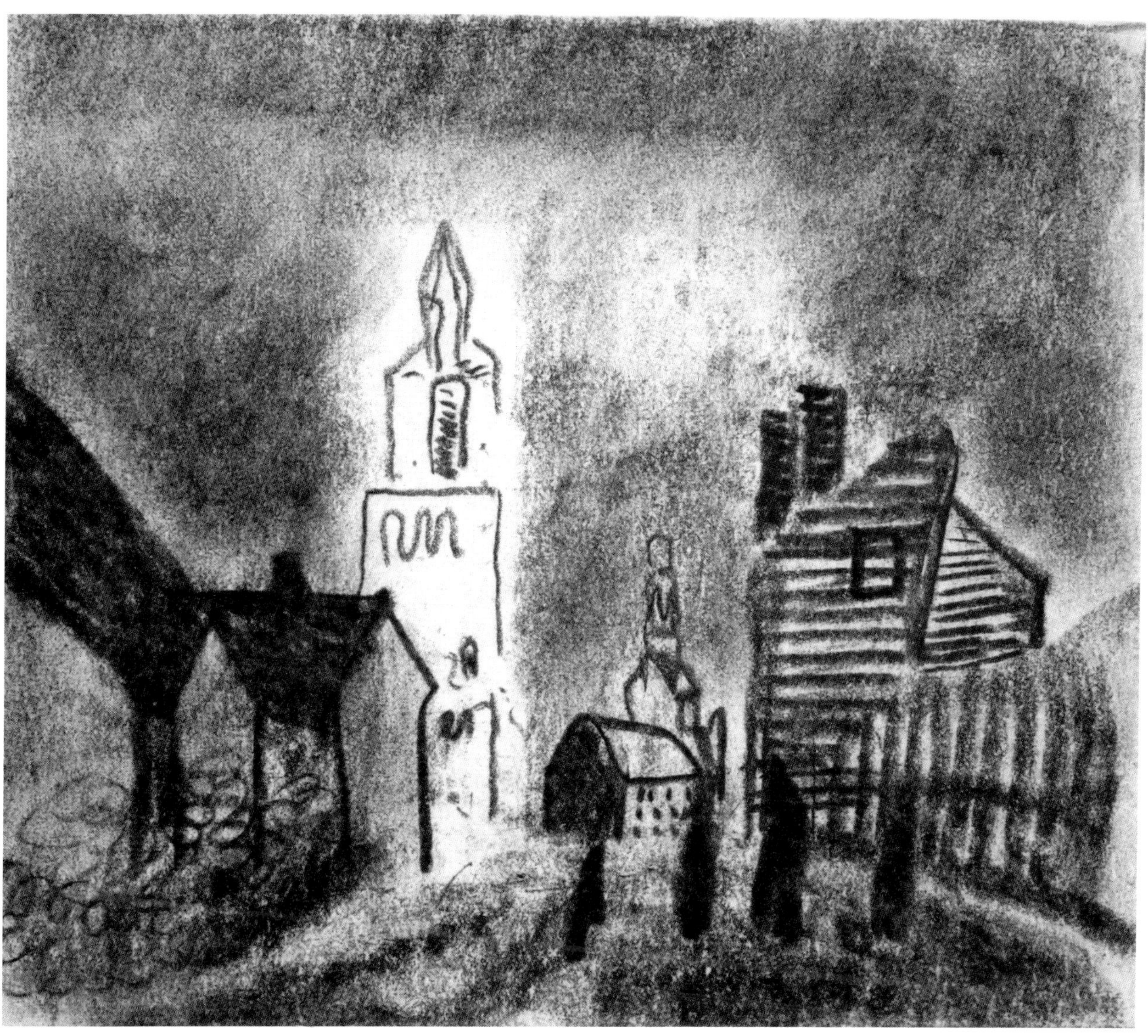

FIGURE 15
WHITE CHURCH, c. 1935,
charcoal on paper (cat. no. 36)

For this reason, Kahn's last major entry at the Pennsylvania Academy's exhibition was far more conventional than those of 1930 or 1931. In 1934 he showed three watercolors: *Evening, Provincetown; In the Berkshires;* and *Sundown, Provincetown,* only the first of which survives (fig. 13).[54] This light and pleasant vignette of the Provincetown harbor had none of the drama and menace of the stormy landscapes he had shown earlier and seems to suggest, if anything, Kahn's relief at being on vacation during these lean and tense years.

Never again would Kahn have so much free time in which to paint, and the mid-thirties form an episode of especially rich experimentation. He dabbled at portraits, played at social realism in a few brooding and uneasy lithographs, produced some competent oil landscapes, and even painted an abstracted version of Esther in a jazzy updating of Modigliani.[55]

Amidst all this playful experimentation, Kahn's painting had yet one more major evolution to undergo, and this appears to have happened around 1935/36. Since the trip to Europe one of his great preoccupations was the depiction of the latent energy in a structure. One device to impart energy to buildings or landscapes was the patterning of brush or ink strokes to form concentric radiating lines, like the waves of a

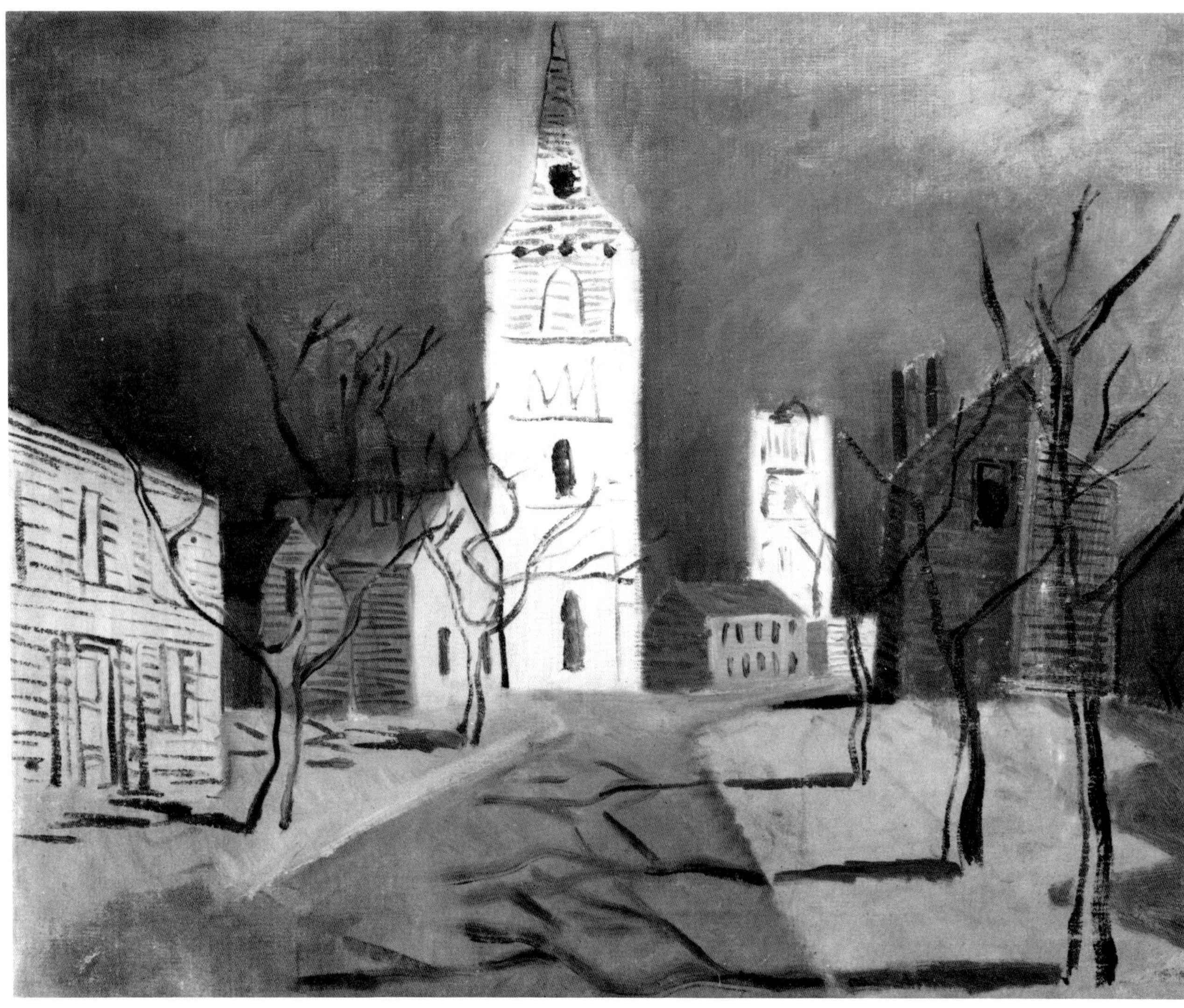

FIGURE 16
WHITE CHURCH, c. 1935, oil on canvas (cat. no. 35)

transmitter, a kind of mysticism of abstract energy. The watercolor of the Spoleto viaduct (pl. 3) extends this effect through trees and clouds; the drawing of the town of Positano, with the forms of the mountain. Another device was to throw everything but the principal monument into darkness and allow it to emerge blazing with light. This he did with his oil painting *Fishermen's houses, Conca dei Marini* (fig. 43). Half a decade later, he was still using the technique in his eerie views of a white church in Massachusetts. Once again, as had sometimes been the case in Italy, a postcard provided the generating idea. This was a view of "An Old Street in Rockport," a town where the Kahns vacationed around 1935 (fig. 14). As subject matter it was not exceptionally promising—an arrangement of vernacular houses, Victorian church towers, and a meandering road—but as an abstract composition of planes and facets it seemed to fascinate Kahn endlessly. He sketched the place repeatedly in charcoal, pencil, and watercolor, and later he prepared an ambitious oil painting of the scene (fig. 16).[56]

Kahn used both the postcard and site observations, making conscientious color notations. Clearly some parts of the composition were more interesting than others. In particular he seemed to enjoy the juxtaposition of the needlelike spire of the central church (now the First Universalist Church of Rockport) and the peculiar Georgian house across the street, with its distinctive cluster of three chimneys and its irregular roof line. As he drew and redrew the site, these elements grew larger and more prominent, until they dominate the scene in his charcoal drawing, the other buildings shrinking into the shadows. As if to live up to his promise to "change cupolas and towers to suit my taste," Kahn made the slender wooden tower squatter and more monumental, and he enlisted a distant cupola from the right edge of the postcard to serve as a buffer between the house and spire. (He even felt free to ignore his own instructions, and the "Venetian red" which he recorded for the church windows turned to deep blue in the oil painting.) In all this moving, simplifying, enlarging, and shrinking, Kahn was acting to maximize the sense of confrontation between the glowing white church and the rather dingy street out of which it emerged. In the charcoal version of *White church* the contrast is most palpable, as the church glistens with an otherworldly incandescence (fig. 15). What had begun as a vignette of a vernacular American street, the kind endlessly recorded by the photographers of the Depression, was now transformed into a confrontation of powerful masses, looming and quivering with energy. Such a predilection for things glowing from internal sources of power was common to the art deco sensibility of the age and was a favorite theme of Georgia O'Keeffe, for example, who perceived crackling energies within cabbages and skulls as well as skyscrapers. With its overexposure of the central subject, *White church* forms a striking link between Kahn's Ferriss-inspired Sesquicentennial rendering of 1925 and his Siena baptistery of 1951 (fig. 64).

But now Kahn began to experiment with a different type of energy. Rather than showing power radiating from within, he began to study the encounter of external light

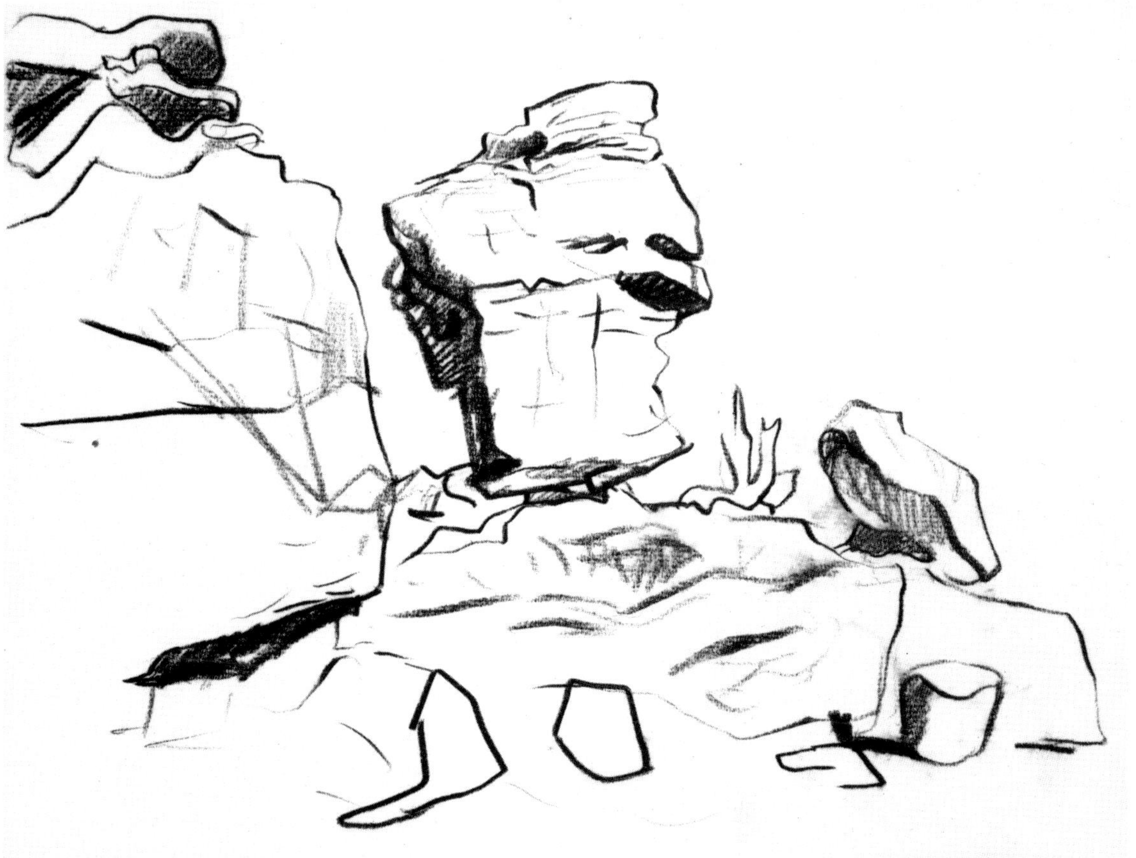

FIGURE 17
ROCK FORMATIONS, GARDEN OF THE GODS, COLORADO,
1948, charcoal pencil on paper
(cat. no. 42)

with the object. In another version of his *White church* he superimposed a red glow to the lines of some trees, added as a kind of afterthought. The idea seems to have been an experiment and shows up in none of the three other versions of the scene. But a year or so later he revived the device with striking confidence, making it the central subject of the work. This was his tempera painting *Coastal village, Isle Madame, Nova Scotia.* Again he prepared several versions in watercolor, but in the tempera version the foreground is taken up by stringy wintry trees that dance with red energy as if recipients of some special variant of sunlight (pl. 5). To enhance the contrast, the shadows on the grass were executed in a highly saturated green, a juxtaposition that was the coloristic equivalent of tossing a match into a pool of gasoline. Here for the first time are intense colors with the level of saturation that Kahn would later use in his pastel drawings of 1951.

These American and Canadian landscapes of the mid-1930s mark the end of Kahn's systematic painting. He continued to draw, but less frequently and with less opportunity to develop his ideas over time. And in particular he ceased to use drawing and painting as a method for exploring architectural ideas systematically. There was the occasional bout of landscape sketching, as in his views of the Garden of the Gods in Colorado from 1948 (fig. 17), but these were more a divagation than a serious theoretical study. In fact, for much of the next two decades, architectural travel sketches of the traditional sort were highly unfashionable. The celebrated renderers of the 1920s passed unlamented from fashion. Any rustle of artistry in the drafting room was now deemed reactionary, as *Pencil Points* recognized when it exchanged its name for a term taken from contemporary politics: *Progressive Architecture.* And so the situation remained until Kahn's own heroic bout of sketching in 1951, which perhaps did more than any other single event to revive the graphic encounter with great architecture as an acceptable pursuit.

It is generally accepted that the late works of Louis Kahn owe much to his Beaux-Arts beginnings and that they represent a personal synthesis of modernism and classicism. This exhibition suggests that Kahn first sought to bridge the worlds of Beaux-Arts classicism and International Style modernism in his sketching and painting during the 1930s. Here in the world of art was a neutral field, apart from the fierce ideological terrain over which architectural modernism advanced, where for a time a kind of truce prevailed, and where Kahn could simultaneously be classicist, modernist, and American regionalist. Given Kahn's abrupt and radical conversion to European modernism, it is astonishing how indifferent he remained to radical abstraction in painting. While he learned with his generation the power of abstraction, his suppression of detail and incident served, if anything, to isolate and emphasize the subject. In his painting he remained committed to a few cardinal principles: the primacy of the subject, a feeling for its monumentality and its internal vital force, a personal sense of the poetry of the encounter of light and matter, and an impulse to unite landscape and structure into a seamless transcendent whole. And these principles, banished for a time in his own modern architecture, lived a submerged existence in his drawings until they emerged bright and diamond-hard in the late 1950s to invigorate the mature works that form the dazzling and sustained crescendo to his career.

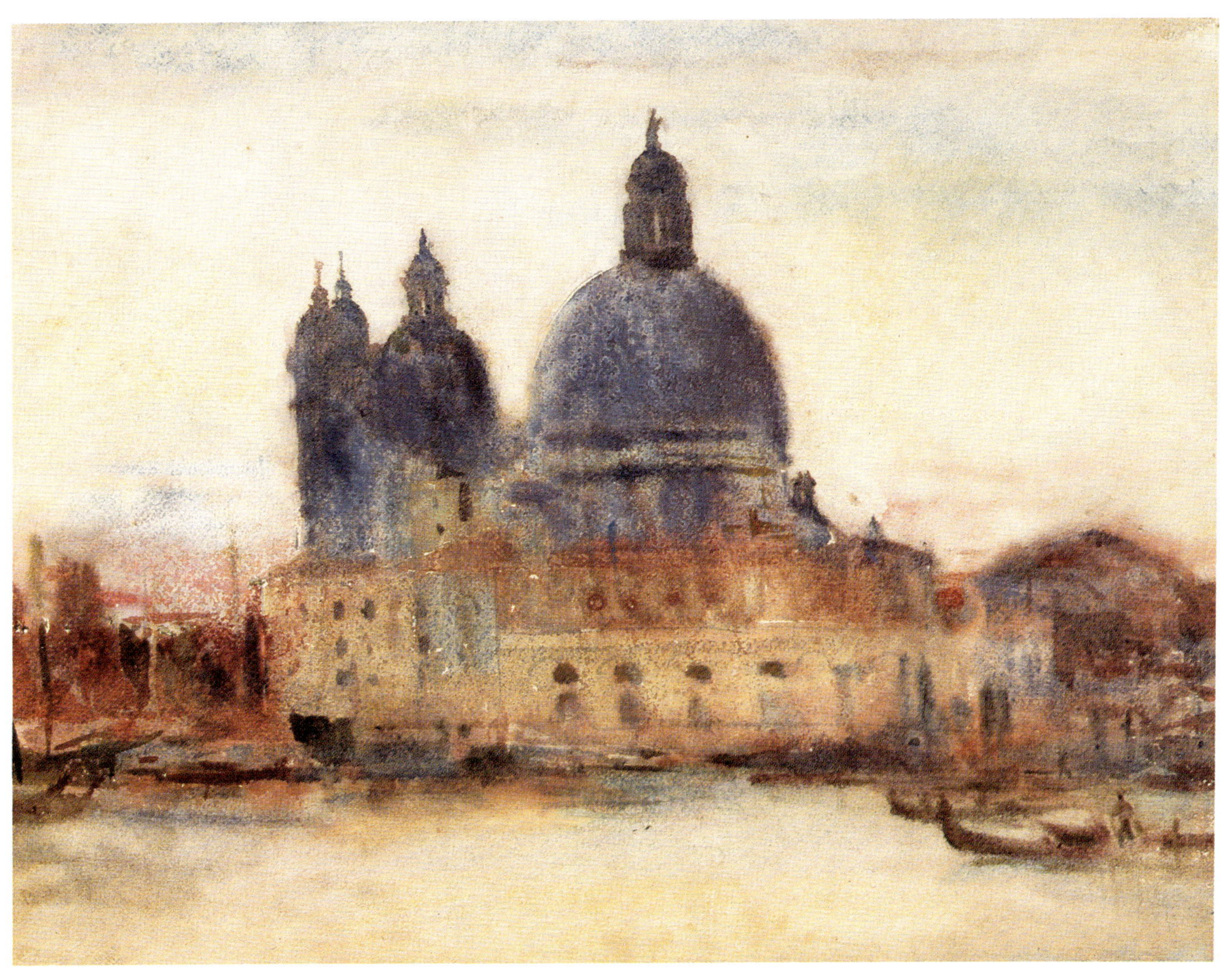

PLATE 1
SANTA MARIA DELLA SALUTE, VENICE, 1928
watercolor on paper
(cat. no. 2)

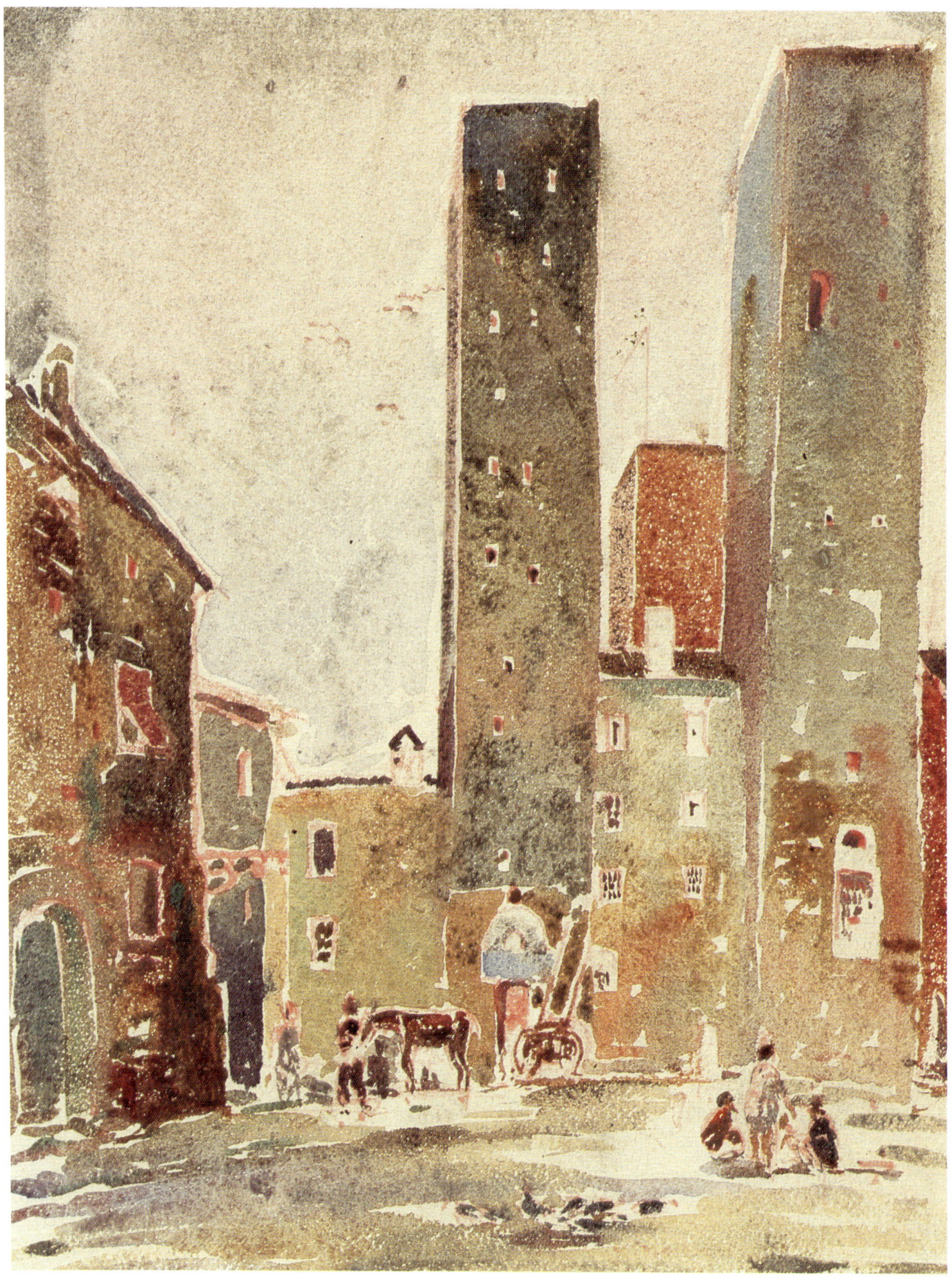

Plate 2
TOWERS, SAN GIMIGNANO, 1928
watercolor on paper
(cat. no. 13)

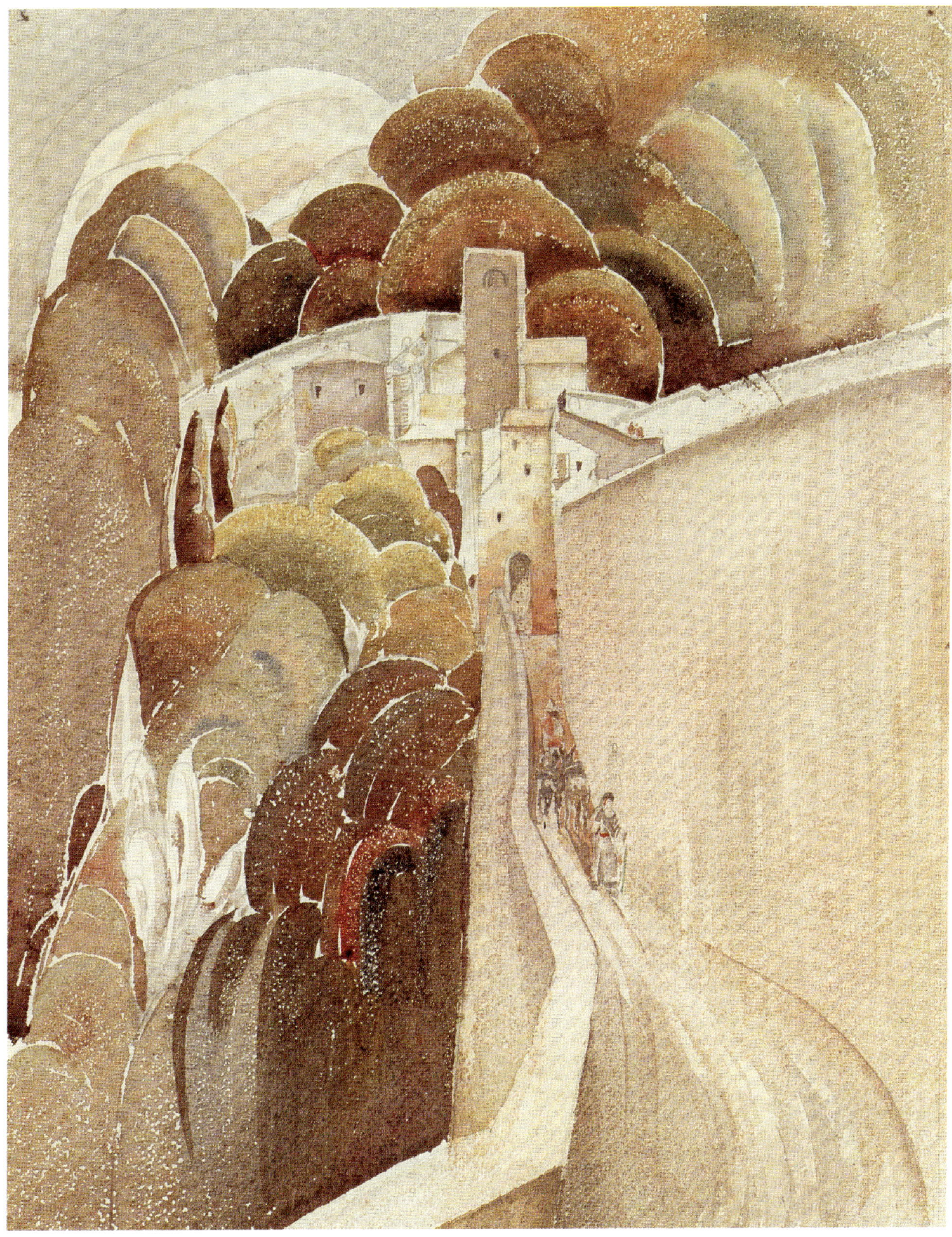

PLATE 3
PONTE DELLE TORRI, SPOLETO, 1928
watercolor on paper
(cat. no. 14)

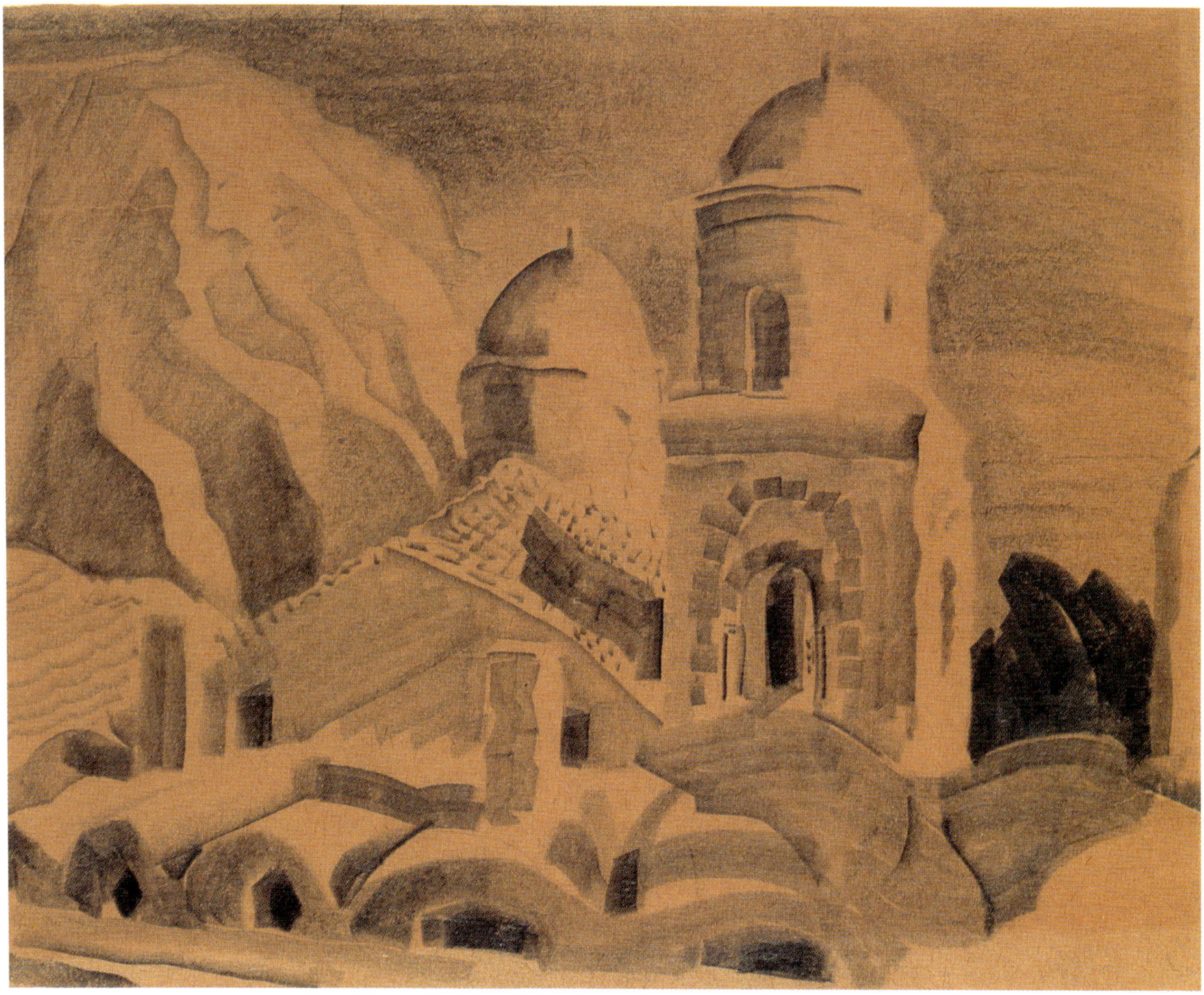

PLATE 4
"CHIESA IN ROVINA," CHIESA DELL'ANNUNZIATA, RAVELLO, 1929
graphite on brown paper
(cat. no. 19)

PLATE 5
COASTAL VILLAGE, ISLE MADAME, NOVA SCOTIA, 1936
tempera on paper
(cat. no. 39)

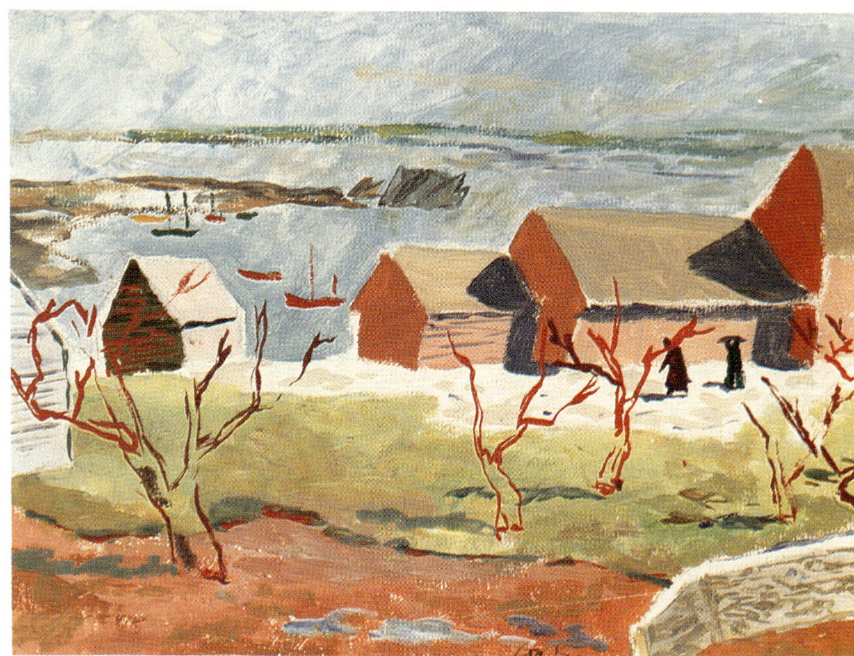

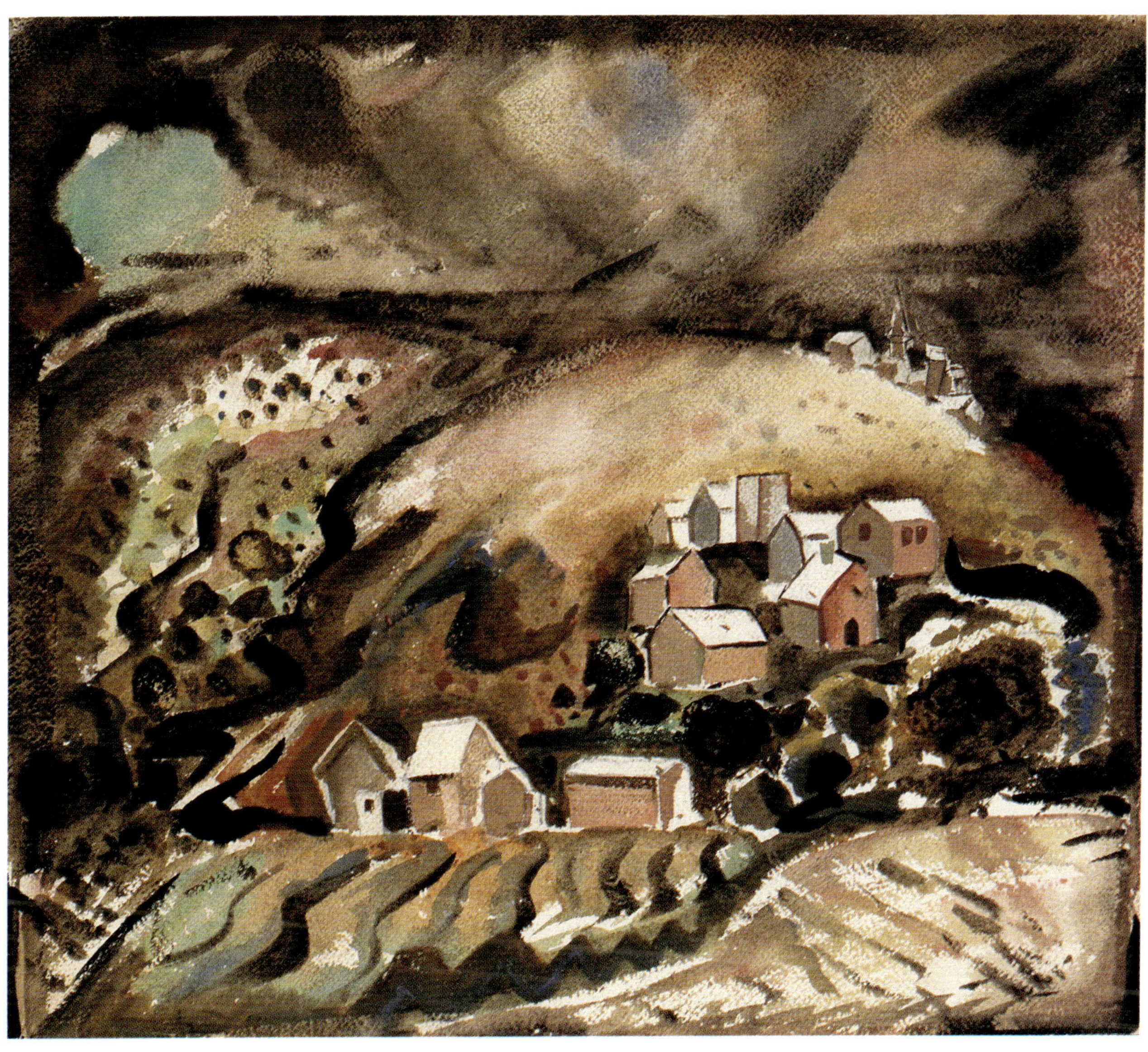

Plate 6
COMING STORM, WOODSTOCK, NEW YORK, 1931
watercolor on paper
(cat. no. 30)

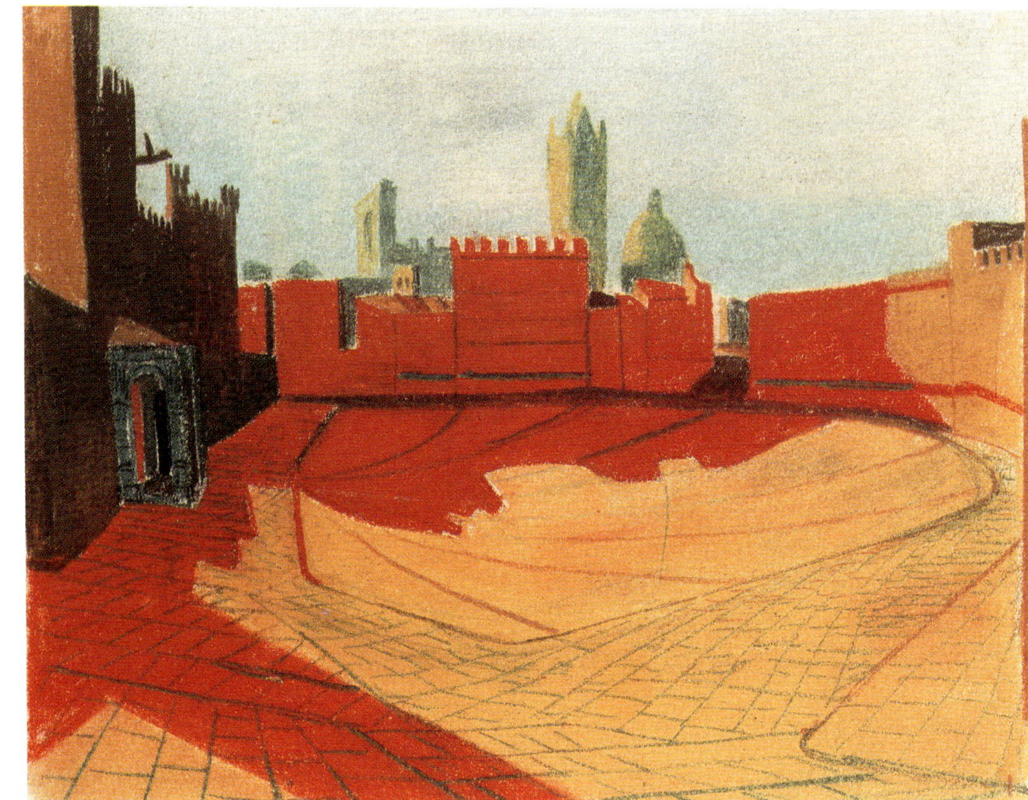

PLATE 7
PIAZZA DEL CAMPO, SIENA, 1950–51
pastel on paper
(cat. no. 46)

PLATE 8
NORTH SIDE, SECOND COURT OF MORTUARY TEMPLE OF RAMESES III, MEDINET-HABU, 1951
pastel and charcoal on paper (cat. no. 52)

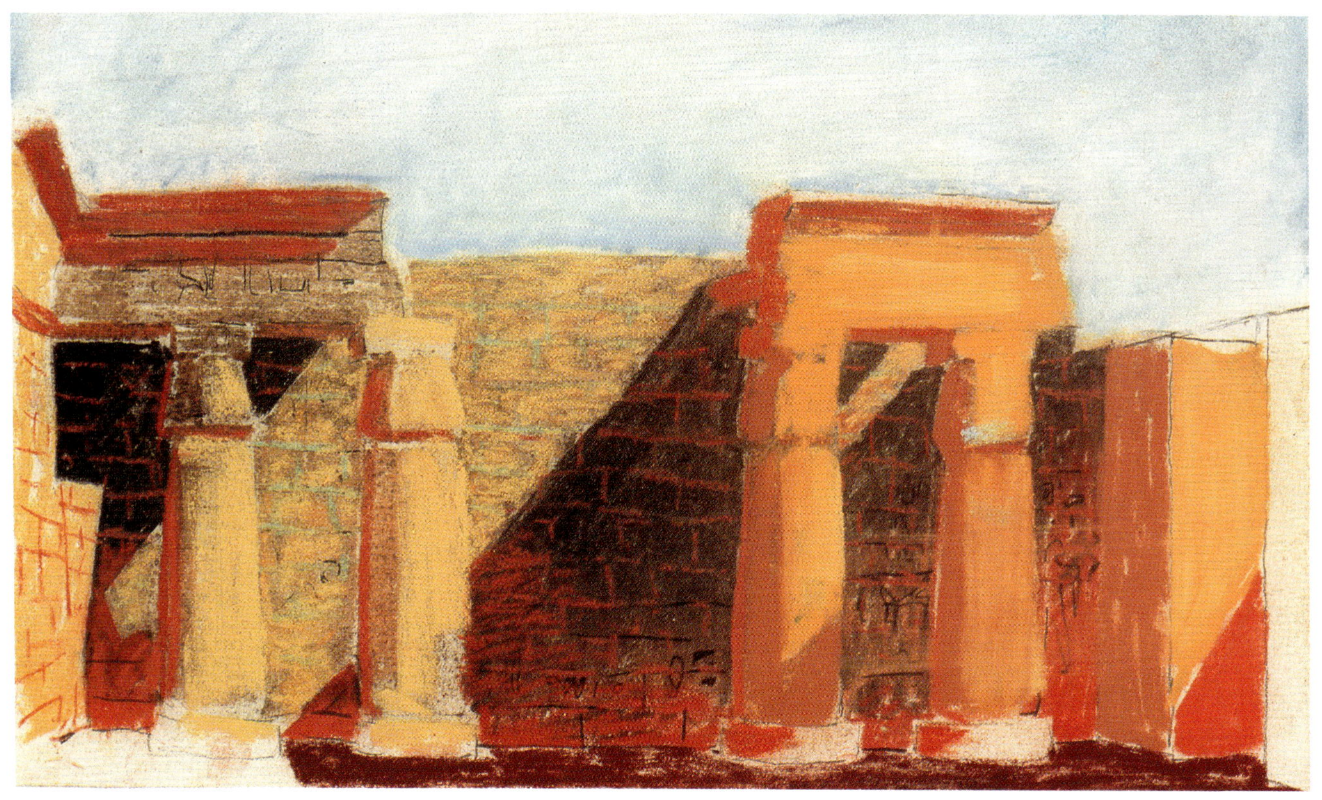

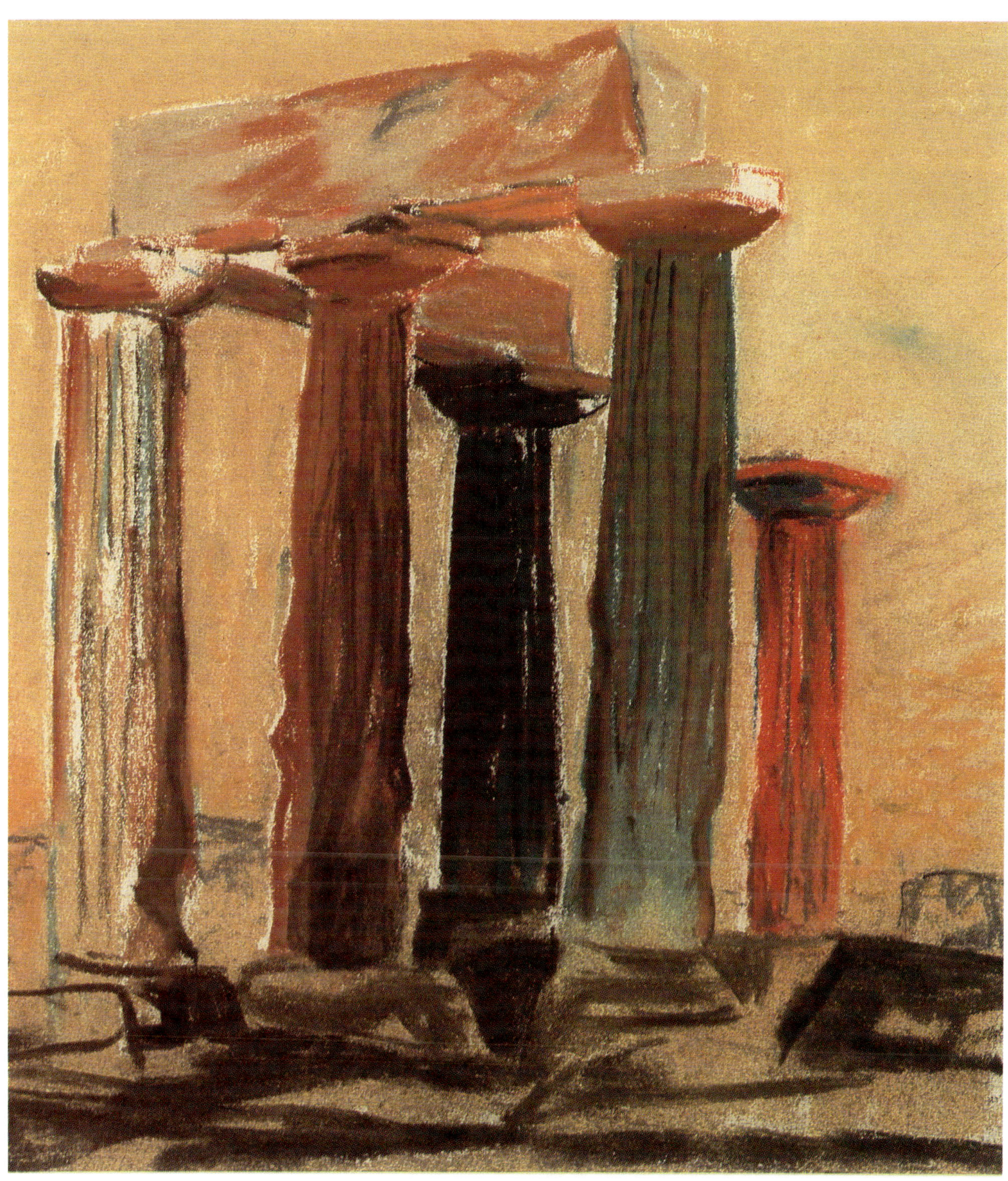

PLATE 9
TEMPLE OF APOLLO, CORINTH, AT SUNRISE, 1951
pastel and charcoal on paper
(cat. no. 59)

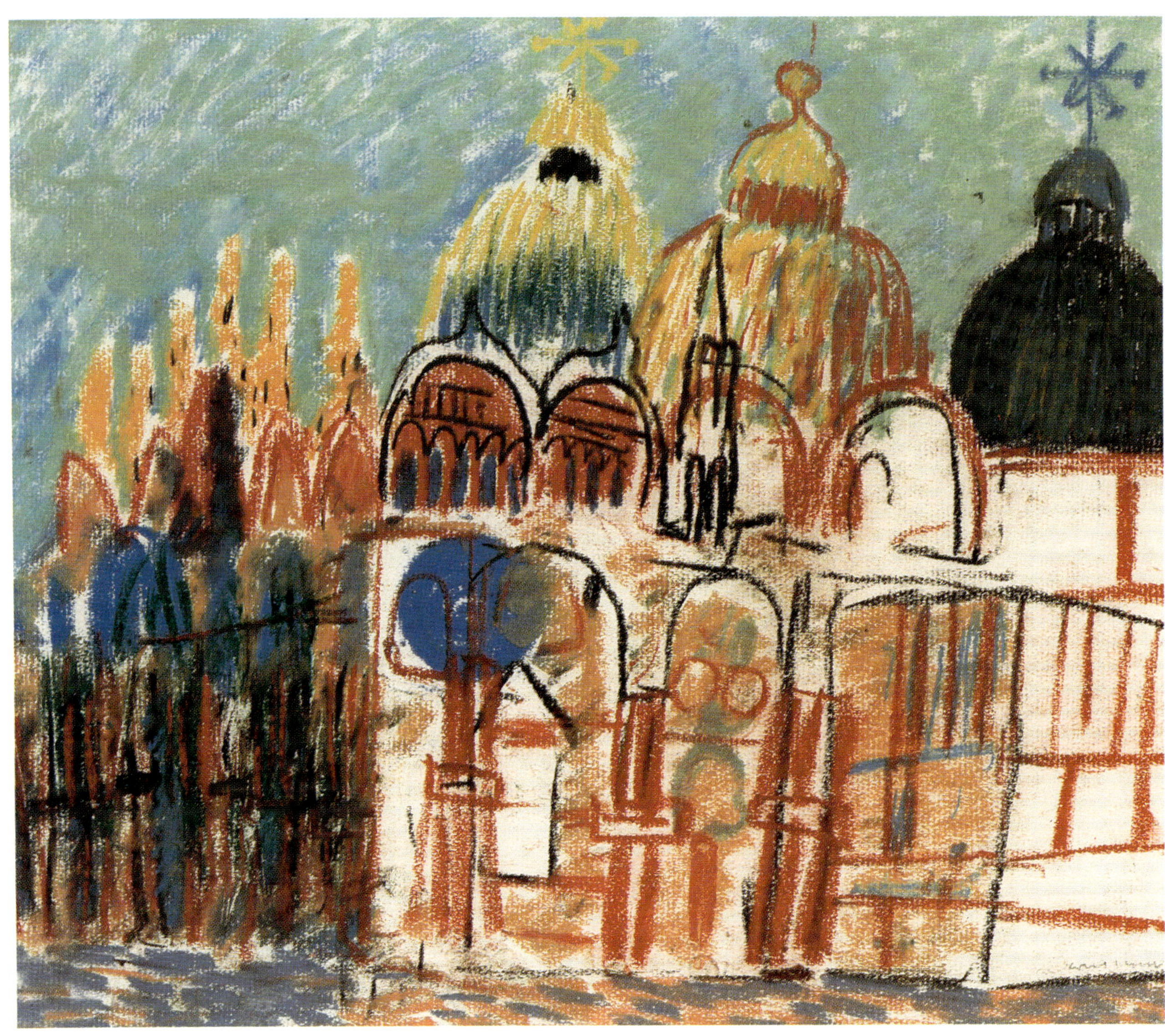

PLATE 10
BASILICA DI SAN MARCO, VENICE, 1951
pastel on paper
(cat. no. 48)

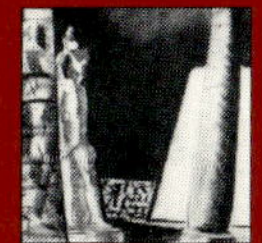

33 • 110

SKETCHING ABROAD

Eugene J. Johnson

THE DRAWINGS OF 1928–29

At the very moment when Louis Kahn, almost sixty years old, finally became an internationally celebrated architect, he chose to recall the sketching trip he had made to Italy thirty years earlier. Invited to give the concluding talk—indeed, to have the last word—at the International Congress of Modern Architecture (CIAM) at Otterlo, the Netherlands, in 1959, Kahn spoke of his early career:

> *Now when I got through with school, I walked around the realm [of architecture] and I came to a little village, and this village was very unfamiliar. There was nothing here that I had seen before. But through this unfamiliarity—from this unfamiliar thing—I realized what architecture was.*[1]

Kahn's "little village" consisted of Italian medieval and vernacular architecture, which he recorded in graphite drawings and watercolors.[2]

Kahn arrived in Europe in 1928 trained in two arts—painting during his high school years and architecture at the University of Pennsylvania, from which he graduated in 1924. He never gave up practicing both arts. We remember him primarily as an architect, but even in the last year of his life, world famous architect that he was, he was hoping to devote more time to painting, and he was planning to turn part of his house into a studio.[3] Kahn made a clear distinction between the roles of painter and architect; according to Anne Griswold Tyng, Kahn's associate for almost thirty years, "Lou always wanted a distinction between things."[4] For Kahn, the work of the architect was closer to that of the musician than to that of the painter because the visual notations on paper which both musicians and architects make represent something outside the paper. A musical score represents sound, an architectural plan the three-dimensional experience of mass, space, and light. A painting, said Kahn, stands for itself and nothing else; it is the representation of the painter's fantasy: a painter could defy gravity, or make a cannon with square wheels to show the futility of war, but an architect had always to use round wheels. According to Kahn, a painter was also free to paint any subject, whereas the architect was always subservient to the laws of physics and the needs of the client. "Giotto was a wonderful painter," he said, "because he painted the skies black in the daytime, and painted dogs that couldn't run and birds that couldn't fly, and people who were larger than buildings."[5] In 1931, shortly after his return from Europe, Kahn argued for a similar level of artistic license: "I have learned to regard it as no physical impossibility to move mountains and trees, or change cupolas and towers to suit my taste."[6] When Kahn made his travel sketches, he was consciously operating as a painter and thus free to move trees and change cupolas, all of which he did with abandon. He argued, however, that there was a greater purpose to painting than flights of fancy. Giotto had been a great painter because his fantasy summoned a world appropriate to the history of Saint Francis; he "combined the life of Saint Francis with the mystical atmosphere which was necessary to bring it to a religious sense, of nobility, of sacrifice, of things which are religious."[7] Making sketches, Kahn argued in 1931, leads one "to understand the intrinsic character, and have respect for the individuality underlying even the things that seemed to create no feeling within us at first."[8]

During the five months he spent in Italy, between October 1928 and March 1929, the arts of painting and architecture informed each other in his work. Kahn the painter found for the first time his own style of drawing, while Kahn the architect discovered the buildings on which he would one day base much of his mature work.[9] His search for a modern, personal way of drawing was accompanied by a growing interest in medieval and vernacular architectural forms that forced him to find an appropriate style in which to render their "intrinsic character." Kahn the painter, then, used the problem of rendering those architectural forms as a means to achieve his own modern pictorial style, which was based largely on cubism; Kahn the architect used the act of drawing to fix in his memory structures that he would one day recall in his own designs.

A trip to Italy had become important for northern Europeans as early as the sixteenth century, when architects such as Philibert de l'Orme came to study both the architecture of antiquity and the new architecture of the Renaissance.[10] Architects' travels to Greece, Egypt, and other countries on the eastern edge of the Mediterranean did not become common until the late eighteenth and early nineteenth centuries. By the early nineteenth century, it was standard for young northern European architects to spend a year or so in Italy, focusing their attention on Rome, and then perhaps go on to Greece, Egypt, and even Asia Minor. In the days before photography, architects made drawings to take home images of what they had admired or what they hoped to use in their careers. Throughout the eighteenth and nineteenth centuries architectural drawings were generally made with care, in order to create an accurate record for the architect's later use and to supplement what was available in illustrated architectural publications. Architects' travel sketches were primarily but not exclusively archaeological records of what actually stood.

By the early twentieth century, photography had largely replaced drawing as a means of acquiring portable images of buildings. In 1914 the young architect Erik Gunnar Asplund, for instance, returned to his native Sweden from Italy and North Africa with over 800 postcards and photographs that he had purchased.[11] Or architects could take their own photographs. On his first trip abroad, to Italy in 1906, Le Corbusier carried both a camera and a sketch pad. Kahn himself never used a camera, although in "The Value and Aim of Sketching" he advised getting one if accurate images were desired. He did collect postcards of landscapes and buildings.[12]

Le Corbusier put the ultimate purpose of making travel sketches of buildings particularly well: "When one travels and works with visual things . . . one uses one's eyes and *draws*, so as to fix deep down in one's experience what is seen . . . all this means first to look, and then to observe, and finally perhaps to discover."[13] This surely is an attitude that Kahn in his own way shared. Both Asplund and Le Corbusier frequently drew plans and views of buildings on the same sheet, and so did many another architect-traveler. In the Kahn travel drawings that have come down to us, there is not a single plan. This fact, in itself, suggests that early in his career Kahn had already clarified in his mind the differences between architecture and painting that he later articulated so clearly. For Kahn the travel sketch was primarily a type of painting. It was not an architectural notation that stood for an experience other than that of the sketch itself, but rather an expression of Kahn's experience of the building when he stood in front of it and of what he understood its purpose to be. The travel sketch for Kahn did not need to be an accurate record of a building, even though his sketches are generally accurate enough to be clearly identified. Kahn seems to have studied buildings to gather impressions that formed the basis either of sketches or of his own architectural designs. Direct copying from prototypes had no more place in his architecture than slavish recording of the visual world had in his drawings. In all these ways his travel sketches are different from the standard architect's travel drawings.

Nineteenth-century architects frequently kept diaries or engaged in lengthy correspondence that aid us in the understanding of their drawings. Le Corbusier even published memoirs of his travels of 1910–11 in a hometown newspaper. In Kahn's case, no preserved diaries or correspondence from his trip of 1928–29 reveal his thoughts. Many architects of the twentieth century wrote fairly extensive notes on their travel sketches to help them remember particulars of a building, such as colors or materials, that are not recorded in the sketches themselves. Sometimes the notes also include direct and immediate reactions to buildings. Even so avid a sketcher as Le Corbusier, for whom making a drawing was an act of memorization and understanding, was given to copious marginalia. Kahn sometimes made color notations on his drawings. Otherwise he wrote almost nothing, a fact that suggests he trusted his memory as long as color was not an issue. Because he believed that drawing itself should contain the artist's reaction to the scene, words would have been superfluous.

Sketching trips were and are so common for architects of the last two centuries that one can easily take Kahn's trip for granted—something an ambitious young architect simply did at the start of a career. But in Kahn's case the trip was quite unusual. He had grown up in grinding poverty; his entry into architecture school had been delayed for a year while he earned enough money to pay the tuition. After gaining his degree at Penn, he worked for four years in various architectural offices in Philadelphia, not only to support himself but also to make the money he would need for a year of travel in Europe. The trip was important enough to him to interrupt what would have been the normal progress of a young architect through the offices of established firms before starting out on his own or seeking a partnership with an established architect. He must have been sure it would be worth the expenditure of his time and savings. When he sailed for Europe in the spring of 1928, he probably foresaw no problem in finding a position once he returned (he could hardly have predicted that the Great Depression would begin in October of 1929). His rendering skills, crucial for success in the profession and already widely appreciated by Philadelphia architects, would be improved by a year of sketching, and his own ability to design would inevitably be enhanced by experiencing important works of architecture. But there was also, and importantly, a social side to the trip. By his own efforts he had raised himself out of poverty to the point where he could send himself to Europe as if he were the offspring of well-to-do parents. A *wanderjahr* in Europe would enhance his social status in a profession still largely populated by "gentlemen" and thus improve his chances of establishing or becoming part of an economically viable, independent practice.

On 25 April 1928 a busy Lou Kahn acquired six visas—for Denmark, France, Hungary, Italy, Norway, and Latvia; he had already received a British visa the day before.[14] England, France, and Italy are countries one might expect a wandering young artist or architect to visit, but the visas for Hungary and Norway suggest that he was planning a not entirely orthodox trip. He gave "visit birthplace" as his reason for requesting a visa for Latvia.

On 3 May Kahn landed at Plymouth;[15] his visa allowed him to stay in England one month. By early June[16] he must have moved on, probably to Belgium, since he entered Holland at Roosendaal, on the Belgian border, on 13 June. On 20 June he received a visa for Germany in Amsterdam, and on the 29th he left Germany at Warnemünde, on the Baltic coast north of Rostock, for Denmark. In Copenhagen, he received visas for

Finland and Sweden. On 4 July he left Denmark, and on the 14th his passport was stamped "Polisei Stockholm." The following day he arrived at Helsinki, where he received a visa for Lithuania. Kahn revised his trip as he went along, adding countries to his itinerary and perhaps also subtracting them, since there is no evidence in his passport that he visited either Norway or Hungary.

On 18 July Kahn left Finland, passing through Estonia and entering Latvia, where his passport was stamped on 19 July at the "Komerc" Hotel, Riga. In later years he recalled that he was "very much moved" by his stay in Riga with his mother's relatives.[17] He spent time with his poverty-stricken maternal grandmother, sleeping on the floor of her one-room house.[18] On 17 August he left Latvia and passed through Lithuania on a transit visa.[19] His travels for the rest of August and September seem to have been largely in Germany, where he later claimed to have looked at new housing projects.[20] At the end of September,[21] his passport was stamped at Gmünd, Austria, on the Austro-Czech border, after he had received a Czechoslovakian visa in Berlin on 28 September. On 4 October he crossed the Brenner Pass into Italy, from which he emerged five month later.[22] On 5 March 1929 Kahn left Italy via Domodossola, passed through Switzerland, and entered France the next day. On 12 April the immigration office in London granted him direct transit through the United Kingdom to the United States.

From Kahn's extensive travels in northern Europe, six months in all, only six drawings are now known, whereas more than ten times as many have come down to us from the five months he spent in Italy. From England come drawings of a gabled manor house, a half-timbered townhouse, and Caesar's Tower at Warwick Castle;[23] from the Netherlands, a sheet showing windmills in the landscape;[24] from Sweden, the Blue Hall of the Stockholm City Hall;[25] and, finally, a nineteenth-century Gothic revival building probably located in a city near the Baltic.[26] From Kahn's month in France at the end of his European stay we have nothing, even though he found himself in the country from which his Beaux-Arts architectural education originated. We do not know if he went around to look at great Beaux-Arts buildings. If he did, no drawings of them are known. In Paris he visited his schoolmate Norman Rice, who was working in Le Corbusier's office. Rice recalls that Kahn showed no interest in Le Corbusier's work at that time.[27]

All three English drawings are splendidly careful renderings that show Kahn's highly developed skills. One suspects he looked on the drawings with some pride simply because they were so well made (such competent drawings might well have been quite salable). The drawing of Warwick Castle (fig. 18) attests to an obsession with medieval fortifications that lasted his entire life. He chose to render Caesar's Tower "tamed" by shrubbery drawn with a clarity that allows us to tell one species from another. Kahn was indulging a passion for boscage kindled not only by personal taste but also by picturesque nineteenth-century renderings of the English landscape that he had seen in books. Art, it would seem, had taught Kahn what to draw in England. In general, Kahn's English drawings show an interest in picturesque forms, in surface texture, and in the relationship between buildings and nature.

The interior of the Blue Hall of Ragnar Östberg's Stockholm City Hall of 1911–23 stands out as a rarity among the drawings made throughout the trip. Only two other interiors are preserved in the whole group of drawings from 1928–29. Moreover, the drawing is of a contemporary building, completed only five years before Kahn's visit. From his entire career only two other drawings of a contemporary building are preserved, both views made in 1959 of the interior of Le Corbusier's church at Ronchamp of 1951–55 (fig. 96). As he would do later at Ronchamp, Kahn chose to make the Stockholm drawing an essay on the penetration of light into an interior. The vaguely historicizing details of the architecture are suppressed so that Kahn can concentrate on effects of light, dark, and atmosphere.

From Kahn's Italian sojourn seventy-five sketches are known. Of these, only one is

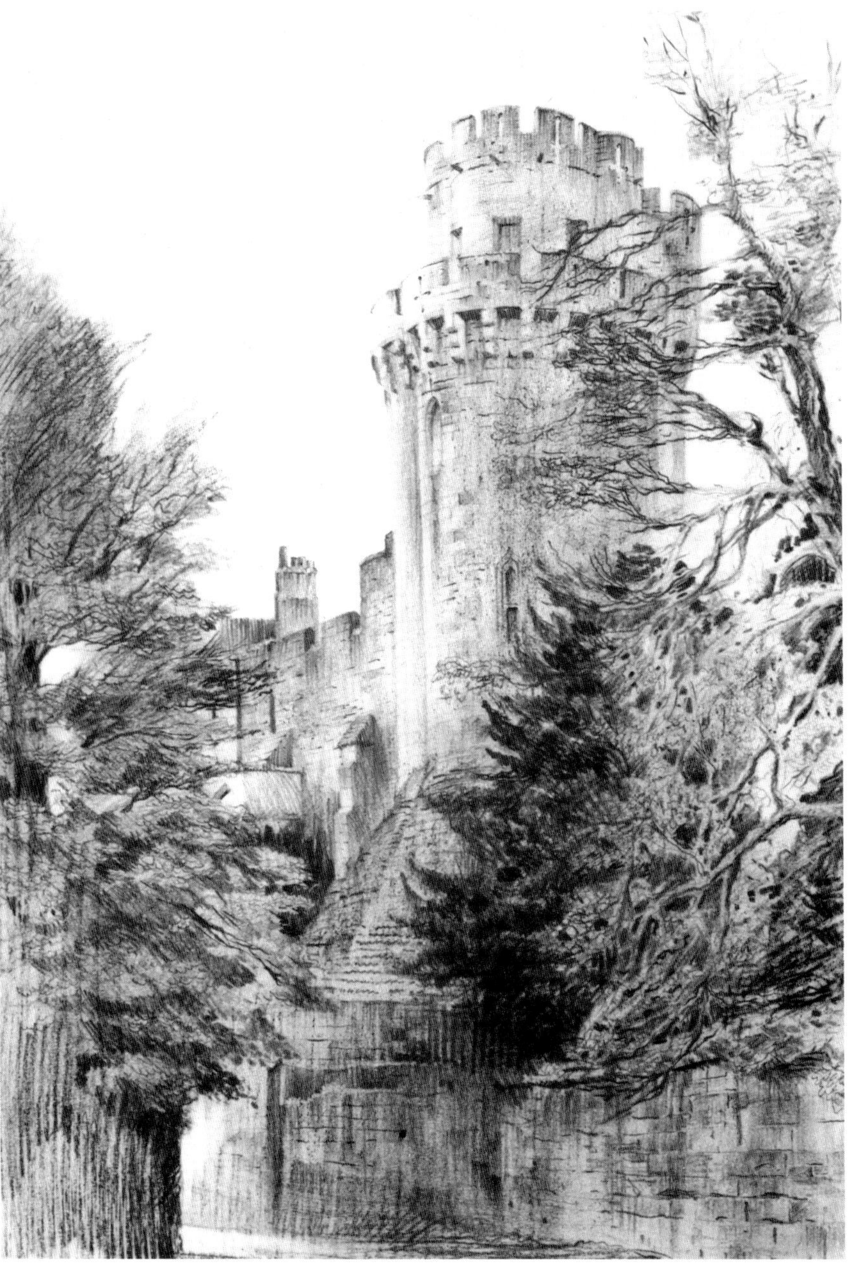

FIGURE 18
CAESAR'S TOWER, WARWICK CASTLE, 1928, pencil on paper (cat. no. 1)

dated to a precise day by an inscription: "Capri 2/7/29."[28] His itinerary in Italy can be reconstructed with some accuracy, however, from the sketches themselves. We can identify drawings that he made in northern Italy at Milan, Verona, Venice, Pavia, and Piacenza. From central Italy come drawings of Florence, San Gimignano, Spoleto, Assisi, and Rome, in which a recently discovered Christmas card places him on 24 December.[29] In the south he sketched at Paestum, Pompeii,[30] and Capri—as well as at several sites on the Sorrento Peninsula, including Amalfi, Positano, and Ravello. Since we know that he entered Italy in early October and was in Rome in December and on Capri in February (the last month of his Italian visit), it seems reasonable to assume that he made his way slowly down the Italian peninsula over the course of the fall and winter, moving south as winter deepened.

Kahn's sketches from his trip of 1928–29 at first glance seem drawn in a hodgepodge of different styles largely because they have not been studied for the internal

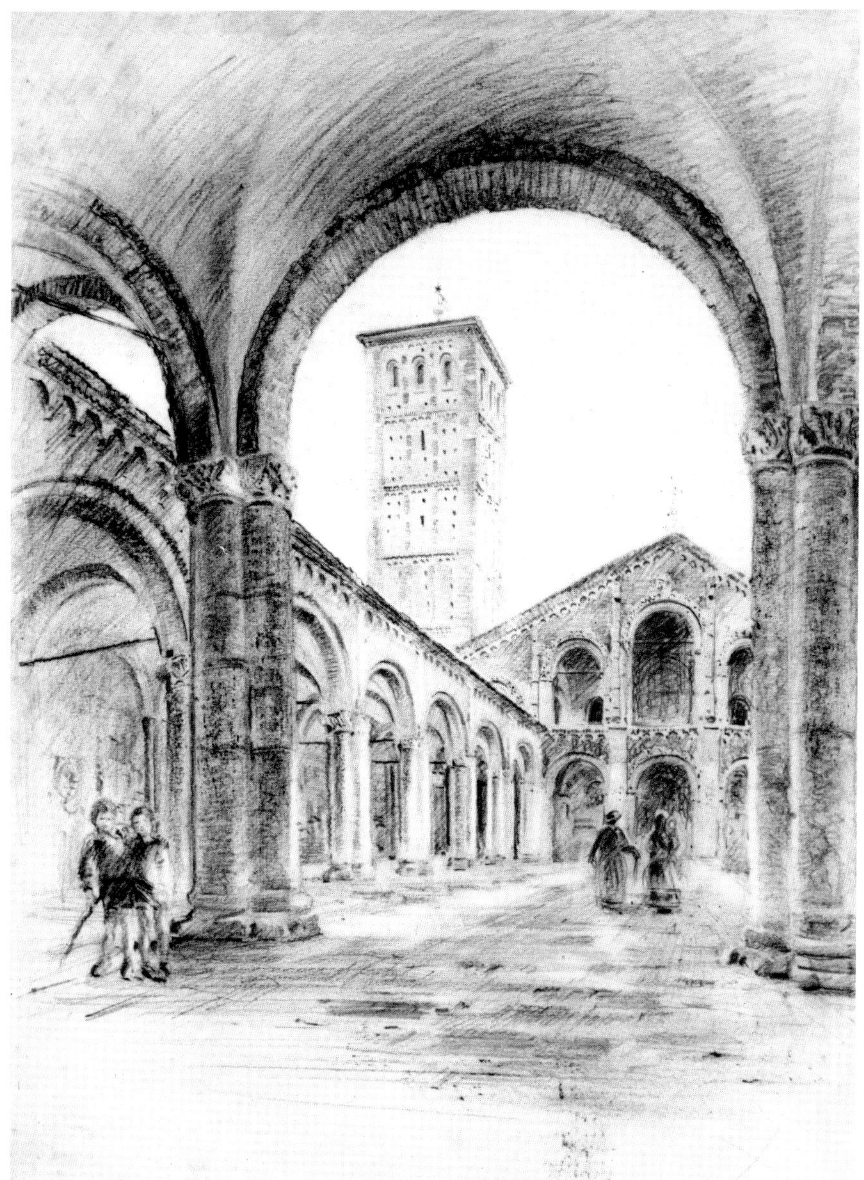

FIGURE 19
ATRIUM OF SANT'AMBROGIO, MILAN, 1928, pencil on paper (cat. no. 4)

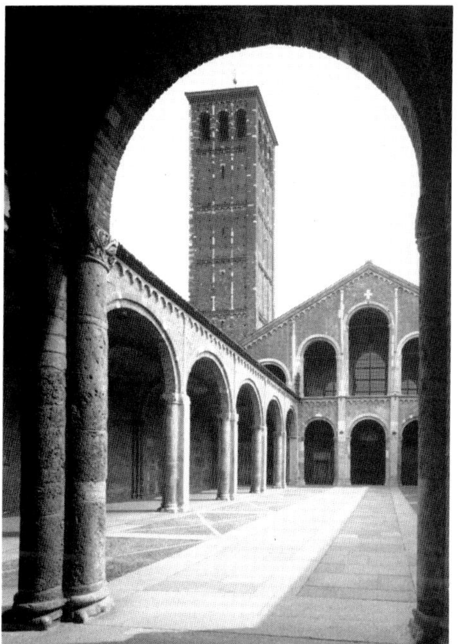

FIGURE 20
ATRIUM OF SANT'AMBROGIO, MILAN; photograph by Ralph Lieberman

stylistic development that takes place within them,[31] or even put in rough chronological order. Jan Hochstim, the author of the standard catalogue of Kahn's two-dimensional works, chose to group the sketches of 1928–29 according to architectural forms depicted: e.g., towers or bridges.[32] This organization obscures a stylistic development that can be grasped once the drawings are grouped chronologically according to places visited. Such a grouping reveals that Kahn's drawings in graphite developed at a different pace from his watercolors. Arranging the drawings chronologically also shows that coeval with the changes in his style were changes in the subjects Kahn chose to draw. Indeed, the shifts in Kahn's subject matter, which reflect his developing ideas about architecture, may have influenced the changes that occurred in his way of drawing.

The attention to detail that one finds in the drawing of Caesar's Tower at Warwick Castle (fig. 18) recurs in the watercolor of the Ponte Scaligero in Verona,[33] the first major Italian city Kahn would have visited after his descent of the Adige Valley from the Brenner Pass. Only slightly less attention to detail and slightly greater freedom in

FIGURE 21
PIAZZETTA AND SAN GIORGIO MAGGIORE (top) and *BASILICA DI SAN MARCO FROM PIAZZETTA* (bottom), *VENICE,* 1928, watercolor and graphite on tissue paper (cat. no. 3)

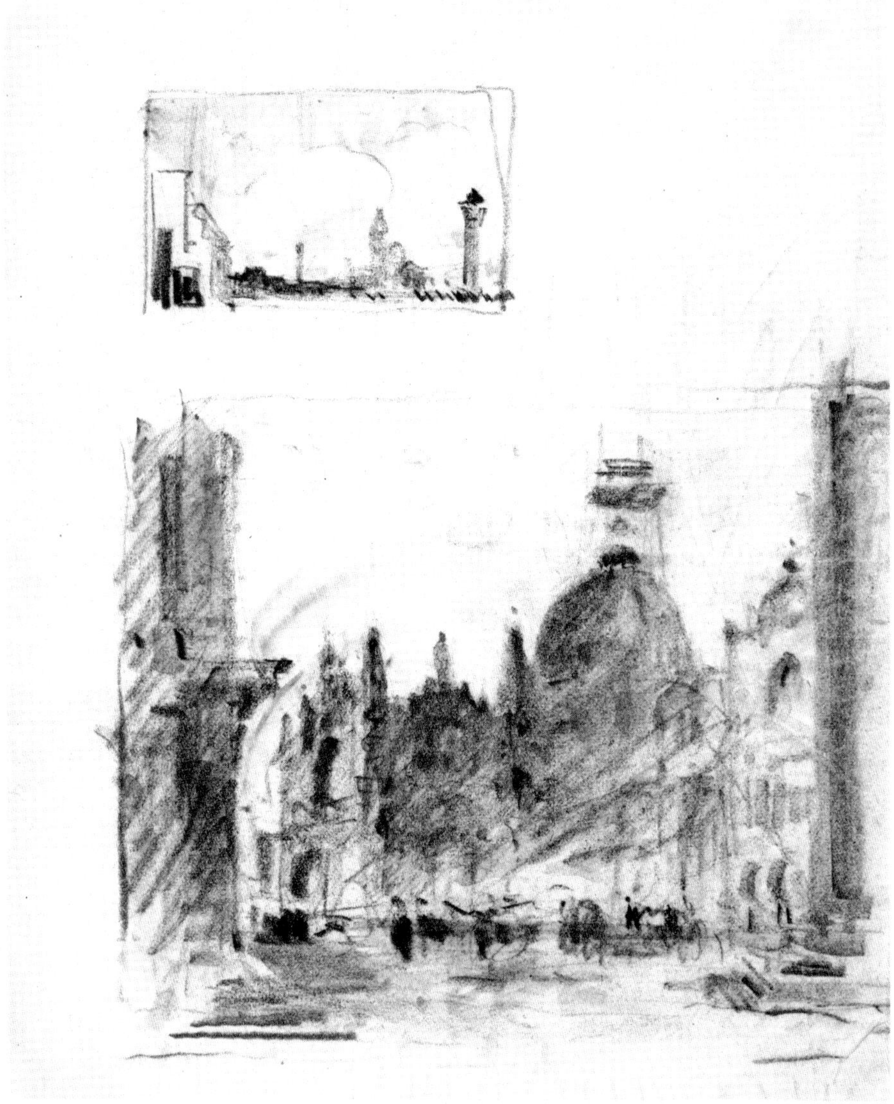

the manipulation of the pencil appear in the drawing of the atrium of Sant'Ambrogio in Milan (figs. 19–20),[34] which Kahn must have made during his first weeks in Italy.[35] On the other hand, conservative as it is, the Sant'Ambrogio drawing shows a certain individuality, for Kahn enhances its expressive power by providing it with more than one vanishing point. The arcade at the left of the drawing focuses on a vanishing point placed just to the right of the pier that separates the lower right arch from the lower central arch of the church façade. The two piers in the foreground of the drawing, however, are not part of this perspective system. The left foreground pier is related to a vanishing point located behind the right foreground pier, while that pier stands on its own, connected to no particular vanishing point at all. By detaching the foreground piers spatially from the rest of the building, and even from each other, Kahn gives them added authority as independent volumes. Three years later Kahn was to write that there was no need to follow the rules of perspective when making sketches.[36]

In northern Italy Kahn worked in a number of styles. An impressionist interest in light and in the atmospheric blurring of architectural forms characterizes drawings that Kahn made in Venice. These include two crayon drawings, now missing,[37] and

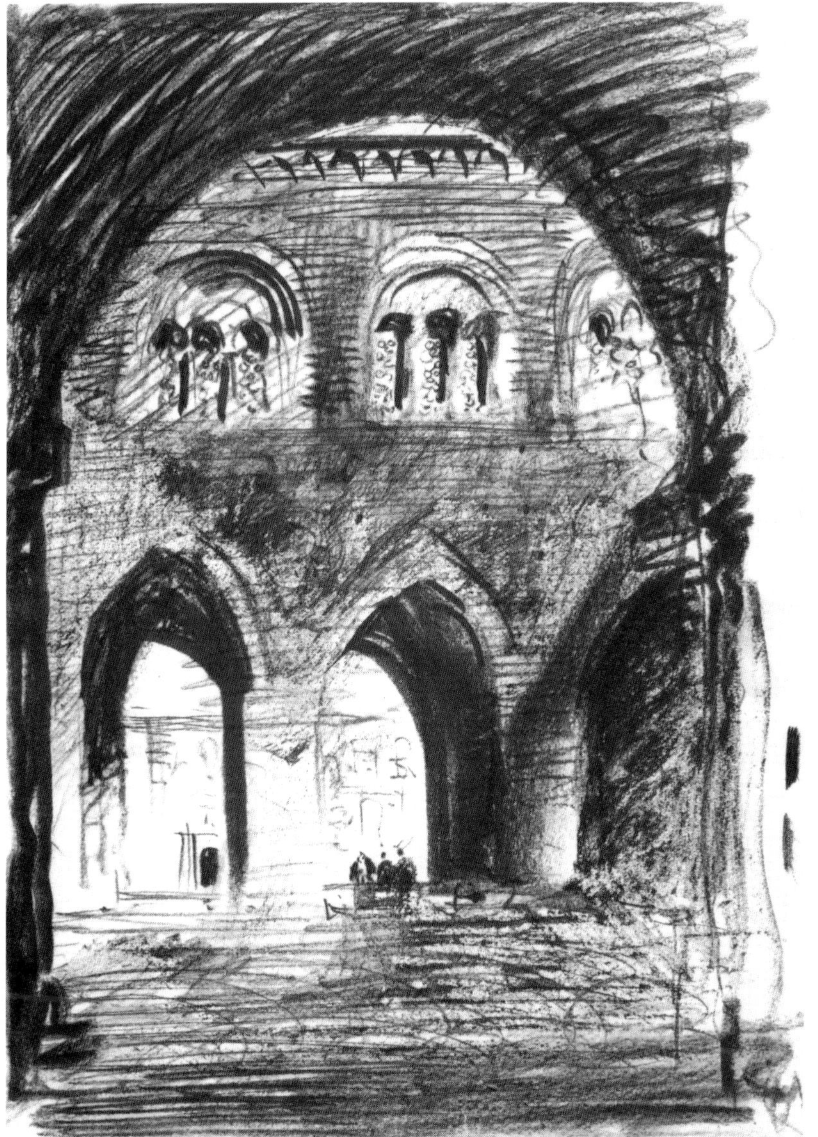

FIGURE 22
CORTILE OF "IL GOTICO" (PALAZZO COMUNALE), PIACENZA, 1928, pencil, graphite, and ink on paper (cat. no. 6)

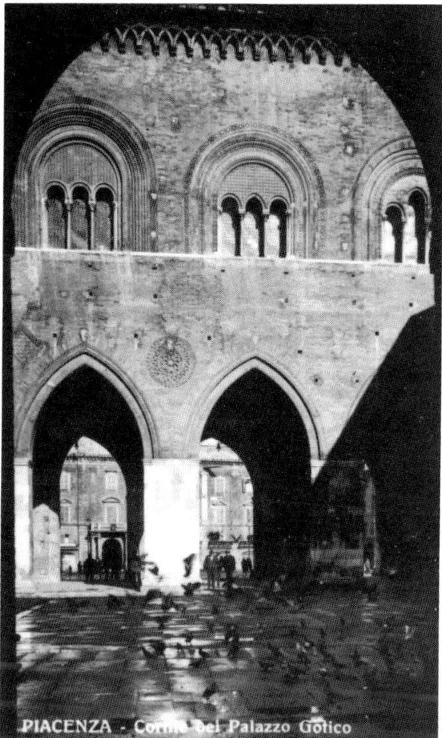

FIGURE 23
CORTILE OF "IL GOTICO" (PALAZZO COMUNALE), PIACENZA, postcard; Collection of Esther I. Kahn

two graphite and watercolor drawings paired on one sheet (fig. 21).[38] In the lower of these drawings, the details of the basilica of San Marco are subsumed in a hazy blur of medium gray shading accented by a few passages of black that indicate deep shadow. The particulars of the architecture of the church, aside from its silhouette, seem to have interested him not at all. Instead, he was trying to render the sparkle of light on the church's polished marble surfaces.

One of the most powerful of the north Italian drawings shows the cortile of "Il Gotico," the Palazzo Comunale in Piacenza (figs. 22–23), enclosed by tall, pointed arches through which one sees the late-eighteenth-century façade of the Palazzo del Governatore across Piazza dei Cavalli.[39] As in many of his drawings from northern and central Italy, Kahn experiments with several media—pencil, graphite, and ink—in an attempt to render space, mass, texture, light, and shade. His strokes are long, thin, and irregular scribbles, the product of his haste to render a strong reaction to the dark arches separated by light-filled voids. There is, however, almost no connection between the shapes of the architectural forms and the shapes of his graphic marks.

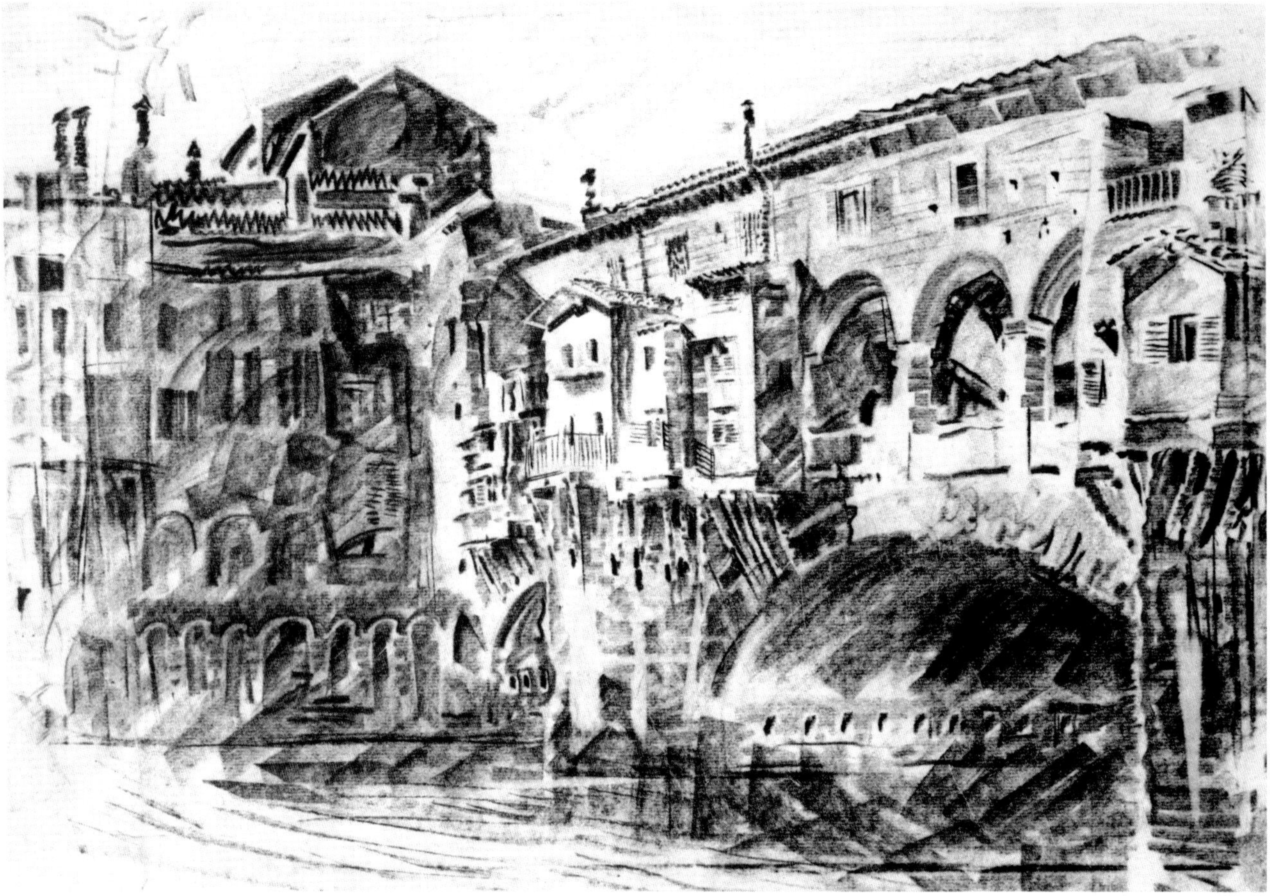

FIGURE 24
PONTE VECCHIO, FLORENCE,
1928, graphite on paper (cat. no. 8)

FIGURE 25
PONTE VECCHIO, FLORENCE;
photograph by Ralph Lieberman

That lack of connection disappears in later work.

Kahn's increasingly free use of the graphite stick as he moved south is clear in the four sketches preserved from his visit to Florence. In his drawing of the Ponte Vecchio[10] (figs. 24–25) short, broad, jabbing strokes define the piers of the arcade in the center of the bridge and render the shadow under the roof above, while nervous zigzags enliven the roof lines to the left. The whole drawing seems both more abstract and more spontaneous than the mixed-media drawing of "Il Gotico." Here, broad strokes of graphite dance with some purpose across the surface, helping to define forms as well as making patterns of light and dark, but still the randomness of the marks often fails to accord with the shapes of the structures rendered.

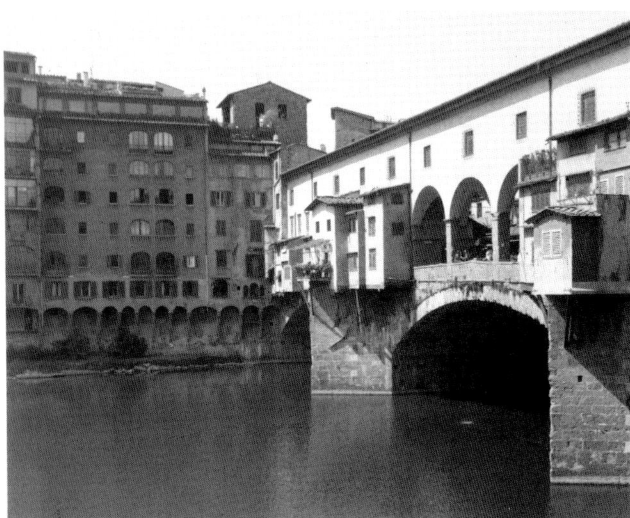

In Assisi, it seems, Kahn found his own way to use graphite. While his drawing of the flank of the church of San Francesco at Assisi[11] (figs. 26–27) is stylistically very close to the sketch of the Ponte Vecchio, the drawing of the façade of the Cathedral of Assisi[12] goes far beyond either (figs. 28–29). Here every architectural surface is rendered with broad, horizontal strokes. Each mark of the graphite defines a cubist plane on the surface of the paper that makes us acutely

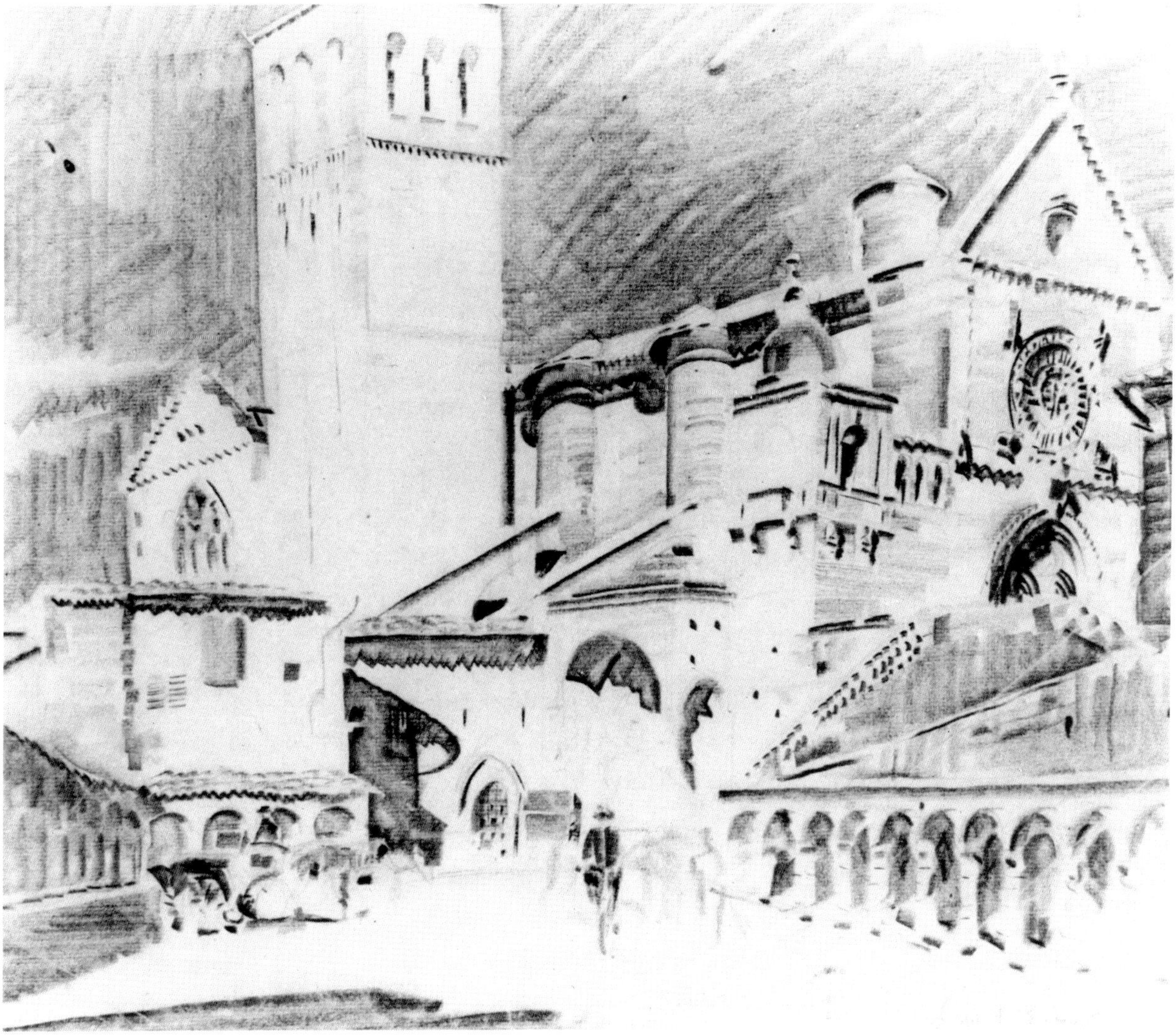

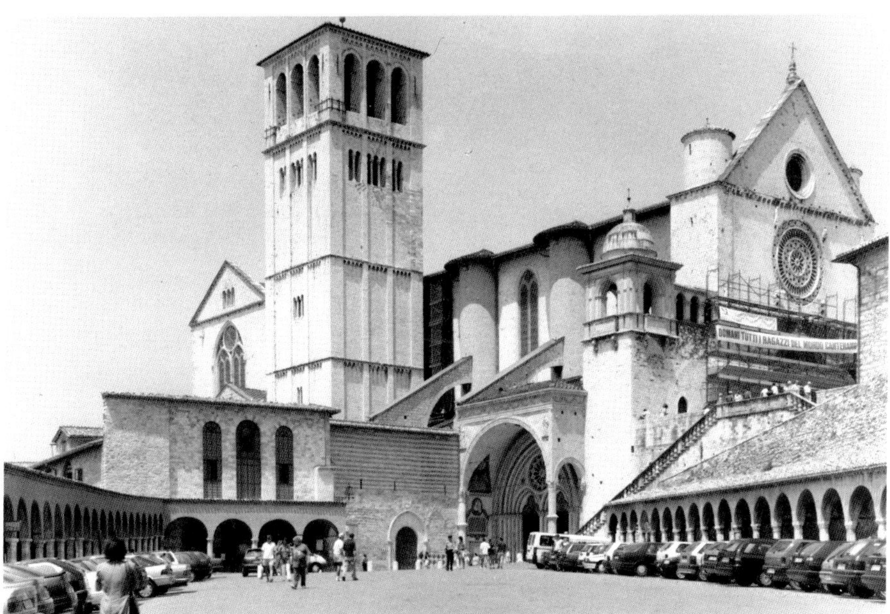

FIGURE 26
SAN FRANCESCO FROM PIAZZA INFERIORE, ASSISI, 1928 [JH70], graphite on paper, 35.3 x 37 cm; photograph courtesy Deutsches Architektur-Museum, Frankfurt

FIGURE 27
SAN FRANCESCO FROM PIAZZA INFERIORE, ASSISI; photograph by Ralph Lieberman

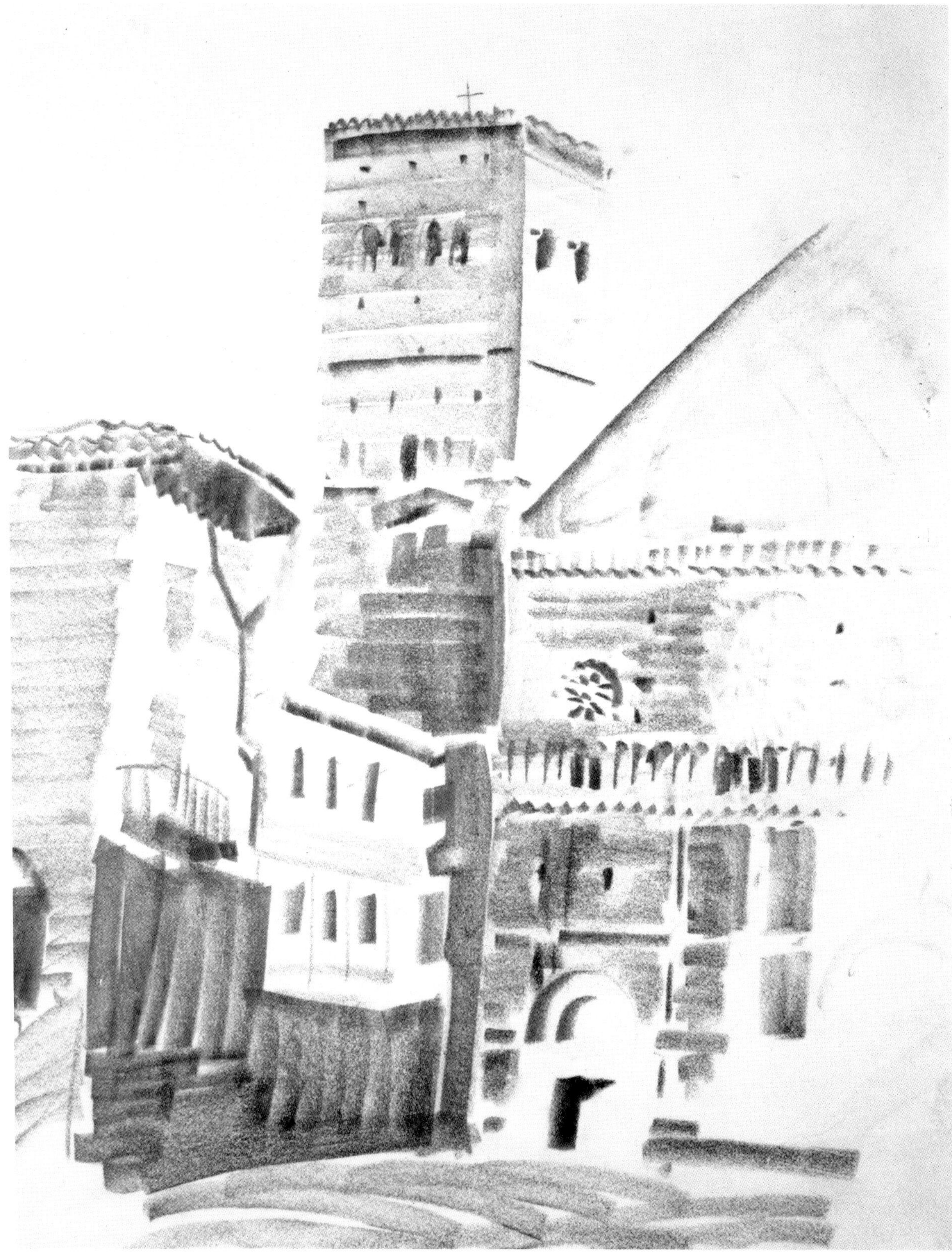

FIGURE 28
CATHEDRAL OF SAN RUFINO, ASSISI, 1928, graphite on ivory paper; photograph courtesy lender (cat. no. 10)

aware, all at once, of the process of making the drawing, of the planarity of the paper, of the flat character of the graphite line, of the rectangular solids of the buildings, and, finally, of the reaction to light of the stone surfaces of the buildings.

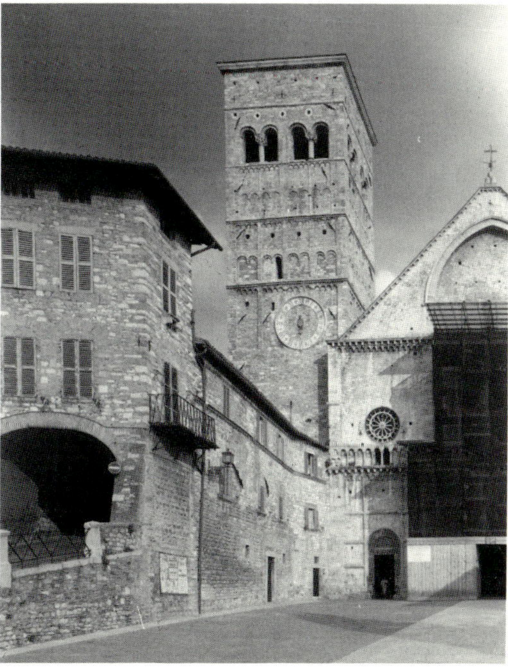

FIGURE 29
CATHEDRAL OF SAN RUFINO, ASSISI; photograph by Ralph Lieberman

This drawing of San Rufino seems to have held particular significance for Kahn. It was one of four drawings from Italy that he exhibited at the 27th Annual Watercolor Exhibition at the Pennsylvania Academy of the Fine Arts in the fall of 1929,[43] and he also chose it as one of six drawings and one lithograph that illustrate the first essay he ever published, "The Value and Aim in Sketching," which appeared in 1931.[44] The drawing was one of two travel sketches from 1928–29 published in Vincent Scully's pioneering book on Kahn in 1962.[45] Kahn's office made a photograph of the drawing available to Scully.[46] Kahn's affection for this drawing suggests that he prized what might seem to be its shortcomings, particularly his apparent indecision in rendering the elements of the cathedral façade. In the sketch, the rose window does not line up with the central portal, and the pointed arch in the pediment is drawn in at least two different sizes.

The pioneering nature of this Assisi drawing may also be signaled by its tense balance between modeling and flatness. Even though Kahn tried to render the volumes of the two towers and to indicate the depth of the arch over the side door, the strongest

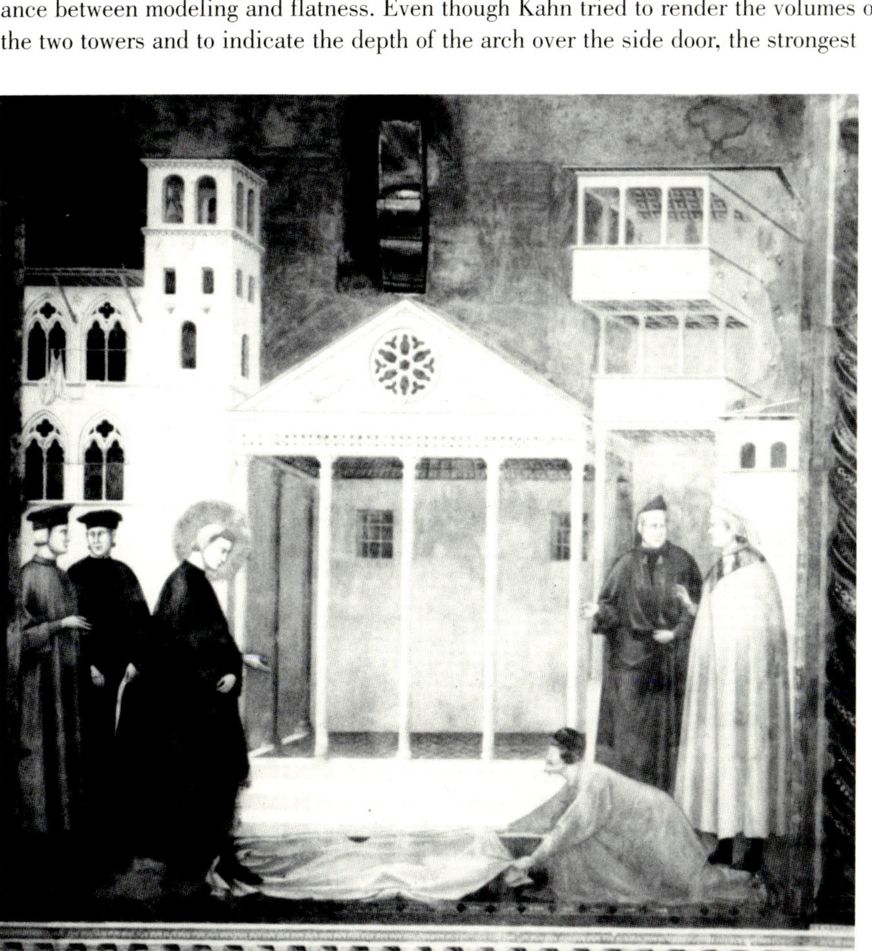

FIGURE 30
SAINT FRANCIS RECEIVES THE HOMAGE OF A SIMPLE MAN, fresco, upper church, San Francesco, Assisi; photograph courtesy Scala/Art Resources

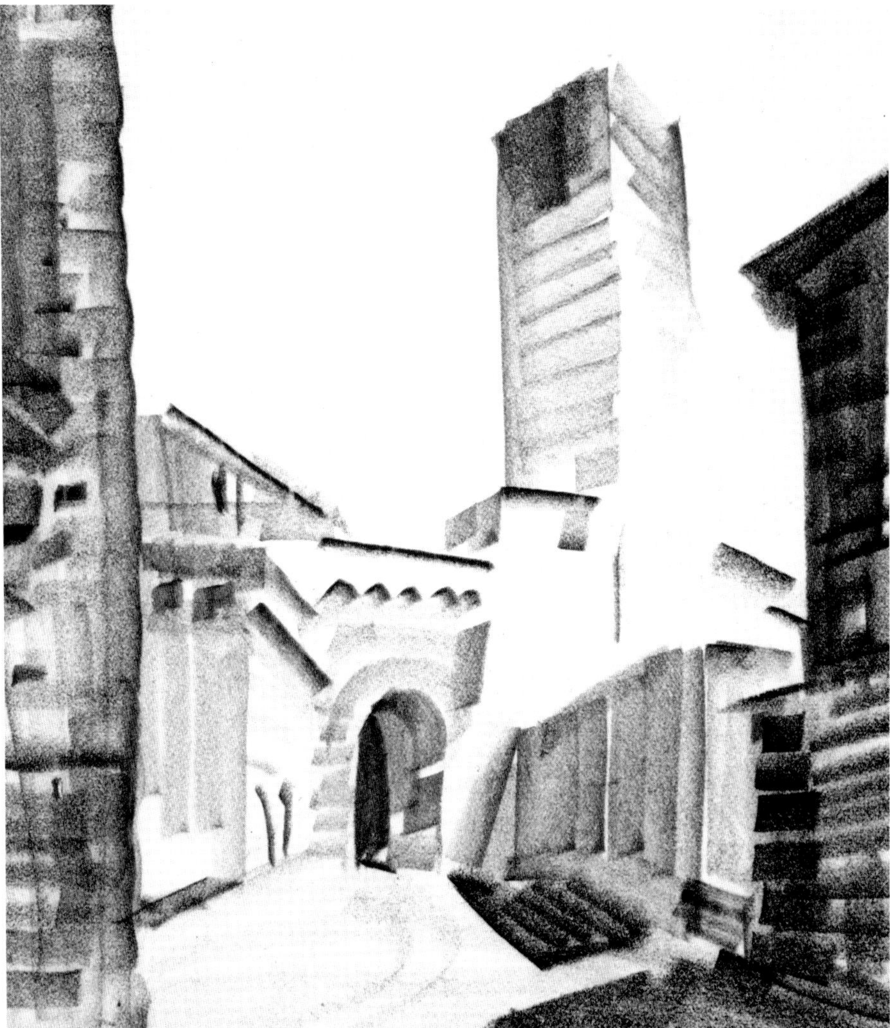

FIGURE 31
STREET AND TOWER, SAN GIMIGNANO, 1928, graphite on paper (cat. no. 12)

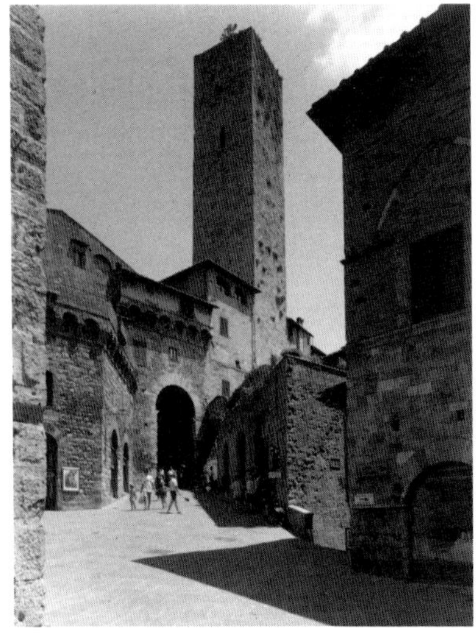

FIGURE 32
STREET AND TOWER, SAN GIMIGNANO; photograph by Ralph Lieberman

impression conveyed by this sketch is one of relentless two-dimensionality; every stroke lies flat on the page, refusing to transform itself into an act of modeling. In another drawing in this manner from San Gimignano (figs. 31–32), which Kahn may have visited just after Assisi, there is a far greater sense of space and of the volume of the structures depicted. *Street and tower, San Gimignano*[17] establishes depth through the powerful verticals of the dark repoussoir forms at either side that play against the lighter forms in the middle ground and the deep, black hole in the center. (Nonetheless, this drawing flattens out considerably the angle of the street as it climbs toward the dark archway.) Most importantly, the drawing now exhibits a complete unity between formal means of drawing and the forms depicted, a unity that occurs just at the point on his trip when Kahn begins to concentrate almost exclusively on medieval architecture and to move away from the drawing of famous set pieces such as San Marco or the Ponte Vecchio to the rendering of less well known works such as the cathedral and the Rocca Maggiore of Assisi.

Kahn's conquest of the graphite stick may well have been speeded up by his experience of the frescoes in the upper church at Assisi (figs. 30, 35). In those paintings buildings are rendered in terms of lighter and darker planes that establish the architectural forms spatially. The planes are not separated by lines; rather, there is simply a clean edge between the lighter and darker colors. Windows appear as areas of black paint. The drawings of the Cathedral of Assisi and the street in San Gimignano use exactly these techniques of modeling and of drawing windows. The architectural forms in the frescoes, grand in their planar simplicity, belong to the same family of Italian Gothic forms that Kahn had already chosen to draw. If, however, the Assisi frescoes helped Kahn find a personal style of drawing buildings, it was his own growing sureness with the graphite stick that gives these drawings, worked at a speed that precludes measured consideration, their spontaneity and urgency.[48]

In Kahn's drawings of the Rocca Maggiore (figs. 33–34), the fortress (a compact, dominant structure not unlike Kahn's Assembly Building at Dacca, Bangladesh, of 1962–83) guards the vernacular houses of the city from its height to the north.[49] Below the Rocca stand the interlocked cubic blocks of ordinary dwellings, jostling each other for place just as the encircling blocks of Kahn's unbuilt Salk meeting house project of the early 1960s would jostle each other in the model.

The dark sky in this drawing probably records an effect of weather that Kahn had experienced. In fall and winter the Umbrian sky is often overcast; sporadically the sun breaks through to illuminate buildings against black clouds. The dark sky may also have been inspired by the frescoes (by Giotto, he thought) that he had seen in the upper church of San Francesco at Assisi; in 1959 Kahn said that Giotto was a great painter because he painted skies black at midday.[50] The way Kahn pulls the Rocca dramatically up into the forward plane of the drawing seems inspired by the way buildings are placed in landscapes in the upper-church frescoes: the scene of Saint Francis giving his cloak to a poor knight (fig. 35) has just such an overscaled building perched on a hilltop in its upper right corner.[51] The published version of Kahn's speech in Otterlo in 1959 is illustrated by a photograph of this very fresco.

Kahn's brilliant drawing of the porch of San Zeno in Verona (figs. 36–37)[52] may seem at first glance to stand outside the development of his drawing style proposed here. Also made with a graphite stick, the drawing has a quality of abstraction that makes it appear far removed from the impressionist glitter of the Venetian crayon drawings or the precise handling of the pencil in *Atrium of Sant'Ambrogio*. Rather, the graphite skips in jazzy art deco rhythms across the surface of the paper to create the abstract contour lines of the lions' manes or the dark patterns of the bronze doors. The strokes, however, are all small, short or relatively narrow, not the long, broad strokes that quickly and abstractly define planes in the Assisi and San Gimignano drawings. Nor is there that interest in flat surface rather than surface detail that characterizes those later drawings. Actually, the San Zeno drawing is all about light, an impressionist drawing made with art deco strokes, as if, say, Claude Monet in his last year of life had taken up the style promulgated by the Exposition des Arts Decoratifs in Paris of 1925. The art deco character of the San Zeno drawing represents Kahn's use of yet another style that he had learned and indeed used in the United States, as Michael Lewis demonstrates in these pages (fig. 4), but the style was not his own. A photograph of the doorway (fig. 37) demonstrates that Kahn shifted positions while he was making the drawing.

By the time Kahn had reached the Sorrento Peninsula, probably in January, he could use the graphite stick not just to create straight, planar strokes but also to form the curved shapes of objects depicted. In the drawing of the Chiesa dell'Annunziata in Ravello (pl. 4),[53] Kahn renders the irregularly curved vaults in the foreground with curved strokes, and he also uses the shapes of his marks to describe the form of the hill in the background. In the most abstract of these drawings from the winter of 1929, a sketch of the Faraglioni at Capri (fig. 38),[54] the curves of the strokes describe the contours of the sea-girt rocks with consummate assurance. On the other hand, some of the drawings from the Sorrento Peninsula, such as *Atrio del Palazzo Rufolo* at Ravello

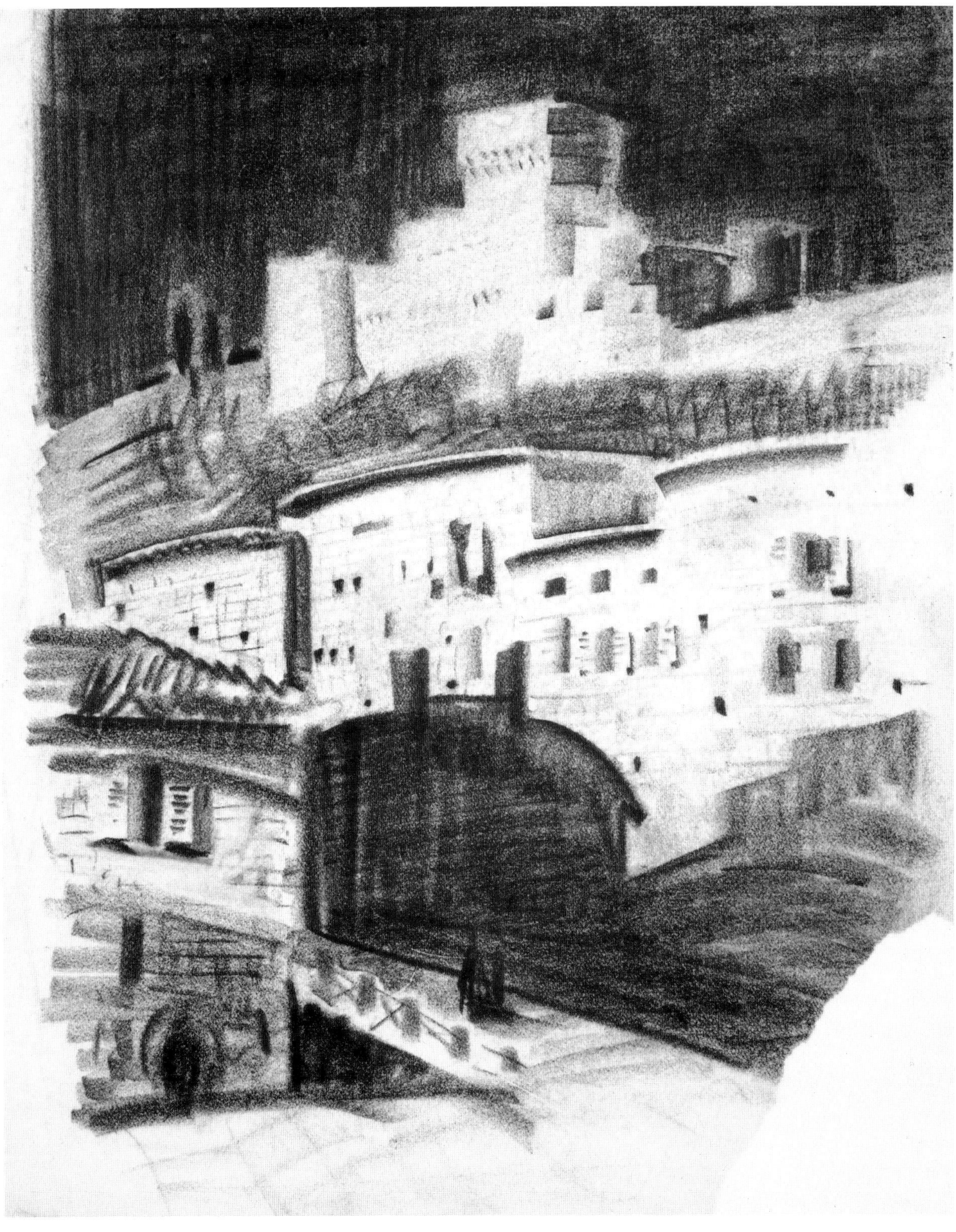

FIGURE 33
ROCCA MAGGIORE FROM PIAZZA SAN RUFINO, ASSISI, 1928, graphite on paper (cat. no. 11)

(fig. 44),[55] show Kahn still struggling with the rendering of trees, a battle that he seems to have won in the powerful drawing of a tree from the Borghese Gardens in Rome,[56] where the strokes of graphite at once describe silhouette, contour, texture, and the play of light and shade. One wonders if these trees from the Villa Borghese may not be the last drawings Kahn made in Italy.[57]

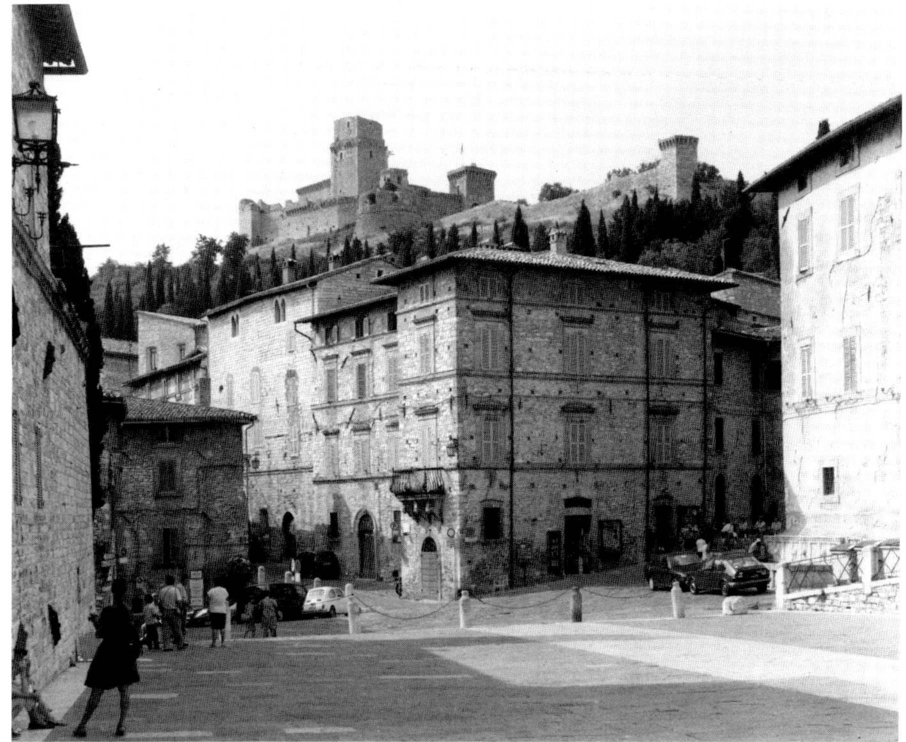

FIGURE 34
ROCCA MAGGIORE FROM PIAZZA SAN RUFINO, ASSISI; photograph by Ralph Lieberman

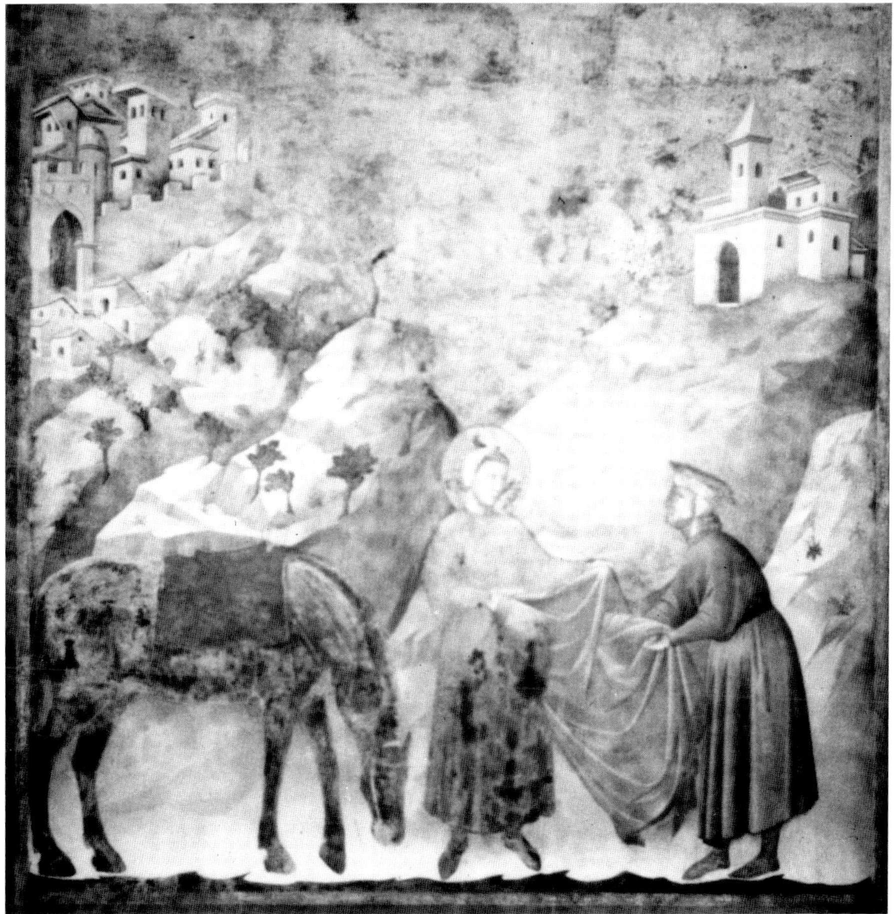

FIGURE 35
SAINT FRANCIS GIVES HIS CLOAK TO A POOR KNIGHT, fresco, upper church, San Francesco, Assisi; photograph courtesy Scala/Art Resources

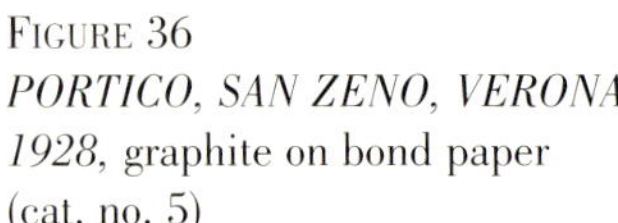

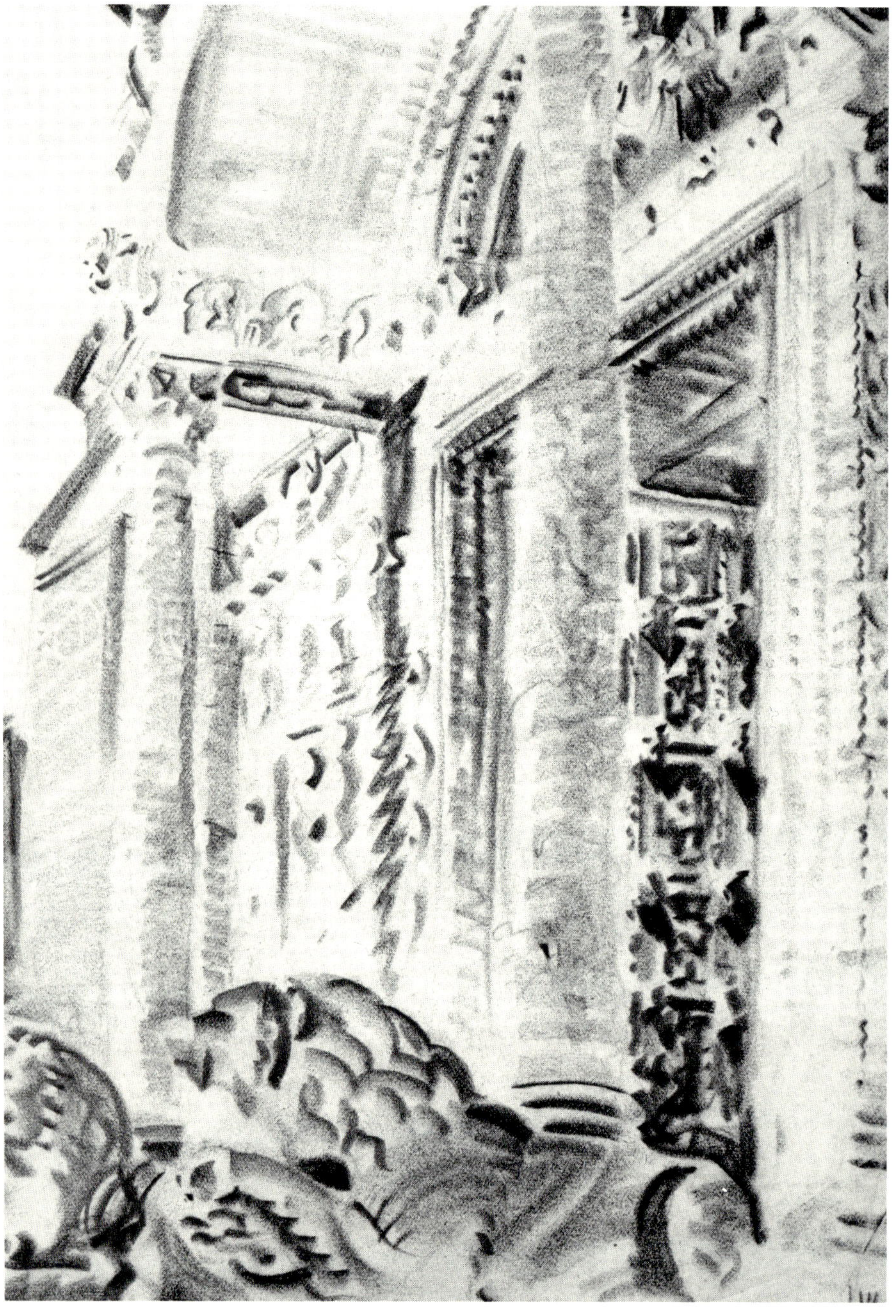

FIGURE 36
PORTICO, SAN ZENO, VERONA, 1928, graphite on bond paper (cat. no. 5)

FIGURE 37
PORTICO, SAN ZENO, VERONA; photograph by Ralph Lieberman

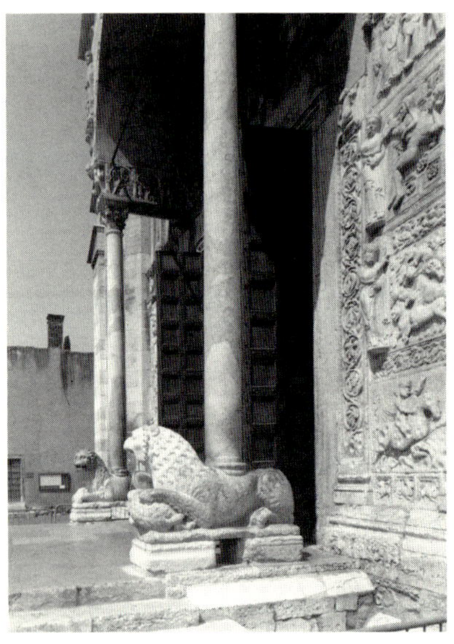

Watercolors form the second large group of sketches that Kahn executed in Italy. Those from Venice are among the earliest, and they show a breaking up of color into little pools that make clear his debt to impressionist painters like Monet, who had also painted Venice, but perhaps Monet's influence was filtered through the work of American watercolorists such as Maurice Prendergast, George

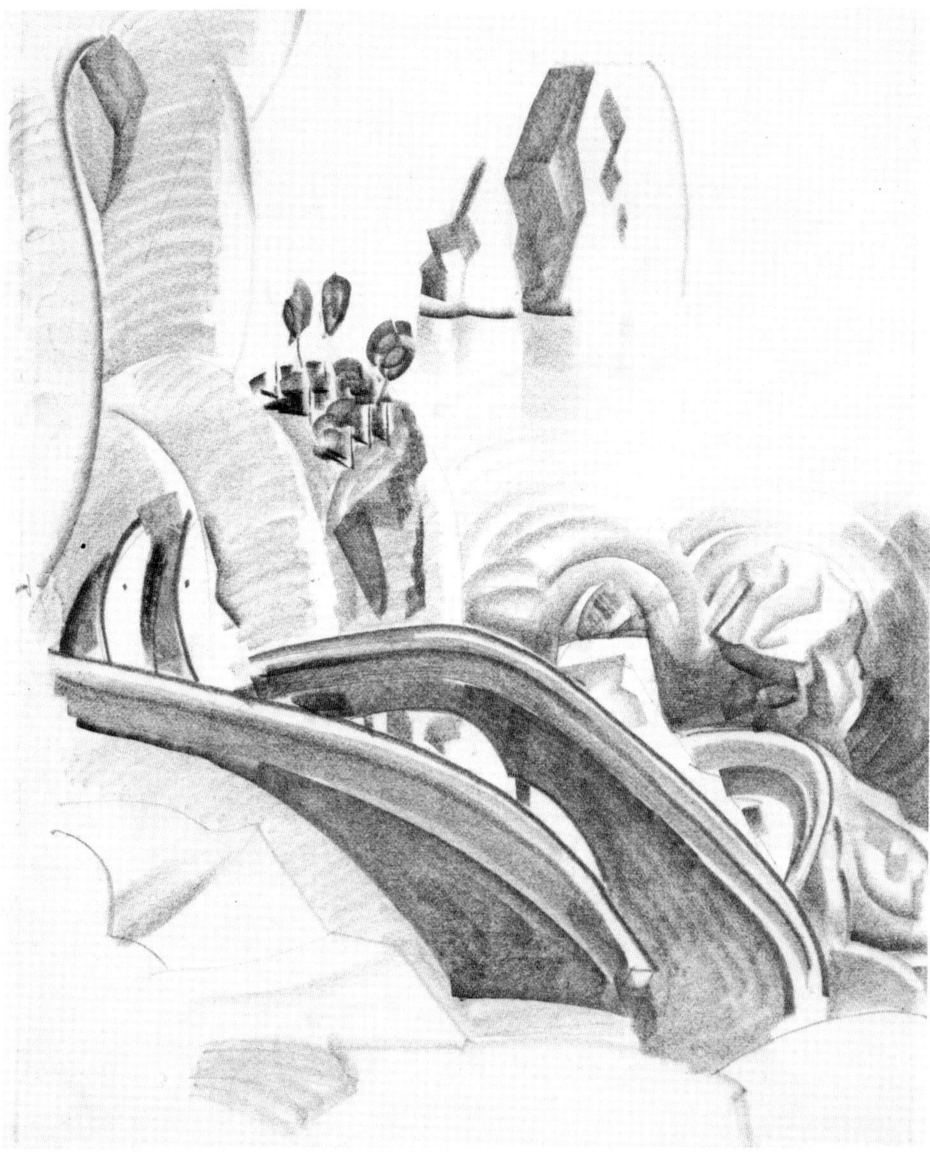

FIGURE 38
I FARAGLIONI, CAPRI, 1929,
graphite on paper (cat. no. 27)

Demuth, or Edward Hopper. Even the subject of two of Kahn's Venetian watercolors,[58] boats riding on the shimmering surface of the lagoons, is a quintessentially impressionist one. For these Venetian views, as for all of his Italian watercolors, Kahn chose the medium for the simple reason that it allowed him to represent the colors of what he was sketching. He frequently liked to work with wet paper to achieve blurred colors. His watercolor of Santa Maria della Salute in Venice (pl. 1) presents the church as a looming mass capped by the blue semicircle of its dome, as if Kahn wanted to transfer the aqueous ground color of Venice to the city's structures themselves.

Kahn did not achieve a mode of personal expression as quickly in watercolors as he had in graphite drawings. *Street and tower, San Gimignano* (fig. 31), one of the finest of his slashing, planar, graphite sketches, is contemporary with the two beautiful but rather more traditional watercolors made in the same town.[59] In one of the watercolors (pl. 2), also of medieval family towers, Kahn treats the surfaces not as abstract, modernist planes but rather as opportunities for the subtle modulation and mingling of colors to create a wonderful sense of tone, texture, and light, all held together by a scaffolding of red pencil outlines that Kahn allows to show through. Two watercolors made slightly later in Rome[60] show a lingering interest in mingling different colors in the same area of the work, but they also exhibit an increasing interest in abstraction and in colors that are less descriptive than the colors in the San Gimignano works.[61]

These characteristics of the Roman watercolors seem to appear first in a sketch made in Spoleto, north of Rome, a watercolor of the Ponte delle Torri (pl. 3), looking east from the city toward the tower that protects the western end of the bridge.[62] The palette is dominated by mauve and lavender, the transparent washes in the upper right of the drawing are particularly delicate, and the forms (especially the trees and clouds) take on the purer geometry we later find in the Roman scenes; the weighty masses of buildings and trees float over a modernist void at the bottom of the page. This void, to be sure, simply signals the presence of the deep gorge crossed by the bridge (fig. 39), but Kahn uses the fact of the gorge as a pretext to create a wholly cubist, antigravitational effect, in which the road that leads into the depth of the drawing actually serves to move the eye flatly and vertically up the plane of the paper.

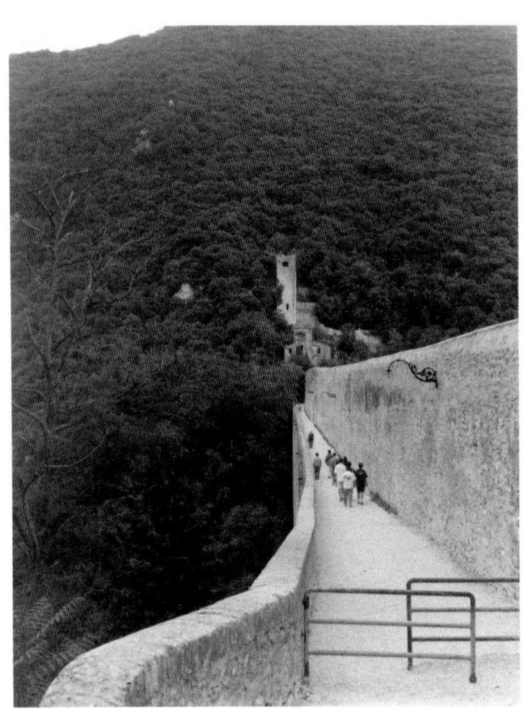

FIGURE 39
PONTE DELLE TORRI, VIEW OF NORTH SIDE FROM WEST, SPOLETO; photograph by Ralph Lieberman

In the watercolors made on the Sorrento Peninsula, Kahn finally achieved a level of personal expressiveness similar to the one he had found in his graphite drawings of Umbria and Tuscany. One of the most remarkable of these is the highly abstract, indeed cubist, *View of Positano*.[63] The palette is restricted to mauves, olive green, and brown, and the forms of the landscape are translated into sharp-edged, flat planes of color. The reduction of means is analogous to that achieved in the graphite drawing of the Cathedral of Assisi. Even in less radical watercolors of nearby scenes, such as *Atrani from Torre Saracena, Amalfi* (fig. 54), or its pendant, *Torre Saracena, Amalfi*,[64] there is a reduction in palette, and the mingling of colors that characterizes the San Gimignano and Roman watercolors has almost completely disappeared.

The watercolor of Positano, even though it is highly abstract, still shows us Kahn's interest in recording precise times of day; the shadows suggest that he made the sketch in the very early afternoon, as the sun began its descent. This interest in the effect of light never left Kahn. We find it again, for instance, in the series of drawings he made of the Temple of Apollo at Corinth in 1951. And we find consistently in his mature buildings a sensitivity to the effects that sunlight and the change of the character of light during the course of a day can have on a structure. We should always keep in mind, however, that the drawings of the Sorrento Peninsula and the pastels of Italy, Greece, and Egypt of 1950–51 all depict winter light; none records the intense sun of high summer in the Mediterranean.

A group of fishermen's houses at Conca dei Marini, a town between Amalfi and Positano, sufficiently caught Kahn's fancy that he bought a postcard of them (fig. 40) on which he based three works: a powerful graphite drawing (fig. 41), a watercolor (fig. 42), and a painting (fig. 43) that he made after his return to Philadelphia.[65] In the watercolor Kahn completely reworked the rocky background of the postcard into angular cubist planes like those of the landscape in the Positano view, while he also raised some of the planes of the buildings to make them read more clearly and to create a more cubist composition.

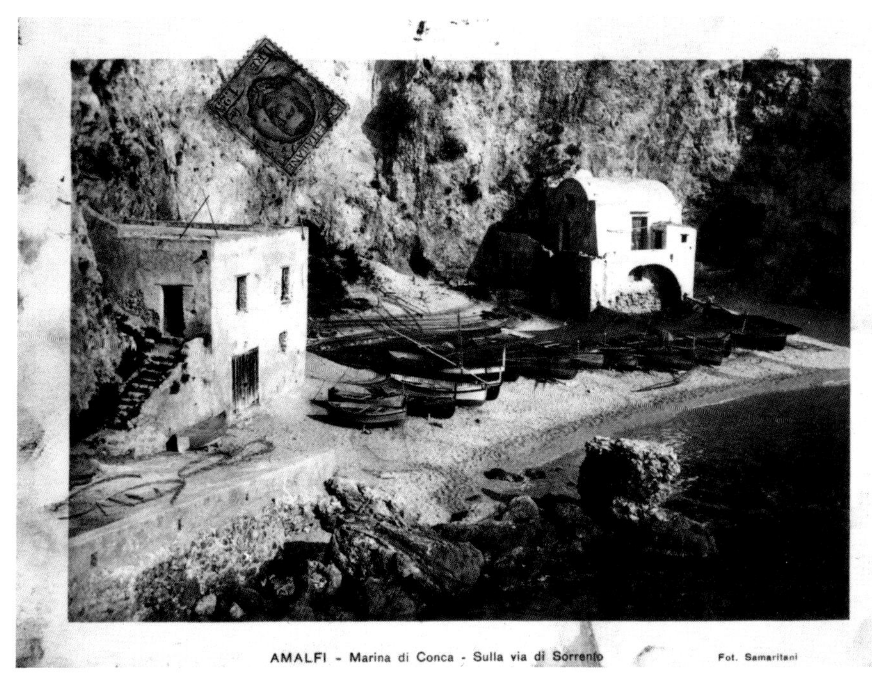

FIGURE 40
FISHERMEN'S HOUSES, CONCA DEI MARINI, postcard; Collection of Esther I. Kahn

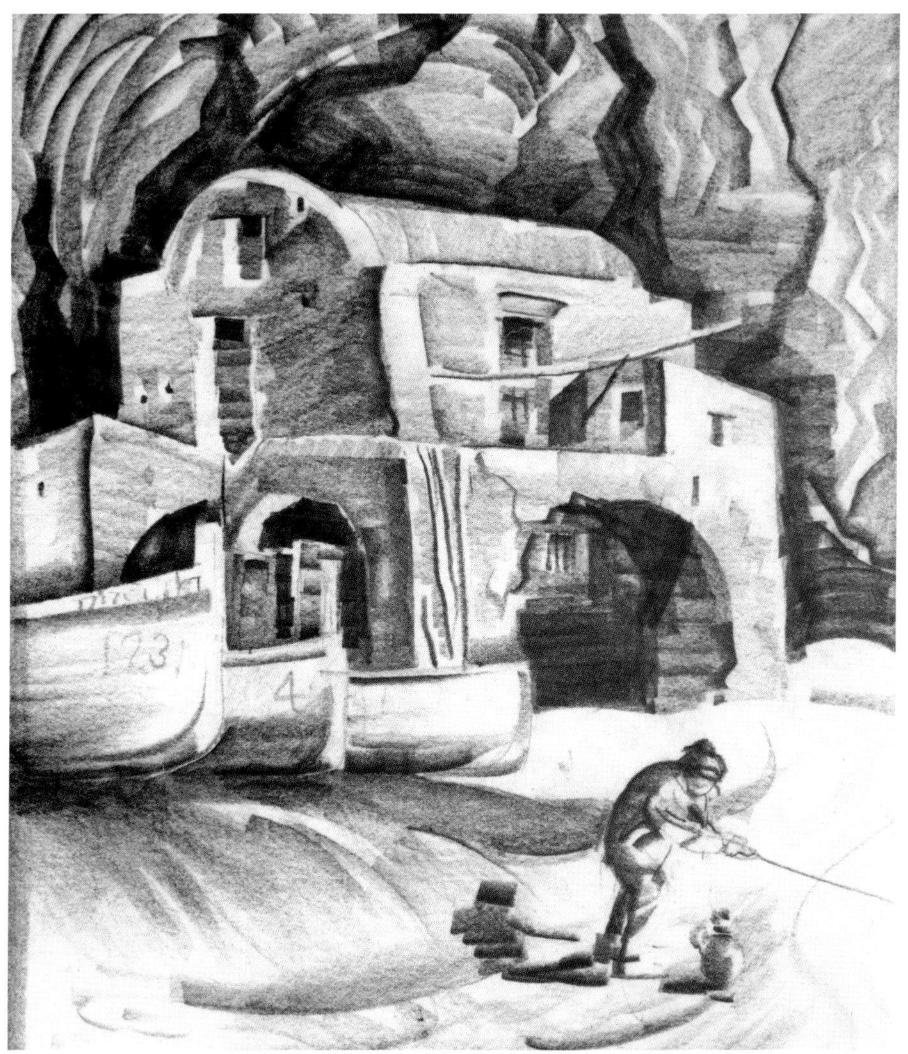

FIGURE 41
FISHERMAN'S HOUSE, CONCA DEI MARINI, 1929, graphite on paper (cat. no. 24)

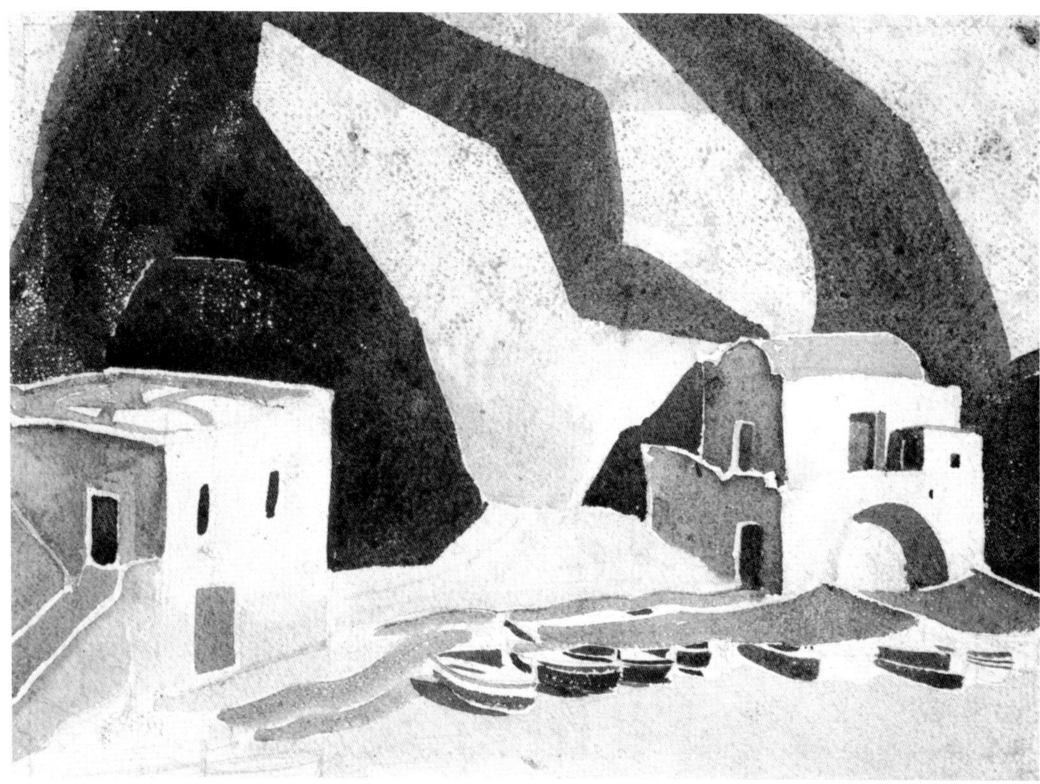

FIGURE 42
FISHERMEN'S HOUSES, CONCA DEI MARINI, 1929, watercolor on paper (cat. no. 25)

Kahn left no written record of his working methods when he was sketching, and the few drawings preserved from most sites are of little help in figuring out how he worked. On the basis of seven sketches that we can now identify as from Ravello, however, one can attempt to reconstruct how he approached—one might even say

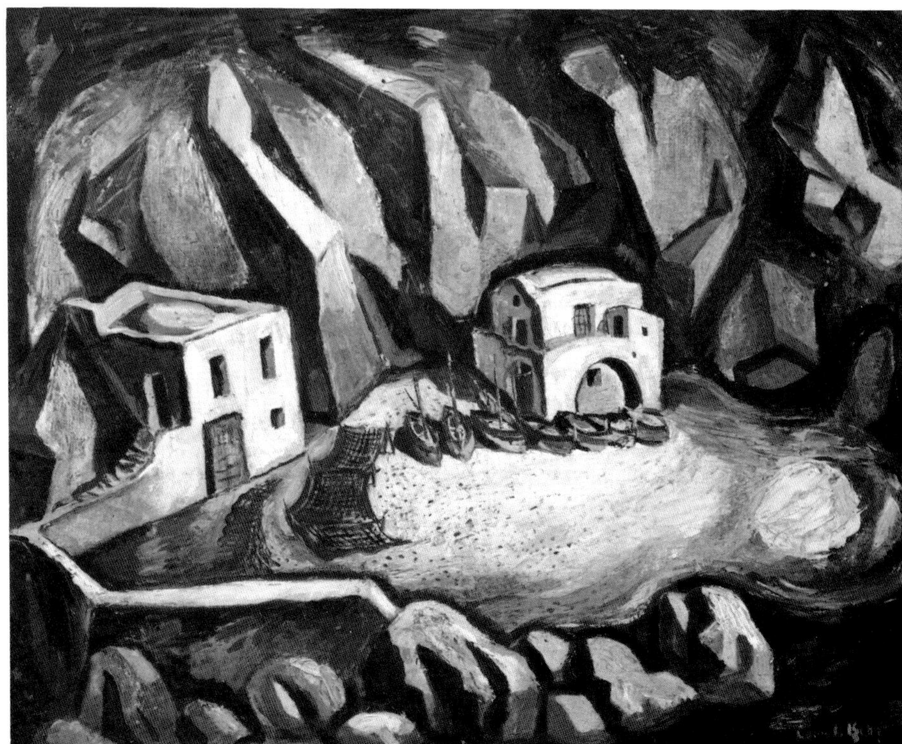

FIGURE 43
FISHERMEN'S HOUSES, CONCA DEI MARINI, 1929–30, oil on canvas (cat. no. 26)

stalked and devoured—a site.[66] All the Ravello drawings (three in watercolor, four in graphite) are either of the Villa Rufolo, a complicated, late-Gothic patrician residence to which a sizable garden was appended in the nineteenth century (Richard Wagner wrote parts of *Parsifal* therein), or of a building visible from the villa, or of a building in turn visible from the one seen from the villa. Kahn concentrated his efforts on a discrete part of the city rather than haphazardly sketching all over town, allowing himself to be drawn away from the focus of his efforts only by buildings that he could see from that focus. This sequence of drawings of Villa Rufolo has its own internal coherence, recording in four, two-dimensional, fixed images enough information to allow Kahn to recall the experience of moving through the complex.

While we cannot know for sure the order in which Kahn made these drawings, we can at least put them in an order that relates to the way one might experience the Villa Rufolo in a visit to Ravello. The villa is entered through a tower that rises across from the southern flank of the cathedral, alongside an extension of the main piazza of the city. In a now missing drawing, Kahn shows the campanile of the cathedral to the left and the entrance tower of the villa to the right.[67] A second drawing (fig. 44), which Kahn inscribed "Atrio del Palazzo Rufolo," shows the inner side of the entrance

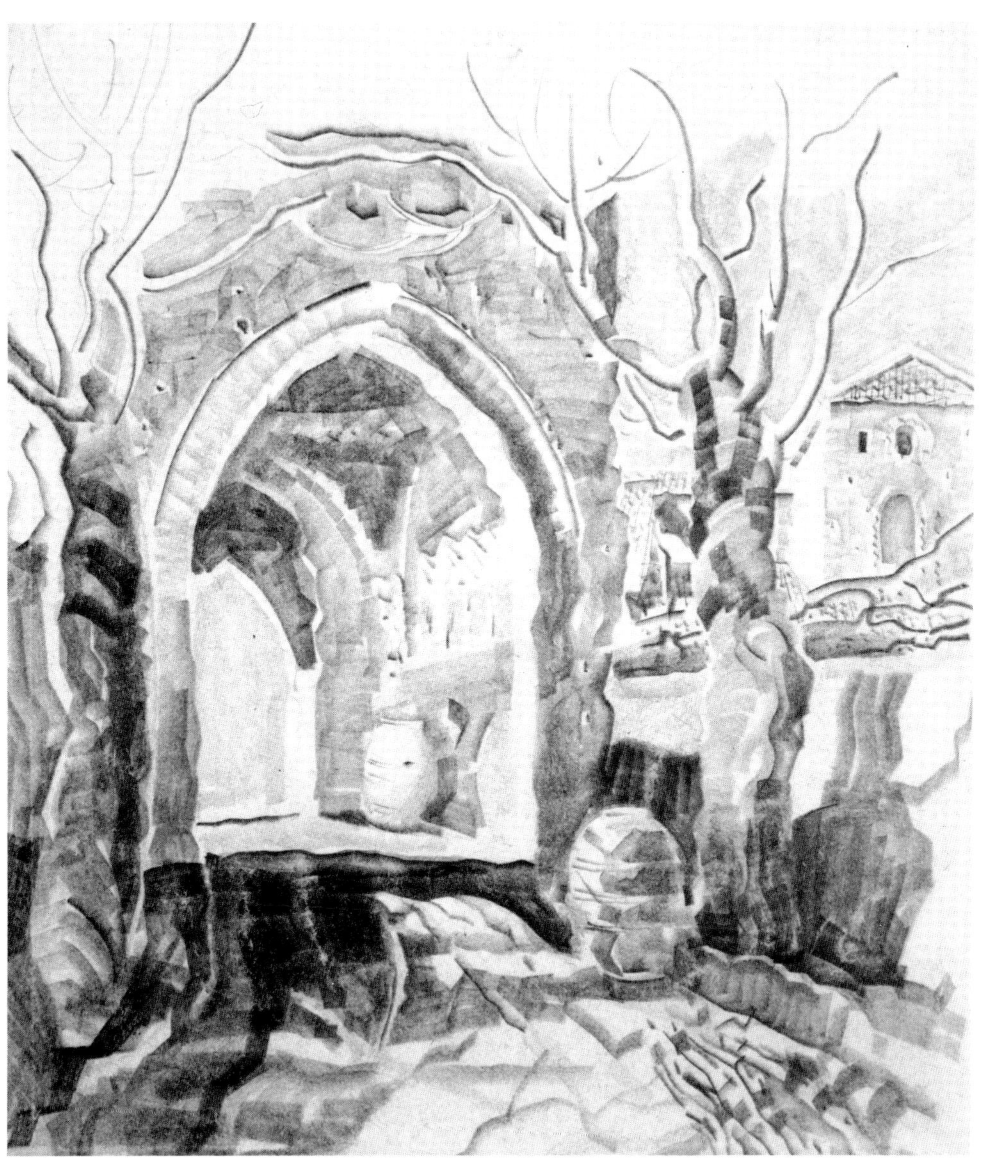

FIGURE 44
"ATRIO DEL PALAZZO RUFOLO," RAVELLO, 1929, graphite on paper (cat. no. 17)

tower, as a visitor sees it looking back from the tree-lined walkway that leads from the tower to the main building of the complex.[68] In that drawing Kahn sketched only the lower part of the entrance tower and its two pointed arches. He omitted the top, but to the right he recorded the south transept of the cathedral.

If one continues down the path and enters the main building, one finds oneself in a tall passageway that opens, on the right, through an elongated Gothic arcade into a cortile. If one walks down this passageway and turns back to look at the door through which one has just passed, the view recorded in a third Ravello drawing (figs. 45–46) is revealed.[69] To the left in this sketch is the tall arcade that brings light from the cortile into the passageway, and on the right wall Kahn drew a pattern of light and shade that seems to be created by the passage of sunlight through the arcade onto the wall.[70] Rays from a sun low enough in the sky to project such a pattern on the right-hand wall would be blocked by structures outside the arcade, and so it seems likely that Kahn invented the pattern of light and shade. Kahn's fourth view of the villa is a watercolor (fig. 47) made from a terrace southwest of the villa.[71] It shows parts of the main building, including the large tower that rises directly outside the wall at the right of Kahn's view of the passageway. In the watercolor, below and to the right of the

FIGURE 45
CORTILE OF VILLA RUFOLO, RAVELLO, 1929, graphite on paper (cat. no. 18)

FIGURE 46
CORTILE OF VILLA RUFOLO, RAVELLO; photograph by Ralph Lieberman

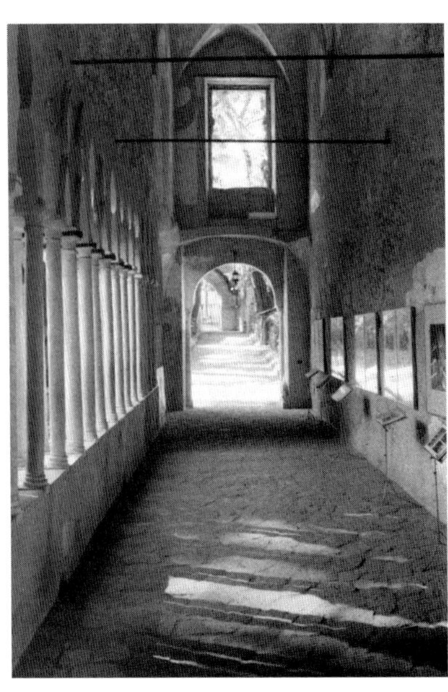

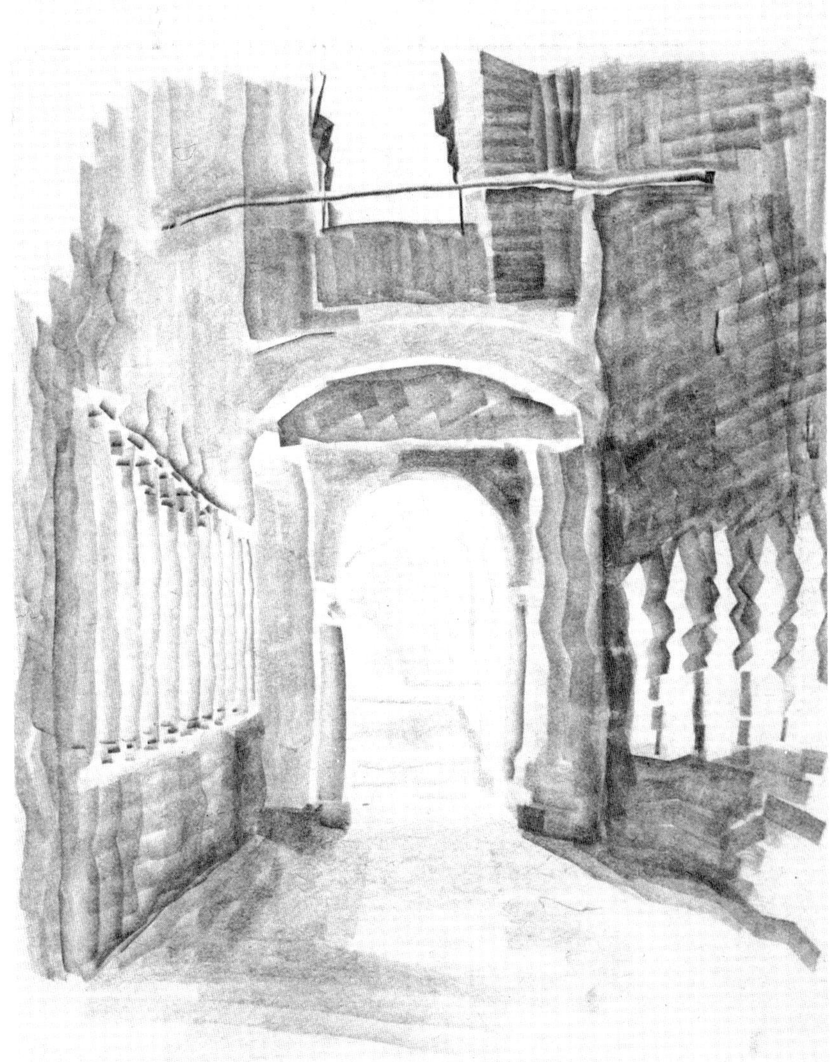

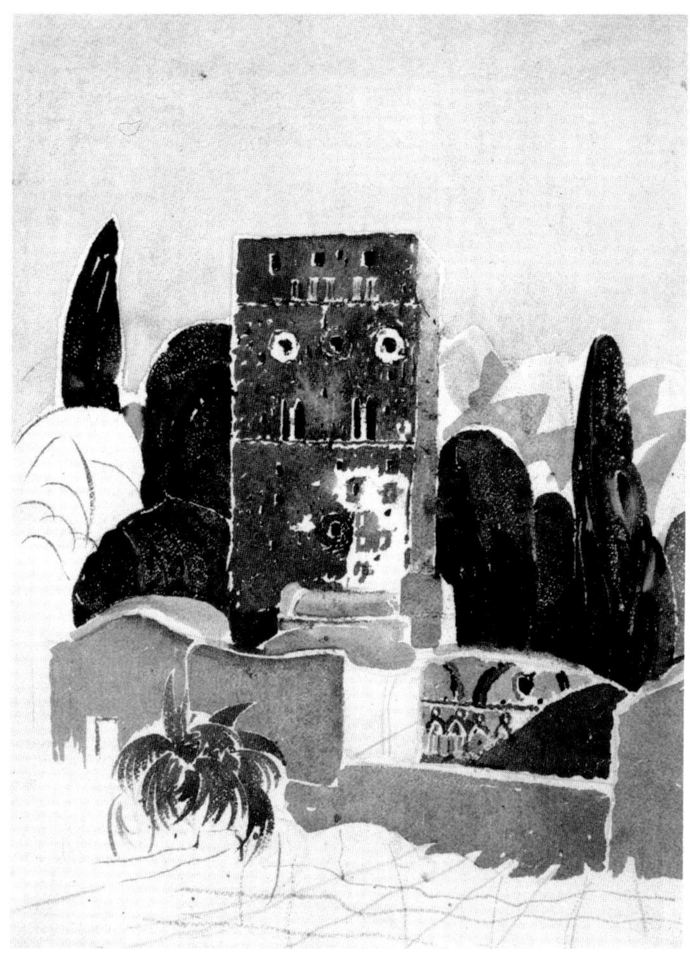

FIGURE 47
TOWER AND CORTILE OF VILLA RUFOLO, RAVELLO, 1929, watercolor on paper (cat. no. 16)

tower, one can see the top of the cortile wall into which the arcade of the passage drawing is set, just below the blind arches visible in the sketch.

A fifth drawing from Ravello shows the Chiesa dell'Annunziata (pl. 4, fig. 101) from the garden of Villa Rufolo.[72] Ravello is built on a steep slope, out of which the entrance into the church is so deeply cut that the irregular vaults of its atrium barely rise above the ground to catch the light. Behind the atrium the drawing shows (left to right) the nave of the church, the dome over the last bay of the nave, and the domed campanile. In the distance are sea and mountains. Curiosity about this building must have led Kahn to walk down the Via Annunziata to visit it. That street, actually a long series of steps, starts at the piazza on which the entrance to the villa stands, just to the left of the entrance tower. The street first descends through a dark, vaulted passageway under the villa garden and then emerges between high, gray, enclosing stone walls. After several twists, turns, and tantalizing glimpses of sky, the street arrives at the atrium of the church. There, where the treads of the steps widen enough to give some sense of a landing, a vista opens up that includes not only sea, sky, and mountains, but also the church of Santa Maria delle Grazie. In his sketch of this scene (fig. 48), Kahn switches from graphite to watercolor to record precisely that release from the monochromatic, stony enclosure of the street to the sun-drenched, color-filled view of landscape and buildings.[73] He even exaggerates the width of the street to increase the sense of openness and freedom. The pergola, essential to defining the space of the drawing and to creating that sense of layers that Kahn frequently sought to record, no longer exists, but the thrill of coming on this view unexpectedly still does.[74]

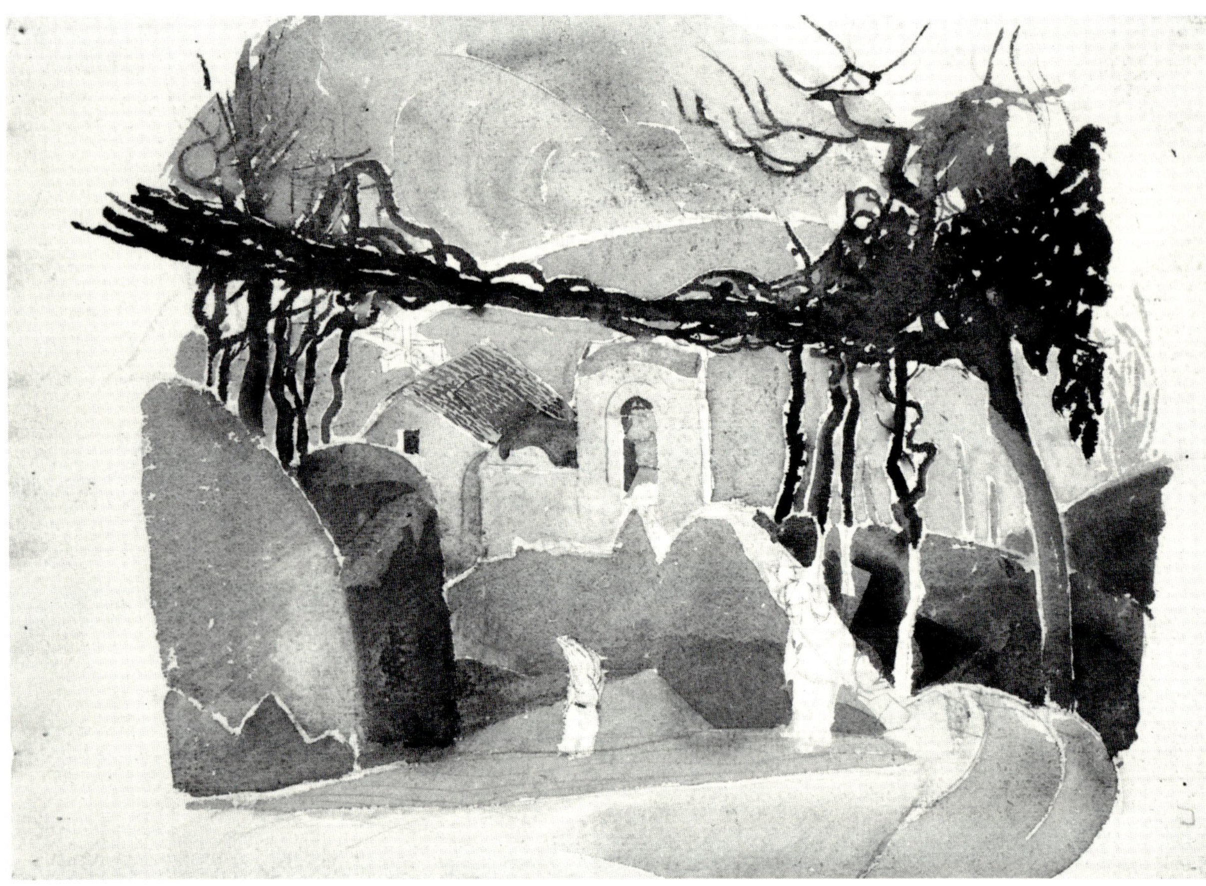

Figure 48
SANTA MARIA DELLE GRAZIE, RAVELLO, 1929, watercolor on paper (cat. no. 20)

In the three sketches that Kahn surely made in nearby Positano we find evidence of a similar approach to a subject—that is, a building that appears in one drawing is recorded from a different point of view in others. The cubist watercolor of Positano shows the west half of the city dominated by the tower and dome of the Chiesa Nuova. That church appears at the top of a graphite sketch that shows the stepped street leading up to its tower (fig. 49), and it reappears at the top of a second sketch (fig. 50) that records one of the deep windows cut into the massive walls of its oval nave.[75]

There is an intimate relationship between the shift in subject matter and the shift in drawing style that occurred during Kahn's stay in Italy. As Kahn made his way south through Italy, he began to concentrate less on famous monuments or tourist views and more on Italian Gothic buildings and vernacular structures. By the time he had reached Rome he seems almost to have given up drawing well-known buildings. The graphic remains of his visit or visits to Rome are mostly sketches of trees in the Villa Borghese and the Pincian Gardens.[76] Only two of the Roman sketches show actual structures. One, of the Fifth Mile of the Via Appia Antica, shows the Tumulo dei Curiazi, a modest masonry cylinder supported on a half-sphere of earth.[77] The other Roman view with structures shows the domes of three famous buildings, those of the twin seventeenth-century churches that stand on the south side of Piazza del Popolo—Santa Maria di Monte Santo and Santa Maria dei Miracoli—and that of Saint Peter's.[78] The view is taken from the Pincio above Piazza del Popolo, from roughly the same place where he made his drawings and watercolors of Roman trees.[79]

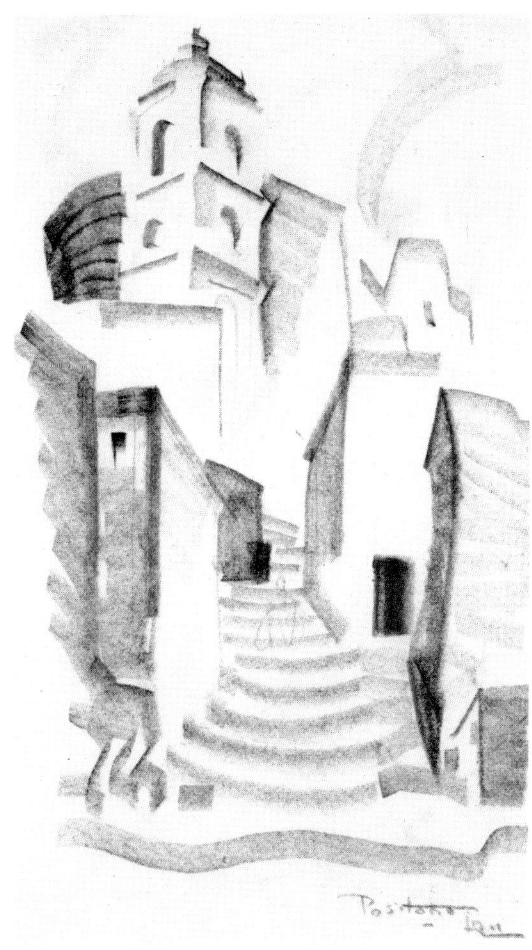

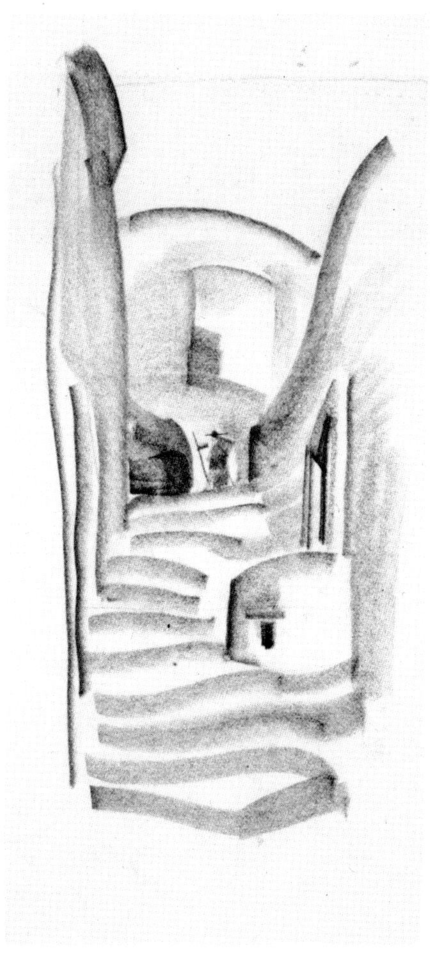

FIGURE 49
STEPPED STREET AND TOWER OF CHIESA NUOVA, POSITANO, 1929, graphite on paper (cat. no. 22)

FIGURE 50
STEPPED STREET AND CHIESA NUOVA, POSITANO, 1929, graphite on bond paper (cat. no. 23)

Kahn's growing interest first in the Italian Gothic and then in vernacular forms seems to have encouraged him to develop a style that could render those kinds of buildings in an original and expressive way. Kahn discarded the artistic baggage he had brought with him in order to make himself an artist of his own time, capable of expressing his interest in the past in contemporary terms. As sympathetic as his graphite drawings are to medieval architecture, they are also expressions of an artistic world forever changed by the advent of cubism. Indeed, cubism as an artistic movement doubtless made Kahn sympathetic to the cubic qualities of the medieval and vernacular buildings he chose to sketch. But it is also likely that he bore within himself an innate taste for such forms that led him to turn to cubism to find a way to render them. There is no evidence that Kahn ever drew any of the great Gothic buildings of northern Europe, although the path of his trip offered him ample opportunities to do so. It was not the skeletal, translucent, seemingly weightless Gothic of France and Germany to which he responded, but rather the planar, opaque, massive Gothic of Italy. Modernist architectural theory, nascent in the 1920s, celebrated French Gothic buildings for their structural honesty and daring but largely ignored their Italian counterparts, which held little interest for the propagandists of a movement devoted to the dissolution of walls into planes of apparently weightless glass.

Kahn partly formed his new sketching style from the way he saw buildings rendered in the frescoes in the upper church at Assisi (figs. 30, 35), but he also turned to the cubism of 1908 of Braque and Picasso. The cubism of transparent planes that Picasso and Braque developed in 1910 had come, through complex routes, to dominate modernist architectural thinking. Kahn, however, chose their earlier cubism of opaque planes because that style worked well for the buildings he wanted to record and also suited his own taste for cubic masses rather than transparent planes, a taste surely in some way engendered by his Beaux-Arts training.

In such drawings as *Street and tower, San Gimignano* (fig. 31), Kahn succeeded in combining the qualities of both the monumentality of the architecture of the past and the fragmented and sometimes weightless visual world of modernity. In the 1940s Kahn would come to understand that in the radical architecture of the previous decades the monumentality of past architecture had been sacrificed in favor of an architecture that used modern materials—steel, glass, and concrete—free plans and antimonumental forms.[80] In his mature architecture, from the mid-1950s on, Kahn recovered the monumentality he had found at San Gimignano, but he made his newly monumental buildings of steel, glass, and concrete, not of stone. Kahn's voyage of artistic self-discovery through Italy,[81] his absorption with its medieval and vernacular buildings, led him to the pioneering path he took as a mature architect thirty years later, when he drew on his memories of Italy as sources for a mode of architectural design in which he reconciled modernity of materials with the grandeur of past architectural forms. In so doing, Kahn helped to change the course of twentieth-century architecture.

The time lag between Kahn's experience of Italian architecture and the appearance of its influence in his work raises the obvious question of how the processes of his memory functioned. We have little direct evidence in his mature project drawings of his reliance on buildings he had seen in Italy in 1928–29, but there is one remarkable example of his ability to recall, vividly, a structure he had drawn more than thirty years earlier. A close approximation of the Gothic viaduct at Spoleto appeared in a sketch Kahn made in the winter of 1960 on a sheet of drawings early in the design process for the Salk Institute in La Jolla, California (figs. 51–52). Jonas Salk and Kahn talked at length about Assisi because Salk saw the monastic buildings there as a prototype for his institute for scientists.[82] They must have reminisced about nearby Spoleto as well, for Kahn sketched the elevation of the viaduct on a sheet on which he was planning a similar structure to bridge a ravine separating two parts of the La Jolla complex, the laboratories and the meeting house.[83] Although Kahn's sketch of the Spoleto viaduct on the Salk sheet represents a rare instance of his sketching another building while designing one of his own,[84] it demonstrates that Kahn carried with him memories of structures he had drawn during his first European sketching trip and, more importantly, that he could summon up images of those structures at will. The sketch on the Salk sheet does not show the same view as either of the preserved drawings of the Spoleto viaduct, but in another sketch for Salk, of Kahn's projected viaduct and the labs as seen from the meeting house,[85] the resemblance to his watercolor of the Ponte delle Torri (pl. 3) is striking.

Kahn's Italian drawings of 1928–29 show a consistent interest in certain architectural issues that became crucial in his mature structures. The sketch of the courtyard of "Il Gotico" in Piacenza (fig. 22) contains some of the earliest evidence we have of Kahn's awakening to these questions. The drawing makes clear his preference for monumental buildings composed of large masses defined by broad planes enlivened by a vigorous play of light and shade and largely devoid of ornament. Almost every building he designed after the late 50s fits this description. Later in his trip he was attracted to subjects like the fishermen's houses at Conca dei Marini (figs. 40–43) because of the simplicity and clarity of their forms.[86] He came to eschew buildings with rich surfaces, such as San Zeno in Verona (fig. 36), and to turn to severe, simple forms that suggested a certain archaism, a certain sense of beginnings rather than of maturity or decadence. Later in his career, Kahn would come to write poetically about the archaic and about "origins," particularly the origins of institutions and of architectural types built to serve those institutions.

In the Piacenza drawing (fig. 22) he was uncertain about the stylistic means to render the shapes and surfaces of the architectural forms he found to his taste, but he

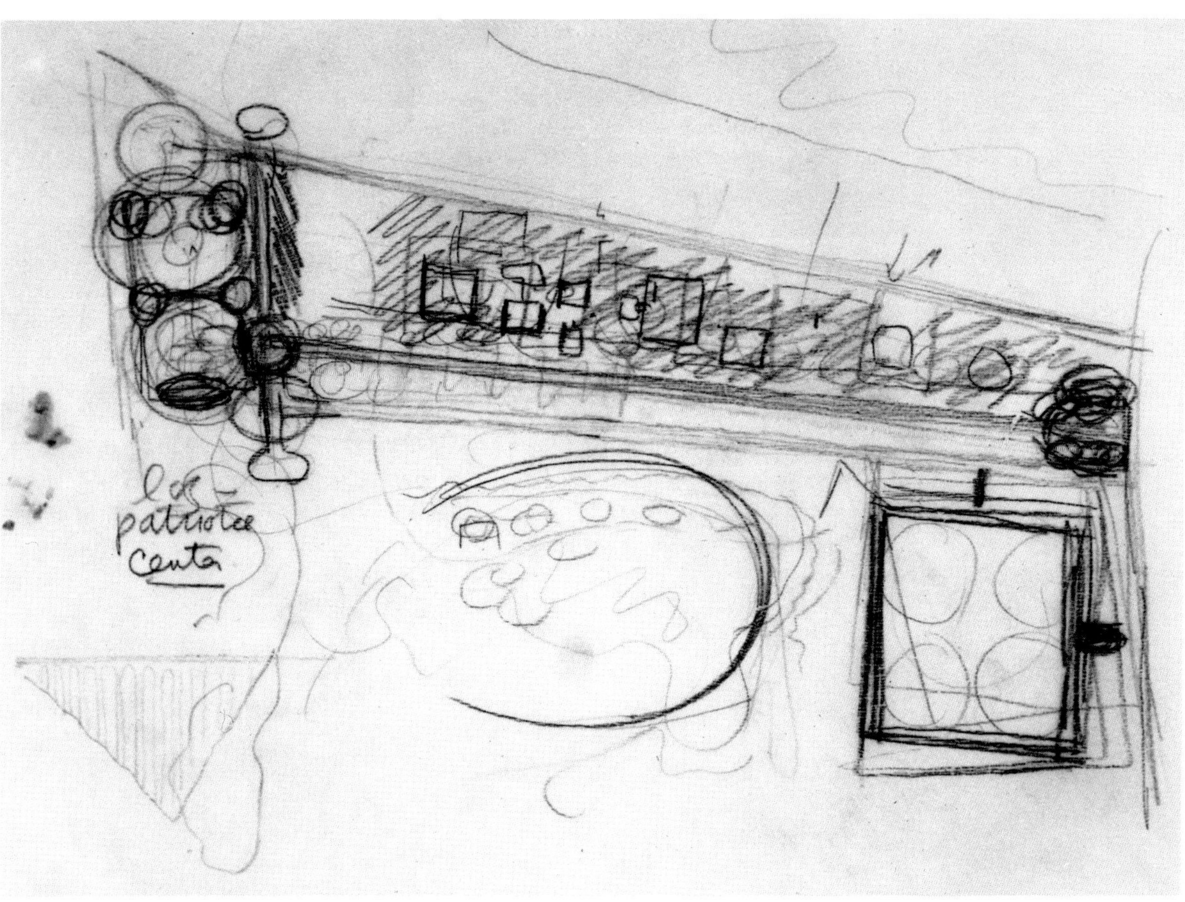

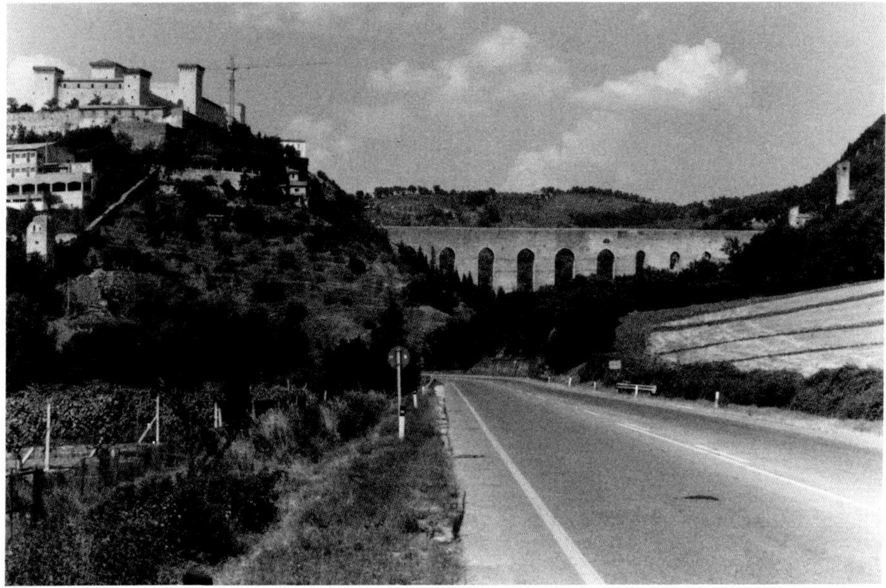

FIGURE 51
SKETCHES FOR SALK INSTITUTE FOR BIOLOGICAL STUDIES, LA JOLLA, CALIFORNIA, 1960, graphite and negro lead on yellow trace; photograph courtesy Louis I. Kahn Collection, Architectural Archives, University of Pennsylvania and Pennsylvania Historical and Museum Commission, 540.4

FIGURE 52
PONTE DELLE TORRI FROM SOUTH, SPOLETO; photograph by Ralph Lieberman

had no problem rendering them spatially. He chose a viewpoint inside the courtyard, so that he could show how the tall vaults, great piers, and sheer walls create sequential spaces—layers of lights and darks, solids and voids, planes and masses. This is precisely the kind of layered spaces that he would develop with consummate skill in mature buildings such as the Exeter Library or the Salk Institute.

Layering is a constant in the drawings of 1928–29. One finds it not only in the drawing from Piacenza, but also in those drawings from the Sorrento Peninsula[87] that show vine-covered pergolas beyond which architectural forms are glimpsed (fig. 48).[88] An entire group of drawings, sketches of the columniated architecture of antiquity, focuses on the issue of layering. The earliest of these is made from the porch of the Temple of Minerva at Assisi,[89] which once faced the Roman forum and now faces the medieval central square of the city (fig. 102). Here Kahn worked from a postcard (fig. 103). The photographer, standing behind ancient columns, had viewed the middle ages, whose buildings Kahn so admired, through a screen of antiquity, an act that recapitulated the way medieval architecture was conceptualized in Italy. We might see this drawing as Kahn's reaction to the way the ancient and medieval pasts coexist (even cohabit) in Italy. What interested Kahn at the Forum at Pompeii[90] and inside the Temple of Hera II at Paestum,[91] sites visited later in the trip, is the same thing that interested him in the Romanesque atrium of Sant'Ambrogio in Milan (fig. 19) or on the porch of the Roman temple at Assisi: the screen of verticals that layers the space and separates the space the viewer occupies from a space beyond, in which yet another enclosed space occurs. These drawings tell us something fundamental about Kahn's understanding of the spatial experience of architecture.

Denise Scott Brown has argued that Kahn's contacts with Robert Venturi in the 1950s led to Kahn's interest in layering: "Through Bob, he investigated the layering of enclosed spaces and the layered juxtapositions of walls and openings, and he discovered that windows could be holes in the wall again."[92] The evidence of the Italian drawings of 1928–29 demonstrates that Kahn had investigated these issues much earlier. His discussions with Venturi, however, may well have brought to the forefront of his consciousness architectural forms that had been displaced in his mind by modernist forms.[93] In 1959, describing his concept of a chapel during his talk at the CIAM meeting in Otterlo, Kahn put his sense of layering into words:

> *A chapel, to me, is a space that one can be in, but it must have excess of space around it, so that you don't have to go in. That means, it must have an ambulatory, so that you don't have to go into the chapel; and the ambulatory must have an arcade outside, so that you don't have to go into the ambulatory; and the object outside is a garden, so that you don't have to go into the arcade; and the garden has a wall, so that you can be outside of it or inside of it.*[94]

As for his realizing that windows could be holes in the wall again, to use Scott Brown's words, his drawings of interiors from Stockholm and Ravello (fig. 45) and of the Bargello in Florence demonstrate this concept forcefully. Kahn's interest in the manipulation of light by passing it through a deep embrasure, obvious in these sketches, became a leitmotif of his mature architecture, from the Unitarian Church in Rochester through Erdman Hall at Bryn Mawr to the mosque attached to the Assembly Building at Dacca. The view of the door and window at the end of the passageway of the cortile at the Villa Rufolo shows a wall pierced by large holes arranged vertically. The concept of controlling light with vertically stacked windows first appears in Kahn's buildings in the keyhole windows of the Tribune Review Publishing Company Building of 1958–62.[95] By the time he designed the unbuilt project for the American Consulate at Luanda, Angola, of 1959–62, Kahn had moved on to the use of discrete holes punched in a wall, one above the other, to protect the building's interiors from the searing tropical sun. Kahn used this pattern frequently thereafter, notably in the unrealized Mikveh Israel Synagogue project in Philadelphia.

Another type of architectural form to which Kahn was attracted was the vaulted element that both gives definition to an interior space and creates a strong identifying silhouette on the exterior. The watercolors of Santa Maria della Salute in Venice (pl. 1)[96] and of the three domes of Roman churches concentrate on such elements. In

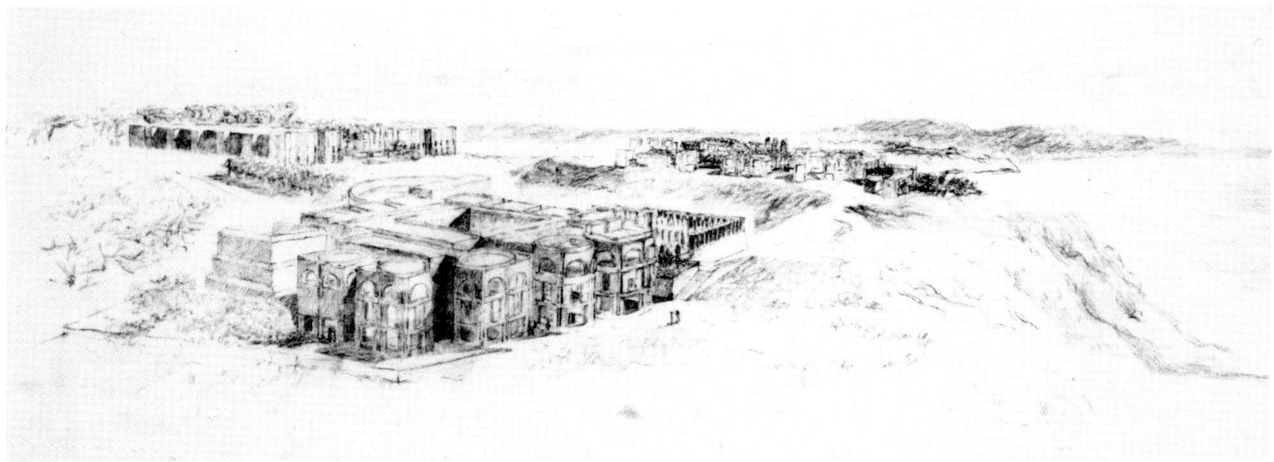

these drawings one sees an inkling of the interest in capping elements that eventually results in the four pyramidal roofs of the Trenton Jewish Community Center Bathhouse—pyramids that in the mid-50s made a decisive break with the flat roofs of modernist architecture.[97] Kahn's fascination with vernacular houses—particularly the now-destroyed fishermen's houses at Conca dei Marini (figs. 40–43)[98]—shows a similar interest that would lead to such remarkable vaulted structures as the Kimbell Art Museum in Fort Worth.

In the Italian sketches there is a constant fascination with the relationship between architecture and landscape. He saw the buildings of Italy as one with their natural environment, and from this unity of building and nature he learned how to fuse his own structures with the landscape. Kahn's drawings of the Amalfi coast hauntingly prefigure his own sketches of the Salk Institute as seen from the sea.[99] When he came to design Salk, Kahn's memory of the cubic outcroppings of buildings on the Amalfi coast (fig. 54) informed the unity of geometry and landscape of the Salk design (fig. 53).

FIGURE 53
AERIAL PERSPECTIVE OF SALK INSTITUTE FOR BIOLOGICAL STUDIES AND SEACOAST, LA JOLLA, CALIFORNIA, c. 1962, graphite and negro lead on mat board; photograph courtesy Louis I. Kahn Collection, Architectural Archives, University of Pennsylvania and Pennsylvania Historical and Museum Commission, 540.20.1

FIGURE 54
ATRANI FROM TORRE SARACENA, AMALFI, 1929, watercolor on paper (cat. no. 21)

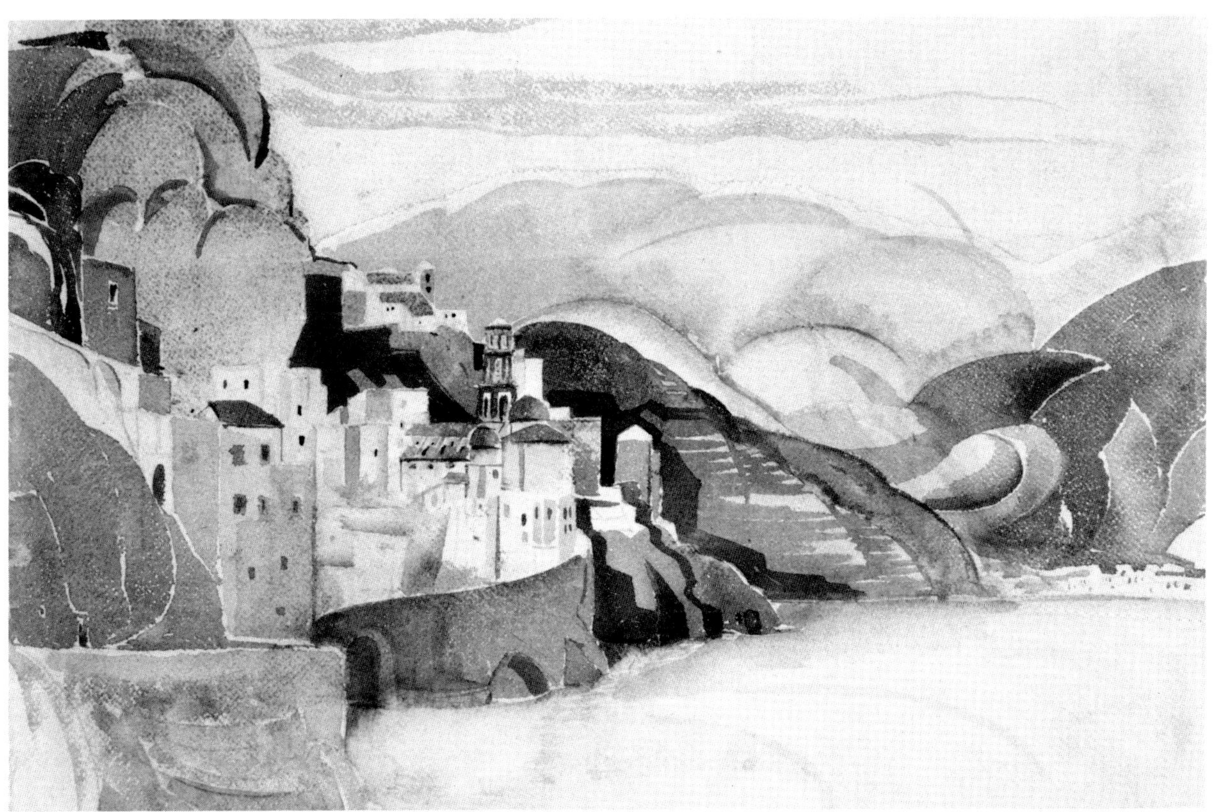

FIGURE 55
PERSPECTIVE VIEW FROM MEETING HOUSE TO LABORATORIES AND HOUSING, SALK INSTITUTE FOR BIOLOGICAL STUDIES, LA JOLLA, CALIFORNIA, c. 1962, charcoal on yellow trace; photograph courtesy Louis I. Kahn Collection, Architectural Archives, University of Pennsylvania and Pennsylvania Historical and Museum Commission, 540.179

FIGURE 56
PERSPECTIVE OF HOUSING, SALK INSTITUTE FOR BIOLOGICAL STUDIES, LA JOLLA, CALIFORNIA, c. 1962, graphite and negro lead on white trace; photograph courtesy Louis I. Kahn Collection, Architectural Archives, University of Pennsylvania and Pennsylvania Historical and Museum Commission, 540.218

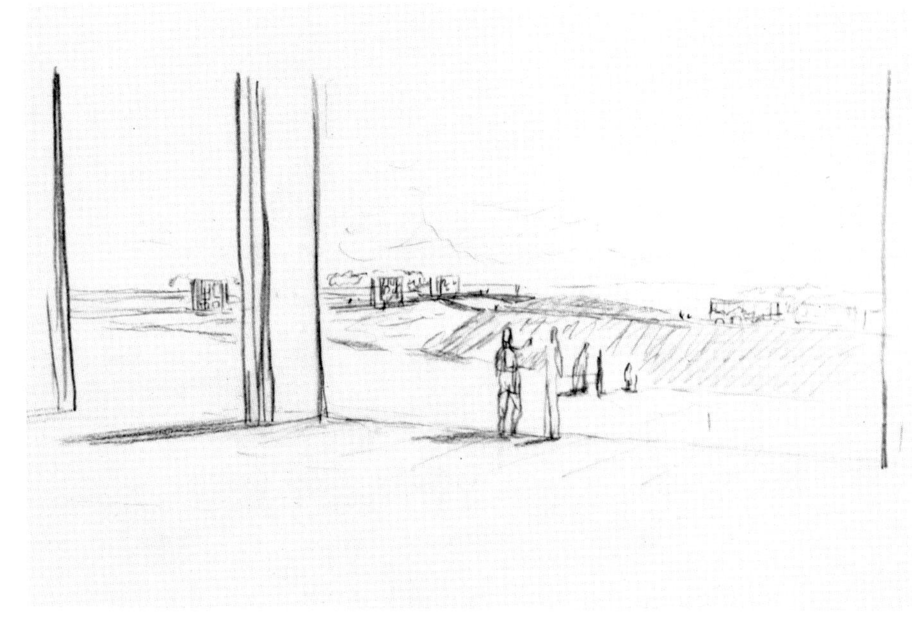

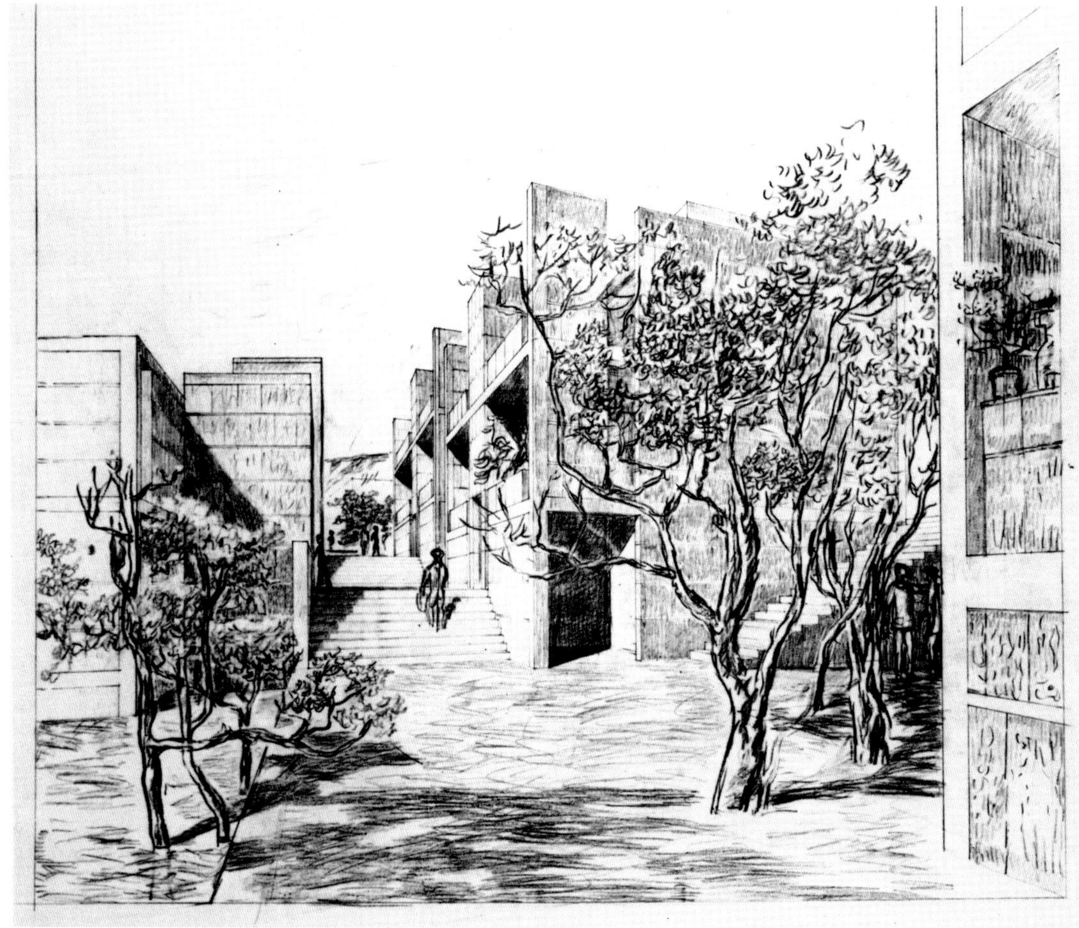

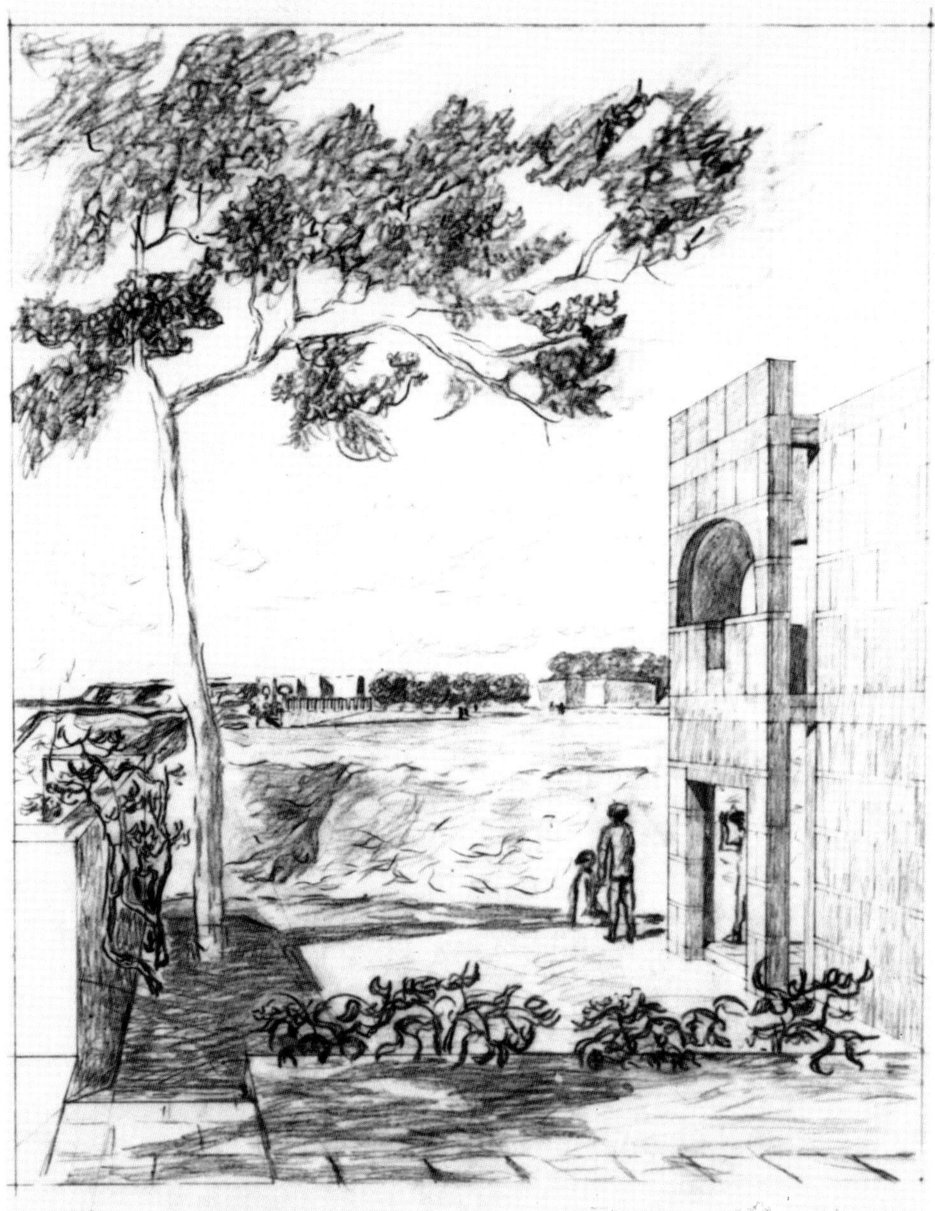

Many of his perspective views of the Salk project recall his Italian drawings.[100] A perspective view through piers of the meeting house to the laboratory and housing complexes (fig. 55)[101] suggests the view through columns of the porch of the Temple of Minerva at Assisi (fig. 102); another perspective of the housing complex (fig. 56), with flights of steps climbing between buildings,[102] recalls the stepped streets Kahn drew in Ravello (fig. 48) and Positano (figs. 49–50); and the tree that frames the view into the landscape from the housing complex (fig. 57) is certainly a descendant of the wooden pergola through which Kahn had sketched Santa Maria delle Grazie at Ravello.[103] He constantly turned to his memory of what he had drawn in 1928–29 to conceptualize the great building complex for Salk, while he also used the skills he developed in Italy as a landscape artist to make his proposals attractive to clients. Surely it is no accident that Kahn thought particularly of the Amalfi coast while working on the Salk Institute, which rises in the locale where the United States enjoys its most Mediterranean climate.

FIGURE 57
PERSPECTIVE VIEW FROM HOUSING TO MEETING HOUSE, SALK INSTITUTE FOR BIOLOGICAL STUDIES, LA JOLLA, CALIFORNIA, c. 1962, graphite and negro lead on white trace; photograph courtesy Louis I. Kahn Collection, Architectural Archives, University of Pennsylvania and Pennsylvania Historical and Museum Commission, 540.219

The relationship among buildings, land, and sea at Salk descends from Kahn's exploration of the same relationships in such sketches as the watercolor view of Santa Maria delle Grazie in Ravello (fig. 48). That view of light, air, ocean, and architecture, experienced after the enclosed passage down the Via Annunziata, is remarkably similar to the view from one of the studies at Salk, achieved only after a complex passage from laboratory to study. In that sketch of Ravello of 1929 Kahn celebrated the very effects of Mediterranean stepped streets that younger architects would come to admire in Siena or on the island of Mykonos some thirty or more years later.[104]

ARCHITECT IN RESIDENCE, THE AMERICAN ACADEMY IN ROME, 1950–51

More than twenty years passed before Kahn found his way back to Italy. He was now a mature architect approaching age 50, a time when hardening of the professional arteries can often set in. He spent only three months as architect in residence at the American Academy in Rome, living and sketching in the city and traveling and drawing in Italy, Egypt, and Greece. But these three months redirected his whole career. Whereas he did not return from his first European trip—at least as far as we can tell—with a new theoretical basis for his architecture, this time around he had as his guide a great scholar of Roman architecture who set Kahn to musing on the relationship between architecture and human institutions that ultimately developed into a major part of Kahn's mature architectural theory. Kahn came face to face with some of the greatest monuments of ancient architecture—Egyptian, Greek, and Roman—at a most fortuitous moment in his career. In the years immediately preceding the trip, he had become more and more disposed to raising fundamental questions about the tenets of modern architecture, which he had accepted eagerly but always a bit uncomfortably in the 1930s and 40s. The architecture of Rome, from antiquity as well as from the sixteenth and seventeenth centuries, convinced him that the architecture of his own day was "tinny," and he came to believe that in his buildings he could recover Roman monumentality of form without abandoning the use of modern materials that modernist theory advocated and to which he was committed. Remarkably, this trip that fundamentally altered his approach to architecture almost failed to happen.

The American Academy in Rome had revived slowly after World War II. The buildings and the library survived the war intact, but reopening required time and planning. Charles Rufus Morey acted as director for one year, 1945–46, and was replaced by Laurance P. Roberts. Because the director in the years immediately prior to the war, Chester Aldrich, had been an architect, there had been no need for an additional person to oversee the work of the fellows in architecture. After the war that changed, and Kahn's former partner, George Howe, was appointed architect in residence for 1947–48. Howe stayed for two and a half years, until he returned to the United States to become the head of the architecture school at Yale in January 1950. After Howe, the Academy found it difficult to find an architect who could spend a whole year in Rome. All, except those who largely supported themselves on academic appointments, were too busy with their own practices to give up that much time to teaching.

Kahn was the first architect in residence to follow Howe.[105] Howe had wanted Kahn to join him in Rome as a fellow at the Academy for 1947–48; he had a joint project in mind for the two of them, and he set about arranging Kahn's appointment.[106]

Undoubtedly at Howe's behest, Philip Johnson had suggested Kahn as a possible fellow (it would have been unseemly for Howe, a member of the Jury of Selection for the fellows, to make the suggestion himself).[107] Kahn sent in his application form on 14 April 1947,[108] but his application was turned down by the board on what can be read as a technicality. Academy policy restricted fellowships to those still at or just beyond the student stage, Kahn was told, whereas he had been a practicing architect for almost twenty years.[109] Kahn's application was blocked by William Platt, who raised the objection to his status and insisted that his application not even be considered by the jury. Apparently Platt on the spot made up the rule that established architects were not eligible to be fellows.[110] One cannot help but wonder if some of the anti-Semitism that had characterized the selection of fellows in earlier years had lingered on to make Kahn another of its victims.[111]

Howe was furious:

> *I wanted to see you last week when I was in Philadelphia but every time I started towards your office I got interrupted. Phil Johnson told me in New York that you had not received any word from the trustees or directors or whatever they are of the Academy in Rome. This fact annoys me extremely as they promised me they would write to you at once explaining that they considered you a contestant for Resident Architect rather than for Fellowship and I could not very well raise any objection to this not unflattering suggestion, but I expressed my disapprobation in no uncertain terms of the dilatory and feckless way of handling the situation. Your name was already placed on the list of competitors before the new proposal was advanced, and I insisted that you must be notified at once of the action taken. Will you let me know if you have received a letter yet? If not, I am going to vent a few of my delicate sarcasms on the head of Mr. William Platt whom I don't particularly like anyway.*[112]

Kahn sent Howe a copy of the rejection letter he had belatedly received from the Academy and expressed his disappointment: "While waiting for word I kept alive the projects which we talked about and I am quite convinced that they are worth while even if they must wait for development later." Excited at the prospect of being resident architect, however, Kahn asked Howe if he should apply formally.[113] Howe advised Kahn not to do so, but "rather leave the matter of proposing your name to your friends. I shall talk to Philip Johnson about the matter and write to Laurance Roberts immediately."[114] That he did, urging Roberts to consider Kahn "as my successor at as early a date as possible. In my opinion it would be difficult to find a more stimulating personality to preside over the meditations and studies of the young men."[115]

This time Howe's maneuvers, which avoided the Academy board in New York entirely, worked. With Howe's departure for Yale imminent, Roberts approached Kahn in the fall of 1949 with a proposal that he be architect in residence for six months the following year, his term to begin around the first of October.[116] Roberts suggested that Kahn apply for a Fulbright grant, and the Fulbright Committee in Washington sent Kahn an application by air mail special delivery. Kahn never filled out the application, probably because he was unwilling to commit himself to so many months away from his practice.[117]

During the winter and spring, negotiations with the Academy continued, and on 30 March Kahn accepted as "entirely satisfactory" an offer of $500 a month for four months beginning October 1950, and $600 for travel.[118] According to Roberts, Kahn's duties would include advising the fellows in architecture, accompanying them on occasional trips, and perhaps supervising the annual collaborative project among the architects, painters, and sculptors. "These duties are not at all time consuming,"

Roberts wrote, "and should leave you ample time for your own sightseeing, work and recreation."[119] October came and went, however, and Kahn was not in Rome. Indeed, in mid-November the executive secretary of the Academy had to ask Kahn to set a definite date of arrival, preferably in the near future: "Mr. Roberts has five young architects on his hands and all of them are eagerly looking forward to your arrival."[120] Finally, on 30 November Kahn boarded a TWA flight for Rome.[121]

One of the most important figures at the Academy was Frank Brown, an historian of Roman architecture who led trips twice a week to Roman sites around the city. Part of what Kahn learned in Rome came from Brown rather than from the experience of Roman buildings themselves. Brown was formulating his remarkable ideas about Roman architecture during the very period when Kahn was at the Academy. For Brown, the earliest Roman architects were priests, who summoned up an invisible and impalpable architecture through the exercise of ritual. In one of the most arresting passages of his book on Roman architecture Brown wrote that, for the Romans, ritual

> *had the power to engender architectural form by the mere fact that it took place in space. Space was informed by ritual. As ritual refined out of crude experience the significant formal pattern, so out of undifferentiated space the significant conformation was precipitated. A particular segment of space took shape from the formal action that occurred in it. It became a capsule, which would reshape itself whenever the ritual was repeated. This spatial form, belonging to a given ritual and established by repetition, acquired independent, architectural existence . . . . Such a shape of space was architecture, even though immaterial.*[122]

Brown's ideas must have made the hair on Kahn's neck stand up, so powerfully did they express the concept of the origins of architectural form in human institutions, a belief that underlay Kahn's entire mature production.[123] For Kahn, the ritual of taking a book from a shelf is the origin of the library: "A man with a book goes to the light," he wrote in 1957. "A library begins that way."[124]

Brown's conception of Roman spaces as independent capsules, shaped by use and ritual, also offered Kahn a theoretical corrective to the modernist notion of universal space, one that was infinitely flexible, that could easily change function as the users of the building might require. Arguably, one can see almost immediately the effect of Brown's notion of Roman space on Kahn's work in the plan of the Yale Art Gallery, the commission for which Kahn received while he was at the American Academy. In that building, the gallery spaces are highly flexible, indeed modernist, to accommodate changing exhibitions. But each gallery space is marked off by blank walls to the north and south and by rows of piers to the east and west. In other words, the modernist spaces of the galleries are framed by structural elements that make of each gallery a separate, discrete unit. In the spine, moreover, the staircase is surrounded by a concrete cylinder that absolutely denies any modernist notions of continuous space. By mid-decade Kahn had abandoned modernist space for Brown's "capsules" in the separate rooms of the Trenton Jewish Community Center Bathhouse, but here, as we shall see, Brown's ideas had been fused with Renaissance concepts of space that Kahn had encountered through the work of another major architectural historian, Rudolph Wittkower.

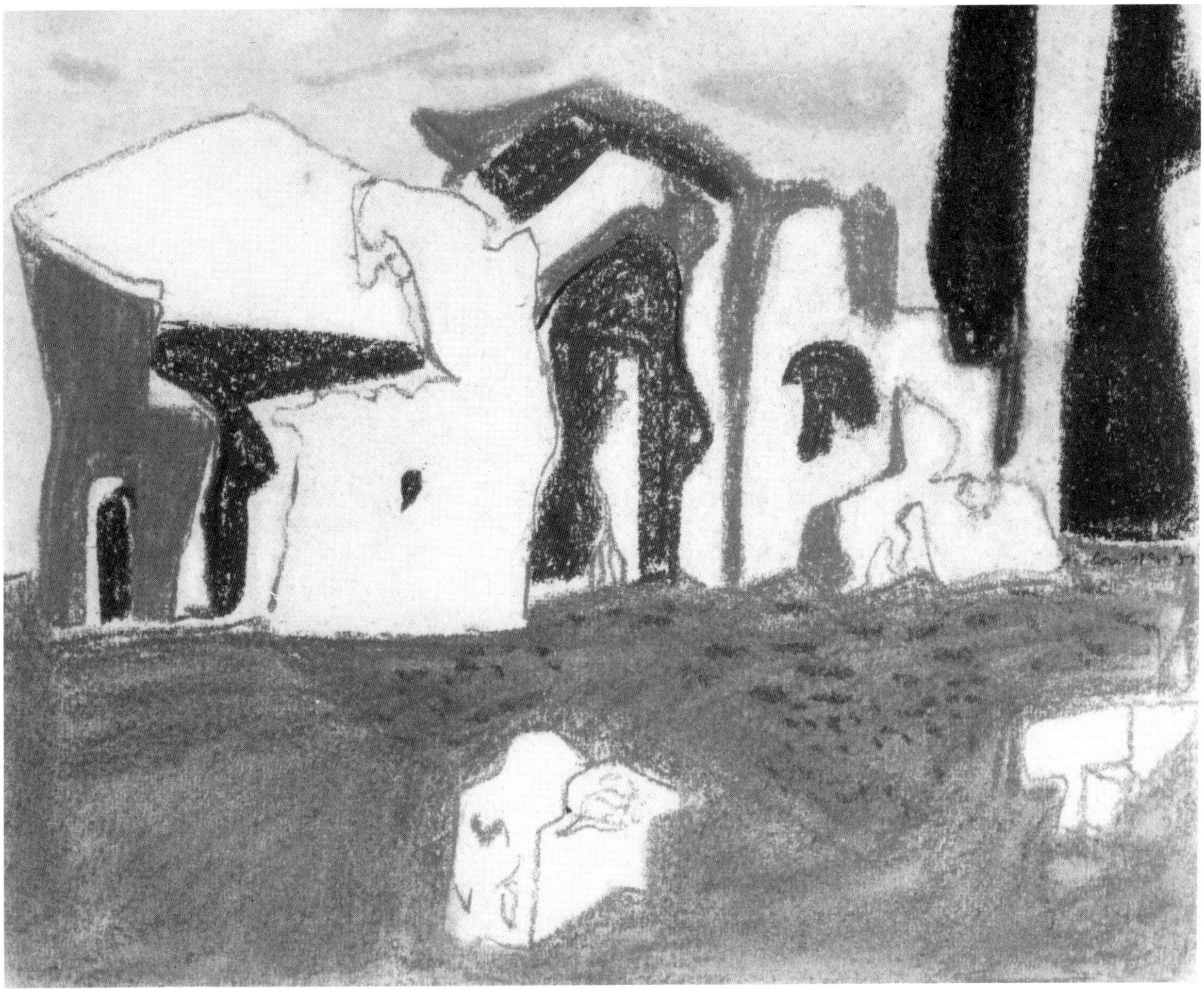

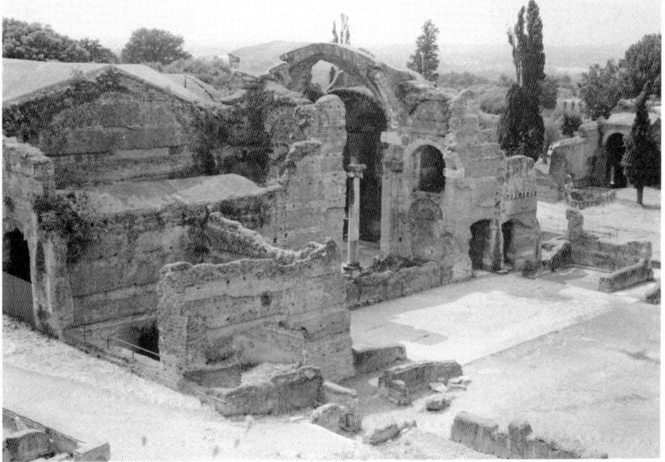

FIGURE 58
LARGE BATHS, HADRIAN'S VILLA, TIVOLI, 1950–51, pastel on paper (cat. no. 43)

FIGURE 59
LARGE BATHS, HADRIAN'S VILLA, TIVOLI; photograph by Ralph Lieberman

Brown's discussion of Roman streets bears an uncanny resemblance to the ideas Kahn published about streets in 1957. For Brown, the Roman street "became a substantive building,"[125] while for Kahn a "street wants to be a building."[126] Brown's Romans conceived the city "as a system of discrete functional enclosures of space, connected by arterial channels. The channels were streets and avenues . . . independent spatial entities, shaped and articulated to instigate directional movement."[127] For

Kahn, "Expressways are rivers that need harbors. Streets are canals that need docks." Streets properly conceived and laid out create an "order of movement."[128] Thus it seems clear that even in terms of concepts of urban planning, Brown supplied Kahn with some of the bases of his mature thoughts.

Of the drawings of Roman ruins that Kahn made while directly under the influence of Brown's ideas, only two can be securely identified. One, with a smoking Vesuvius in the background, shows a scene near Naples, perhaps at Pompeii.[129] The second is a rather free rendering of the Large Baths at Hadrian's Villa, Tivoli (figs. 58–59), as seen from the Praetorium.[130] Of the others, *Classical sculpture* may be a somewhat fanciful view of the Piazzale delle Corporazioni at Ostia[131] and *Ruins*, a free and rather surreal variation on the so-called Biblioteca Greca at Hadrian's Villa.[132] The location of *Roman wall* remains unidentified.[133] *Interior view with statue* shows a mosaic pavement very close to one in a niche in the dressing room immediately to the south of the plunge pool at the Baths of Caracalla (the mosaic at Caracalla, however, does not have the straight lines that frame the curved lines in Kahn's drawing),[134] and *Interior view* shows the interior of a tavern, or *caupona*, perhaps at Ostia.[135] Kahn expressed admiration for the Pantheon and, particularly, for the Baths of Caracalla,[136] but if he drew these buildings, those drawings are not now known. In the case of all the other drawings Kahn made of buildings in Italy, Egypt, and Greece in 1950–51, the subjects can be identified. Why the drawings of Roman ruins are so difficult to identify is not clear. These were the only drawings Kahn ever made under the tutelage of a great expert in the history of the buildings depicted. That circumstance, one can speculate, may have allowed Kahn to be freer, more fanciful, more interpretive in what he drew. At this point we simply do not know.

The pastel of the Large Baths at Hadrian's Villa (fig. 58) certainly shows Kahn dealing with issues of geometry and of the interplay of mass and space in strong light and deep shadows. This drawing demonstrates that Kahn made at least one sketch at Hadrian's Villa, to which Brown must have taken him, since the villa was one of the primary structures on which Brown erected his ideas about Roman architecture. It would seem, however, that Kahn never came to much of an understanding of the villa's plan. During the long process of design for the Salk Institute, a member of Kahn's office staff used a part of the villa's plan to organize the various buildings of the Salk complex on its site. Kahn liked the suggestion but at first he did not recognize its source.[137]

Kahn's charcoal sketch of a Roman wall pierced by arched openings (fig. 60) is little more than an archaeological record, but it is extremely significant for his later work. We know that he explored the concept of the window as a hole in a wall in his drawings of the 1920s, and here he returns to the same question. This drawing records the encounter with Roman ruins that led Kahn to his very important notion of wrapping a building in a "ruin" in order to protect it from the force of direct sunlight, as in his design for the American Consulate in Luanda, Angola.[138] Many of the masonry walls of his buildings of the 1960s are foretold in this sketch.

In Rome Kahn also made two drawings of sixteenth- and seventeenth-century Roman public spaces. One is a brilliantly colored pastel of the Campidoglio;[139] the second shows the piazza in front of Saint Peter's viewed from the southernmost bay of the atrium of the church, under the south campanile[140]—a view that fragments the carefully wrought balance of the piazza into a tense asymmetry (figs. 61–62). To the right looms Bernini's statue-surmounted wall that forms the south side of the trapezoidal forecourt of the church. In the left foreground the steps of the church project

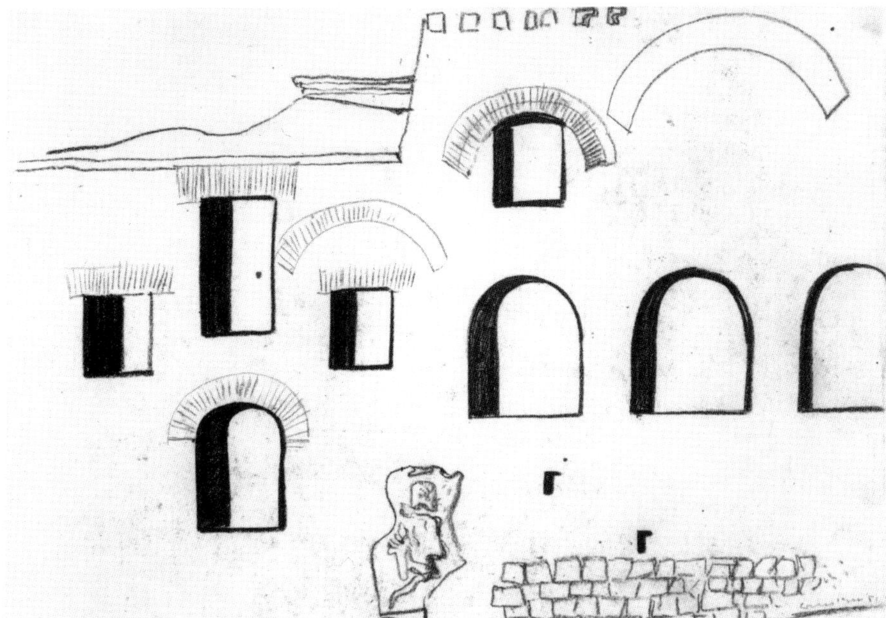

FIGURE 60
ROMAN WALL, 1950–51, charcoal on paper (cat. no. 44)

westward to end at the base of the statue of Saint Peter. In the middle distance are the obelisk and the north fountain that mark the cross axis of the piazza, while in the background part of Bernini's colonnade enters from the left. Behind the obelisk and the statue of Saint Peter is one of the buildings erected by Pius XII for the Jubilee year of 1950, the year Kahn arrived in Rome, to complete the west end of Mussolini's Via della Conciliazione. On a postcard of G. B. Piranesi's bird's-eye view of the square that Kahn sent to his office (fig. 63), he wrote, "There is so much to see and feel here which can influence the work of any architect. Not so much the modern but the old original source."[141] Kahn's drawing of the square is rendered with that haunting sense of emptiness with which Giorgio de Chirico had imbued his paintings of

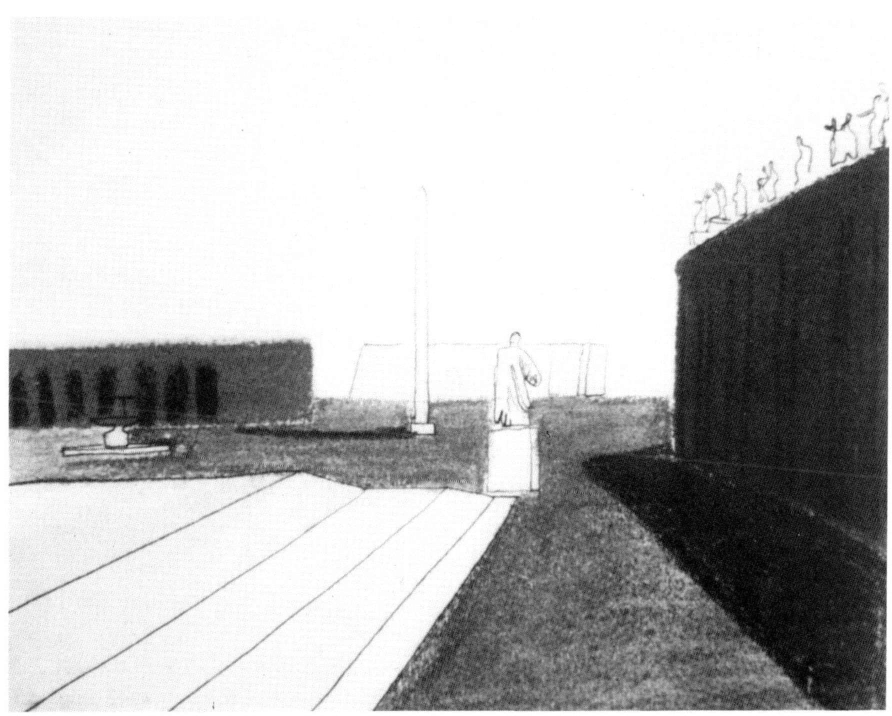

FIGURE 61
PIAZZA SAN PIETRO FROM ATRIUM OF SAINT PETER'S, ROME, 1950, pastel on paper; photograph courtesy lender (cat. no. 45)

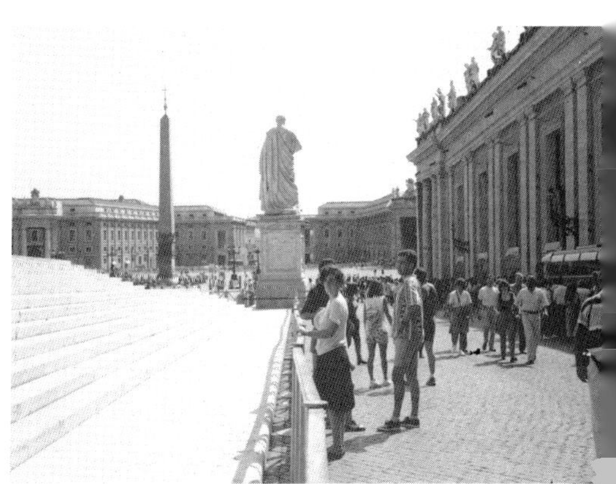

FIGURE 62
PIAZZA SAN PIETRO, FROM ATRIUM OF SAINT PETER'S, ROME; photograph by Ralph Lieberman

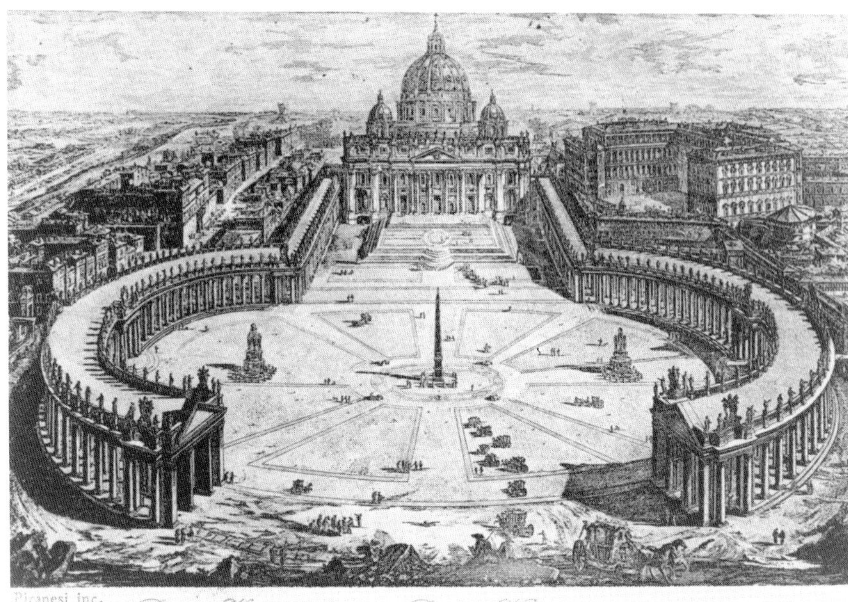

FIGURE 63
G. B. Piranesi. *VEDUTA DELL'INSIGNE BASILICA VATICANA COL PORTICATO E LA PIAZZA, ROMA*, postcard from Louis I. Kahn to his office, postmarked 1951; from "Rome, 1951," LIK Box 60; photograph courtesy Louis I. Kahn Collection, University of Pennsylvania and Pennsylvania Historical and Museum Commission

imaginary piazzas from the second decade of the century. One of the fellows who accompanied Kahn recalled that Kahn had a deep admiration for De Chirico's work.[142]

Ideas about older architecture had already formed in his mind after his first few days in Italy, as we know from a letter he wrote to his office.[143] The letter is worth quoting in its entirety.

> *Wednesday, Dec. 6 1950*
>
> *Dear Dave*
> *Anne*
> *Alice*
> *Bill*
> *Armstrong*
>
> *I should write to you separately but I must conserve time in light of the many things I find I have to do now that I am here. When I go over the list of possible projects laid before me including must travel ideas it will take careful selection to accomplish only a part of what I visualize my presence here can mean to the Academy.*
>
> *For one—I firmly realize that the architecture in Italy will remain as the inspirational source of the works of the future. Those who don't see it that way ought to look again. Our stuff looks tinny compared to it and all the pure forms have been tried in all its variations.*
>
> *What is necessary is the interpretation of the architecture of Italy as it relates to our knowledge of building and needs. I care little for the restorations (that kind of interpretation) but I see great personal value in reading ones [sic] own approaches to the creation of space modified by the buildings around as the points of departure. I find it of little difficulty translating the masonry construction into steel and concrete and I intend to have the Fellows explore their reactions to what they see into similar aims. They are quite excited about the idea.*

I live in the Villino Aurelia—a complete house attached to the Villa Aurelia out of the 5 rooms and bath I can use only 1. It is on the uppermost point on the Giniculum [sic] and my bedroom window overlooks Rome. It has been sporadically sunny and cloudy with occasional rain. I have tried to sketch but find the weather and the duties don't go together. When I take my travel jaunts I believe I will do better

---

I hope everything is going smoothly—I hope everyone really works hard to clean up the nasty chores so we can see light out of the mess I left behind. Please write often to keep me informed—I will feel much better. Don't expect too much mail from me

Good luck

Lou

The most remarkable part of this extremely important letter lies in Kahn's comments on the historical architecture of Italy and how he foresaw using it in his own work. By "our stuff" that "looks tinny" he meant the modern, International Style architecture he had been trying to design in the previous two decades. The masonry forms of Roman and Renaissance architecture he saw little trouble in translating into the modern materials of steel and glass. He had already sought to put steel and glass at the service of a new monumentality in his article of 1944, "Monumentality";[144] but in that essay he was thinking in modernist structural terms of a skeletal architecture based on French Gothic buildings. Those were the same terms he employed when he wrote in the spring of 1947 his statement of purpose as a candidate for a fellowship at the American Academy:

I should consider work in Rome, away from practice, as the opportunity I have looked for to develope [sic] thoughts I have on architecture of to-day. These thoughts are about the frames and enclosures of new architectural spaces, their effect and relation to painting, sculpture and the crafts, their significance to the people and their place in the continuing evolution of traditional forms.[145]

In Rome, he put that notion of frames behind him and turned to what he called, in the letter to his office staff, "the pure forms . . . in all its variations."

To Michael Graves Kahn later spoke clearly about the effect his experience of Roman architecture in 1950–51 had had on his work.

[Kahn] once said to me that he regretted having wasted so much of his time trying to be a modern architect. He said, "Michael, I tried and tried and tried all my life to make the wall thinner and thinner and thinner." It wasn't until he went to Rome and saw the Domus Aurea and other Roman villas in the Forum that he realized the strength of the wall, the power of chiaroscuro, the interest in light, and all of what architecture eventually held for him. He said he finally felt he was at home with architecture. He realized that the structural, technical, and social aspects of architecture didn't work well for him. There had been a mismatch . . . .[146]

But at this point in Kahn's career, there was not yet a mismatch with modernist notions of free-flowing space. His drawing of the Piazza San Pietro (fig. 61) makes this apparent. There, the strength of the wall and the power of chiaroscuro are fused with a modernist, asymmetrical disposition of solids to create a sense of a space not enclosed but rather modulated by screen walls that allow the space to flow around and even bounce off them, as if "space" were a ball rolling around a pinball machine.

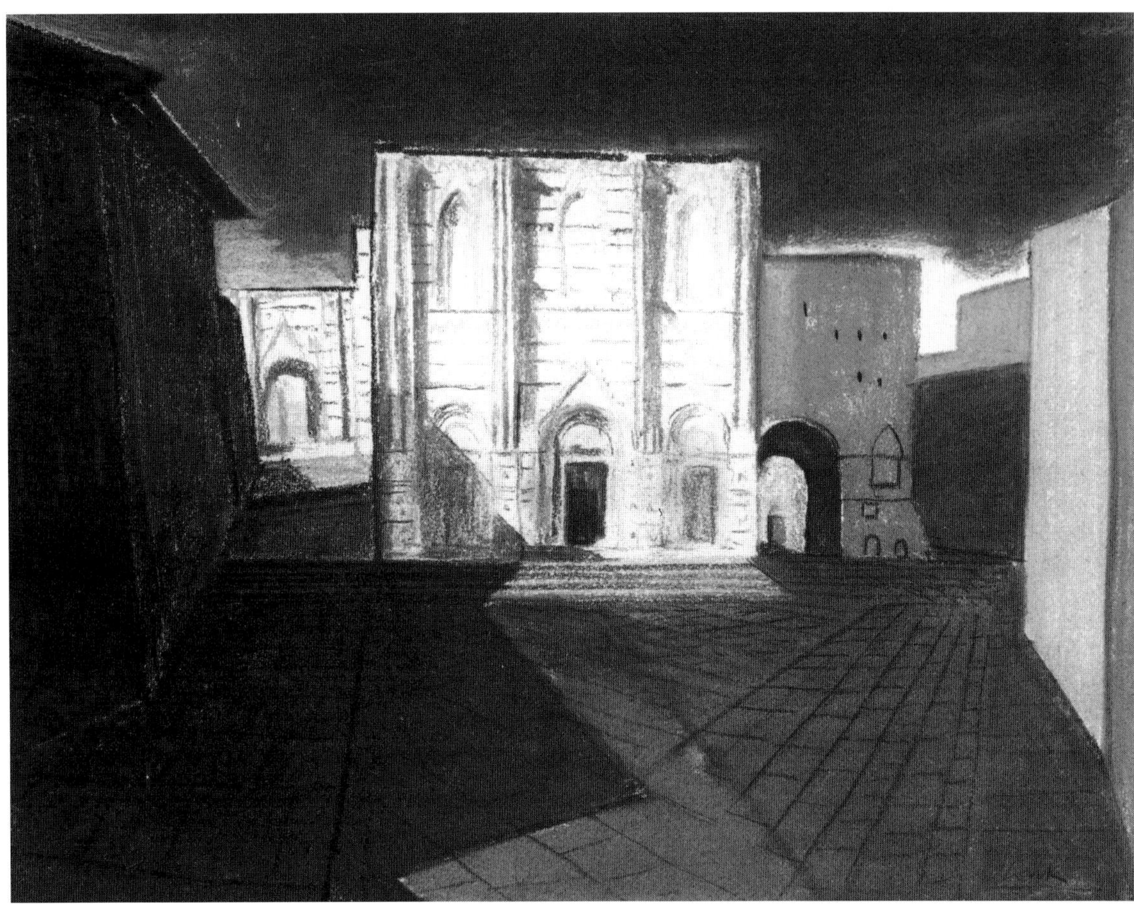

FIGURE 64
BAPTISTERY OF SAN GIOVANNI, SIENA, 1950-51, pastel on paper (cat. no. 47)

While the spatial conception is very close to that of Mies van der Rohe's Project for a Museum for a Small City of 1942, the planes that inflect the space are the substantial masonry of Bernini's wall and colonnade rather than the almost diaphanous planes of Mies's design.

Kahn's fusion of the mass of older architecture with the free-flowing space of modernism may reflect the project that George Howe had in mind for the two of them to work on in Rome in 1947–48. In the late forties the question of space was much on Howe's mind.[147] In a talk of 1948 called "Flowing Space: The Concept in Our Time," Howe said: "Flowing space can neither be enclosed nor excluded—not even limited by thought or fact. It can only be directed." For Howe, the forms that define the space "turn out to be, not objects to be looked at in the light, but aggregates of planes of references defining the movements, whether in or out or through, of certain portions of universal curvilinear space."[148] That is precisely the kind of space Kahn drew in his pastel of Piazza San Pietro. This is also the kind of space that Howe had designed in his Speiser House of 1935 in Philadelphia, in which a clever use of planes allowed pockets of privacy within a completely modernist, flowing space.[149] While Howe was at the American Academy, he tested his theories of space against the buildings of Rome, often in the company of the Italian architect Bruno Zevi.[150] Surely those theories would have been tested in the company of Lou Kahn, had Kahn been granted a fellowship. Kahn's interest in this kind of modernist space is evinced by several drawings and paintings Kahn made in the years when Howe was at the Academy.[151]

With the exception of the sketches of Roman ruins, the drawings that Kahn made in Italy in 1950–51 focus almost entirely on public spaces. There are the three justly famous pastels of Siena—two views of the Campo (pl. 7)[152] and one of the baptistery

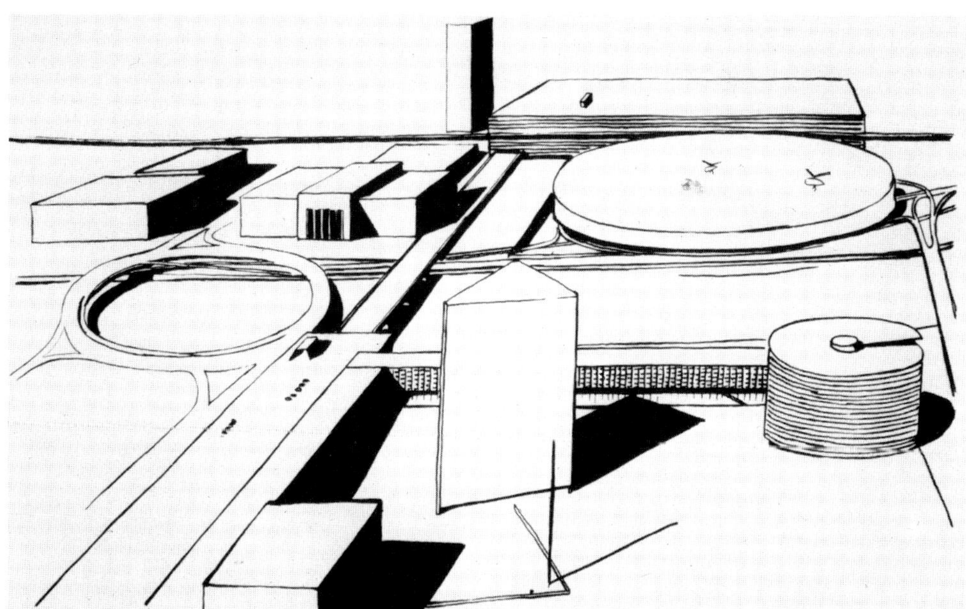

FIGURE 65
AERIAL PERSPECTIVE, PROJECT FOR CIVIC CENTER ON SCHUYLKILL RIVER, PHILADELPHIA, c. 1951–52; photograph courtesy Louis I. Kahn Collection, Architectural Archives, University of Pennsylvania and Pennsylvania Historical and Museum Commission, 365.0.1

and its piazza (fig. 64)[153] We know seven black crayon drawings of Florence, all unfortunately now missing.[154] Of these, four show open spaces around Palazzo Vecchio; one, the piazza in front of the cathedral; and the other two focus on particular buildings, the dome of the cathedral and Palazzo Strozzi. There is a crayon drawing of the baptistery and cathedral in Pisa as monuments in an open public space, and four drawings in the same technique record the squares and buildings of the civic center of Venice: the Piazza San Marco, the Piazzetta, the Basilica di San Marco, and the Doge's Palace. All of these drawings of Pisa and Venice are missing.[155] The two preserved pastels of Venice do not, however, show public spaces. One is filled with an angled view of San Marco (pl. 10)[156] and the other, one of Kahn's most imaginative sketches (fig. 83), is a fantasy on a theme of Venetian Gothic tracery.[157]

In Florence, Siena, Pisa, and Venice Kahn concentrated on the civic cores of the cities, while the two pastels of public spaces in Rome are of its secular center at the Campidoglio and its religious center at Saint Peter's. Such focused drawing could hardly have been accidental; clearly, core urban spaces preoccupied Kahn. His colleagues in Philadelphia understood this from afar. One wrote, "P.S. Wish I could see some of the Italian Piazzas right now!"[158] Another had more sober advice: "You may find it very difficult when you first get your hooks in one of these city planning assignments, to hold yourself down to the scale of things here vs those you are looking at right now."[159] Urban planning much concerned Kahn in these years, when Philadelphia was seeking to turn itself into a modern city.[160] From October of 1946 until two days before his departure for Europe he had been deeply involved in efforts to redesign the Triangle, the northwestern area of the city bordered by Market Street, the Schuylkill River, and the Benjamin Franklin Parkway. Kahn was primed for *piazze*.

Once back in Philadelphia, Kahn put his experiences of Italian spaces to use. A drawing he made for a proposed new Philadelphia Civic Center on the banks of the Schuylkill in 1951–52 (fig. 65) shows a bird's-eye view of a large square surrounded on two sides by buildings with loggias—Piazza San Marco in Penn's town.[161] Inside the square are three buildings of pure form and a tall, slender shaft, all arranged in an asymmetrical fashion. Every structure casts a dark shadow to the northwest. (It's morning in Philadelphia.) Here we see the fragmentation that Kahn wrought from Bernini's symmetry in his pastel of Piazza San Pietro deliberately designed into his own square. He had abstracted certain principles from historic Italian designs—primary forms, large open spaces surrounded by walls and arcades, isolated monuments that cast shadows—and used them in a design that owed no small debt to De Chirico.[162] There was also a lingering debt to Le Corbusier.[163] The isolated monuments in the square would have created the flowing space modulated but not defined by objects of which George Howe had spoken. As the decade wore on, Kahn kept Italian public spaces in mind as he continued to do planning projects for central Philadelphia. On a sheet from 1957 on which he drew a plan for the Philadelphia Civic Center he also sketched, at the same scale, a plan of the church and piazza of Saint Peter's. He must have been working from memory (or possibly from the bird's-eye-view postcard he had sent his office from Rome) rather than from a plan, for he drew the end of the western arm of Saint Peter's as a rectangle rather than the actual semicircle.[164]

Kahn was not alone in his interest in Italian urban spaces in these years. He had an ardent young Romanist colleague in his fellow Philadelphian, Robert Venturi. Six months after Kahn's return, Venturi sent Kahn a copy of *Architectural Review* for February 1950, an issue that had featured a long article on Rome by Henry Hope Reed.[165] From Venturi's accompanying letter[166] it is clear that he had just enjoyed a visit with Kahn during which Rome must have been a major topic of discussion. A few months later Venturi, who was working in the Saarinen office in Michigan, wrote: "Eero has returned with some wonderful color slides of Italian piazzas, especially that of San Marco, and four copies of engravings of maps of Rome of different periods which give you palpatations [sic] of the heart."[167] In the fall semester of 1952 Kahn and Christopher Tunnard jointly taught a course in urban planning at Yale, and in that course some of the material that Tunnard included in his exhibition of 1953, "Ars in Urbe," on Roman civic art and its progeny, must have appeared.[168] Kahn's drawings of Italian public spaces and Roman ruins came, then, at a crucial moment when things Roman and Italian were at the forefront of the latest thinking in the American architectural profession.

In January 1951 Kahn and the fellows in architecture left Rome for a sketching trip in Egypt and Greece, the first such excursion for the fellows since the war.[169] No part of Kahn's stay at the Academy, by all accounts, was a greater success than this journey, which seems to have been Kahn's idea. The director, Laurance Roberts, wrote Kahn a belated but ecstatic letter of thanks: "[W]hen I returned here early in March I had never seen before such an excited and interested group of architects as those whom you took to Egypt and Greece. You gave the Academy just the right shot in the arm and gave the architects the most exciting winter that any group has had here since I've been in Rome."[170] In the annual report Roberts went even farther: "Mr. Kahn most generously took the architects on an extended tour of Egypt and Greece at the end of January. All the Fellows returned from this trip excited not only by what they had seen, but also by the discussions which Mr. Kahn's comments and observations provoked. For the architects this was perhaps the high point in the Academy's postwar history."[171]

From Egypt, the first stop on the trip, Kahn, an indifferent correspondent at best, sent a second postcard to his office, with a view of "Thebes—The famous Colossi of Memnon representing the King Amenhotep III." Kahn's message was enthusiastic but brief: "Luxor and the Temples and Monuments . . . are really terrific. The scenic beauty of the Tropical country equals easily the magnificance [sic] of the monuments. I must wait when I return before getting details, but believe me is wonderful and instructing."[172]

Kahn did find the temples at Karnak and Luxor wonderful and instructing, and perhaps most instructing of all were the pyramids (fig. 81), which he had a whole week to sketch because one of the fellows fell ill and had to be hospitalized for a few days.[173] Thirteen sheets of drawings of pyramids, a large group of drawings of one subject from Kahn's hand, have come down to us—ten of Giza,[174] two of Saqqara,[175] and one probably of Dashur.[176] Both Scully[177] and Hochstim have insisted on the centrality of these drawings for Kahn's later work, but Anne Griswold Tyng has challenged such interpretations as art-historical oversimplifications, because she views Kahn's forms as based on archetypes rather than specific structures.[178] Scully and Tyng remember Kahn saying slightly different things about the pyramids. One can imagine that his reactions to them may have been complex and that his listeners tended to hear statements that matched their own interests. It seems inescapable, however, that his encounter with the pyramids had an effect on his design of the Trenton Bathhouse, with its quartet of pyramids that serve as roofs—just compare a distant view of the bathhouse with Kahn's drawing of six pyramids, perhaps at Dashur, seen from afar. But it seems rather less likely that the Egyptian pyramids stand behind the complex geometry of his concrete ceiling structures in the Yale Art Gallery.

Kahn and the fellows went as far south as Aswan, and his preserved drawings from their trip up the Nile can be identified as from Edfu,[179] Luxor, Karnak,[180] Medinet-Habu, and Deir el-Bahri.[181] Kahn's encounter with the Temple of Amon at Luxor pro-

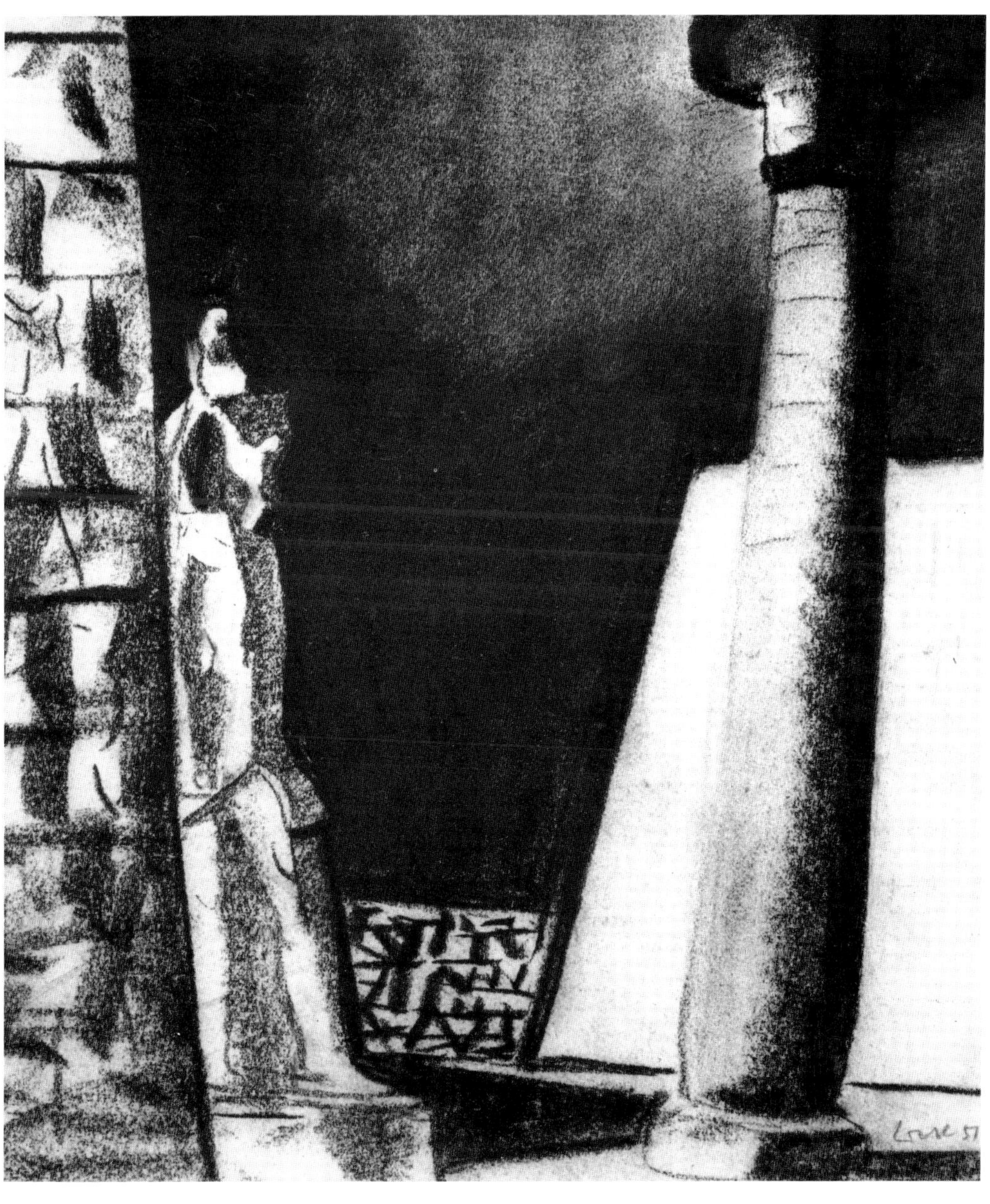

FIGURE 66
COMPOSITION WITH STATUE, COLUMN OF TAHARKA, AND PYLONS, FIRST COURT, TEMPLE OF AMON, KARNAK, 1951, charcoal on paper (cat. no. 53)

duced at least five drawings, three taken from essentially the same point on the west side of the complex, a viewpoint that renders this highly axial architectural composition as asymmetrical as his view of Piazza San Pietro[182] or the view he would subsequently make of the Propylaea in Athens. Skewed views, as we have seen, destroy symmetry and create fragmentation.

Kahn used fragmentation to produce a sense of mystery in a brooding drawing of the first court of the Temple of Amon at Karnak (fig. 66) that shows a standing figure against a wall to the left and a single column, poised against the white plane of a pylon, to the right. This Egyptian drawing is a fantasy; Kahn had to stand in one place to draw the statue and in another to see the single papyrus column of the Nubian pharaoh of the XXV Dynasty, Taharka, against the pylon.[183]

In Egypt the color of shadows seems almost to have overwhelmed Kahn. On one of the Luxor drawings he wrote "sand brown in shade,"[184] and his pastel of Luxor is distinguished by green and brown shadows in the foreground. In terms of color and light, the pastel of the second court of the Mortuary Temple of Rameses III at Medinet-Habu (pl. 8) is one of his most magical and complex.[185] While compositionally the drawing recalls layered sketches such as *"Il Gotico," Piacenza*, from 1928 (fig. 22), the handling of light and shadow goes way beyond anything he ever attempted on his first European trip. The sand is also brown in the shade, but the light that infuses the shadows creates red reflections on the rear wall, which itself is plunged into a green shadow against which the red joints of the masonry vibrate. The power of the color of this drawing, however, should not make one ignore the physical substance of the architecture or the powerful rhythm of the paired columns, which is not the original spacing, for the central column is now missing. This rhythm is similar to the one that Kahn will use at the end of the decade on the four towers of the rear wall of the Richards Medical Research Center at the University of Pennsylvania.

Athens apparently was Kahn's first stop in Greece, followed by visits to Corinth, Mycenae, Epidaurus, and, finally, Delphi. The party split up in Greece. All of the fellows except William H. Sippel took off for the islands, and Kahn and Sippel wandered around the mainland for three weeks. According to Sippel, Kahn always carried a sketch pad and a box of charcoal and pastels, and he worked so rapidly on site that he could complete a pastel in no more than twenty minutes.[186]

In Athens Kahn drew on and around the Acropolis to produce a dozen known drawings,[187] seven from outside the sanctuary, and five inside. Five of the first group show the Acropolis rather close up from the north, west, and south, while the two views from the east are from far away, from the park surrounding the Temple of Olympian Zeus.[188] These views of the Acropolis present only fragments of the structures inside its walls, so that the prize that awaits the visitor who finally mounts the stairs to the sanctuary is suggested but not revealed. The play is consistently between the solid planes of the surrounding wall and the openness of the colonnaded temples. It is almost as if Kahn wanted, in these drawings, to give visual form to the difference between a wall and, to paraphrase his own words, a wall that has parted to become columns.

The view from the south was taken in the afternoon from the Theater of Dionysos (figs. 67–68), looking up from its ruins to the enormous retaining walls erected in the fifth century B.C. to contain the vast area of fill that surrounds the deep substructures of the Parthenon on its south side.[189] Above the wall, punctuated by the dark shadows of the projecting buttresses, one gets only a glimpse of the superstructure of the temple itself. (In the drawing, Kahn eliminated a tree growing next to the temple that surely had been there for many years before 1951.) This drawing, like a similar drawing of the sanctuary at Delphi (fig. 76), is about layers in both two and three dimensions. There are the horizontal layers of stone and rock and earth that form strong parallels on the surface of the paper, and there are also the layers in depth of the same horizontal strata, which move back in space as they rise above one another.

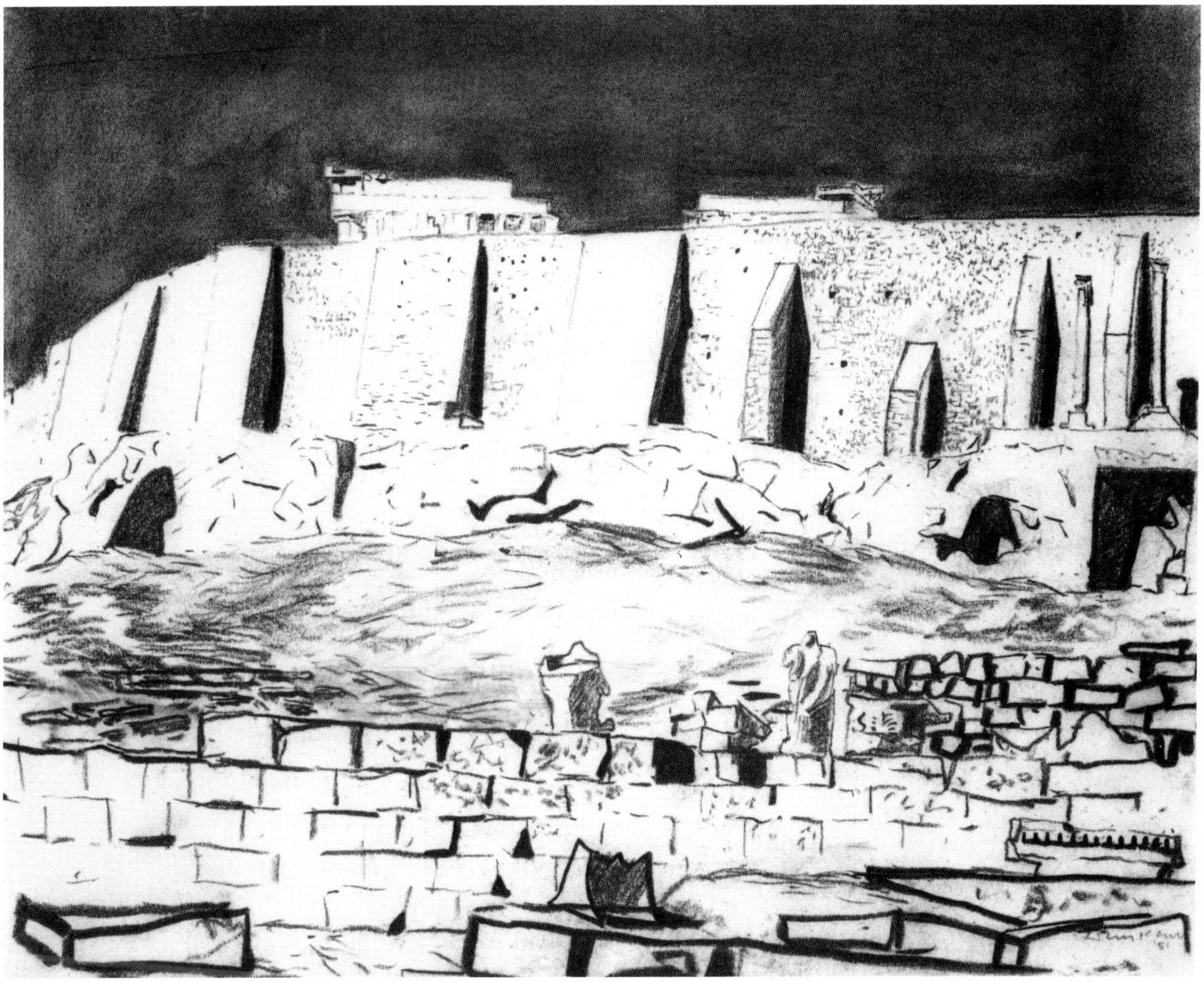

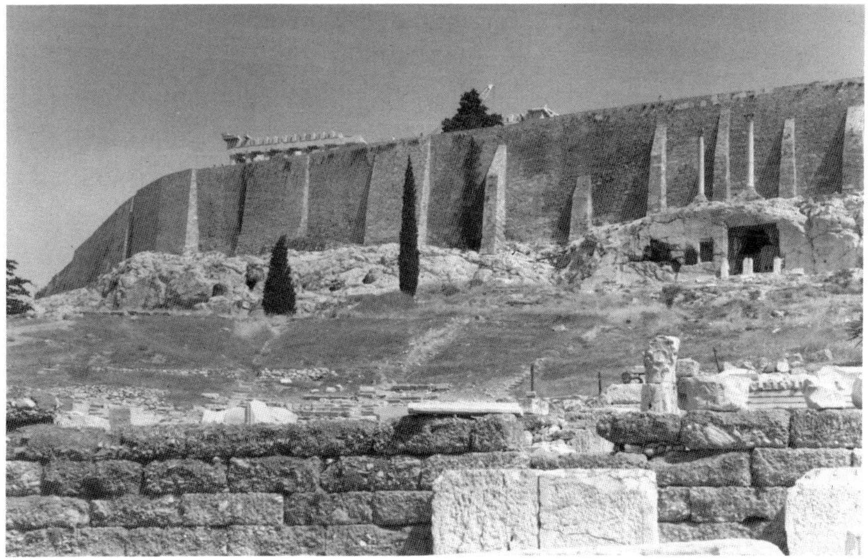

FIGURE 67
ACROPOLIS FROM THEATER OF DIONYSOS, ATHENS, 1951, charcoal and black crayon on paper (cat. no. 58)

FIGURE 68
ACROPOLIS FROM THEATER OF DIONYSOS, ATHENS; photograph by Ralph Lieberman

This is a different concept of layering from the one we so frequently encountered in the drawings of 1928–29. Here there is no screen in the foreground that acts as a foil to the extension of the scene in depth.

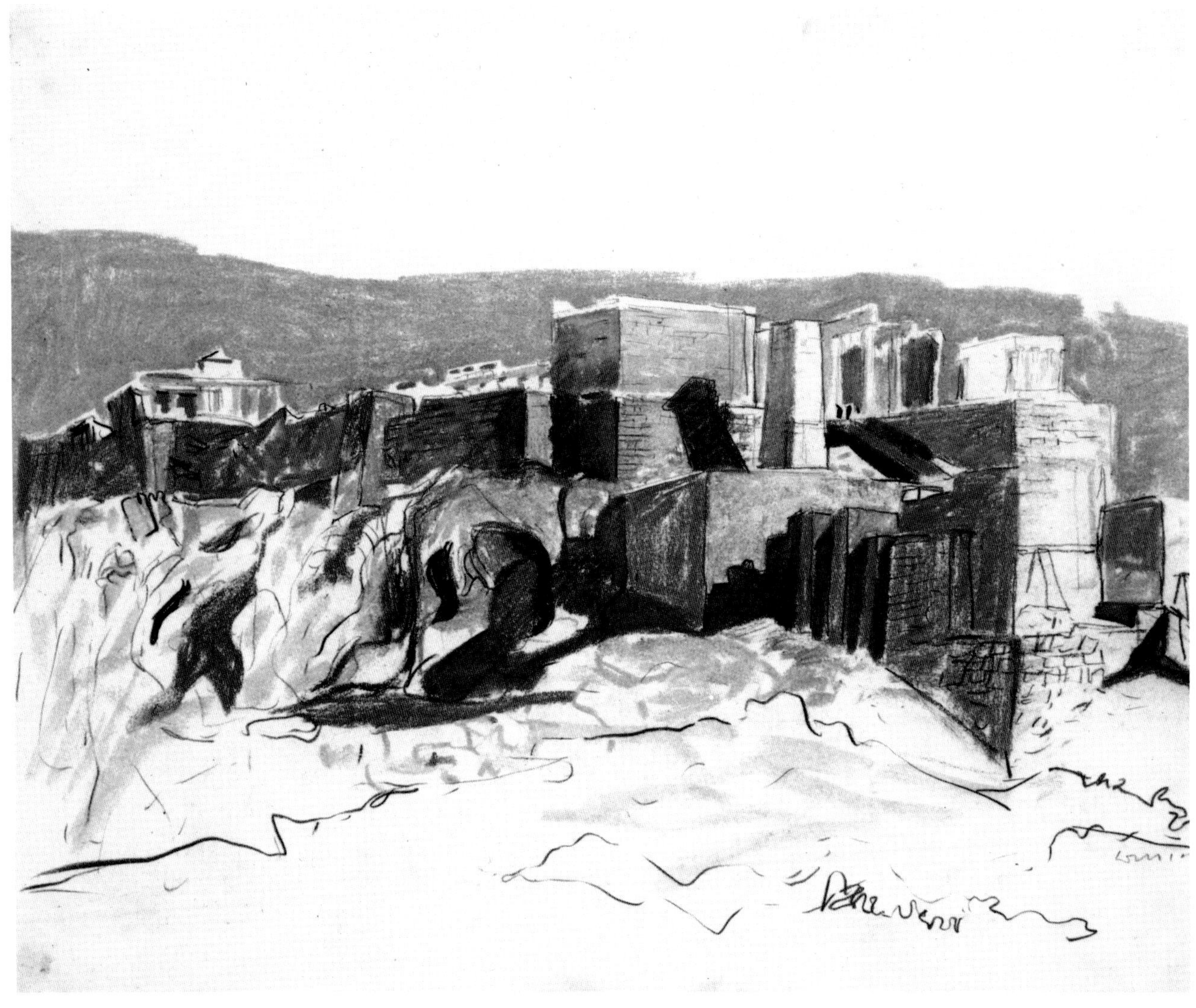

FIGURE 69
ACROPOLIS FROM AREOPAGUS, ATHENS, 1951, pastel and charcoal pencil on paper (cat. no. 57)

Opposite page:
FIGURE 70
COLUMNS AND WALLS OF PROPYLAEA FROM EAST, ACROPOLIS, ATHENS, 1951, pastel on paper (cat. no. 55)

Perhaps the finest drawing of this group is the pastel made after noon of the Acropolis from the Areopagus,[190] the rocky outcropping that stands just to the northwest of the sanctuary (fig. 69). Kahn sketched the slippery, irregular rock on which he stood with such light lines that the viewer or the artist seems to be levitated. By only suggesting the Areopagus, Kahn was able to concentrate his energies in one horizontal band into which the rock of the Acropolis, its buildings, and the sky are compressed. The buildings of the western approach come forward, their angled corners pointing aggressively at us.[191] Here we see another favorite compositional device of Kahn's in these drawings, advancing angles that slice the line of vision,[192] a prefiguration of the visual effect of looking at the Unitarian Church in Rochester of a decade later on angle.

We have three pastels that Kahn drew inside the sanctuary of the Acropolis. One shows the Erechtheion and the Parthenon bathed in the peachy glow of late afternoon light,[193] and a second was made inside the Parthenon, looking east.[194] The third is one of the most disorienting drawings he ever made (fig. 70). He stood inside the Propylaea, looking west through its eastern portico and two of its doors into the mostly broken columns of its west side.[195] The drawing is hard to read, even if one stands on the very spot where Kahn stood, with a reproduction of it in hand, but it is sufficiently remarkable to warrant a careful, even lengthy, analysis of its complexities.

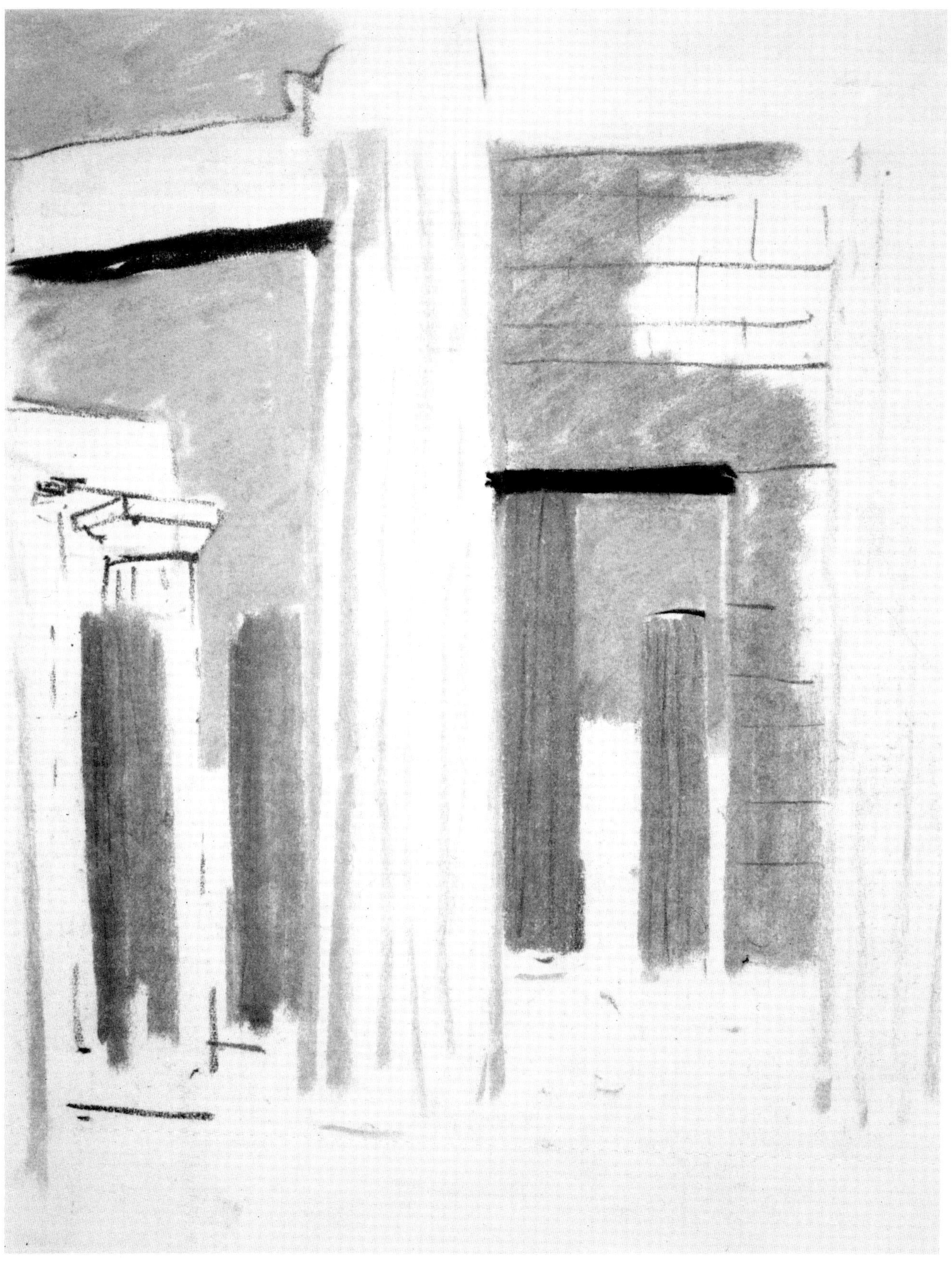

Six Doric columns form the eastern portico of the Propylaea; they are subdivided into two groups of three by the passageway that passes through the center bay of the colonnade. Kahn stood far to the right of the central bay, almost in line with the column at the right, or northern, end of the row. In the foreground plane of the drawing he sketched in very lightly the right-hand column at the right edge of the paper. Almost in the center of the paper he drew the first column in from the right corner, and at the left-hand margin he indicated the edge of the second column from the right corner. His position afforded him a view through the two northern intercolumniations of the portico to a second plane, created by the wall behind the columns. This wall is pierced by two rectangular doors: at left the doorway of the central passageway, at right the doorway immediately to the north of the central portal. Through these two doors Kahn had a diagonal view into the ruined columns that stand on the west side of the wall. The central passageway is lined by six columns of the Ionic order, three to each side, while the west porch of the Propylaea is created by a row of six Doric columns that correspond to the six Doric columns of the eastern portico. Of these twelve columns, Kahn drew the five he was able to see. Through the central door, to the left in the drawing, he sketched the stumps of two of the Ionic columns as dark slabs. Beyond them he drew the outline of the Doric column that stands at the south end of the western portico, as well as the architrave which that column still carries. To the left of this column, Kahn indicated the anta that stands behind this column and supports the other end of the architrave block. Through the other door Kahn sketched, again as darker shapes, two of the Ionic columns that line the north side of the central passageway. Of these, the one to the left still maintains its full height, and so Kahn shows it rising beyond the top of the intervening door. The other is a stump, and he shows it as such.

If one plots these columns on a plan of the Propylaea, one discovers that Kahn has included six different planes in depth: the plane of the east portico, of the wall and doorways, of the first and second pairs of Ionic columns flanking the central passage, of the anta that corresponds to the southernmost column of the west portico, and that column itself. Despite the fact that the drawing represents six planes in space, its effect is more of flatness than of depth. Kahn creates this flatness partly by failing to draw any connection between the foreground columns and the ground, and so the columns float ambiguously on the plane of the paper. The wall and the other columns have an equally tenuous relation to the ground, and they too float. At the top of the drawing Kahn leaves out the entablature of the eastern portico, which would have given the foreground columns some weight to bear and might have countered their tendency to float.

Of the three pastels that Kahn made in 1950–51 from a viewpoint chosen to be disorienting and to disrupt the symmetry and axiality of the subjects, this drawing of the Propylaea is the most extreme, because it also disrupts our perception of three-dimensional space itself. The pictorial sophistication of the Propylaea drawing makes clear that Kahn had not abandoned the notion of drawing for its own sake during this trip. But the drawing also shows us how Kahn was seeking to force what he admired about the architecture of antiquity—its solidity and its pure forms—into a radically asymmetrical, and thus modern, composition.

Kahn also made at least two charcoal drawings that include the Propylaea, one from the north steps of the Parthenon[196] and one, recently given to the Herbert F. Johnson Museum at Cornell University, of the Nike Temple and the south wing of the Propylaea (fig. 71). On the verso of the Cornell drawing is a counter-impression of the drawing Kahn made from the north steps of the Parthenon, a fact that indicates the Cornell drawing was made first, since the drawing with the Parthenon steps must have been on the next sheet in the sketchbook Kahn was using for its charcoal lines to have been transferred to the back of the sheet on top. A comparison of the ghost impression on the Cornell drawing with the actual sketch demonstrates that Kahn's drawings were often cropped after they were removed from the sketchbook. The upper parts of the columns and the entablature of the Parthenon have been cut off the Cornell sheet, which suggests that Kahn (or someone else) trimmed the Nike Temple drawing in order to improve the composition. On the other hand, the Cornell sheet shows more at the base of the Parthenon than the present drawing provides, which suggests that the drawing of the Parthenon steps in turn was trimmed at the bottom to improve its composition. The sizes of Kahn's drawings tend to vary a great deal. It would now seem clear that this variety was created by careful cropping of sketches after they were removed from their sketchbooks.

At Corinth Kahn spent most of a day focusing on the Temple of Apollo, the structure that dominates the excavations of the ancient city. He began drawing the temple at dawn when the sky at Corinth can be the deep yellow of the pastel (pl. 9) that focuses on five columns of the temple.[197] Always happy to leave out a detail that interfered with a good composition, Kahn eliminated one of the capitals of the rear row (fig. 72). The columns themselves are dark, as they become during the winter when they absorb the water of the seasonal rains. By giving each dark column a different color, Kahn makes the sketch vibrate with an expressionist power he only rarely achieved.

Drawing the columns from a point so close that they crowd the margins of each sheet, Kahn stalked the temple of Apollo, circling it as Apollo in his chariot circled the sky. When the sun was still low, Kahn made a second sketch, in charcoal on the right-hand page of a spiral-bound sketchbook, of the temple from the west. The sun's orb appears in the upper right, and the dark columns, seen against the sun, cast long shadows on the ground. Landscape forms are indicated summarily in the background, as they are in the next sketch, made on the left-hand page of the same sketchbook.[198]

FIGURE 71
NIKE TEMPLE AND SOUTH WING OF PROPYLAEA, ACROPOLIS, ATHENS, 1951, charcoal on paper; photograph courtesy lender (cat. no. 56)

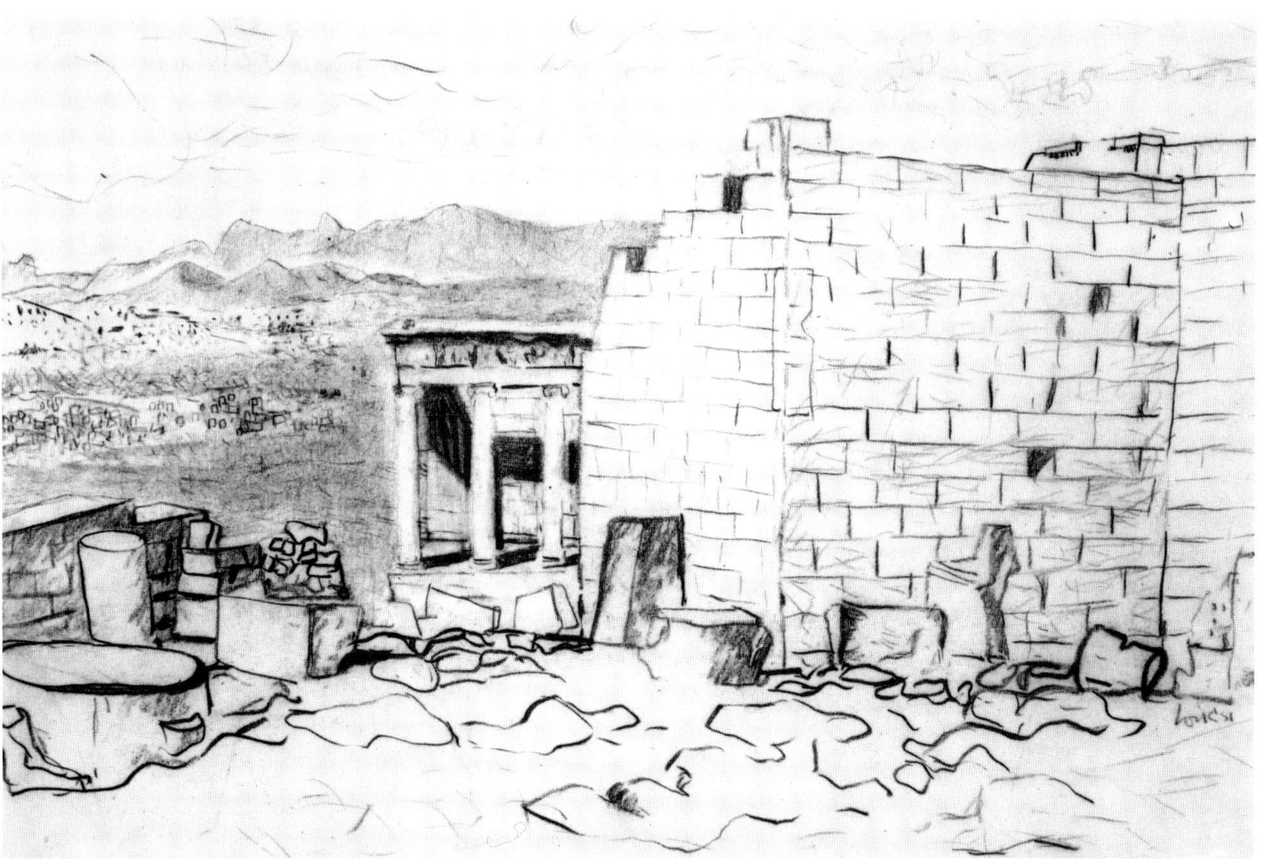

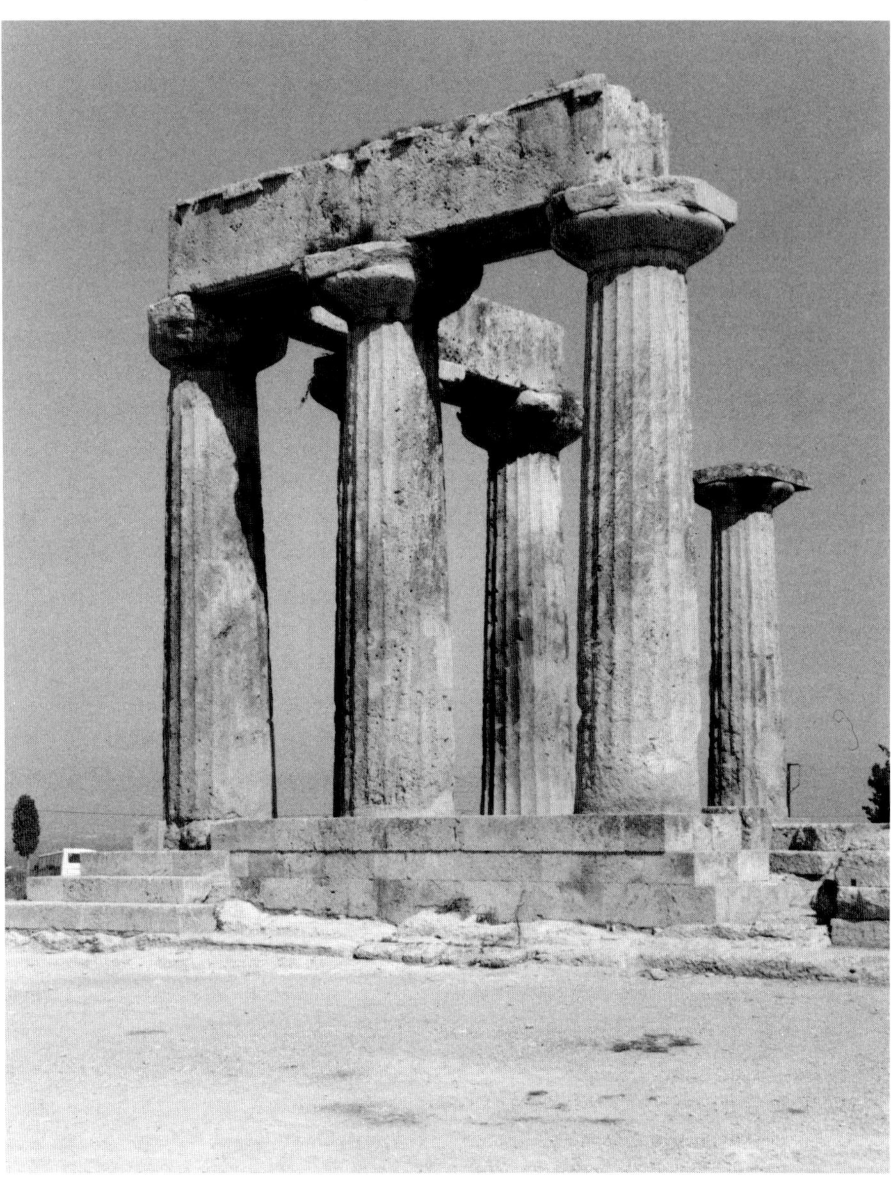

FIGURE 72
TEMPLE OF APOLLO, CORINTH;
photograph by Ralph Lieberman

It is now about 10 A.M., with the sun high enough to cast the shadows Kahn recorded inside the southern columns. Toward noon—the steep angle of the shadow on the entablature gives away the hour—Kahn made a second pastel from inside the temple (figs. 99–100), looking toward its southwest corner.[199] Kahn has pulled the vibrant blue of the overhead sky down behind the columns like a window shade, obliterating Acrocorinth, the mountain that forms a brown and green backdrop to the shafts.[200] He denies the very landscape he recorded in most of the other Corinthian drawings in order to pose the columns against a blue ground that brings to mind the frescoes in the upper church at Assisi that he had admired in 1928.

Finally, in the afternoon, Kahn stood on a wall next to the museum at Corinth and made the famous pastel (fig. 73) that puts the temple in the context of its site.[201] The seven columns stand against the deep blue of the Gulf of Corinth, the ruddy colors of the Perachora Peninsula that enters from the right, and the hilly northern shore of the gulf. A snowcapped range of mountains rises far in the distance. The time is January, and the day is one of those extraordinarily clear ones that occur in Greece in the winter after a storm has passed. Even the greens in the sky probably record colors that Kahn saw. This is one of Kahn's finest landscape drawings, and it shows as well as

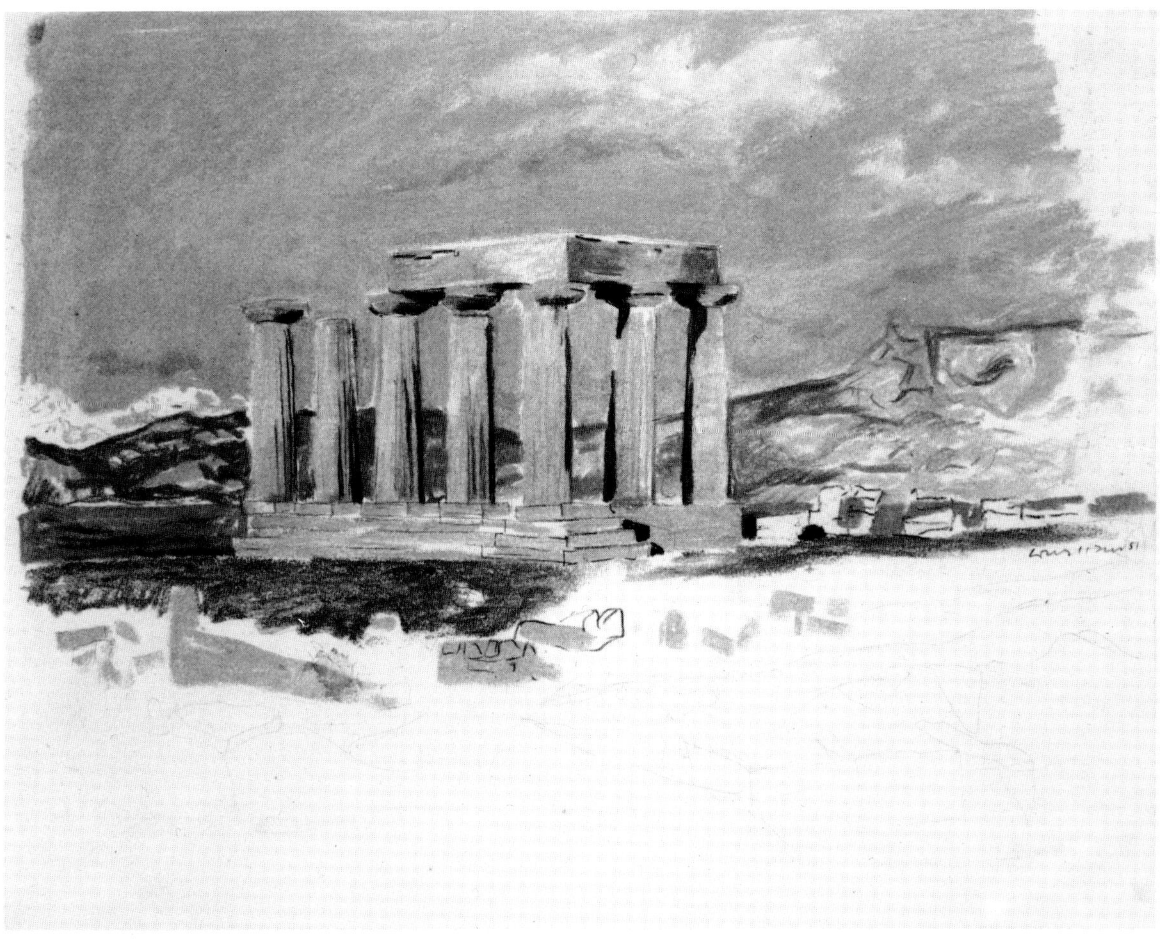

FIGURE 73
TEMPLE OF APOLLO, CORINTH, AT MIDAFTERNOON, 1951, pastel and charcoal on paper (cat. no. 61)

any drawing he ever made his sensitivity to the effects of color, light, and atmosphere on our perception of landscape and architecture alike.

As a group the Corinthian drawings demonstrate, as no other set of Kahn's drawings quite does, the sensibility that will one day give us, inside the Kimbell Art Museum, the changing hues and shifting intensities of light as the sun moves or clouds pass overhead. The interest in light and color that Kahn manifested through impressionist techniques in his first Italian sketches of 1928 stayed with him throughout his life, adapting itself to different artistic modes but constantly focusing on the changeability of nature and on the effects of light and atmosphere that Kahn sought to trap in his own structures. It became a matter of principle to Kahn that no room could be architecture unless it contained the changing effects of daylight.

From Delphi, Kahn's last stop in Greece, five drawings with architectural elements are known.[202] Three, made from the main road at a point near the Castalian Spring, focus on a round, stone-lined hole that Kahn places against the panorama of the surrounding mountains (figs. 74–75).[203] The hole is the remains of the plunge bath that formed part of a gymnasium complex located between the upper sanctuary and a lower sanctuary that contains a round temple dedicated to Athena. In this evocative site the ruins, remains of one moment in human history, are surrounded by ancient olive trees, traces of a later moment that continues into the present, while the mountains represent geological time. These drawings capture the ability of excavations to make us ruminate on time and history. They also signified for Kahn an act of reverence for the forces that govern nature. The line of the hill in this drawing, he told Hochstim, was "an absolute end line of conscious being, . . . the manifestation of evi-

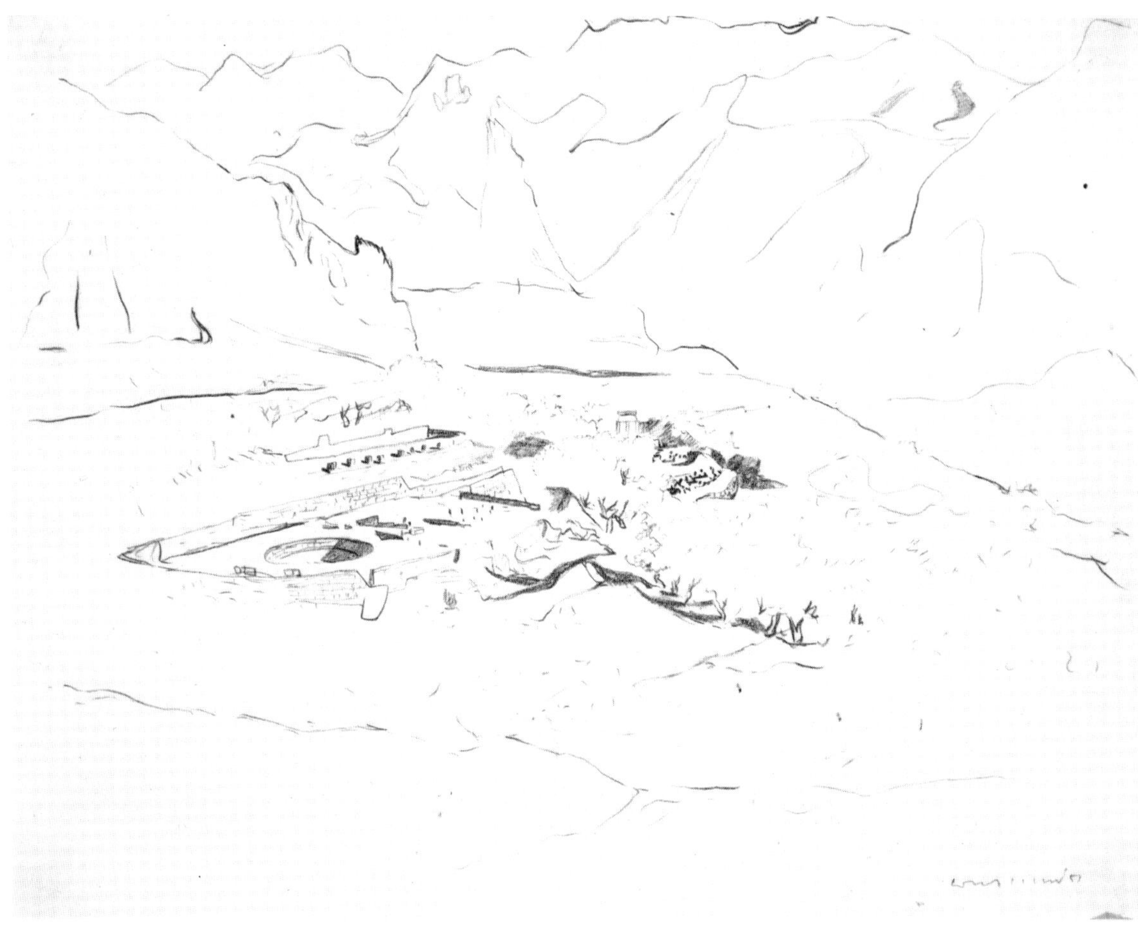

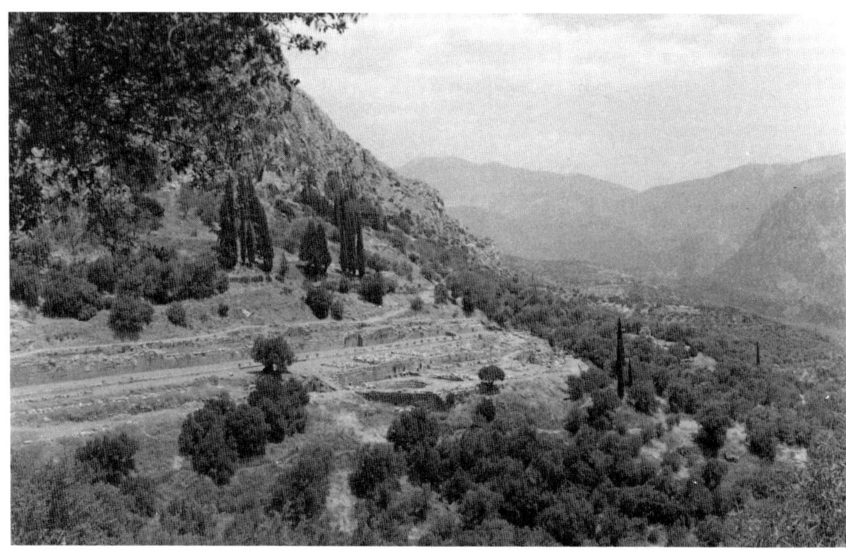

FIGURE 74
PLUNGE POOL OF BATH BUILDING, LOWER SANCTUARY, DELPHI, 1951, charcoal pencil on paper (cat. no. 62)

FIGURE 75
PLUNGE POOL OF BATH BUILDING, LOWER SANCTUARY, DELPHI; photograph by Ralph Lieberman

dence of being . . . in drawing this line you draw your reverence for that which is also devised as the maker of all things."[204] While his language contains typical Kahnian contortions, his meaning is fairly clear. The line that forms the edge of a mountain represents the boundary—the end—of that mountain as established by nature. In drawing that boundary Kahn believed he had represented the very principles on

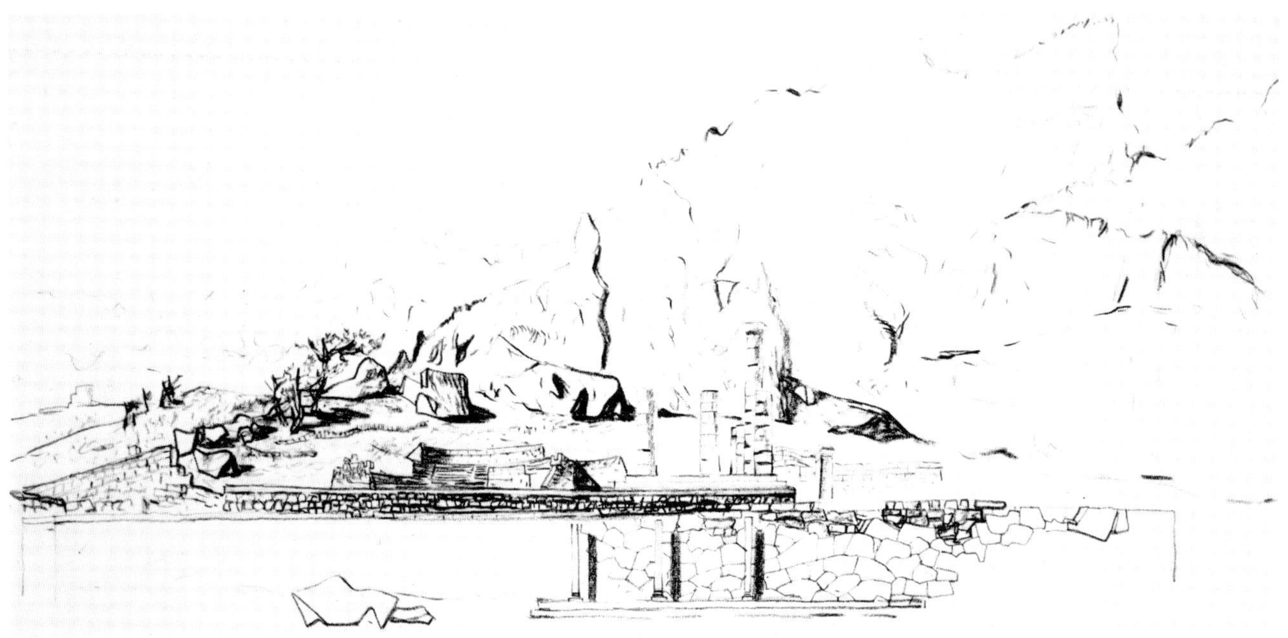

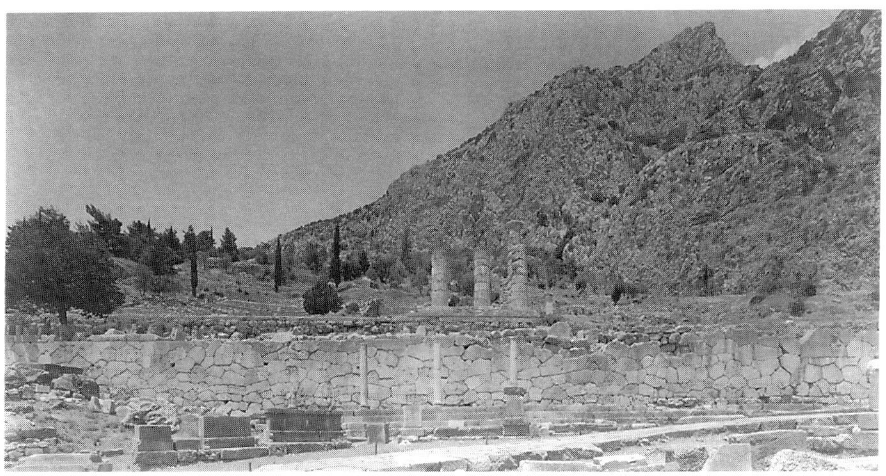

FIGURE 76
PORTICO OF ATHENIANS AND TEMPLE OF APOLLO, DELPHI, 1951, charcoal pencil on paper; photograph courtesy lender (cat. no. 63)

FIGURE 77
PORTICO OF ATHENIANS AND TEMPLE OF APOLLO, DELPHI; photograph by Ralph Lieberman

which nature operates, and for him that act had been "a great privilege." The round hole of the plunge bath and the surrounding olive trees, in turn, represent the very modest ways humans operate within the realm of nature. If one theme runs through almost all of the drawings Kahn made in Greece, it is the relationship between structures made by humans and the nature in which they placed those structures. It is not a new issue in Kahn's travel sketches—many drawings of the 1920s take up the same theme—but the Greek drawings suggest that the landscape of Greece gave Kahn a new reverence for nature itself.

The circular hole of the plunge bath is powerful as a purely formal element against nature's irregularities. Excavation holes held an attraction for Kahn. James Ackerman, fellow in art history at the American Academy in 1950–51, recalls Kahn's fascination with excavation holes in the Roman Forum when the two of them stood side by side looking at the ruins.[205] Although Kahn manipulates and changes the forms of the landscape very little in these drawings, he does adjust the position of the hole, lifting it up from the rear to bring it more into the plane of the paper so that its circular shape is more obvious, more "perfect"—to demonstrate the durability of a Platonic form that has survived the passage of time. That circle, to Kahn, may have represented the human search for order, a word that was to come to play its own very peculiar role in the oracular language he later developed to talk about the process of creating architecture. "Order is," he would pronounce.[206]

In his sketch of the Portico of the Athenians and the Temple of Apollo (figs. 76–77)[207] Kahn represents on a sheet 36.2 cm wide a distance so great—the upper step of the stylobate of the temple alone is 58.18 m long[208]—that three separate photographs with a 28 mm lens are required to encompass it. Behind the three columns of the Portico of the Athenians rises the polygonal masonry of the retaining wall above which the Temple of Apollo stands. In sketching the wall, Kahn went to great pains to distinguish between the large polygonal blocks of the original wall and the smaller stones of later repairs. As one studies the drawing, however, one comes to realize that he has changed the distances between the portico's columns, narrowing the intercolumniations to something he found more pleasing or acceptable.[209] One suspects that he was also trying to make a better vertical relationship between the columns of the portico and those of the temple above, a relationship that is far more discordant in actuality.

Kahn's experience of the non-orthogonal planning of Greek sanctuaries had an immediate effect in his own work. When he returned to Rome from Greece, he found a letter, dated 18 January 1951, from Kenneth Day, an architect with whom he had been corresponding the previous month about the Mill Creek Housing Project in Philadelphia. In the letter Day had sent a plot plan of the project for Kahn's perusal.[210] On the back of the first sheet of that letter Kahn sketched his own version of this orthogonal plot plan (fig. 78). Then, at the same scale and in the same blue ink, he made a second sketch on half a sheet of letterhead of the American Academy in Rome.[211] On this second sketch (fig. 79) he rejected the orthogonal planning that he had received from Day for a much looser plan, in which the apartment blocks stand at various angles to each other as, say, the treasuries of Greek cities had stood at a variety of angles to each other along the Sacred Way at Delphi. Although Kahn's scheme was never executed, it prompted Day to reply: "the little odd-shaped courts attract me."[212] The little odd-shaped courts signaled a farewell to Corbusian Ville Radieuse

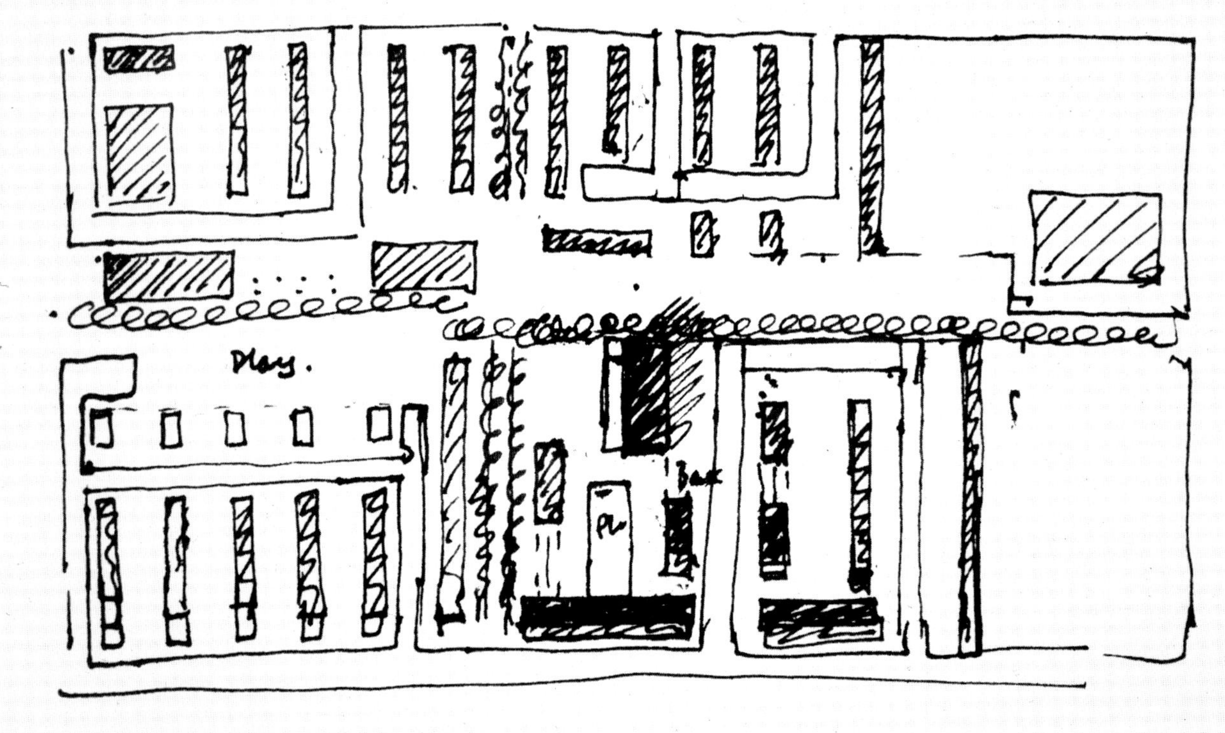

FIGURE 78
SKETCH PLAN OF MILL CREEK HOUSING, January 1951, ink on typewriter paper, letter from Kenneth Day to LIK, 18 January 1951, "Letters to L. I. Kahn," LIK Box 60; photograph courtesy Louis I. Kahn Collection, University of Pennsylvania and Pennsylvania Historical and Museum Commission

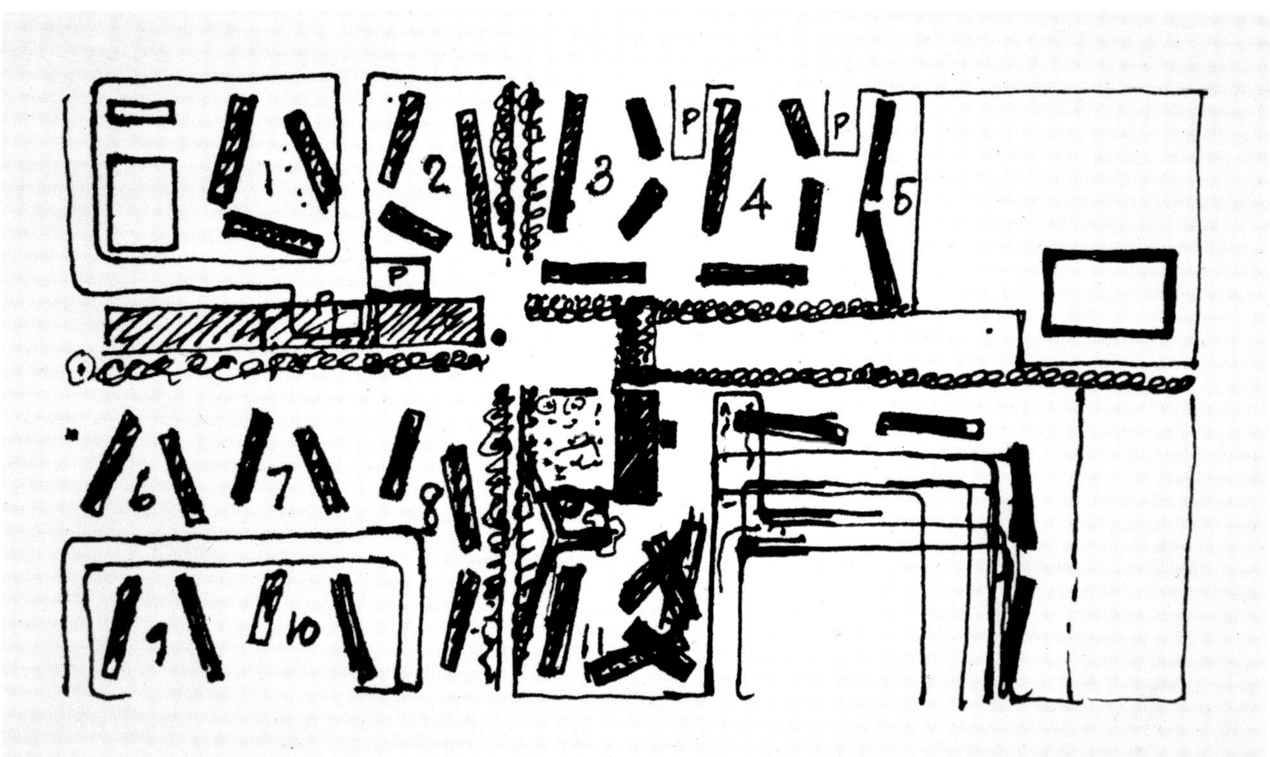

FIGURE 79
SKETCH PLAN OF MILL CREEK HOUSING, January 1951, ink on letterhead of American Academy in Rome, "Letters to L. I. Kahn," LIK Box 60; photograph courtesy Louis I. Kahn Collection, University of Pennsylvania and Pennsylvania Historical and Museum Commission

planning on Kahn's part, a farewell that the experience of Greece had clearly led him to take. One might argue that the tendency to asymmetrical composition that Kahn had taken from De Chirico and used in the sketches of the Piazza San Pietro and the Propylaea had been reinforced by the experience of the architectural power of the asymmetrical sanctuaries of ancient Greece. In the Mill Creek sketch plan Kahn tried to transfer that powerful informality to low-cost housing.

All during his trip of 1950–51 Kahn restricted himself to three media: charcoal, black crayon, and pastel. The first two he had used, although sparingly, in his sketches of the 1920s, when his favorite media were graphite and watercolor, and he had employed them with some frequency in his North American sketches of the 1930s. Pastel, however, seems to be a medium he almost never used prior to 1950. Of the 330 items that Hochstim has catalogued that predate Kahn's arrival in Rome in December 1950, only three employ pastel, and always in the company of another medium.[213] In the mid-thirties, while he continued to work frequently in watercolor, Kahn also began to work in tempera on paper to obtain more opaque planes than watercolor can readily produce (pl. 5); it may be that this interest in producing opaque planes stands behind his adoption of pastels in his travel sketches of 1950–51. In his watercolors of the mid and late thirties Kahn was attempting to achieve a level of saturated color for which the medium is not entirely suited. For saturated color, tempera stood him in better stead, as did pastel in the travel sketches of 1950–51. By the 1940s Kahn seems to have abandoned watercolor entirely. There are no North American travel sketches from the forties, however, because wartime gasoline rationing had rendered impossible a continuation of the automobile trips to the New England and Canadian coasts that the Kahns had enjoyed in the previous decade.

But none of this really explains Kahn's decision to use pastels instead of his previously beloved watercolors after he arrived in Rome. Vincent Scully has proposed that the impact of European modernism after World War II "entirely killed off his urge to do watercolors. They were undoubtedly all too irrevocably associated with the bad old

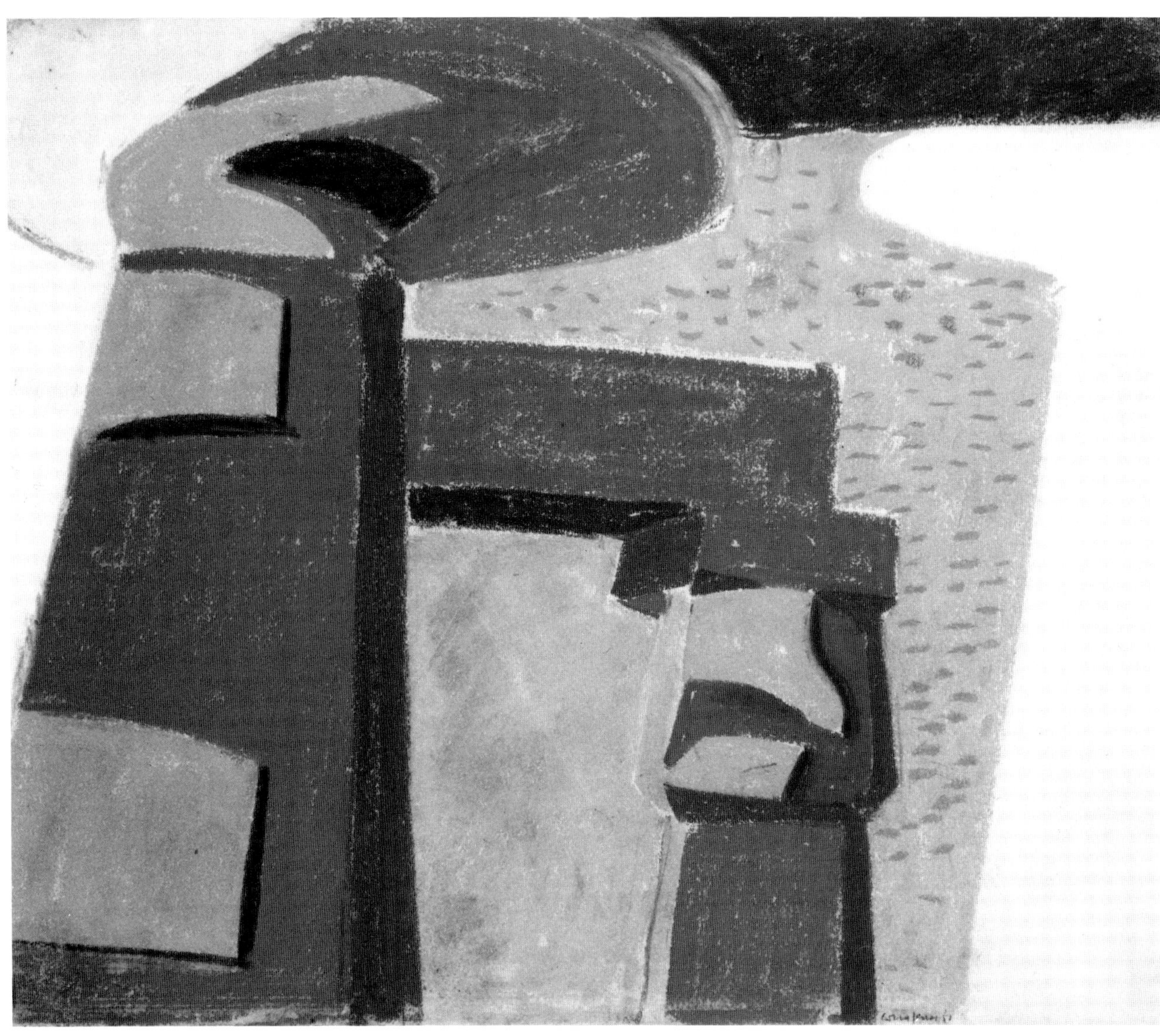

FIGURE 80
CAPITALS, HYPOSTYLE HALL, TEMPLE OF AMON, KARNAK,
1951, pastel on paper (cat. no. 54)

picturesque Beaux-Arts way."[214] This explanation is both attractive and problematic, for Kahn had continued his prolific production of watercolors in the mid-1930s, during the very years his architecture came under the heavy influence of the work of Le Corbusier, the standard bearer of European modernism among architects. The summer and fall of 1936 found him working on drawings for the Jersey Homesteads in Roosevelt, New Jersey, one of the most progressive housing projects of the decade and one for which he made a particularly Corbusian sketch.[215] That same summer's vacation produced a wonderful series of watercolors of Nova Scotia.[216] It is possible, however, that Kahn may have clung to a more traditional medium in his two-dimensional work at the very moment when he took up more radical architectural forms. One must always remember that he kept the two activities separate in his mind.

One clue to Kahn's reasons for adopting pastel may lie in his admiration for the paintings of Giorgio de Chirico. De Chirico's opaque planes and often saturated colors could hardly be approximated in watercolor, but they could be approached in pastel, a medium also highly agreeable to the needs of the traveler who wants to make a quick sketch. This hypothesis is supported by what seems to be the most obvious stylistic development within the pastels themselves. Of all his pastels of 1950–51, the sketch

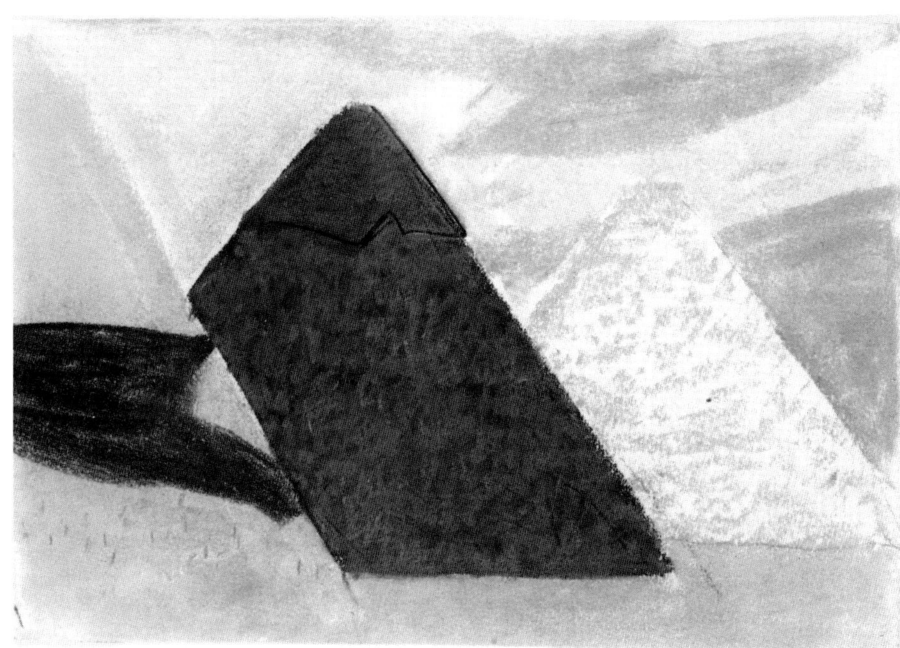

FIGURE 81
PYRAMIDS, GIZA, 1951, pastel on paper (cat. no. 50)

of the Piazza San Pietro (fig. 61) is most blatantly imitative of De Chirico. In this drawing Kahn's handling of the medium seems particularly hesitant—the work of a novice. He first sketched in a few defining lines in charcoal or pastel, and then he colored in separate areas with discrete hues. Much of the surface of the paper is left blank, as if he were not quite sure what to do with it. There is none of the bold interlocking of areas of saturated color almost covering the entire sheet that marks his more fully developed pastels, such as those of Siena (pl. 7). Moreover, in the Saint Peter's sketch Kahn fails to exploit the way linear variety can be achieved with pastel, an aspect of the medium he quickly learns to use with considerable skill. In this respect, a good contrast to the Saint Peter's drawing is offered by the pastel of the five columns of the Temple of Apollo at Corinth at dawn (pl. 9), in which he draws loosely, surely, and with energetic, varied lines. Saint Peter's is an easy walk from the American Academy, and so it is easy to imagine that he strolled down to the church to sketch shortly after he had arrived in Rome.[217] He must have made his other drawing of a Roman square, that of the Campidoglio, considerably later in his stay, for stylistically it is a far cry from the drawing of Saint Peter's.[218] Indeed, in its looseness it comes much closer to the two pastels of Venice, which are the loosest of them all.

A stylistic analysis of the pastels suggests the following chronological sequence: Piazza San Pietro, the drawings of Siena, the Roman ruins dated 1951, the drawings of Egypt, the drawings of Greece, and finally the Campidoglio and the two pastels of Venice.

We know that Kahn visited Egypt before Greece, and so that part of the chronology is sure.[219] From this fixed point we can work both forward and backward to try to establish a relative chronological relationship. Of the Egyptian pastels, the view of the temple at Luxor seems to share many characteristics with the view of the Siena baptistery, including the dark blue, lowering sky, the strong black lines that outline dominant planes parallel to the picture plane, the dark lines that separate the ochre ashlar blocks. In his pastel of the temple at Edfu[220] Kahn makes use of the same strong, clear, black outlines and, in addition, throws a sharp-edged orange shadow across the foreground that recalls the shadows in his views of Siena. The interlocked flat planes of color in the Edfu drawing are likewise analogous to those in the Siena sketches. In the pastel of the courtyard of the Mortuary Temple of Rameses III (pl. 8), the vibrant play of colored shadows, enlivened by the complementary colors that mark the interstices between ashlar blocks, develops more fully the way Kahn drew the shadowed pavement stones of the Campo (pl. 7). Because the pastels of Siena are close to some made in Egypt, but quite different from those made in Greece, it seems sensible to date the Sienese sketches before rather than after the trip to the eastern Mediterranean.[221]

In Egypt Kahn learns to use pastel to model with color—as in the splendidly glyptic columns of the mortuary courtyard at Medinet-Habu—something that he seems as yet unable to do in his view of Hadrian's Villa and that he tentatively explores in the forms of Siena Cathedral that loom over one view of the Campo. That use of color to model is apparent in two of the three closely related pastels of capitals and entablatures from the Hypostyle Hall at Karnak. In one of these drawings[222] Kahn uses color to model the roundness of the columns and capitals, although in the bud capital to the rear the highlights begin to approach abstraction. In a second drawing[223] the abstraction of the highlights of the bud capital into flat pattern is carried farther. In the third in the series (fig. 80), one of the boldest drawings Kahn ever made in terms of color, the columns have been almost entirely flattened out into abstract patterns, so much so that the one at the right foreground is indicated only by bare paper silhouetted against the bright blue of the ground.[224] Kahn never achieved quite the same degrees of abstraction and flatness in another drawing of an architectural subject.

FIGURE 82
MORTUARY TEMPLE OF HATSHEPSUT, DEIR EL-BAHRI,
1951, pastel on paper (cat. no. 51)

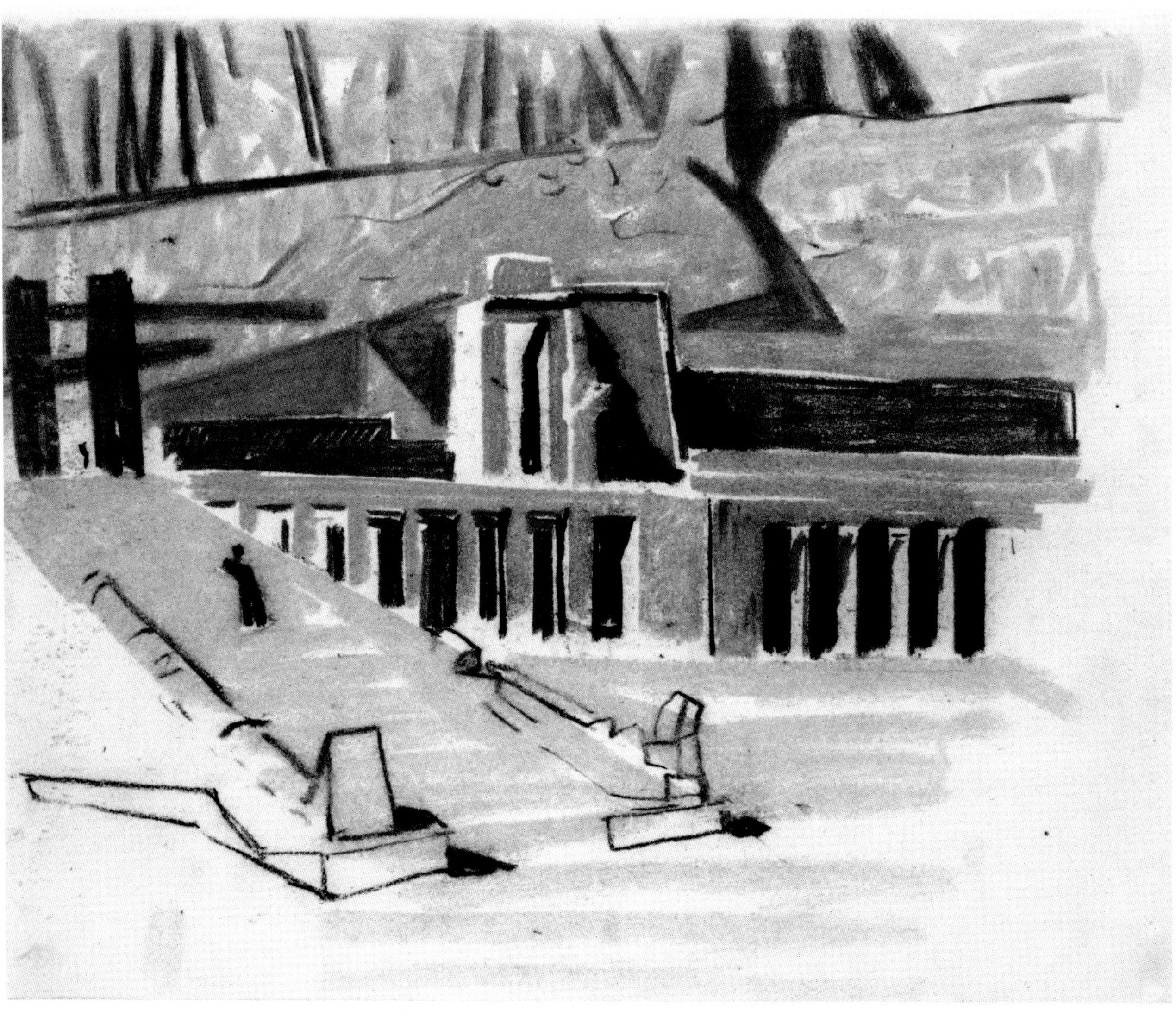

Of the Egyptian pastels, those of the pyramids are most problematic and least successful. In most he tries to render the rough texture of the stone of the pyramids by short jabs of the pastel stick,[225] or in some cases by long lines[226] that are as unconvincing as the squiggles he drew years before on the walls of "Il Gotico" in Piacenza (fig. 22). Both the jabs and the lines undercut the sense of the monumentality of the forms. One might argue that because the pyramid sketches are so tentative, they come before the other Egyptian drawings. One aspect of the pyramid drawings certainly does foreshadow what he will do commonly in Greece: leave the foreground bare to focus our attention on the pyramids, which appear either in a middle register[227] or take up the upper half of the compositions.[228]

Kahn's view of the Temple of Hatshepsut at Deir el-Bahri (off-axis like the view of Saint Peter's square) appears to represent a new freedom in his handling of pastel (fig. 82), just as his view of the façade of the Cathedral of Assisi (fig. 28) seems to repre-

FIGURE 83
GOTHIC TRACERY, VENICE,
1951, pastel on paper (cat. no. 49)

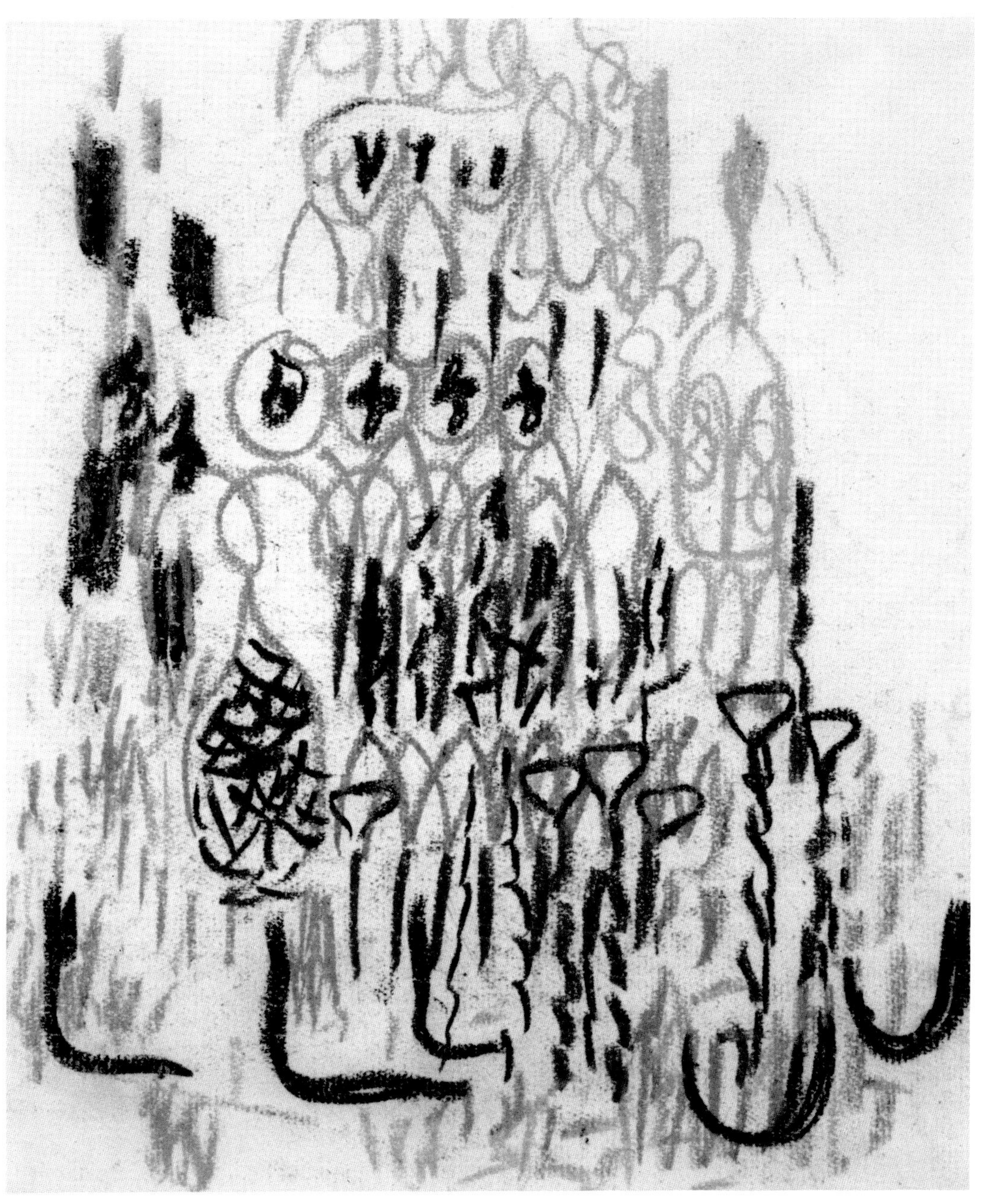

sent a breakthrough in his handling of a graphite stick in 1928. Instead of the tightly controlled areas of color that one finds in the Edfu or Luxor sketches, Kahn handles the medium much more loosely. A few strokes indicate the cliffs behind the temple, quick notations with dark color create areas of shadow in the colonnades, and a lot of paper is left bare as highlight, rather than just empty, as in the drawing of Piazza San Pietro. This technique, hard won in Egypt, Kahn carries with him to Greece.

In his views of the Acropolis from the Areopagus and of the Propylaea (figs. 69, 70), Kahn displays the mastery of pastel he achieved in Egypt. In both drawings there is a skillful use of blank paper as a compositional and coloristic device. There is also a growing flexibility of line and sureness of modeling with colors. And in the view of the Propylaea there is a level of abstraction, albeit not flattened abstraction, that goes beyond even the third of the Karnak capital sketches (fig. 80). No less sure are the pastels from Corinth,[229] of which the view of the temple at sunrise (pl. 9) marks a high point for Kahn as a colorist.

When Kahn visited Venice sometime in February, he made a pastel of San Marco that is so rapidly and loosely sketched that the architectural forms seem to dissolve in a haze of colored lines (pl. 10). He seems to have recast his earlier impressionist drawings of Venice into a more vigorous, more expressive, and coloristically more explosive mode. A second drawing, a close-up view of Venetian Gothic tracery (fig. 83), is more ground than figure, more atmospheric and evanescent than anything he had ever drawn. Never in his architecture did he approach the dissolution of form he perpetrated here. Kahn the painter let himself wallow in the pictorial possibilities of Venice. One cannot help but think of paintings by Philip Guston,[230] who finally achieved his mature style of shimmering strokes of color in 1951, the very year that Kahn presumably made this drawing.[231]

Kahn left Italy in early March and returned to the United States by way of Paris, repeating his route of 1929. From shipboard he wrote a letter to the fellows in Rome, who must have still been digesting their sweep through Egypt and Greece.[232] Kahn's letter was all about Paris, about the greatness of that city, about the lessons to be learned from its urban patterns. A man whose mind never stood still, Kahn had already moved on to absorb yet another experience. But once again, it seems, he did not draw Paris.

ALBI, CARCASSONNE, AND RONCHAMP, 1959

The visits to Egypt, Greece, and Rome, which led Kahn to seek a way out of the "tinniness" of modernism, marked the beginning of a decade of extraordinary development in his work, when he moved from being a respected teacher who had done a few buildings of minor interest to a major figure on the international architectural scene. He accomplished this leap in his career on the basis of two completed buildings, the Yale Art Gallery and the Trenton Bathhouse; one almost-completed structure, the Richards Medical Research Institute; and a few publications in *Perspecta: The Yale Architectural Journal.*[233] In 1959, when he made what turned out to be his last sketching trip in Europe, Kahn was in his late fifties. He was still a learner—indeed he was always a learner—but he was on the verge of what the British architects Alison and Peter Smithson predicted in 1960: "Louis Kahn will soon be a very great architect."[234] A measure of Kahn's achievement of international status during the 1950s was the invitation to address what turned out to be the last meeting of

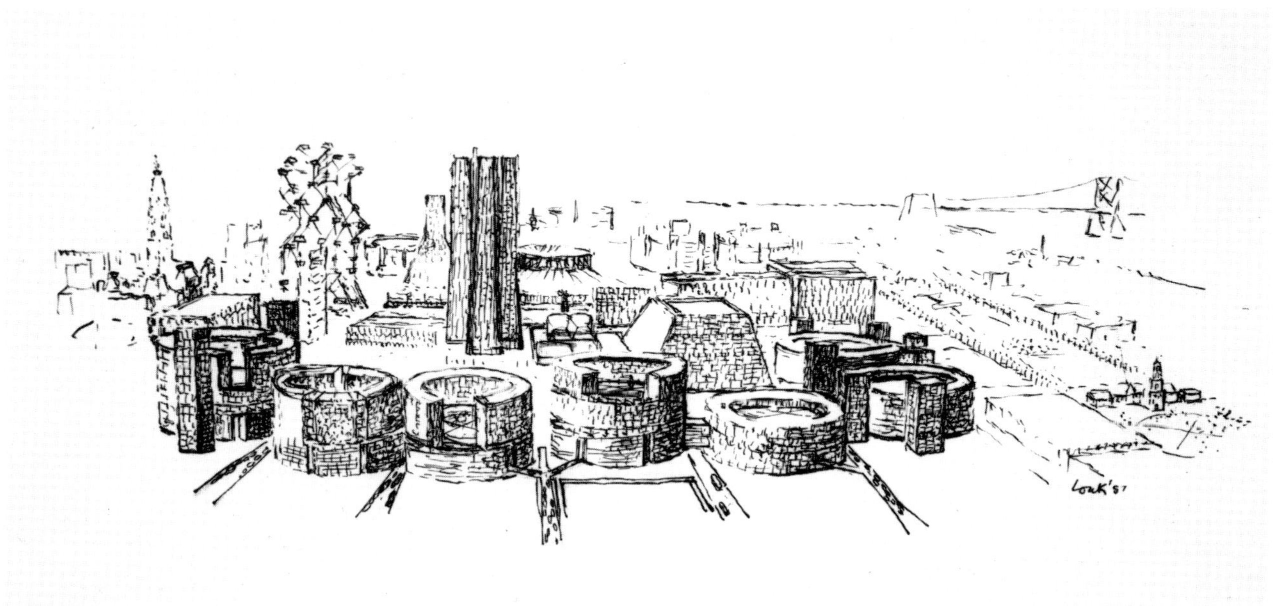

FIGURE 84
PENN CENTER PLANNING STUDIES, CENTER CITY, PHILADELPHIA, PA, Project, 1957; ink on white tissue, 27.9 x 35.5 cm; The Museum of Modern Art, NY, Gift of the architect. Photograph © 1996 The Museum of Modern Art, NY

the International Congress of Modern Architecture (CIAM), held at Otterlo in September 1959.[235] Before going to the Netherlands for the meeting, Kahn made a six-day trip in France to sketch the cathedral of Albi and the medieval walled city of Carcassonne, and while he was in Europe he visited Le Corbusier's church at Ronchamp.[236] The sketches Kahn made of Albi, Carcassonne, and Ronchamp closed this crucial period of his life, just as the drawings from his months at the American Academy opened it.

During the 1950s the effect of Egypt, Greece, and Rome on Kahn was slow to emerge in his work. Outside of the project for the Civic Center in Philadelphia of 1951–53, of which we have already spoken, there was little evidence in his designs of influence from ancient or Renaissance architecture until 1955. Instead, Kahn moved away from International Style modernism by experimenting with structural and geometric ordering influenced both by the ideas of Anne Griswold Tyng, who had entered Kahn's office in 1945 after being trained under Walter Gropius at Harvard, and by the meditations on structural forms of Buckminster Fuller, who was teaching at Yale. Around the middle of the decade influences from earlier architecture begin to creep into these experiments. Kahn's plan of a triangle inscribed in a circle for the Adath Jeshurun Synagogue project of 1954–55 seems dependent on a plan of Claude Nicholas Ledoux,[237] and in 1955 plans derived from Italian Renaissance architecture, which Kahn came to know from Rudolph Wittkower's *Architectural Principles in the Age of Humanism*, began to emerge on his drawing table.[238] While works deeply influenced by the ideas of Tyng and Fuller largely made use of a geometry of triangles and polygons, those influenced by Renaissance and neoclassical sources tended to employ the circle and the square. Such forms make up the Greek Cross plan of the Trenton Bathhouse of 1955, over which four pyramids rise to form the roofs.

Drawings that Kahn made in 1956–57 for another projected Civic Center in Philadelphia—this one located along Market Street east of City Hall—show exactly the formal confusion of his work of the mid-fifties (fig. 84). At left rear is the skewed, skeletal City Tower that he and Anne Tyng first conceived around 1952, whose triangulated diagonal structural units cause it to rise in a sequence of zigzags that express the geometric logic of its bracing against the wind.[239] In the same drawing there are buildings based on the geometries of the circle, the square, and the pyramid: an office tower with a Greek Cross plan, several cylindrical structures, and a truncated pyramid.[240] Here, one might argue, every tendency that was floating around in Kahn's mind poured out into a project that is fascinating precisely because it is unresolved.[241] The reminiscences of both European sketching trips are clear. Some of the cylindrical buildings have San Gimignano-like towers attached to them. The truncated pyramid is Egyptian in origin,[242] and the hollow cylinders recall the circular stone hole of the plunge bath at Delphi. The seemingly random layout of the buildings on the site suggests an attentiveness to Greek principles of planning rather than to Egypto-Roman axiality and symmetry, while at the same time the layout harks back both to the way he sited individual buildings in the Civic Center project of 1951–53 (fig. 65)[243] and to the way he proposed to site apartment blocks in the plan for Mill Creek that he conceived in Rome in 1951 (fig. 79).

As the decade grew older, more ideas that Kahn must have picked up on his European trips began to surface in his work. The plan, from 1957, of the day camp for the Trenton Jewish Community Center consists basically of abstracted Greek temples and treasuries set at the seemingly accidental angles one finds in Greek sanctuaries; the barbecue pit even calls to mind a Greek outdoor altar. Also from late 1957 are early perspectives for the Richards Medical Research Building in which some of the servant towers are rather fussily articulated and others are pure rectangular solids.[244] In the end, driven by a need to meet budget requirements, Kahn opted for simplicity over complexity and made all the towers pure rectangles.[245] That he deliberately sought inspiration from his thirty-year-old drawings of San Gimignano while designing the Richards towers we do not know; indeed, he need not have pulled out his drawings and looked them over. As we have seen in the instance of his sketching the Spoleto viaduct on a sheet of drawings for the Salk Institute, the buildings that he had drawn in 1928–29 had so thoroughly penetrated his consciousness that he was capable of recalling their images at will. One simply cannot imagine that someone of Kahn's remarkable visual intelligence was unaware of the similarity of what he was designing to what he had once drawn in San Gimignano. Moreover, Richards had to be inserted into a long, narrow space lined with turn-of-the-century buildings by Cope and Stewardson. Opposite the Richards site rose Gothic dormitories to whose shapes the Richards towers, even though clearly modern, were sympathetic. Kahn needed an abstract shape reminiscent of medieval buildings to make his building compatible. As he wrote on an aerial perspective of the Richards complex, the "towers present a silhoette [sic] complimenting the many chimneys and tower accents of the Jacobian [sic] dormitories nearby."[246] To insist only on the medievalism of Kahn's towers, however, makes the story too simple, for it seems likely that Kahn was also thinking of Frank Lloyd Wright's corner towers of the Larkin Building in Buffalo.[247] Here the source not only works formally but also in terms of function, for the Larkin towers, like Kahn's, served for the circulation of people and air.

By the first half of 1959, Renaissance architectural forms had come to play an ever more important, but hardly exclusive, role in Kahn's thinking. His plan for the unexecuted Fleisher House, from the winter of that year, is Palladian in its symmetry, and the Fleisher House makes use of thick walls more typical of Renaissance masonry structures than of twentieth-century buildings.[248] In June Kahn made his first sketch plan for the Unitarian Church in Rochester, a centrally planned building with an eight-point vault over a circular core surrounded by eight rectangular spaces.[249] The relationship to centrally planned churches of the Renaissance, which he would have known from Wittkower's book, is perfectly clear. One of the most important contributions of Wittkower's book was its insistence that the geometry used by Renaissance architects was chosen not merely for visual reasons but also because it symbolized the perfection of God himself. In other words, Kahn would have found in Wittkower's text a precedent for the kind of cosmic justification for formal choices that he was seeking for his own work.[250]

Kahn's trip to Europe came at a moment of profound doubt about the future of modern architecture. By 1959 the "old masters" of modernism had achieved not only maturity of years but also maturity of style, as in Mies's just completed Seagram Building in New York or Le Corbusier's church at Ronchamp that had opened four years earlier. At Otterlo Kahn criticized the Seagram Building, and while he was in Europe he visited and drew Ronchamp. The generation of architects that came of age during the years of World War II had to confront the new situation that existed in the wake of the war, including the remarkable triumph of an architecture that before the war had been widely unbuilt. This new generation believed that while their forebears—Mies, Gropius, and Le Corbusier—had sought to deny architectural history, they could not. At the same time, they feared that if they tried to use historical forms in their new architecture, history would hold their buildings in its thrall, just as they believed history had enthralled the eclectic architecture of the late nineteenth and early twentieth centuries. They felt compelled to make an architecture that was both new and also compatible with the old urban cores of the European cities in which they had to operate, but they were not sure how to do so. Kahn found himself at the very center of this dilemma, for his Trenton Bathhouse had made use of historical forms, but not in a sentimental or regional sense, or even in a typological sense. His pyramidal roofs at Trenton did not signal a burial ground, nor his Greek Cross a Renaissance church. At Trenton Kahn had used old forms in an abstract way, for the sense of shelter and order and geometry that the roofs and the plan defined.

Some of the sharpest battles at CIAM were between a group led by Alison and Peter Smithson, who continued to reject all historical architectural forms in their search for new ones, and a group of Italians, principally Ernesto Rogers and Giancarlo de Carlo, who were trying to integrate new structures into old urban situations by recalling, more or less directly, indigenous structures. The building that caused the most controversy was the Torre Velasca in Milan, a skyscraper with projecting upper stories that clearly recalled Lombard fortress towers of the middle ages, designed by Banfi, Belgiojoso, Peressutti and Rogers (B.B.P.R.). Ernesto Rogers argued, a bit disingenuously, that the form of the building had largely been determined by functional rather than historical considerations. Peter Smithson took a strong moral stance against the building, seeing its historicism as a dangerous precedent: "Such a development contains the possibility of other people's doing similar things in a worse way."[251] According to Smithson, the architect had a moral responsibility to create a methodological model that would help other architects (implicitly lesser ones) make the right (read "no historicizing, please") choices. For Smithson, such a model had to operate within what he perceived as an historical given: the fundamental and irrevocable differences between the twentieth century and all other ages. For the Smithsons, such differences made any reference to past architectural forms in new buildings unthinkable.

At Otterlo the attack on Giancarlo de Carlo's housing project for the Calabrian city of Matera, while similar to the critique of the Torre Velasca, also reprised another modernist refrain, that of architecture as a means of cultural uplift for the masses. The architect André Wogensky criticized De Carlo for "betraying" the Calabresi who lived in his project. "These people have not received an education into the new plastic relationships of our epoch, and do not understand the poetry of modern space and movement," argued Wogensky. "You must, if you hope to lead them to the future, introduce this new plastic expression, and fight to make it clear and understandable to them. The plastic conception of architectural space cannot be independent of the culture of our day with its advances in scientific and artistic thinking."[252] What De Carlo claimed to have tried to achieve was a contemporary building that suited its site in an old city as well as the lives of the people who were to live in it. He had rejected the architectural salvationism still preached by Wogensky. So had Kahn.

Peter Smithson expressed particularly clearly one aspect of the dilemma faced by the congress: ". . . in the reality of the present we are confronted with a peculiar difficulty, and that is, that there is a knife-edge between two conceptions of architecture. The one is the concept of an architecture of social engineering, and the other the concept of an architecture of art. We exist at this moment on the knife-edge between these two concepts . . . we are face to face, not with accepting the old forms of architecture, but with the need for a genuine invention of a new formal vocabulary—a new architecture."[253]

Into this not always polite debate stepped Kahn, one of only two American architects invited to Otterlo.[254] Fresh from sketching Carcassonne, as picturesque a medieval site as one might hope to find, he talked not about style, not about regional traditions, not about modern conceptions of space, not about architecture as social or aesthetic engineering, but about architecture as an investigation of human institutions. He sought a higher road, albeit one ultimately grounded on issues of function, than the one taken by the others at the congress by insisting that there is one fundamental concern that no architect can overlook—the search for the best form to accommodate a particular institution. Kahn included, to be sure, critiques of the classic modernist position—in his insistence that each space have an identifiable shape, in his stress on all the old forms of architecture that can still make sense in a modern context, in his relegating the question of choice of materials to a secondary role. In the Trenton Bathhouse Kahn's use of old forms for their abstract geometry had essentially denied the significance of their architectural typology. At Otterlo, however, his discussion of old architectural forms was in terms of building types, an issue obviously related to the question of how architecture could best serve human institutions.

In his talk Kahn enunciated, perhaps for the first time, his now famous distinction between Form and Design. For Kahn, Form had to do with the general question of institutional purpose, Design with the particulars of realizing a given building on a given site for a given client. Most of the issues over which the participants had quarreled Kahn relegated to the "easy" area of Design. By so doing, he surely hoped both to encourage some to think more profoundly about their profession and to put himself above such relatively petty disputes. Even though he was giving the "wrap-up" speech, he said very little about specific projects that had been presented at the meeting. For praise he singled out the Smithsons' grasp of urbanism and Aldo Van Eyck's penetrating analysis of the nature of a fundamental architectural detail, the doorway.[255] For censure he pointed (although not by name) to the designs of the team of Georges Candilis, Alexis Josic, and Shadrach Woods for new quarters at Bagnols-sur-Cèze. There he found the architects guilty of not thinking through the nature of the types of buildings they were designing. They had placed a group of Corbusian apartment buildings at the entrance to an existing town, whereas Kahn's analysis of the situation argued for some sort of symbolic gate.[256]

The medieval building types Kahn drew in Albi and Carcassonne actually had some relevance to modern problems of function that he himself had faced or might face. Recently he had been called on to find the Form of a religious structure—in mid-June he had presented his first preliminary sketches for the First Unitarian

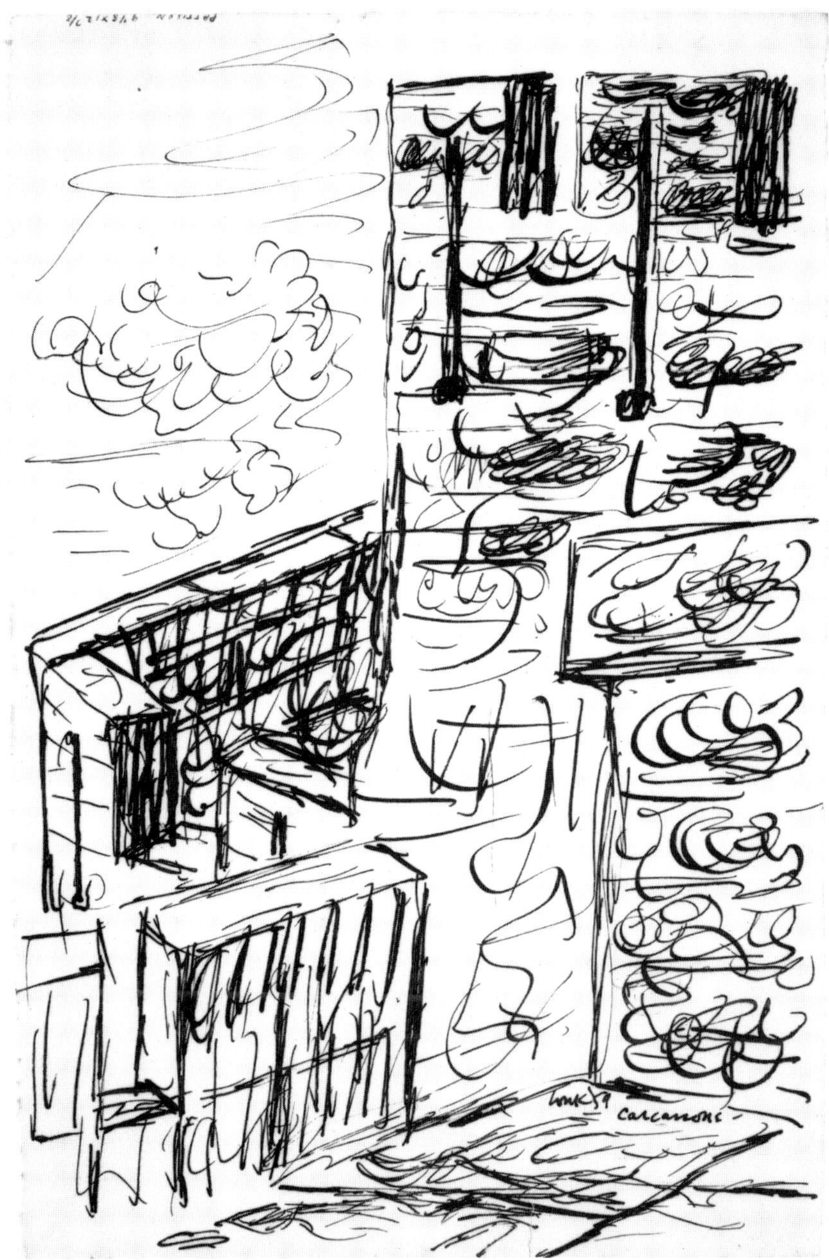

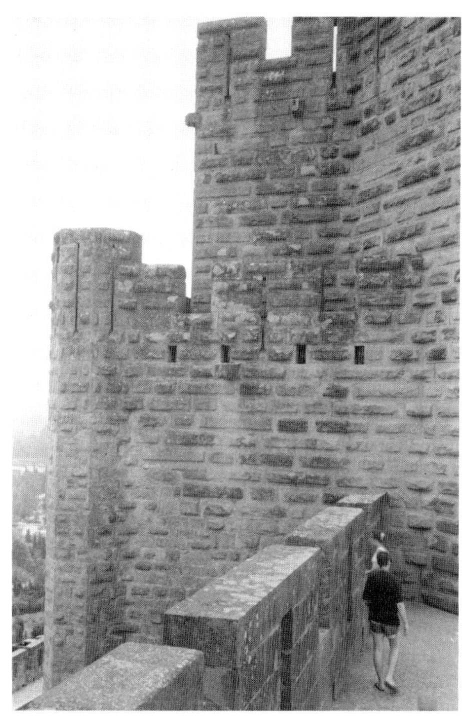

the more famous Gothic cathedrals of the Île de France, the cathedral of Albi (figs. 93, 95) is mural rather than skeletal, because it had to serve as a fortress as well as a church. In this sense, it is the French equivalent of the Italian Gothic structures Kahn had chosen to draw thirty years earlier. By choosing to draw Albi instead of, say, Chartres or Beauvais, Kahn once again threw his allegiance to a form of Gothic he had learned to love as a young man. The decision to draw Albi at this moment in his career is revealing. He did so just when he was about to abandon the skeleton and skin structural systems that he had devised in the 1950s[274]—for Yale, for the Philadelphia City Hall project, for the supports of the laboratory towers of the Richards Medical Research Center (still under construction)—in favor of the masonry walls, in which structure and skin are one, that would soon surround the Unitarian Church at Rochester as well as a host of subsequent buildings. Drawing Albi signaled that Kahn was ready to give up trying to achieve monumentality through clearly

Figure 89
DETAIL OF RUSTICATED MASONRY, TOUR SAINT NAZAIRE, CARCASSONNE, 1959, pen and ink on paper (cat. no. 67)

Figure 90
TOUR SAINT NAZAIRE, CARCASSONNE; photograph by Ralph Lieberman

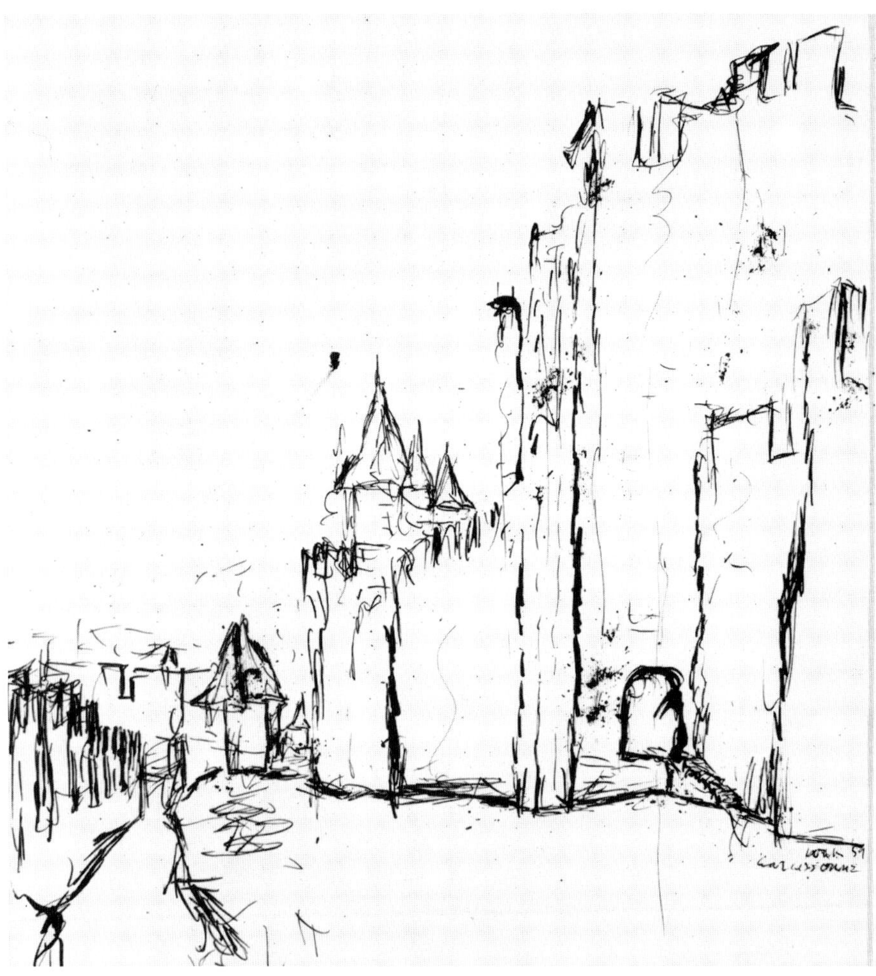

Figure 91
TOUR AND PORTE SAINT NAZAIRE FROM THE LICES, CARCASSONNE, 1959, pen and ink on notebook paper; photograph courtesy lender (cat. no. 66)

expressed structure, a procedure he suggested in his essay of 1944, and to return to that monumentality created by walls that he had perhaps first recognized at Piacenza.

In a remarkable series of five drawings from across the river Tarn (fig. 92), Kahn sketched the cathedral and the walled palace that occupies the slope between the church and the river.[275] The cathedral's great western tower rises from four enormous round buttresses that form the corners of its square plan (fig. 93). Stretching to the east, the nave wall is articulated by smaller, semicircular buttresses that receive the thrust of the nave vaults and support their weight, making possible the relatively thin curtains of brick into which tall windows are punched. The walls surrounding the Berbie essentially repeat this theme, with large towers that anchor their ends and smaller buttresses that punctuate the planes of the intervening curtain wall. Inside the palace walls rises the irregular bulk of the Berbie. This is the last group of sketches in which Kahn took up the theme of layering that had preoccupied him since 1928, but in these five drawings from Albi there is also a sense that the cathedral is a building within a building, an idea that surfaces again and again in his later work.[276] This notion of the building or buildings that exist in layers, crucial to Kahn's description of his concept of the Form "chapel" that he presented at Otterlo, is just as fundamental to the way Kahn designed his own buildings as it is to the way he drew buildings from earlier times. Once Kahn came to understand what lay at the core of a human institution—once he knew what the building wanted to be—his architecture could serve that institution by surrounding its core with layers of space that accommodated layers of functions.[277]

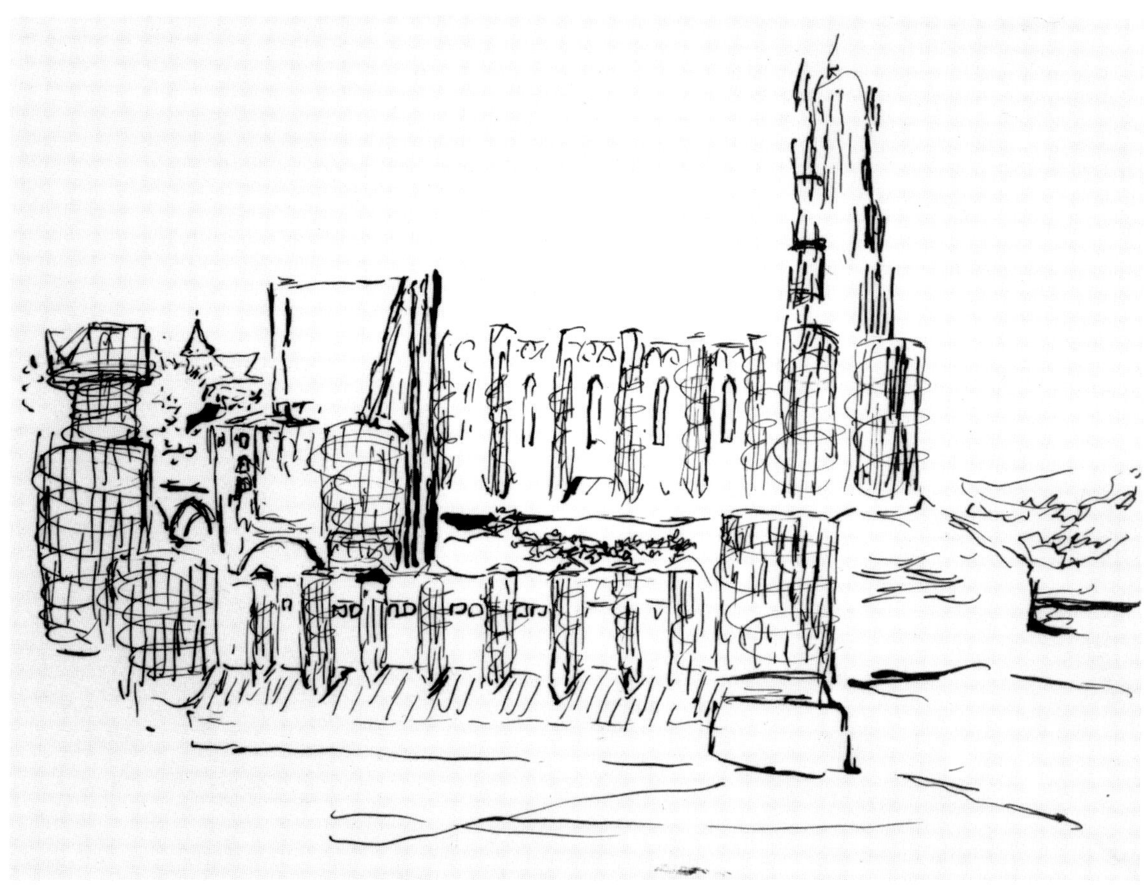

Kahn claimed a few years later that when he drew Albi he was trying to capture the excitement in the mind of its architect:

> *In the presence of Albi, I felt the belief in the choice of its architectural elements, and what exhilaration and patience were combined to begin it and work towards its completion. I drew Albi from the bottom up as though I were building it. I felt the exhilaration. The patience it took to build, one didn't need, for I drew it without bothering about corrections or correct proportions. I wanted only to capture the excitement in the mind of the architect.*[278]

FIGURE 92
CATHEDRAL OF SAINTE CÉCILE FROM NORTH, ALBI, 1959, pen and ink on notebook paper (cat. no. 69)

FIGURE 93
CATHEDRAL OF SAINTE CÉCILE FROM NORTH, ALBI; photograph by Ralph Lieberman

In a more abstract sense, the drawings are about cylinders—the big towers or buttresses—connected by flat planes punctured by holes—the walls and windows. In the group of drawings, Kahn experimented with different ways of getting these ideas across, varying the weight of his lines and, in one case, defining the towers and buttresses by rapidly sketched spiral lines (fig. 92). Graphically, these spirals are the most interesting aspect of the Albi drawings.[279] Kahn repeated them in a view of the Berbie, in two views of the cathedral apse (fig. 94), and in a view of the cathedral and Berbie copied from the guidebook photograph. Formally, the spirals allowed him to build the church from the ground up, their rising curving lines capturing the excitement in the mind of its architect as he

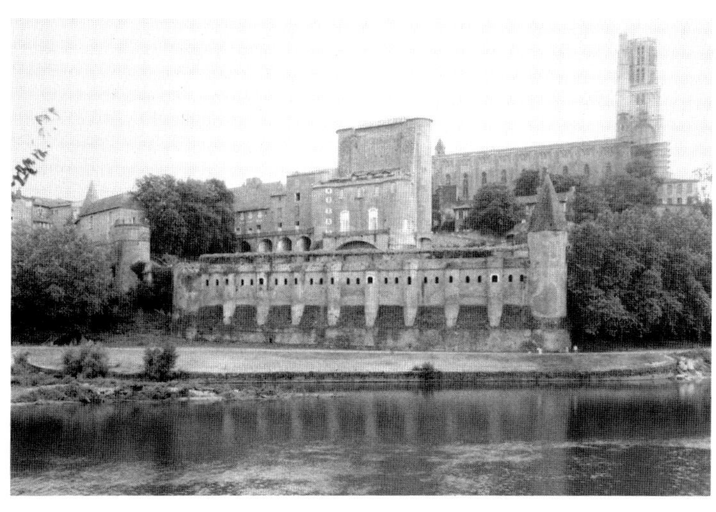

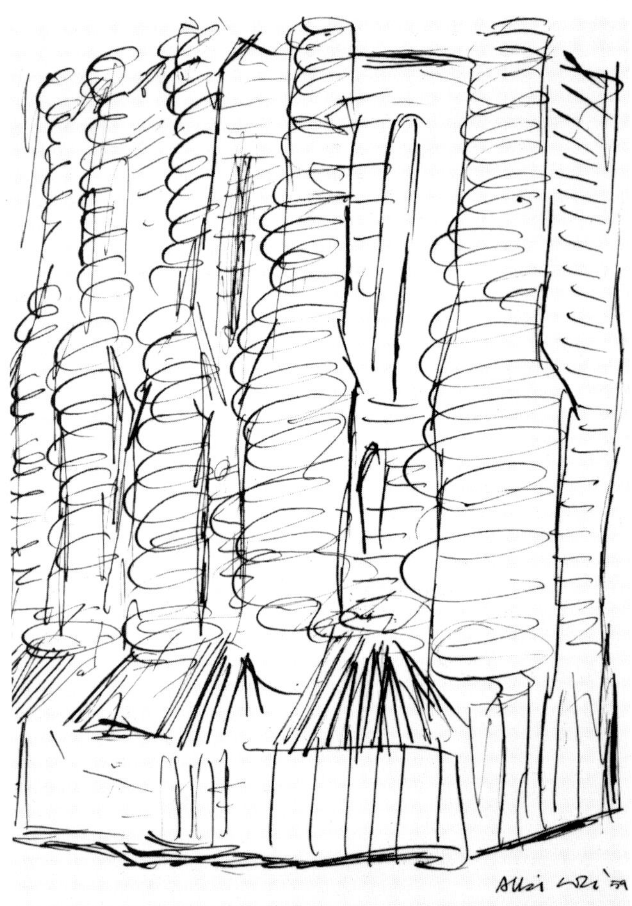

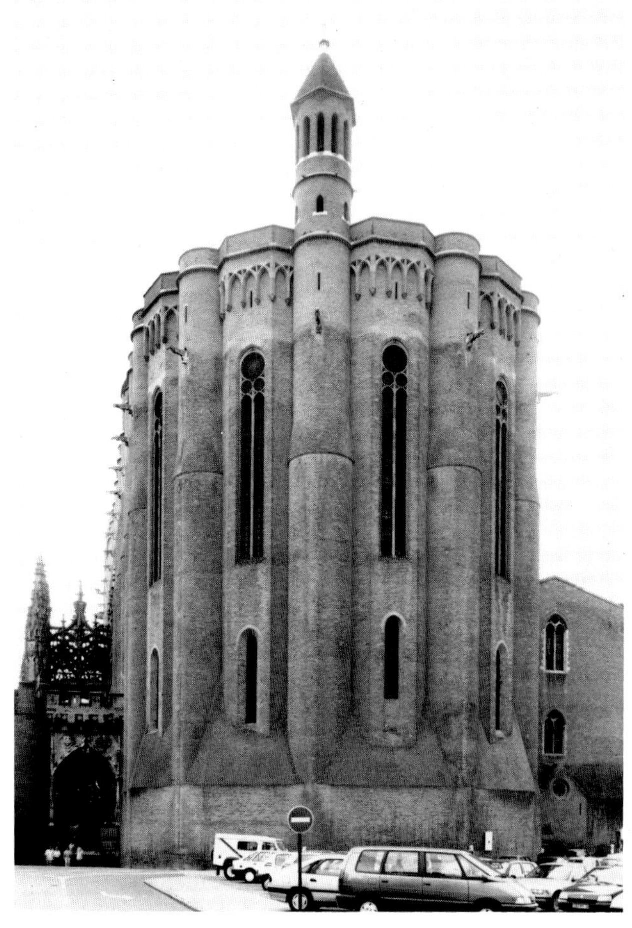

FIGURE 94
APSE, CATHEDRAL OF SAINTE CÉCILE, ALBI, 1959, pen and ink on paper; photograph courtesy lender (cat. no. 70)

FIGURE 95
APSE, CATHEDRAL OF SAINTE CÉCILE, ALBI; photograph by Ralph Lieberman

watched his building grow. Spirals are rare in Kahn's sketches. The closest Kahn comes in other drawings to the Albi spirals are those that indicate garages in his traffic study drawing of 1951–53 for the center of Philadelphia. There the spirals stand for the coiled-up ends of streets that receive traffic roaring off expressways and bring it to a halt before it enters and destroys the center of the city. The coiled streets embrace a void, the garage in which the cars will be parked. In Kahn's mind the concepts of city and cathedral were intertwined. "The Center is the cathedral of the city," he had written in 1957.[280] If the walls of Carcassonne were analogous to the walls he intended to erect against modern traffic in Philadelphia, then the buttressed walls of the fortified cathedral of Albi could just as well protect the cathedral that was the center of his city. At Albi as at Carcassonne, Kahn had found a typological connection between old and new structures.

Kahn's spirals transformed the solid brick buttresses of Albi into what he had come to call "hollow stones," forms that served not only as structure but also as a space for servant functions—for the accommodation of all the technology that a modern building required. "In Gothic times," Kahn wrote, "architects built in solid stones. Now we can build with hollow stones. The spaces defined by the members of a structure are as important as the members. These spaces range in scale from the voids of an insulation panel, voids for air, lighting and heat to circulate, to spaces big enough to walk through or live in."[281] In contrast, the towers under construction at that very moment for the Richards Medical Research complex performed the servant but not the structural function. By dissolving the Albi buttresses into spirals he adapted

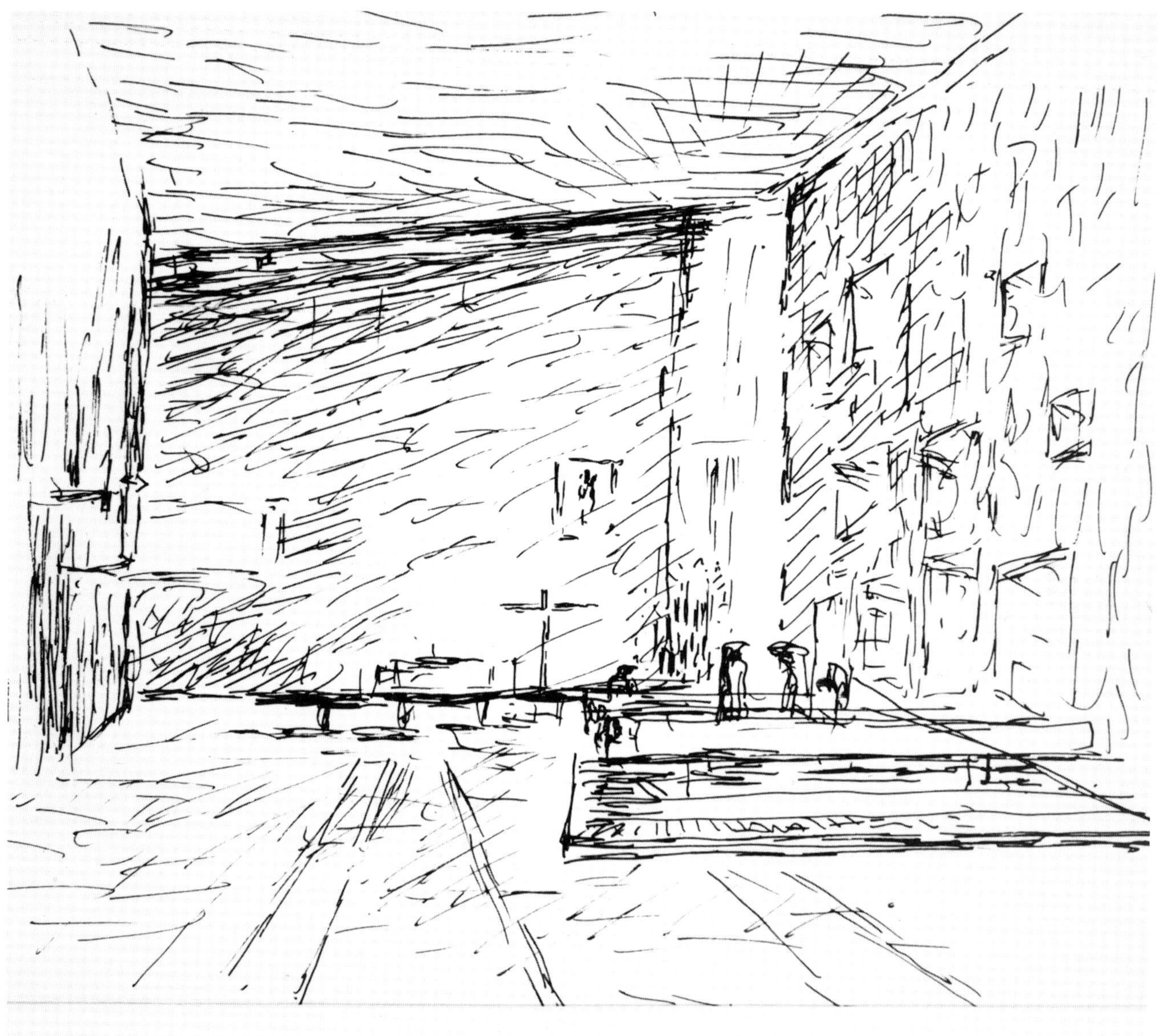

FIGURE 96
INTERIOR, NÔTRE DAME DU HAUT, RONCHAMP, 1959, pen and ink on notebook paper; photograph courtesy lender (cat. no. 71)

old architectural form to the new purposes required by modern buildings. In precisely this spirit, Kahn advocated adapting Renaissance forms to modern uses in his speech at Otterlo. To paraphrase what he said then, in his drawings of Albi with spirals "the buttresses are not the same in character because structure today demands different things."

From these Albi drawings it becomes clear why Kahn no longer thought of his travel sketches as independent works of two-dimensional art. They had become, instead, a way to consider some of the most pressing architectural problems that confronted him and the part of the international architectural community to which he belonged. He had crossed a boundary into a world in which recording an architectural thought in a drawing was more important than making a drawing for itself.[282] His travel sketches had undergone a metamorphosis from *vedute* featuring architectural subjects to direct recordings of his own architectural thoughts through on-site redesigning of older structures.

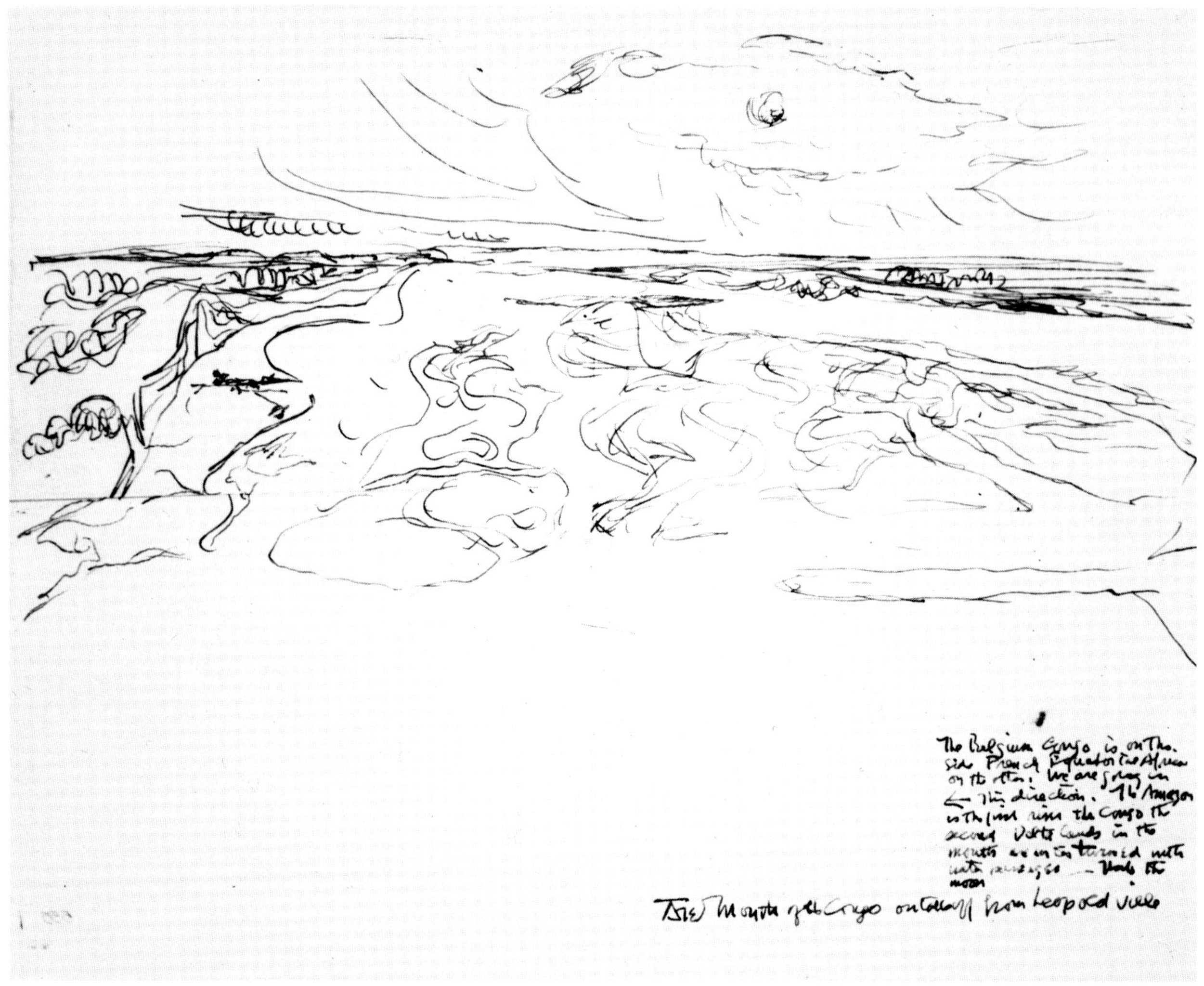

FIGURE 97
THE MOUTH OF THE CONGO ON TAKEOFF FROM LEOPOLDVILLE, January 1960, pen and ink on paper; photograph courtesy lender (cat. no. 72)

Kahn's drawings of Ronchamp, highly unusual in his oeuvre both because they are interiors and because they are of a contemporary building, have to be understood in the context of his visit to Albi and Carcassonne and in terms of the debate that took place at Otterlo. Of all the great masters of twentieth-century architecture, Le Corbusier had been the most important for Kahn. Oscar Stonorov, Kahn's early architectural partner, had been one of the editors of the first volume of the publication of Le Corbusier's works, the *oeuvre complète*,[283] and from Stonorov, as well as from Norman Rice, who had worked in the Corbusier office, Kahn must have learned about the Corbusian brand of modernism. In later life Kahn told Alison Smithson that in the 1930s he had lived in a beautiful city called Le Corbusier. By 1959 the traces of Corbusian influence had by and large disappeared from Kahn's work. On a previous trip to Europe he had gone to Marseilles to see Le Corbusier's Unité d'Habitation while it was under construction.[284] If he made drawings of the Unité they have not survived, but he did speak of it with admiration. Ronchamp, of course, had caused great consternation when it opened in 1955. To many it seemed that with Ronchamp Le Corbusier had abandoned all the great principles of modern architecture for which he had once stood. Some critics even called Ronchamp "baroque," about the most damning adjective one could hurl at a contemporary building in the mid-1950's. Kahn decided to see for himself. He may well have wondered if the slippery old master's seeming recantation of principles actually offered a way out of the dilemma in which Kahn and younger architects found themselves.

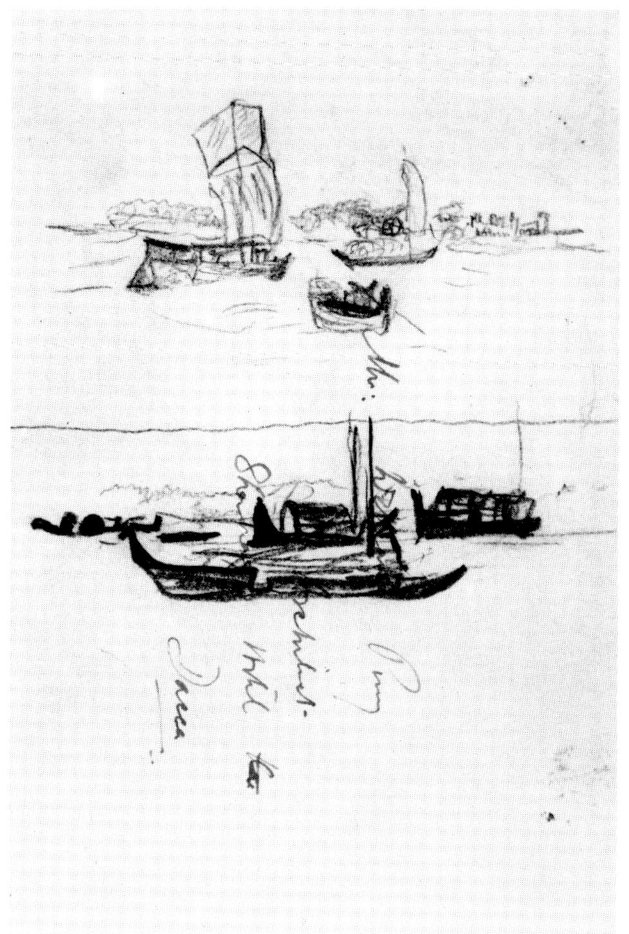

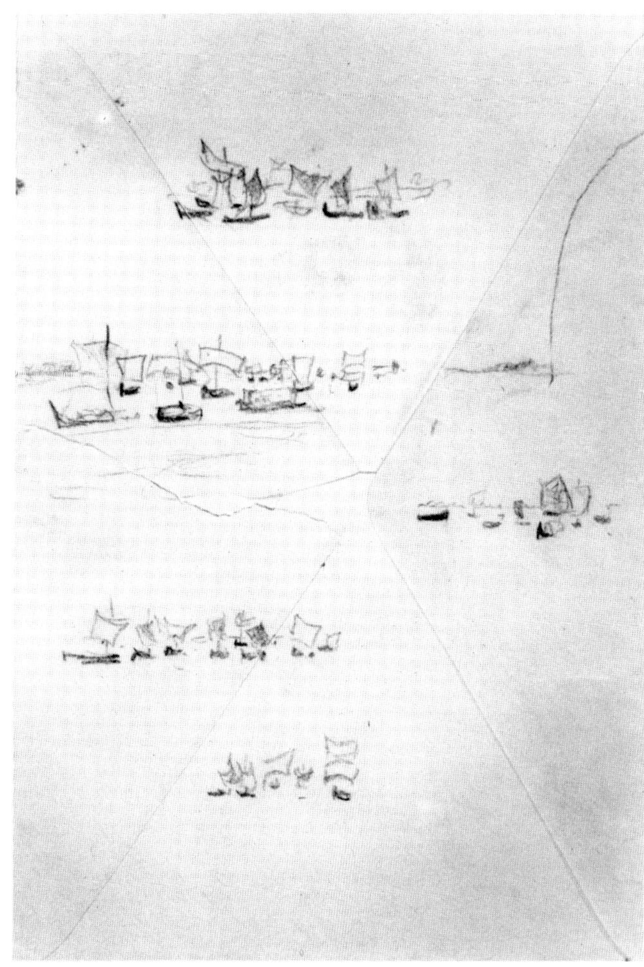

FIGURE 98
SKETCHES FROM THE RIVER, DACCA, March 1963, graphite on paper envelope; photograph courtesy lender (cat. no. 73)

Kahn's two drawings of the pilgrimage chapel are almost identical views of the interior looking east toward the altar and the window that holds an image of the Virgin Mary, to whom the church is dedicated (fig. 96). Although Kahn said, "I fell madly in love with" Ronchamp, Anne Tyng had criticized it for not being derived from an order,[285] and Kahn also noted that "in Marseilles order was strong . . . . At Ronchamp order is only dimly felt in order born of dream."[286] Perhaps in response to Tyng's evaluation of the church, Kahn chose not to sketch its "disorderly," dreamlike (in a surrealist sense) exterior, with its extravagantly eccentric towers, biomorphic forms, and swooping roof; the cylinder and planes of Albi and Carcassonne would serve him better. For Kahn, the lesson of Ronchamp lay in its light.

In his sketches Kahn concentrated on the passage of light through the relatively flat east wall into the interior. At the side of the drawing one also gets some sense of the magical entrance of light through the deep embrasures of the southern wall. "Light is the key," Le Corbusier said of his design at Ronchamp, and Kahn's two sketches show that he clearly understood. In these very years Kahn was wrestling with the problem of controlling light by controlling the shapes of openings in masonry walls. The east and south walls of Ronchamp present one of the most masterly displays of light control through the manipulation of masonry in the architecture of this century. Of the lessons he had learned about light at Ronchamp Kahn continued to make use. Although we have no drawing by Kahn of the interiors of the towers, which Le Corbusier used to trap light and bring it down onto the altars placed in their bases, it was the towers of Ronchamp that Kahn modified to make the four light hoods that illuminate the sanctuary of the Unitarian Church in Rochester. The Kimbell was Kahn's ultimate statement of the power of Ronchamp's light on his imagination. *Light Is the Theme* is the title of the book published to celebrate the opening of that museum, the year after Kahn's death.[287]

POSTLUDE

When Kahn visited France in 1959 he was on the verge of becoming a very famous and busy architect, whose commissions and renown would send him traveling around the world. Even though after 1959 he had far more opportunity to make travel sketches than he had had previously, he seems almost entirely to have abandoned the endeavor.[288] In the winter of 1960 he flew to Luanda, Angola, to visit the site of the United States Consulate he had been commissioned to design. When his plane took off from a refueling stop at Leopoldville, he made a very quick sketch of the view he had from its window of the delta of the Congo, a vast panorama of channels and islands that seems to suggest all the rhythms of nature itself (fig. 97). Here Kahn shows the same reverence for nature we found in the drawings of the landscape around Delphi of 1951 (fig. 74). In 1963, on a trip to Dacca, he sketched small boats in pencil on both sides of an envelope that contained an invitation to an official event related to the construction of his new capitol buildings (fig. 98). The shapes of the sails fascinated Kahn—curved shapes that recall the way he had drawn the leaves of trees all his life. These wonderfully sure, rapid sketches of boats—of forms made by humans that approximate forms found in nature—are the last travel drawings we know by Louis Kahn.

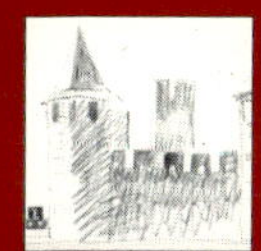

IN THE FOOTPRINTS OF THE MASTER:

The Photographic Campaign

Ralph Lieberman

The most interesting investigations almost never produce the results anticipated at the start; they are characterized instead by great surprises, and the more successful they are, the more informative are the unexpected discoveries. In preparing an exhibition of Louis Kahn's travel drawings, it seemed a fine idea that someone go to the sites he visited and photograph them from exactly where he stood when he drew them. The obvious assumption was that the material gathered on such a campaign would allow us to see what Kahn saw, and supplement our understanding of his drawings. That expectation was completely fulfilled, and we now understand better than ever before what Kahn actually did when drawing a building. But we learned as well as number of things that could not have been predicted.

There is no evidence that Kahn ever used a camera; he did not carry one while traveling abroad. Yet on his three journeys to Europe, particularly the first of them, he made more use of photographs than had been known.

Long before the research and photographic campaign for this exhibition began, it was clear that one of Kahn's pictures had been copied from a postcard; among the drawings he made at Carcassonne in 1959 is a bird's-eye view of the wall circuit of the town that could only have been made from an aerial photograph. Until now, that was the only unambiguous evidence of Kahn's use of ready-made images. But while this catalogue was being prepared, Kahn's daughter, Sue Ann, found in the attic of her mother's house in Philadelphia a box of old postcards that her father had collected, and three of them are irrefutably the sources for drawings he made on his first trip to Europe in 1928–29. It must not be imagined from this, however, that all of Kahn's drawings, or even the majority of them, were made from postcards, for the photographic evidence demonstrates clearly that most of the time he drew on the spot.

Kahn was not interested, as most traveling architects are, in visual notation or the collection of design and siting solutions. He was trained as a painter, and his chief interest was the conversion of what he saw into pictorial compositions. Over the thirty years that separate the earliest from the latest works in this exhibition, Kahn's drawing style and the nature of his reactions to the things he saw changed dramatically, but what most of his architectural drawings have in common is their pictorial quality. Kahn the architect is not consistently present in the drawings until 1959, the date of the last of the pieces in this exhibition, when he began actively to analyze in architectural terms the buildings he drew. Before then, he was mostly concerned about creating pictures.

The idea of the photographic campaign was to photograph Kahn's subjects to match the drawings, but once the field work was under way it quickly became clear that the undertaking was based on an incomplete awareness of how he worked.

The page is blank when an artist begins to draw, and only what he puts on it will be there; nothing ever appears that was unnoticed on the site, or that has to be admitted begrudgingly. Photography is precisely the opposite; the difficult part is to keep things out. What a painter does not want goes away, in effect, but a photographer often has to accept things—like electric wires and poles, neon signs, and tour

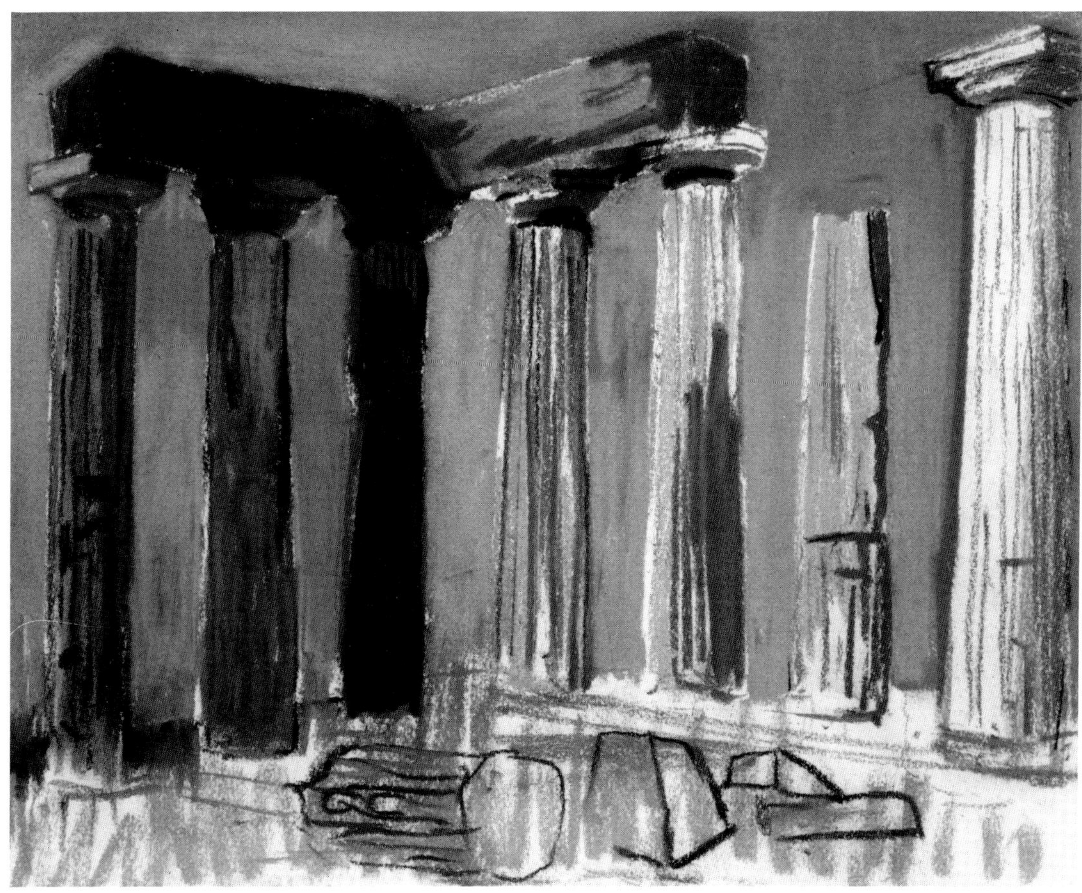

buses—that he would prefer not to see, because they cannot be separated from the ones he wants to record. Nor is the outright elimination of objects the only advantage the painter has over the photographer; the painter can with ease change the position of objects, their scale, and their relative importance. In one of Kahn's views of the remaining columns of the Temple of Apollo at Corinth (fig. 99), he must have been standing right in front of the fragment of a fallen column that, in the photograph of the site (fig. 100), dominates the foreground and vies with the surviving architecture in

FIGURE 99
TEMPLE OF APOLLO, CORINTH,
1951, pastel and charcoal on paper
(cat. no. 60)

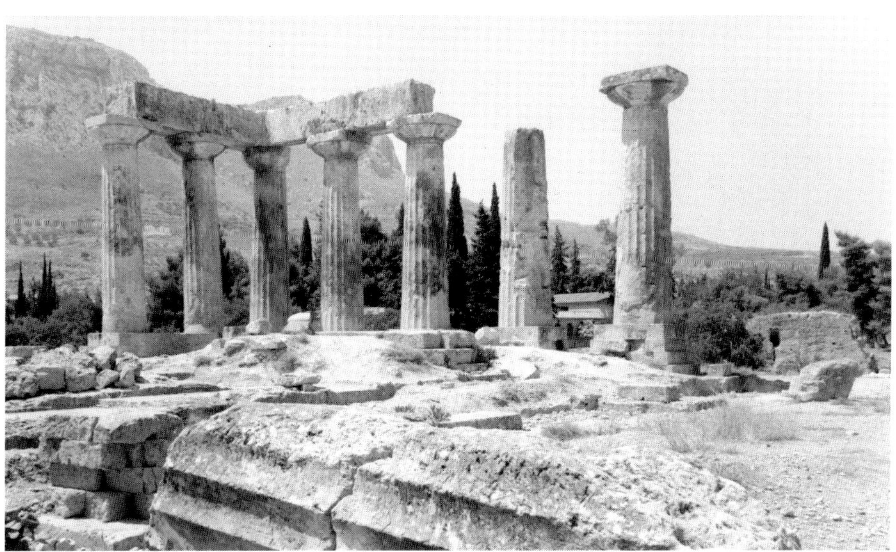

FIGURE 100
TEMPLE OF APOLLO, CORINTH;
photograph by Ralph Lieberman

the middle ground. He recorded the presence of the fragment but was free to give it a scale proportionate to his interest in it, so that it appears much smaller than the camera makes it and does not diminish the importance of the columns. Beyond all these liberties, there is the fact than an artist can walk about as he makes a drawing, viewing from different angles elements that will appear in a single, apparently unified scene.

Because Kahn did all of these things, sometimes singly, sometimes at once, his drawings do not have a consistent relationship to their subjects; anyone trying to duplicate the drawings with a camera soon learns that each has its own idiosyncrasies and none of them is to be taken literally. As a result, the guiding idea behind the photographic component for the exhibition changed in the course of the campaign. It became clear that the more informative and thought-provoking aspects of the photographs would be their differences from what Kahn drew, rather than their similarities to it. What began as a plan to document what Kahn saw became a means to reveal, even to emphasize, what he altered, so that we might understand better the nature of his reactions.

Even when Kahn was recording structures in a relatively straightforward manner, he often showed them from angles at which, in terms of the actual scene before him, they could not have been visible. A quick comparison of his drawing of the Ravello church (pl. 4) and the photograph of the building (fig. 101) reveals why it was both difficult and instructive to photograph the sites to match his drawings: architectural forms appear in the drawing in mutually exclusive ways and it was impossible to find a single spot from which the elements lined up exactly as Kahn presents them. When the camera was placed at a point where the relationship of the two domes was the same as it is in the drawing, the tower on the right was seen from too far to the left, and the gabled roof on the left from too far to the right. When we could see the window in the right side of the bell tower, the two domes overlapped differently from the way Kahn drew them. The photographic evidence makes it obvious that he changed position slightly when he wanted a more complete view of some aspect of his

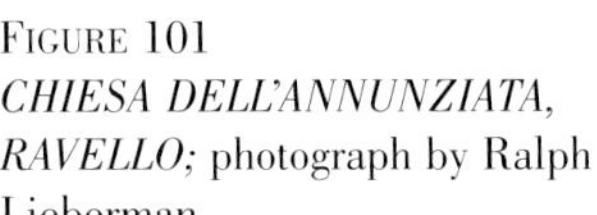

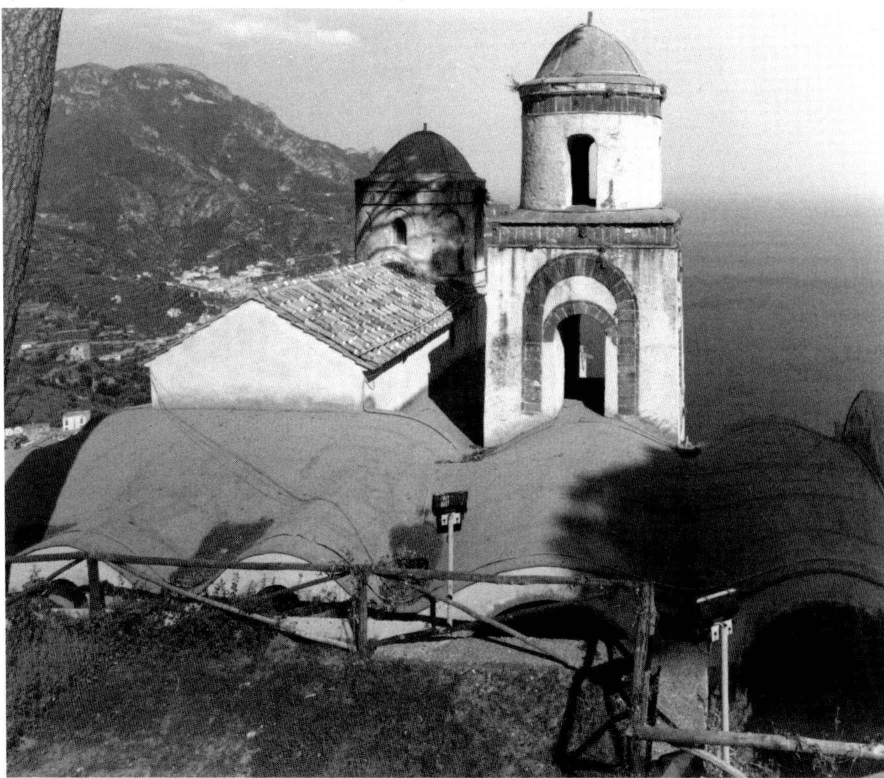

FIGURE 101
CHIESA DELL'ANNUNZIATA, RAVELLO; photograph by Ralph Lieberman

subject. It is worth recalling that Kahn was trained as a painter in the 1910s, which means that he would have been familiar with the paintings of Cézanne, and perhaps as well with cubism and its basic tenets. Whether or not he ever studied cubism carefully, he clearly did not hesitate to combine multiple viewpoints in a single drawing by the simple expedient of moving around in front of a building while recording it. A photographer cannot do that and has no practical alternative but to find a reasonable compromise, making an image that can be precise in only one respect, inaccurate in all others. The choice of which aspect of the drawing will be accurately reported in the photograph is the photographer's, and it depends on his judgment about what is important.

Kahn's training as a painter appears to explain another curious aspect of his drawings: his inconsistent use of shading. One tends to assume when looking at pictures that shaded areas correspond to shadows on the subject, but this is not always so with Kahn. In the drawing that shows the left side of the façade of San Rufino in Assisi (fig. 28), there is a narrow vertical strip of wall to the left of the façade proper that looks to be in shadow; the photograph (fig. 29) reveals that it is set at an angle between the façades of the church and the building next to and perpendicular to it. When Kahn made the drawing, this section of wall could not have been in shadow if the building to the left of it was as brightly lit as it appears to be; his treatment was a means to indicate differences in plane rather than real differences in illumination. The shadows above the door on the left side of the church façade suggest that sunlight is coming from two directions at once, until we understand that the portal is shaded not to indicate a light source but to reveal the forms that Kahn knew to be there.

At the same time that Kahn was making reinterpretive drawings in which he arranged the elements he saw according to his own vision, he would now and then find a photograph or postcard to use as a starting point for a drawing. There is in fact a tradition of painters working from postcards and photographs; Utrillo and Braque made paintings after postcards, and Gaugin based many of his images of Tahitian women on photographs of Egyptian art in Paris that he carried to the South Seas to serve as compositional suggestions. It seems that Kahn did not always look for an original composition either, and the drawing he made in 1928 of the piazza seen from inside the colonnade of the Temple of Minerva in Assisi (fig. 102) is based closely on one of the postcards that has recently turned up (fig. 103). There are many reasons why Kahn might have used it: perhaps he liked the shadows of the columns in the postcard better than they way they appeared when he was there; perhaps he was at the temple in the early morning, before the sun backlights the columns, and decided it was not worth waiting several hours for the sun to create that effect, so he just used the image he had found; or he may have spent his time looking at the site, drawing it later and using the postcard to recreate the scene. When working from a photograph Kahn could not change the perspective by walking around, but he nonetheless altered things. There is more light and air in the drawing than in the postcard, and he improved the composition by extending the skyline of the buildings on the piazza so that it is visible between the left and center columns.

Until the rediscovery of the postcard on which it was based, Kahn's drawing of one wing of the Palazzo Comunale, or "Il Gotico," the town hall of Piacenza (fig. 22), was particularly curious and difficult to understand. The drawing shows a characteristic Lombard brick structure with three arches on its ground story. The wing is framed by an arch, but there is now no analogous arch through which Kahn could have seen his subject. On the opposite side of the courtyard from the wing Kahn drew, there is a series of arches that had been filled in by the time he got to Piacenza in 1928,[1] which led to the conclusion that Kahn was simply imagining the way the main part of the building would have looked through one of the arches if they had still been open. Such an arch-framed arrangement could have appealed to him because it is part of a tradition of architectural views dating back to the Renaissance; for his own drawing of

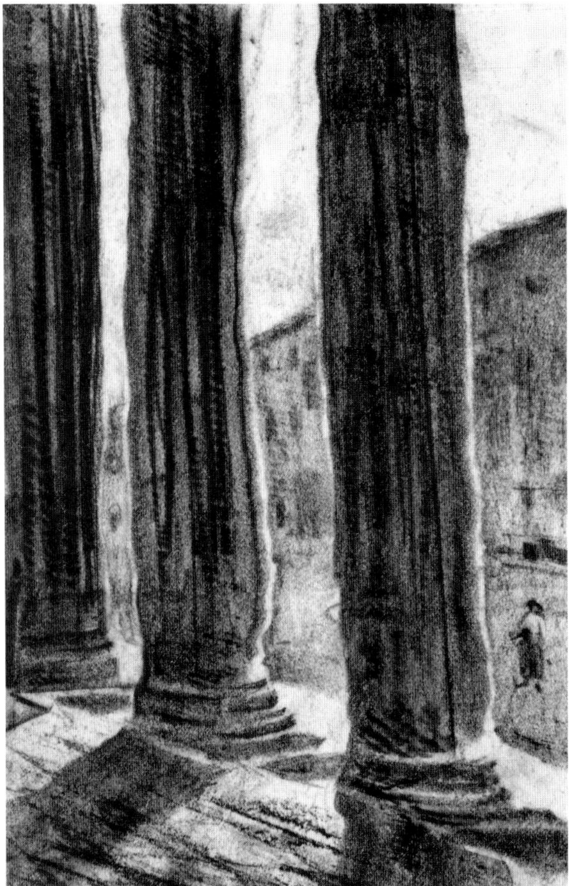

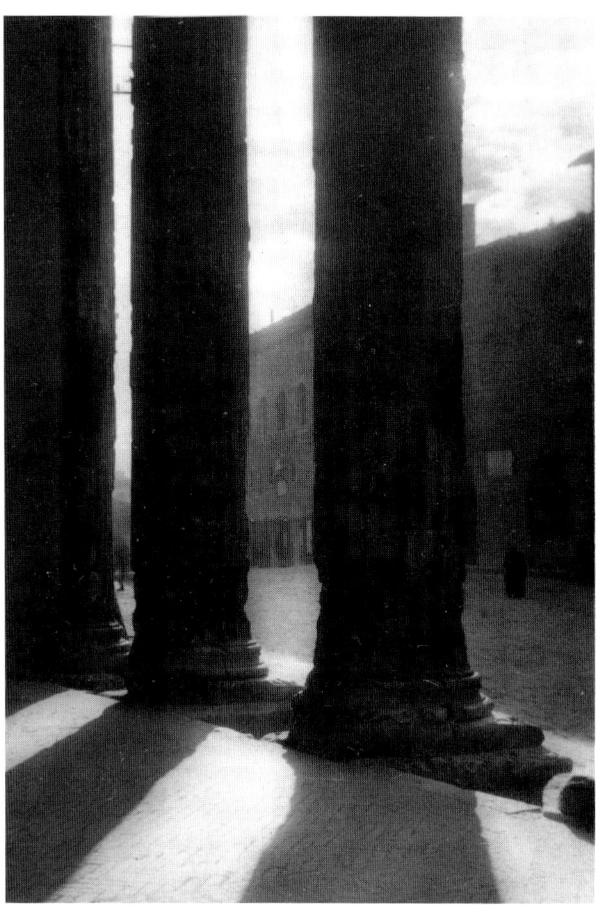

FIGURE 102
VIEW FROM PORTICO, TEMPLE OF MINERVA, ASSISI, 1928, graphite and crayon on paper (cat. no. 9)

FIGURE 103
VIEW FROM PORTICO, TEMPLE OF MINERVA, ASSISI, postcard; Collection of Esther I. Kahn

the atrium of Sant'Ambrogio in Milan (fig. 19) he had stood under the arcade opposite the façade so that the church and campanile would be framed by an arch. Now that we have the image on which the drawing is obviously based, however (fig. 23), we know that Kahn was simply making use of a postcard that showed a view through the arcade before it was closed.[2] But his presentation is still curious, for it is one of the few examples we have in which it is clear that Kahn seriously misdrew a subject. Two of the windows of the upper story have been moved to the right and are not centered over the points of the arches below them. This is especially odd in view of the fact that Kahn, who was often startlingly precise when dealing with wall openings, drew the asymmetrical shapes of the dark vaults under the ground-floor arches, and the distant opening that is seen through the left arch, quite exactly. He even included the group of figures that appears under the central arch. How, then, did he get the upper story of the palace so wrong? The best answer seems to be that he began with the black framing arch and then the ground-floor of the palace, and only discovered when he began to draw the details of the upper story that he had not left himself enough room to put them where they should have been, so he pushed them to the right. Kahn is unlikely to have made such a mistake if he had been drawing on the site itself rather than from a postcard.

Although in the course of Kahn's career the character of his drawings changed, they did not necessarily become more accurate. On the site at Carcassonne (fig. 105) it was clear that in his 1959 drawing of a corner of the Château Comtal (fig. 104), Kahn played fast and loose with the basic forms. The square tower in the middle is both higher and wider in the drawing than it ought to be, the corner of the building

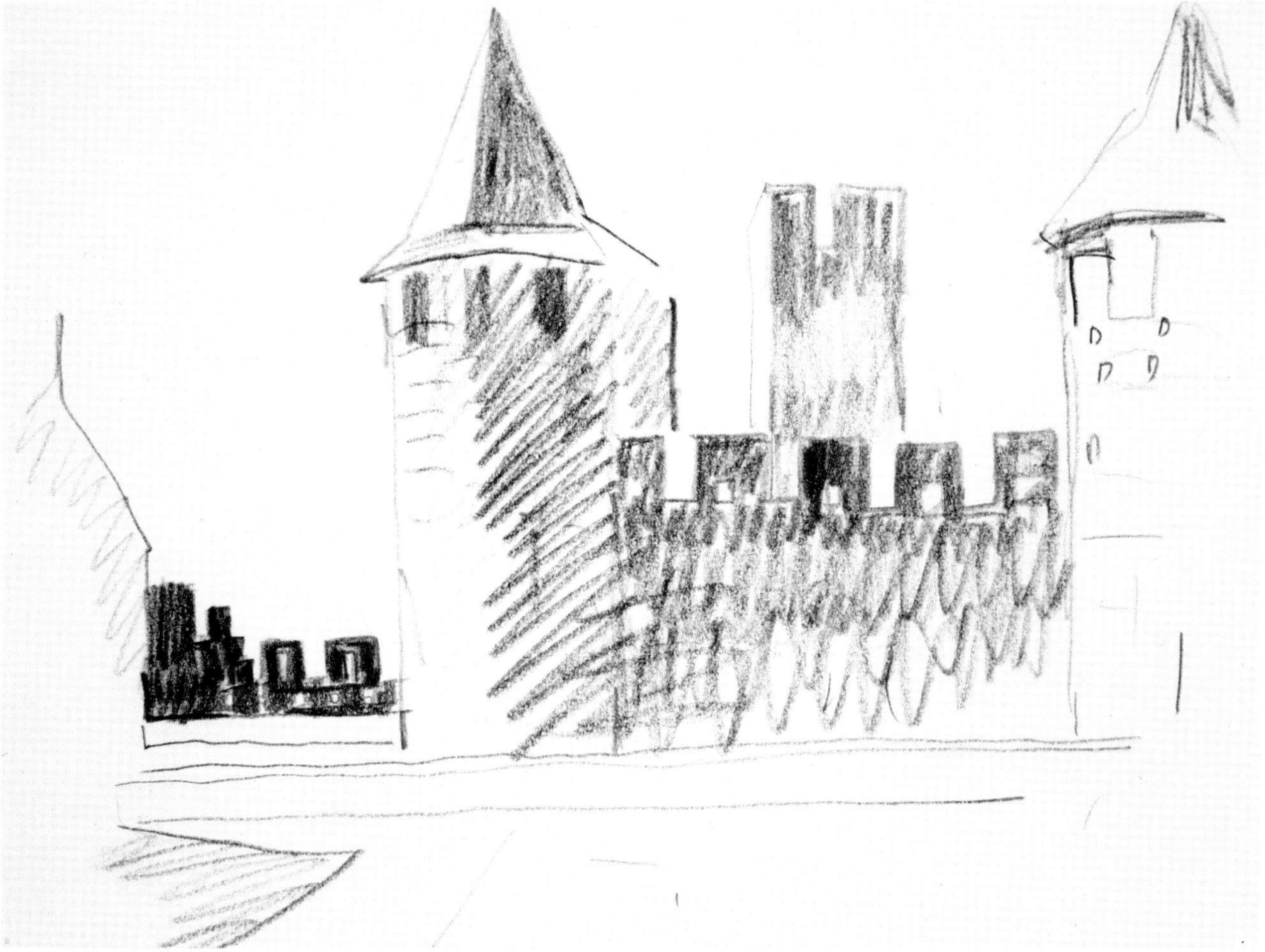

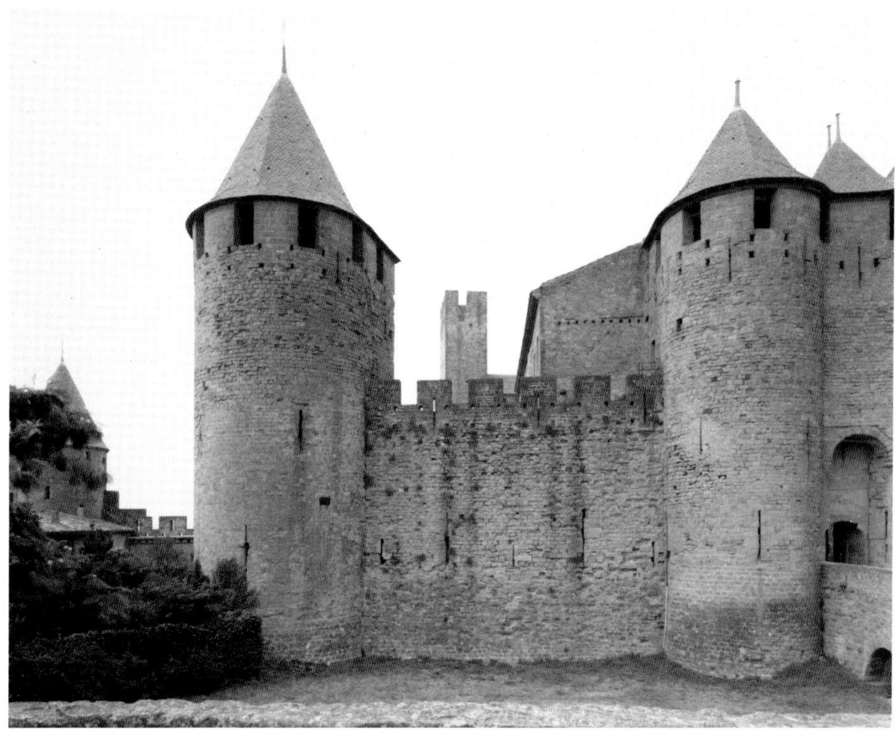

FIGURE 104
TOUR DE SAINT PAUL, TOUR PINTE, AND SOUTHERN TOUR DE LA PORTE FROM BARBICAN, CHÂTEAU COMTAL, CARCASSONNE, 1959, pencil on sketchbook paper; photograph courtesy lender (cat. no. 64b)

FIGURE 105
TOUR DE SAINT PAUL, TOUR PINTE, AND SOUTHERN TOUR DE LA PORTE FROM BARBICAN, CHÂTEAU COMTAL, CARCASSONNE; photograph by Ralph Lieberman

that extends toward the central tower from the turret on the right is gone without a trace, there are too few crenelations between the turrets, and the tower on the left side of the drawing is much too high. It was obvious that there was not going to be any photograph that corresponded to the drawing because in this case Kahn's thoughts were mostly about how he could improve the design.

The Louis Kahn of 1959 did not suddenly appear from nowhere. Here and there in his earlier drawings are hints of the approach that characterizes this Carcassonne drawing; in a 1928 pastel of the Piazza della Signoria in Florence, for example, Kahn altered the Bargello tower behind the foreground sculpture, making it shorter and thicker.[3] But these changes are for pictorial purposes, and they reinforce the conclusion that on his 1928–29 trip Kahn approached his subjects primarily as a painter—recording what he saw from multiple points of view and using shadow to suggest things other than light.

By 1959, however, Kahn was a completely different artist; he was very sure of himself and had long experience as a teacher of architecture. In the Carcassonne drawing he transformed a cluttered view into a handsome and forceful arrangement by boldly simplifying things and shifting the scale of the original elements so that they more effectively contribute to the whole ensemble. Kahn did not accept the built forms, nor did he consider them in their own terms and context in order to learn from them; rather than draw Carcassonne he redesigned it. In this sketch, a masterpiece of graphic simplicity and power, with tonal gradations that cover the full range from light gray to near black, the corner of the château is better than it is in the photograph, or in person, for Kahn saw in an unimpressive and weak jumble of misproportioned components the potential strength they fail to convey, and brought it out. In the thirty years since he had made his first drawings in Europe, he had become one of the great architects of the twentieth century.

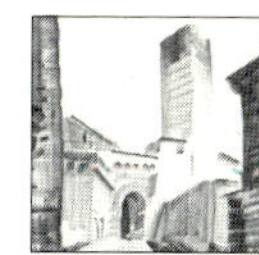

EXHIBITION CHECKLIST

The bracketed JH number that follows most titles in this listing represents the number given the work in Jan Hochstim, *The Paintings and Sketches of Louis I. Kahn* (New York: Rizzoli, 1991).

LOUIS ISADORE KAHN (American, 1901–1974)

1. *Caesar's Tower, Warwick Castle,* 1928 [JH39]
pencil on paper
53.3 x 38.4 cm
Collection of Sue Ann Kahn
Figure 18

2. *Santa Maria della Salute, Venice*, 1928
watercolor on paper
28.8 x 37.7 cm
Collection of Sue Ann Kahn
Plate 1

3. *Piazzetta and San Giorgio Maggiore* (top) and *Basilica di San Marco from Piazzetta, Venice*, 1928 [JH101]
watercolor and graphite on tissue paper
26 x 20.9 cm
Collection of Sue Ann Kahn
Figure 21

4. *Atrium of Sant'Ambrogio, Milan*, 1928 [JH67]
pencil on paper
53.3 x 38.4 cm
Collection of Sue Ann Kahn
Figure 19

5. *Portico, San Zeno, Verona*, 1928 [JH75]
graphite on bond paper
27.2 x 20 cm
Collection of Sue Ann Kahn
Figure 36

6. *Cortile of "Il Gotico" (Palazzo Comunale), Piacenza*, 1928 [JH83]
pencil, graphite, and ink on paper
31 x 22.3 cm
Collection of Sue Ann Kahn
Figure 22

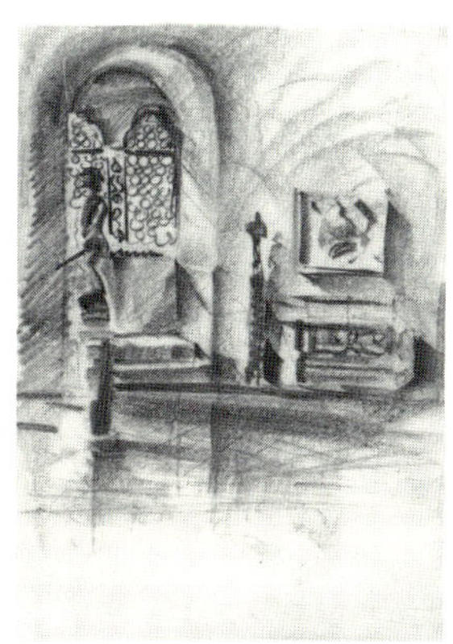

7. *Interior of Palazzo Bargello, Florence,* 1928 [JH81]
graphite on paper
31 x 22.5 cm
Collection of Sue Ann Kahn

8. *Ponte Vecchio, Florence*, 1928 [JH33]
graphite on paper
40 x 58.7 cm
Collection of Sue Ann Kahn
Figure 24

9. *View from Portico, Temple of Minerva, Assisi,* 1928 [JH87]
graphite and crayon on paper
20 x 13.4 cm
Collection of Sue Ann Kahn
Figure 102

10. *Cathedral of San Rufino, Assisi,* 1928 [JH69]
graphite on ivory paper
27.9 x 22.2 cm
Courtesy of the Museum of American Art of the Pennsylvania Academy of the Fine Arts, Philadelphia; Gift of Mrs. Louis I. Kahn
Figure 28

11. *Rocca Maggiore from Piazza San Rufino, Assisi,* 1928 [JH72]
graphite on paper
28 x 22 cm
Collection of Sue Ann Kahn
Figure 33

12. *Street and tower, San Gimignano*, 1928 [JH94]
graphite on paper
17 x 16 cm
Collection of Sue Ann Kahn
Figure 31 and Cover

13. *Towers, San Gimignano*, 1928 [JH95]
watercolor and red pencil on paper
30.8 x 23.5 cm
Museum purchase with funds provided by an anonymous donor and with the J.W. Field Fund, John B. Turner '24 Memorial Fund, Joseph O. Eaton Fund, Karl E. Weston Memorial Fund, Bentley W. Warren Fund; 94.14
Plate 2

14. *Ponte delle Torri, Spoleto*, 1928 [JH42]
watercolor on paper
30.8 x 23.2 cm
Collection of Sue Ann Kahn
Plate 3

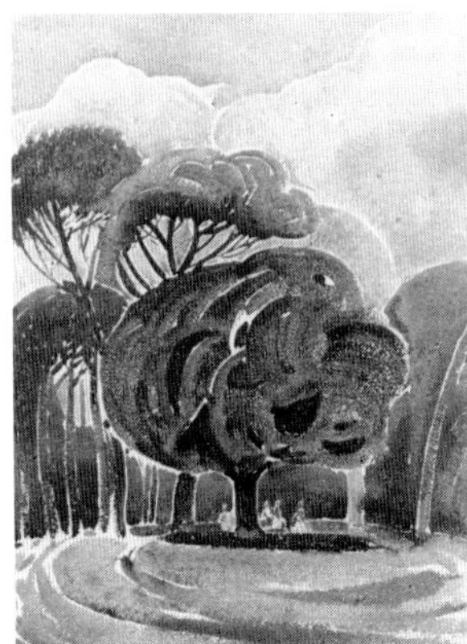

15. *Borghese Gardens, Rome*, 1928–29 [JH27]
watercolor on paper
36.2 x 27.9 cm
Collection of Sue Ann Kahn

16. *Tower and cortile of Villa Rufolo, Ravello*, 1929 [JH43]
watercolor on paper
36.8 x 27.3 cm
Collection of Sue Ann Kahn
Figure 47

17. *"Atrio del Palazzo Rufolo," Ravello*, 1929 [JH85]
graphite on paper
41.9 x 29.5 cm
Collection of Sue Ann Kahn
Figure 44

18. *Cortile of Villa Rufolo, Ravello*, 1929 [JH84]
graphite on paper
30.5 x 22.6 cm
Collection of Sue Ann Kahn
Figure 45

19. *"Chiesa in Rovina," Chiesa dell'Annunziata, Ravello*, 1929 [JH73]
graphite on brown paper
22.5 x 30.5 cm
Collection of Sue Ann Kahn
Plate 4

20. *Santa Maria delle Grazie, Ravello*, 1929 [JH32]
watercolor on paper
28 x 38.5 cm
Collection of Sue Ann Kahn
Figure 48

21. *Atrani from Torre Saracena, Amalfi*, 1929 [JH49]
watercolor
28 x 38.7 cm
Collection of Sue Ann Kahn
Figure 54

22. *Stepped street and tower of Chiesa Nuova, Positano*, 1929 [JH57]
graphite on paper
27.6 x 19 cm
Collection of Sue Ann Kahn
Figure 49

23. *Stepped street and Chiesa Nuova, Positano*, 1929 [JH56]
graphite on bond paper
28.2 x 21.9 cm
Collection of Sue Ann Kahn
Figure 50

24. *Fisherman's house, Conca dei Marini*, 1929 [JH55]
graphite on paper
28.3 x 20.6 cm
Collection of Sue Ann Kahn
Figure 41

25. *Fishermen's houses, Conca dei Marini*, 1929 [JH60]
watercolor on paper
16.8 x 25.4 cm
Private collection
Figure 42

26. *Fishermen's houses, Conca dei Marini*, 1929–30 [JH61]
oil on canvas
60.9 x 76.2 cm
Collection of Esther I. Kahn
Figure 43

27. *I Faraglioni, Capri*, 1929 [JH46]
graphite on paper
28.2 x 22 cm
Collection of Sue Ann Kahn
Figure 38

28. *Paradox Lake, Adirondacks*, 1930 [JH17]
graphite on paper
26.7 x 21.9 cm
Collection of Sue Ann Kahn
Figure 6

29. *Sketches for Coming storm*, 1931 [JH124]
charcoal pencil on bond paper
27.5 x 21.2 cm
Collection of Sue Ann Kahn
Figure 9

30. *Coming storm, Woodstock, New York*, 1931 [JH126]
watercolor on paper
34 x 39.3 cm
Collection of Sue Ann Kahn
Plate 6

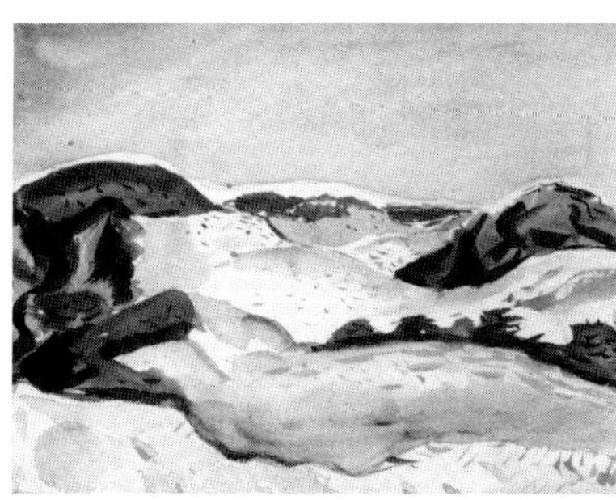

31. *Sand dunes, Provincetown, Massachusetts*, 1934 [JH134]
watercolor on paper
21.5 x 28.2 cm
Collection of Sue Ann Kahn

32. *Evening, Provincetown*, 1934 [JH181]
watercolor on paper
21.6 x 28.6 cm
Collection of Olivia Israeli Abelson and Milton Abelson
Figure 13

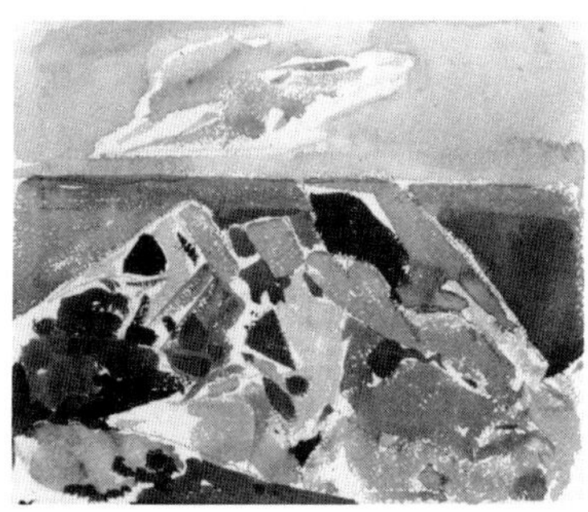

33. *Rock formations, Massachusetts*, 1934–35 [JH142]
watercolor on paper
18 x 22 cm
Collection of Sue Ann Kahn

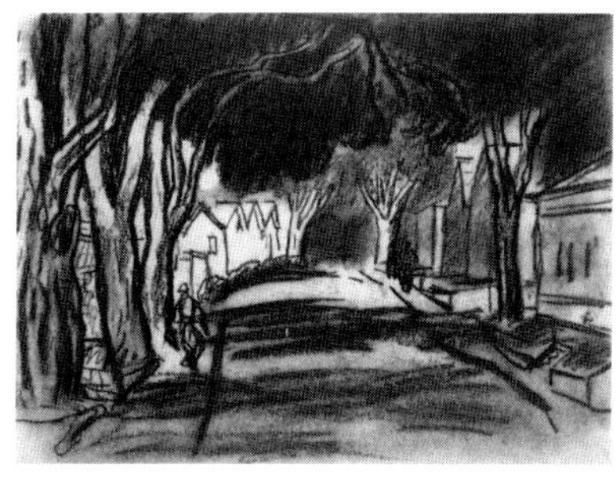

34. *Street with elms, Gloucester, Massachusetts*, 1934–35 [JH116}
charcoal on paper
22.2 x 30 cm
Collection of Sue Ann Kahn

35. *White church*, c. 1935 [JH253]
oil on canvas
60.9 x 76.2 cm
Collection of Esther I. Kahn
Figure 16

36. *White church*, c. 1935 [JH250]
charcoal on paper
15 x 17.5 cm
Collection of Sue Ann Kahn
Figure 15

37. *Factory, Philadelphia*, c. 1930–35 [JH261]
graphite on paper
22.3 x 17.2 cm
Collection of Theodore T. Newbold and Helen Cunningham
Figure 12

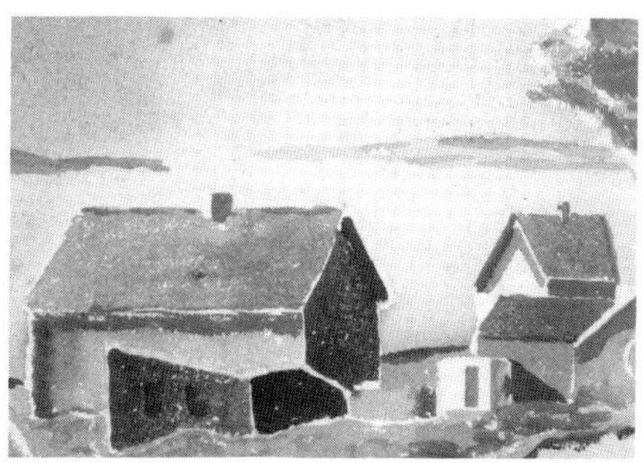

38. *Houses on the bay, Isle Madame, Nova Scotia*, 1936 [JH200]
watercolor on paper
14.5 x 21 cm
Collection of Sue Ann Kahn

39. *Coastal village, Isle Madame, Nova Scotia*, 1936 [JH203]
tempera on paper
18.1 x 27.9 cm
Collection of Esther I. Kahn
Plate 5

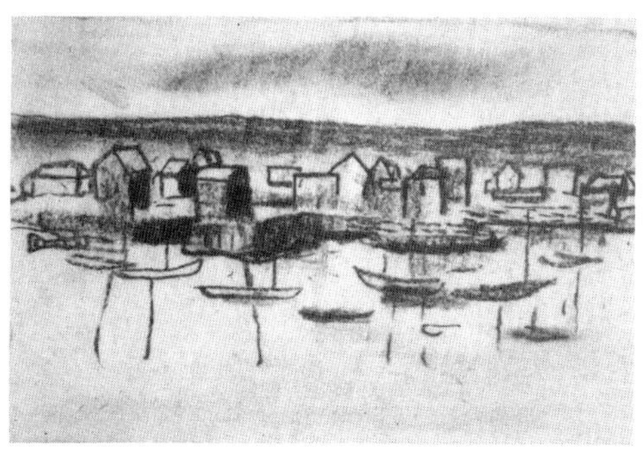

40. *Moored boats, Cape Breton Island, Nova Scotia*, 1936 [JH166]
charcoal on brown paper
11 x 16.5 cm
Collection of Sue Ann Kahn

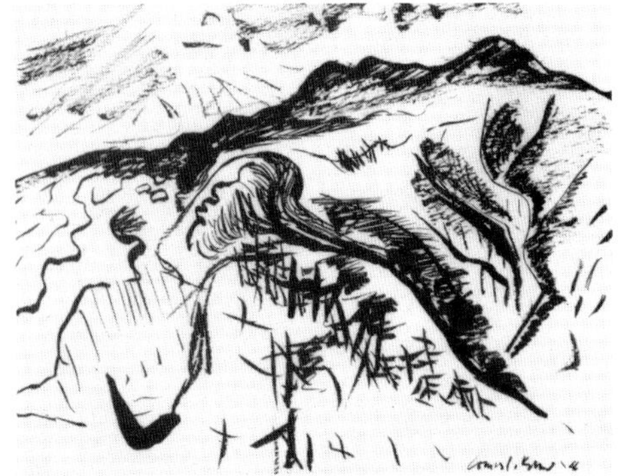

41. *Woodstock, New York*, 1946 [JH147]
brushed ink on onion skin paper
21.6 x 27.9 cm
signed and dated 1946
Collection of Sue Ann Kahn

42. *Rock formations, Garden of the Gods, Colorado*, 1948 [JH239]
charcoal pencil on paper
22.5 x 30.4 cm
Collection of Sue Ann Kahn
Figure 17

43. *Large Baths, Hadrian's Villa, Tivoli*, 1950–51 [JH332]
pastel on paper
19 x 22 cm
Collection of Sue Ann Kahn
Figure 58

44. *Roman wall*, 1950–51 [JH335}
charcoal on paper
28.9 x 37.8 cm
Collection of M. Louis Goodman
Figure 60

45. *Piazza San Pietro from atrium of Saint Peter's, Rome*, 1950 [JH336]
pastel and charcoal on paper
19 x 22 cm
Louis I. Kahn Collection, University of Pennsylvania and Pennsylvania Historical and Museum Commission. Special Purchase Fund, 1995. LIK 945.21
Figure 61

46. *Piazza del Campo, Siena*, 1950–51 [JH338]
pastel on paper
29 x 37.5 cm
Collection of Sue Ann Kahn
Plate 7

47. *Baptistery of San Giovanni, Siena*, 1950–51 [JH340]
pastel on paper
29 x 38.5 cm
Collection of Sue Ann Kahn
Figure 64

48. *Basilica di San Marco, Venice*, 1951 [JH353]
pastel on paper
31.7 x 39.4 cm
Collection of Sue Ann Kahn
Plate 10

49. *Gothic tracery, Venice*, 1951 [JH354]
pastel on paper
30.5 x 25.5 cm
Collection of Sue Ann Kahn
Figure 83

50. *Pyramids, Giza*, 1951 [JH416]
pastel on paper
17.5 x 25.4 cm
Collection of Mr. and Mrs. James Gubelmann
Figure 81

51. *Mortuary Temple of Hatshepsut, Deir el-Bahri*, 1951 [JH404]
pastel on paper
29 x 37.5 cm
Collection of Sue Ann Kahn
Figure 82

52. *North side, second court of Mortuary Temple of Rameses III, Medinet-Habu*, 1951 [JH401]
pastel and charcoal on paper
18.5 x 31 cm
Collection of Sue Ann Kahn
Plate 8

53. *Composition with statue, Column of Taharka, and pylons, first court, Temple of Amon, Karnak*, 1951 [JH403]
charcoal on paper
27.9 x 24.1 cm
Private collection
Figure 66

54. *Capitals, Hypostyle Hall, Temple of Amon, Karnak*, 1951 [JH407]
pastel on paper
28.6 x 36.2 cm
Collection of Sue Ann Kahn
Figure 80

55. *Columns and walls of Propylaea from east, Acropolis, Athens*, 1951 [JH373]
pastel on paper
29.8 x 23.5 cm
Collection of Sue Ann Kahn
Figure 70

56. *Nike Temple and south wing of Propylaea, Acropolis, Athens*, 1951
charcoal on paper
22.2 x 35.2 cm
Herbert F. Johnson Museum of Art, Cornell University. Gift of Dr. Aaron and Rosa Esman, 94.022
Figure 71

57. *Acropolis from Areopagus, Athens*, 1951 [JH374]
pastel and charcoal on paper
28.3 x 37.5 cm
Collection of Sue Ann Kahn
Figure 69

58. *Acropolis from Theater of Dionysos, Athens*, 1951 [JH378]
charcoal and black crayon on paper
29 x 36.3 cm
Collection of Sue Ann Kahn
Figure 67

59. *Temple of Apollo, Corinth, at sunrise*, 1951 [JH382]
pastel and charcoal on paper
27.5 x 26 cm
Collection of Sue Ann Kahn
Plate 9

60. *Temple of Apollo, Corinth*, 1951 [JH383]
pastel and charcoal on paper
28.5 x 36.8 cm
Collection of Sue Ann Kahn
Figure 99

61. *Temple of Apollo, Corinth, at midafternoon*, 1951 [JH384]
pastel and charcoal on paper
28.6 x 37.5 cm
Collection of Sue Ann Kahn
Figure 73

62. *Plunge pool of bath building, lower sanctuary, Delphi*, 1951 [JH363]
charcoal on paper
29 x 37.5 cm
Collection of Sue Ann Kahn
Figure 74

63. *Portico of Athenians and Temple of Apollo, Delphi*, 1951 [JH367]
charcoal on paper
28.9 x 36.2 cm
Louis I. Kahn Collection, Architectural Archives of the University of Pennsylvania, Gift of Richard Saul Wurman, 1985, LIK 945.22
Figure 76

64a. *Gate and bridge from barbican, Château Comtal, Carcassonne*, 1959 [JH438]
pencil on sketchbook paper
17 x 22 cm
Louis I. Kahn Collection, Architectural Archives of the University of Pennsylvania. Gift of Richard Saul Wurman, 1984, LIK 945.10
Figure 87

64b. *Tour de Saint Paul, Tour Pinte, and southern Tour de la Porte from barbican, Château Comtal, Carcassonne*, 1959 [JH452]
pencil on sketchbook paper
17 x 22 cm
Louis I. Kahn Collection, Architectural Archives of the University of Pennsylvania. Gift of Richard Saul Wurman, 1984, LIK 945.11
Figure 104

65. *Château Comtal and Porte d'Aude, Carcassonne*, 1959 [JH449]
pen and ink on paper
26.2 x 21.8 cm
Collection of William S. Huff
Figure 85

66. *Tour and Porte Saint Nazaire from the Lices, Carcassonne*, 1959 [JH446]
pen and ink on notebook paper
24.1 x 20.3 cm
Louis I. Kahn Collection, Architectural Archives of the University of Pennsylvania. Gift of Richard Saul Wurman, 1984, LIK 945.3.3
Figure 91

67. *Detail of rusticated masonry, Tour Saint Nazaire, Carcassonne*, 1959 [JH460]
pen and ink on paper
24.8 x 16.8 cm
Private collection
Figure 89

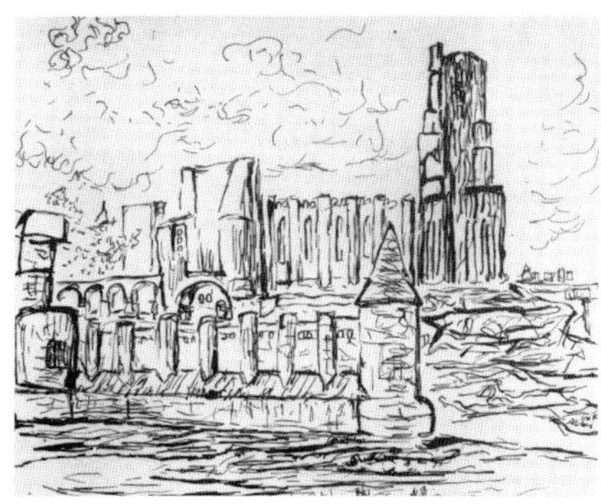

68. *Cathedral of Sainte Cécile from north, Albi*, 1959 [JH467]
pen and ink on notebook paper
21.9 x 26 cm
Collection: Der Scutt, New York

69. *Cathedral of Sainte Cécile from north, Albi*, 1959 [JH470]
pen and ink on notebook paper
21.1 x 26.2 cm
Museum purchase from the Joseph O. Eaton Fund, 82.17
Figure 92

70. *Apse, Cathedral of Sainte Cécile, Albi*, 1959 [JH476]
pen and ink on paper
28 x 24 cm
Collection of Robert Venturi
Figure 94

71. *Interior, Nôtre Dame du Haut, Ronchamp*, 1959 [JH479]
pen and ink on notebook paper
21.3 x 26 cm
Louis I. Kahn Collection, Architectural Archives of the University of Pennsylvania. Gift of Richard Saul Wurman, 1984, LIK 945.21
Figure 96

72. *The mouth of the Congo on takeoff from Leopoldville*, January 1960
pen and ink on paper
21.8 x 28 cm
Louis I. Kahn Collection, University of Pennsylvania and Pennsylvania Historical and Museum Commission, 555.1
Figure 97

73. *Sketches from the river, Dacca*, March 1963
pencil on paper envelope
18.7 x 13 cm
Louis I. Kahn Collection, Architectural Archives of the University of Pennsylvania, Gift of Henry Wilcots, 1994, 650.1.1
Figure 98

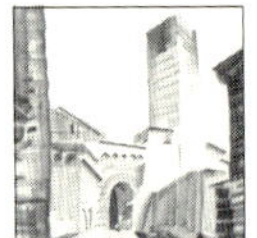

NOTES

Works frequently cited in the essays by Lewis and Johnson have been identified by the following abbreviations:

B&D
David B. Brownlee and David G. De Long, *Louis I. Kahn: In the Realm of Architecture* (New York: Rizzoli, 1991).

Holman
William G. Holman, catalogue entries in PAFA.

JH
Jan Hochstim, *The Paintings and Sketches of Louis I. Kahn* (New York: Rizzoli, 1991).

Kahn Archive
The Louis I. Kahn Archive: Personal Drawings, 7 vols. (New York: Garland Publishing, 1987).

Kahn Collection
Louis I. Kahn Collection, University of Pennsylvania and Pennsylvania Historical and Museum Commission.

Kahn, "Monumentality"
Louis I. Kahn, "Monumentality," in *New Architecture and City Planning, A Symposium* (New York: Philosophical Library, 1944), 577–88.

Kahn, Otterlo
Louis I. Kahn, "Talk at the Conclusion of the Otterlo Congress," in Newman *CIAM*.

Kahn, "Value and Aim"
Louis I. Kahn, "The Value and Aim of Sketching," *T-Square Club Journal* 1, 6 (May 1931): 18–21.

Latour, *l'uomo*
Alessandra Latour, *Louis I. Kahn, l'uomo, il maestro* (Rome: Edizioni Kappa, 1986).

Latour, *Writings*
Louis I. Kahn, Writings, Lectures, Interviews, Alessandra Latour, ed. (New York: Rizzoli, 1991).

Newman, *CIAM*
Oscar Newman, *New Frontiers in Architecture, CIAM '59 in Otterlo* (New York: Universe Books, 1961).

PAFA
Pennsylvania Academy of the Fine Arts, *The Travel Sketches of Louis I. Kahn*, Introduction by Vincent J. Scully, Catalogue by William G. Holman (Philadelphia: Pennsylvania Academy of the Fine Arts, 1978).

Protetch
Max Protetch Gallery, *Louis I. Kahn: Drawings* (Los Angeles: Access Press, 1981).

Reed, diss.
Peter Shedd Reed, *Toward Form: Louis I. Kahn's Urban Designs for Philadelphia, 1939–1962*, Ph. D. dissertation, University of Pennsylvania, 1989.

Scully, Introduction
Vincent Scully, "Introduction," PAFA 1978.

Scully, *Kahn*
Vincent Scully, *Louis I. Kahn* (New York: George Braziller, 1962).

Wurman and Feldman
Richard Saul Wurman and Eugene Feldman, *The Notebooks and Drawings of Louis I. Kahn* (Philadelphia, 1962; reprinted Cambridge, MA, and London: MIT Press, 1973).

KAHN'S GRAPHIC MODERNISM

Michael J. Lewis

1. The definitive monograph on Kahn is David B. Brownlee and David De Long, *Louis I. Kahn: In the Realm of Architecture*. For Paul Cret, see Theophilus B. White, *Paul Cret, Architect and Teacher* (Philadelphia: Art Alliance Press, 1973); Elizabeth Grossman's long-awaited monograph on Paul Cret is to be published by Cambridge University Press.
2. See *Winning Designs, 1904–1927, Paris Prize in Architecture*, edited by the Society of Beaux-Arts Architects with an introduction by John F. Harbeson (New York: Pencil Points Press, 1928). The winners were Douglas D. Ellington (1911), Donald Kirkpatrick (1912), Grant M. Simon (1913), and Harry Sternfeld (1914).
3. Unlike his mentor, Julian Guadet, Cret himself wrote no manual of architectural theory. Nonetheless, his loyal pupil John Harbeson published an extended treatise on the Beaux-Arts method which is a meticulous compendium of the method taught at the University of Pennsylvania. John F. Harbeson, *The Study of Architectural Design* (New York, 1926).
4. Kahn also received two second medals from the New York Society of Beaux-Arts Architects as well as the Arthur Spayd Brooke memorial prize.
5. *University of Pennsylvania, School of Fine Arts, Architecture* (Philadelphia: University of Pennsylvania, n.d. [1928?]), 32. Copy in collection of Susan Glassman.
6. The key event was the "Exhibition of Paintings and Drawings showing the Later Tendencies in Art," held in May 1921, which also highlighted the work of Joseph Stella, Arthur Dove, Marsden Hartley, Edward Steichen, Max Weber, and others.
7. David B. Brownlee, *Building the City Beautiful: The Benjamin Franklin Parkway and the Philadelphia Museum of Art* (Philadelphia: Philadelphia Museum of Art, 1989).
8. William was George Hewitt's younger brother and was chief draftsman in the office of Frank Furness between 1872 and 1876. See George Thomas, Jeffrey A. Cohen, and Michael J. Lewis, *Frank Furness: The Complete Works* (New York: Princeton Architectural Press, 1991), 359.
9. E. L. Austin and Odell Hauser, *The Sesqui-Centennial International Exhibition* (Philadelphia: Current Publications, 1929), 73ff., 479. Vincent Scully's assertion that Kahn was "given the job because he was the best renderer in Philadelphia" should be taken as an exaggeration. Scully, *Kahn*, 12.
10. Mrs. Kahn remembers one aerial rendering of the Fair that hung in their living room for years until the family moved to Clinton Street, when Kahn threw it away.

Mrs. Esther Kahn, interview with author, 29 September 1995 (hereinafter cited as E. Kahn interview).

11. The Palace of Liberal Arts housed a great deal of modernist art, including works by Kandinsky and Malevich that were selected by the Société Anonyme.

12. William H. Lee (1884–1971) studied at the University of Pennsylvania. The only physical record of Kahn's term in the office is a sheet of details for a theater in Philadelphia. Collection of Athenaeum, Philadelphia.

13. For example, Magaziner designed the vast Eva Stotesbury summer house in Bar Harbor. See James T. Maher, *The Twilight of Splendor* (Boston: Little, Brown, 1975), 81. Also see Sandra Tatman and Roger Moss, *Biographical Dictionary of Philadelphia Architects: 1700–1930* (Boston: G. K. Hall, 1985).

14. The classic study of Philadelphia's social elite is E. Digby Baltzell, *Quaker Philadelphia and Puritan Boston: Two Protestant Ethics and the Spirit of Class Authority and Leadership* (New York: Free Press, 1979).

15. Photolithography was the first technology that eliminated the transitional step of carving drawings as woodcuts. By 1868 the *British Building News* was already using the new technology. Still it was not until the turn of the century that photographic halftones became widely used, allowing for the reproduction of wash drawings.

16. Mrs. Esther Kahn, interview with author, 28 December 1995.

17. In the office was another Jewish architect Kahn would have known from the University of Pennsylvania, Alfred Bendiner (1899–1964). Bendiner had been a fellow in Architecture at the American Academy in Rome when Kahn passed through the city in 1928; could he have helped bring Kahn to Cret's attention?

18. This is the one role particularly remembered by Mrs. Kahn, over a half century after the fact. Incidentally, although Kahn was a former pupil and employee, Cret seems to have treated him with his customary Gallic reserve and sense of protocol, and they did not regularly socialize. Mrs. Kahn recalls a single meeting with Cret, late in life, when he was already suffering from his fatal illness. E. Kahn interview.

19. Ibid.

20. These seven works are tersely recorded in the files, and the names do not always correspond to those in Hochstim's catalogue. They are designated as *Torello; Assisi* (JH69); *Study of a tree, Borghese Gardens* (JH30); *Fishing village on Amalfi Coast* (JH55); *Ravello* (JH64); *Entrance to Palazzo Rufolo;* and *A church, Ravello.* The last two listed may be JH85 and 73, respectively, or vanished versions of them. File card, record of exhibiting artists, Pennsylvania Academy of Fine Arts, Philadelphia, PA.

21. 28th Annual Watercolor Exhibition, Pennsylvania Academy of the Fine Arts (1930), catalogue no. 1881. File card, record of exhibiting artists, Pennsylvania Academy of Fine Arts, Philadelphia, PA. JH128.

22. JH, 24.

23. Kahn, "Value and Aim," 4, 18–21; Louis I. Kahn, "Pencil Drawings," *Architecture* 63 (January 1931): 15–17. Hochstim catalogued these drawings, with the exception of an unidentified American landscape in the *T-Square Club Journal* piece, closely related to the honeymoon series from the Adirondacks.

24. Kahn, "Value and Aim," 21.

25. Rayne Adams, "The Drawings of Ernest Born," *Pencil Points* 10, no. 7 (July 1929): 438–52; Rayne Adams, "Some European Drawings by Ernest Born," *Pencil Points* 10 (November 1929): 740–52.

26. JH, 74.

27. Kahn prepared a draft of an article about the Highstown, New Jersey, housing development for *Shelter*, the successor to the *T-Square Club Journal*, but it never appeared. See file, "Louis I. Kahn," Archives of *Shelter*, Collection of the Canadian Centre for Architecture, Montreal.

28. Kahn, "Value and Aim," 21.

29. Kenneth Conant, "Drawing in Pencil," *Pencil Points* 5 (February 1924): 27.

30. Kahn, "Value and Aim," 21.

31. JH127. Preparatory sketches are JH124, 125, and 126.

32. According to the records of the Academy, *Coming storm* (PAFA catalogue no. 1789; JH127) is the only work exhibited by Kahn in 1931. Nonetheless, his oil on canvas *Fishermen's houses, Conca dei Marini* (JH61) bears the PAFA catalogue number 1027 and the date 6 January 1931. It remains uncertain whether or not this was also shown.

33. Kahn, "Value and Aim," 21.

34. During this period Kahn's exhibiting activity dwindled. In 1932 he exhibited a scratchboard portrait of his father at the Pennsylvania Academy, but he seems to have shown nothing in 1933. JH, 204.

35. The University of Pennsylvania graduates were Hyman Cunin ('24), J. Robert Buffler ('25), Joseph Rovner ('25), Willis Humphrey Church ('28/M. Arch. '34), Henry Bryan Stevens ('31), and Urban Anthony Bowman ('32). The other three members were Dominique Berninger, Herman Polis, and George R. Copeland. See *Book of the School, Department of Architecture, University of Pennsylvania, 1874–1934* (Philadelphia: University of Pennsylvania Press, 1934). According to G. Holmes Perkins, other members were Kenneth Day and George Daub. G. Holmes Perkins, interview with author, 17 February 1983.

36. H. Barrett Pennell, Jr., interview with author, 25 July 1995.

37. Berninger was from Alsace-Lorraine and originally a close friend of the Kahn family. Esther Kahn recalls a subsequent falling out over the early support of Berninger's wife for Hitler. Berninger went on to act as supervising architect for the French Pavilion at the New York World's Fair of 1939. E. Kahn interview. Also see *The Book of Small Houses*, compiled by the editors of the *Architectural Forum* (New York: Simon and Schuster, 1936), 130-31.

38. Ibid. Kahn also ran into a number of German émigrés during the mid-thirties. Among them were Alfred Clauss, Peter Blach, and Henry Klumb, with whom he was later associated in Magaziner's office or in the Architectural Research Group. Clauss's wife had worked in the office of Le Corbusier, and Clauss was already in Philadelphia by 1931 when he exhibited a modernist gas station in the T-Square Club exhibition. Klumb was typical of these restless and mobile architects: a German immigrant to America who seems to have briefly passed through the office of Frank Lloyd Wright, then worked with Kahn and Magaziner in 1937 on plans for a prefabricated house before moving to Puerto Rico.

39. Robert Reiss, "Air Castles Rise in 'Clinic,'" *Philadelphia Record*, section 2 (14 May 1934): 1.

40. Soviet architecture was of intense interest in the early 1930s. Among the important early accounts were Alfred H. Barr, "Notes on Russian Architecture," *The Arts* (1929): 1, 103; S. T. Woznicki, "USST—On Problems of Architecture," *T-Square* 2 (November 1932): 80–83; and R. Byron and B. Lubetkin, "The Russian Scene," *Architectural Review* 71 (May 1932): 173–214. See the extensive bibliography in Selim O. Khan-Magomedov, *Pioneers of Soviet Architecture* (New York: Rizzoli, 1987), 592–94; 598–600.

41. Khan-Magomedov, 592–94; 598–600.

42. E. Kahn interview. For Ladovsky, see Kahn-Magomedov, 107–8; 144.

43. Kastner was trained in Hamburg and emigrated to the United States in 1924; he then worked as a draftsman with Raymond Hood and also Joseph Urban. Stonorov was born in Frankfurt and studied in Zurich before emigrating in 1929; in 1932–34 they built the Carl Mackley Houses, America's first fully realized examples of social housing on the European modernist model—and an important early source of inspiration for Kahn.

44. E. Kahn interview.

45. Reiss, op. cit.

46. JH317.

47. Norman Rice, interview with author, 21 March 1983. A childhood friend and classmate of Kahn's, Rice was the first American in Le Corbusier's office in the spring of 1929 when Kahn passed through. He recalled Kahn's striking lack of interest in Le Corbusier's work.

48. *T-Square* suspended publication in 1932 before the cover could be used. Kahn nonetheless remained in close contact with the journal's editor, Maxwell Levinson, and in 1938 served on the board of the reconstituted journal, then dubbed *Shelter*. See the archives of *Shelter* Magazine, collection of the Canadian Centre for Architecture.

49. Reiss, op. cit.

50. Brownlee and Delong, 25, 47. Bernard J. Newman, "Northeast Philadelphia Housing Association," *Housing in Philadelphia, 1933* (Philadelphia: Philadelphia Housing Association, 1934), 22–23.

51. This is confirmed by Henry Magaziner, the son of Louis Magaziner. Henry Magaziner, interview with author, 8 March 1983.

52. This was for the design of the Jersey Homesteads, Highstown, NJ (1935–37). Kahn acted as co-designer and seems to

have had a role in the design of the community school. Here, also, came his first collaboration with an important American painter, Ben Shahn, who contributed the school's mural and who himself moved to Highstown. See Brownlee and DeLong, 26–27.

53. *Factory*, JH261 (where it is misidentified as Collection of the Philadelphia Maritime Museum).

54. File card, record of exhibiting artists, Pennsylvania Academy of Fine Arts, Philadelphia, PA. Apparently this is JH181, entitled *Beach houses in Provincetown*.

55. *Portrait of Esther*, JH286; *Medical lecture*, JH262).

56. See JH248, 250–53.

SKETCHING ABROAD

Eugene J. Johnson

1. Kahn, Otterlo, 213. Reprinted in Latour, *Writings*, 81–99. The passage continues: "Not right then, because I was then dealing with answers, but Le Corbusier raised the question for me, and the question is infinitely more powerful than the answer. So through the question—the power of it—the real thing was brought out."
2. Kahn's paintings and drawings have been catalogued by JH. Some of the travel sketches were shown in an exhibition (PAFA) put together by the Pennsylvania Academy of the Fine Arts.
3. Esther Kahn, interview with Alessandra Latour, in Latour, *l'uomo*, 27.
4. Anne Griswold Tyng, interview with Alessandra Latour, ibid., 43. Tyng was referring specifically to materials, but her statement consistently holds true for all aspects of Kahn's work and thought. Cf. B&D, 55.
5. Kahn, Otterlo, 211.
6. Kahn, "Value and Aim," 18–21. Reprinted in Latour, *Writings*, 10–12.
7. Kahn, Otterlo, 212.
8. See n. 6.
9. There seems to be no systematic study of what it may mean for an architect to have been trained first as a painter, as Kahn, like many other architects, was. From the evidence of his drawings from 1928–29, one may hypothesize that Kahn used his training as a painter later in his career when he needed to make convincing perspective drawings of a project for a client (see the discussion of the Salk Institute, below). Later in life, when designing a new building, Kahn, as his Beaux-Arts training had taught him, concentrated on drawing plans rather than elevations or perspectives. But did he visualize the appearance of a building in painterly terms as he was drawing its plan? If so, what difference might that have made in his designs? The flip side of these questions may well be represented by the fact that we have no plans from his *wanderjahre* (if he drew any plans, he apparently did not keep them). Mark Hewitt, "Representational Forms and Modes of Conception, An Approach to the History of Architectural Drawing," *Journal of Architectural Education* 39 (Winter 1985): 7, provides a starting point for consideration of such complex issues: "Architects, unlike painters, are not involved in directly representing or even abstractly depicting aspects of the visual world, except as they must visualize their invented objects within it. Nevertheless, they must use similar representational forms, types and media. It is important to recognize that both similar and different psychological operations are involved in the two arts."
10. A brief history of the effect of travels in Italy on architects is offered by Paul Kruntorad, "Broadened Horizons: The Paradigm of Travel in Italy," *Lotus International* 68 (1991): 122–28, but there seems to be no systematic study of this important subject.
11. Luca Ortelli, "Heading South: Asplund's Impressions," *Lotus International*, 68 (1991): 24.
12. In the Kahn Collection at the University of Pennsylvania there are three photographic reproductions, in postcard format, of etchings of medieval buildings in Germany: Verkleinerte Wiedergabe aus dem Mappenwerke: Wachauer Bildern von Ulf Seidl. Würthle Verlags G. m. b. H. München-Wien; 9. Aus Krems a. d. Donau; 22. Ruine Weitenegg in der Wachau; 55. Melk a. d. Donau: Alte Verteidigungsturm. "Louis I. Kahn, Personal Greeting Cards, Personal Letters," LIK Box 60, Kahn Collection. It is probable that Kahn acquired these views in 1928. Ulf Seidl (1881–1960) was an Austrian painter and printmaker.
13. Le Corbusier, *Creation Is a Patient Search*, J. Palmes, trans. (New York: Praeger, 1960), 37. The "crucial relationship between drawing, memory and design" is stressed by Norman A. Crowe and Steven W. Hurtt, "Visual Notes and the Acquisition of Architectural Knowledge," *Journal of Architectural Education* 39 (Spring 1986): 3–16. They argue, 7, that one understands and remembers a building better if one draws it and that "these remembered experiences and understandings constitute the architectural memory that we call upon in order to design." Further, 12, they note that the "sketchbook captures thoughts and observations that might contribute to projects yet to arise."
14. Passport #517916, issued 2 April 1928. LIK Box 57, Kahn Collection.
15. According to the lists published in the *New York Times*, several ships sailed from New York to England on the days immediately following 25 April, but it is not entirely clear which one Kahn took, since Plymouth was not given as the final destination for any of them. He may have sailed on 28 April on the Rotterdam, which normally called at Plymouth on its voyages between New York and Holland.
16. A portrait drawing, JH89, is inscribed "June '28 London."
17. LIK interview with Jaime Mehta, 22 October 1973, in Richard Saul Wurman, *What Will Be Has Always Been: The Words of Louis I. Kahn* (New York: Access Press and Rizzoli, 1986), 225. One wonders if the "Komerc" Hotel may have been the one that once belonged to his maternal grandfather that Kahn mentioned in this interview.
18. Kahn's statement on his Latvian visa that he intended to "visit birthplace" presents something of a problem. By all accounts, Kahn was born on the island of Ösel, where his father and mother had settled after Kahn *père* had left his position as paymaster in the Russian army. At the time of Kahn's birth in 1901, the island was part of the Russian province of Estland, which became the independent country of Estonia in 1918. Kahn's father's family was from the province of Estland (not Ösel specifically), and his mother's family was from Riga, in present-day Latvia. (Kahn was therefore born a Russian citizen.) Ösel is the largest and westernmost island in the archipelago that lies to the west of mainland Estonia. At the time of Estonian independence Ösel, the German name of the island, was substituted by Saaremaa, the Estonian name (in the Middle Ages the island had belonged to the Teutonic knights before passing in succession to Denmark, Sweden, and Russia). At no point in that succession of rulers has the island been part of what is now Latvia. According to Kahn's passport, he was in Estonia only to pass through it on July 18, and the passport contains no Estonian visa. Kahn may not—as B&D, 22, would have it—have visited his birthplace on Saaremaa in 1928 at all. Rather, the entire month he spent in the Baltic countries may have been passed among his mother's family in Latvia.

   The confusion lies in the disorganized account of his birth on Saaremaa and of his travels in 1928 that Kahn gave to Jaime Mehta in 1973. In one paragraph Kahn recalled his birth on an island off the coast of Estonia, which we know to be Saaremaa from other sources. Because the next paragraph begins with the statement: "I went to visit my grandmother in 1928," it is easy to assume that he visited her on the island he had just been talking about in the previous paragraph, but a close reading of what he actually said suggests that such an assumption may be unwarranted. In the next paragraph Kahn spoke about his poverty-stricken maternal grandmother, who was supported by her relatively more prosperous children in Riga, whom Kahn identified as "her daughters and sons, my mother's brothers and sisters." The reasons for the grandmother's poverty are explained in a third paragraph that follows the first two: the confiscation of the family hotel by the Russians after the death of Kahn's maternal grandfather.

Kahn, however, did tell the engineer August Komendant, also Estonian by birth, "that his grandmother was at least part Estonian and he had visited her on Saaremaa Island in 1928 or 1929—he did not remember exactly—for a few months." (August E. Komendant, "'First Contact,' Eighteen Years with Architect Louis Kahn," in Latour, *l'uomo*, 117.) Kahn's account of his trip of 1928 to Komendant, however, was probably just as confusing as the account he gave Mehta, and in both cases he was wrong in saying that his visit to his grandmother had lasted for months.

19. His memory that he had spent "months" on his grandmother's floor (see n. 18 above) is not reliable.

20. B&D, 47, n. 17. It is not clear how seriously we should take this claim, given Kahn's complete lack of interest in seeing Le Corbusier's work when he was in Paris in the spring of 1929 (Michael Lewis interview with Norman Rice). When Kahn pointed to his experience of the German *Siedlungen*, he was being interviewed for a job designing housing projects.

21. The precise date is unreadable.

22. B&D, 23.

23. JH25, JH65 and Holman 5, and JH39 and Holman 4, respectively. Sue Ann Kahn has identified JH65 as Harvard House, Stratford-on-Avon, on the basis of a postcard Kahn had bought.

24. JH18.

25. JH80. Hochstim suggests that Kahn made the drawing from a photograph, and, according to Sue Ann Kahn, he used a postcard that he had purchased in Stockholm as the source for the drawing.

26. JH41 as *Gothic courtyard, England*, Holman 28 as *Europe. 1928*. This drawing awaits proper identification.

27. See n. 20.

28. JH23, Holman 14. Of the 75 drawings listed by Hochstim from this Italian trip, 13 are of sites he did not try to identify. Unfortunately, several of his identifications are inaccurate, as are some of Holman's.

29. Christmas card, LIK to Is Mohl, postmarked Rome, 24 December, but the year is illegible. The handwriting on the card is datable to 1928 rather than to 1950, the only other Christmas season that Kahn was in Rome. Kahn Collection. We are very grateful to Julia Moore Converse for bringing this card to our attention. On it Kahn writes in part: "Today I have a date with a Russian countess with elegant lines. Not doing so bad for a little fellow."

30. It is generally stated in the Kahn literature (as early as the first monograph on Kahn, Scully, *Kahn*, 13) that all of his drawings of Paestum have disappeared. Hochstim, however, photographed one (JH88) when he was in Kahn's office in December 1972. When Hochstim came to publish his catalogue of the drawings, the one of Paestum, like many others he had photographed, had disappeared.

31. Scully, Introduction, 10–20 (reprinted as "Marvelous Fountainheads. Louis I. Kahn: Travel Drawings," *Lotus International* 68 (1991): 48–63; Holman, 23: "What is more revealing than the number of works which were made on this trip [the trip of 1928–29] is the variety of styles and techniques which Kahn made use of."

32. There seems to be no guiding principle behind Holman's groupings of the drawings from this trip.

33. JH35.

34. JH67, Holman 7.

35. Once in Verona, Kahn could have turned east to Venice or west to Milan, and he probably passed through Verona a second time as he moved between the latter cities. It seems slightly more logical, given the fact that we know he also visited Pavia and Piacenza, to postulate that he went first to Venice and then to Milan, from which he traveled through Pavia and Piacenza on his way south to Florence. Such a route is partly confirmed by a recently discovered postcard from Piacenza, on which Kahn had penned an unfinished note to his parents, stating in part that he had recently encountered friends from Penn in Milan. See n. 39.

36. Kahn, "Value and Aim," 19–21.

37. JH97–98. Wurman and Feldman, n. 6, identify JH98 as *1928, Venice, Italy*. Their dates, which can be checked out, are quite accurate, perhaps because they had the benefit of Kahn's own memory when they published this book. Their placing Kahn in Venice in 1928 instead of 1929 is further evidence for the argument that he was there earlier rather than later in his Italian trip. Fortunately the travel sketches they included are reproduced at actual size, since many of those shown in their book have subsequently disappeared.

38. JH101.

39. JH83, called *Romanesque foyer;* I am grateful to Robert Russell for the correct identification, confirmed by Sue Ann Kahn's discovery of a postcard in her father's collection on which he based the drawing. See Lieberman essay for a discussion of this postcard.

40. JH33, Holman 8. JH106, called *Arcade, Italy* and dated c. 1930, is a watercolor of the central arcades of the Ponte Vecchio, looking east toward Uffizi Gallery. On the left of the drawing, the arches of Vasari's *corridoio* are marked by strong black shadows. Presumably this sketch was made in 1928 when Kahn was in Florence. I am grateful to Ralph Lieberman for recognizing the subject.

41. JH70, Holman 15.

42. JH69, Holman 17.

43. JH30 and Holman 12, JH55 and Holman 22, JH64, JH69 and Holman 17. All were graphite drawings rather than watercolors.

44. Kahn, "Value and Aim," 4 (JH69), 18 (JH307, the lithograph, a still life), 19 (JH56), 20 (JH44, 59, and 64) and 21, a drawing of an American landscape scene with trees and gabled houses not recorded by Hochstim.

45. Scully, *Kahn*, fig. 1, called *Siena*. The other was JH93, which Hochstim called *"The Plaza," San Gimignano, Italy* and Scully, fig. 9, identified simply as *San Gimignano*. Kahn published JH93 in 1931. See n. 6.

46. Correspondence about the book is contained in "Braziller, George—Publications (Scully book) 1962," LIK Box 68, Kahn Collection.

47. JH94.

48. I am grateful to Mike Glier for his illuminating comments on these drawings.

49. JH72, called *Town with a castle, Italy*. The Rocca appears at the left side of JH37, a drawing of the convent of San Francesco.

50. See n. 5.

51. Kahn, Otterlo, 211.

52. JH75, correctly identified. Holman 26 called it *Portico façade, Italy*.

53. See n. 72.

54. JH46, called *Rocky coast, Amalfi Coast*. I am grateful to Ralph Lieberman for recognizing the Faraglioni.

55. JH85, Holman 20. The drawing is inscribed "Atrio del Palazzo Rufolo" on the recto.

56. JH30, Holman 12.

57. Esther Kahn suggested that Kahn's sketch of a seated man with a pipe, JH91 and Holman 24, may be of his friend John Richards, whom she remembered Kahn had met up with in Rome in the spring of 1929. If the drawing in question was indeed made in Rome at that time, then Kahn would have been in the city on his way north to France. Certainly the style of JH91 is close to that of the drawings of Roman trees.

58. JH99, 100. Another watercolor impressionist in technique and subject is JH66, Holman 29, which shows the Corso Vittorio Emanuele in Milan, with the spires of the cathedral in the background.

59. JH95 and 96, correctly identified. JH96 is Holman 10.

60. JH27 and Holman 13, *Borghese Gardens, Rome*, and JH31 as *Italian landscape*, and Holman 6 as *Europe. 1928–29*, but actually a view of the Via Appia Antica. See n. 77.

61. Hochstim noted the stylistic similarity between these two works.

62. JH42 as *Town walls, Amalfi Coast*, which follows Holman 21, *Amalfi Coast, Italy*. Hochstim did realize, however, that the subject was probably the same as that in JH40, a graphite drawing that shows the south side of the viaduct, whereas the watercolor shows the north side.

63. JH53, correctly identified.

64. JH49 and 48, respectively, identified as *Coastal town, Amalfi Coast* and *Cliff fortifications, Amalfi Coast*.

65. JH55, 60, and 61. The postcard was recently found by Sue Ann Kahn.

66. JH32, 38, 43, 71, 73, 84, 85. Of these, only JH85 was recognized by Hochstim as being of Ravello. JH64, called *Rustic house, Ravello, Italy*, was recognized by no one to whom I showed it in Ravello, but the countryside around the city is so changed since the late 1920s that what Kahn saw may no longer be recognizable. Because JH64 was identified as Ravello when Kahn exhibited it in 1929 in Philadelphia, one should not dismiss the identification lightly. The drawing is

inscribed "Rustic Houses" in Kahn's hand on the verso. I am very grateful to Prof. Vincenzo Palumbo for his help in identifying buildings and scenes that Kahn drew along the Amalfi Coast.

67. JH71, called *Street scene with a church tower*. A better title might be *Campanile of cathedral and entrance tower of Villa Rufolo, Ravello.*

68. JH85, Holman 20, correctly identified thanks to inscription on recto.

69. JH84, called *Passage, Italy.*

70. In February 1995 parts of the random masonry of the wall were exposed where the stucco covering had fallen off. There was no evidence of earlier holes in the wall where Kahn had drawn the bright patches framed by the dark shadows of the arcades.

71. JH43, called *Tower, Positano, Italy*, which follows Holman 18, *Positano, Italy.*

72. JH73, called *"Chiesa in Rovina," Rovina, Italy*, a misunderstanding of Kahn's inscription on the verso, "Chiesa in Rovina," i.e., "church in ruins." The church has since been restored.

73. JH32, called *Pergola, Italy.* Kahn made a sketch of a town called Torello (see Lewis essay) which *The Blue Guides, Southern Italy*, Findlay Muirhead, ed., (London: MacMillan & Co., 1922), 356, notes can be reached from Ravello by continuing down the Via Annunziata. It is likely that Kahn used this guide.

74. From the center of town a second stepped street, the Via Magruni, descends past the western side of Villa Rufolo. If one follows this street to a level below that of Santa Maria delle Grazie, a groin-vaulted house very similar to the one Kahn sketched in a third watercolor from Ravello appears off to the left (JH38, called *Bay houses, Amalfi Coast*). Such groin-vaulted houses are peculiar (but not unique) to Ravello.

75. JH57, called *Stepped street with a church, Positano, Italy.* JH56, *Stepped street, Positano*, shows a fragmentary view of the Chiesa Nuova from a second stepped street that approaches the building from roughly the opposite side from which it is shown in JH57. JH56 and 57 were published together in Louis I. Kahn, "Pencil Drawings," *Architecture* 63, no. 1 (January 1931): 17, with the caption: "Each of the two drawings shows a street in Positano." JH56, in isolation, graced the first page of text (19) of Kahn, "Value and Aim." I was not able to verify that JH63, *Street, Positano, Italy*, was made in Positano, but it may have been. Two other graphite drawings with stepped streets, JH58 and JH59, also await secure identification. The style of JH58, with many parallel strokes of the graphite stick, suggests that it was made about the same time as the drawings from Assisi and San Gimignano, while JH59 may well have been made later. JH52, called *View of town, No. 1, Positano, Italy*, whatever it may show, does not show a view of Positano. The two lithographs, JH50 and 51, may well be based on a scene Kahn recorded along the Amalfi coast or on Capri, but both must have been made after Kahn returned to Philadelphia. Hochstim dates JH51 "1928–29." JH55 and JH60–61 show fishermen's houses at Conca dei Marini, a town on the coast between Amalfi and Positano. The houses, I was told, were subsequently destroyed by "un'ondata di mare" and rebuilt along somewhat different lines. JH55 is Holman 22, called *Fishing village, Amalfi Coast, Italy.*

76. JH26–30.

77. JH31, called *Italian landscape, Italy*, and assigned a date of 1929, even though the drawing is signed and dated 1928. Holman 6 noted the signature and date but identified the sketch as *Europe. 1928–29.* The scene today is far different from the one Kahn recorded. J. Ripostelle and H. Marucchi, *La Via Appia à l'époque romaine et de nos jours, histoire et description*, 2nd ed. (Rome: Desalée et C.ie, 1908), 236, contains a photograph of the site that corresponds closely to what Kahn drew. Holman 27, *Figure in a landscape*, a watercolor not listed in Hochstim, is now in the Philadelphia Museum of Art. Stylistically it is close to the view of the Via Appia Antica.

78. JH102, called "Cupolas of Basilica di San Marco, Venice."

79. The style of JH31, the view of the Via Appia, and of JH27, *Borghese Gardens*, are so close that they must have been made only days apart. The style of JH26, which probably shows the cypresses that line the edge of the Pincian Gardens above Piazza del Popolo, seems very different. The monochromatic nature of this watercolor suggests a kinship with the *View of Positano*, JH53, and therefore a date in the winter of 1929. Such a date would correspond to the later date one would like to assign to the three graphite drawings of trees, JH28–30, which, as suggested above, seem more advanced than the drawings of trees Kahn made on the Sorrento Peninsula. Perhaps Kahn returned to Rome on his way out of Italy and made more drawings. If that were the case, then JH102, with its Pincian cypress tree on the right and its experimental (for Kahn) use of very wet paper, may also date from the last days of his stay in Italy. It would have been typical for Kahn to make two drawings from nearby places on the same day.

80. Kahn, "Monumentality," 577–88. Reprinted in Latour, *Writings*, 18–27.

81. On the other hand Scully, Introduction, 10, argues that Kahn's travel sketches made before 1950 "have very little to do with Kahn's buildings."

82. Daniel S. Friedman, "Salk Institute for Biological Studies," in B&D, 330.

83. *Kahn Archive*, vol. 2, 540.4. See Friedman, "Salk Institute," n. 12, who was unable to connect the sketch on 540.4 with the travel drawing because the drawing had not yet been published by Hochstim. In the same note Friedman points out that on another Salk sketch, 540.10, Kahn wrote the word "Assisi."

84. Another instance is the plan of Saint Peter's he sketched on a drawing of 1957 for the Philadelphia Civic Center, ibid., vol. 1, 455.1.

85. Ibid., vol. 2, 540.5.

86. He may also have compared this house in his mind with the one-room house his grandmother lived in, near a fish market or fishing dock. See n. 18.

87. For example, JH32, the view of Santa Maria delle Grazie, Ravello, JH38, a groin-vaulted house probably at Ravello, and JH63, called *Street, Positano.*

88. Other examples are JH78, *Church interior*, which probably is not a church interior but a view from a portico (perhaps in the cloister of the cathedral of Amalfi) through a *bifora* into a sunny cortile with a well; JH84, 85, 105, and 106. Something similar occurs in drawings of trees in Rome, JH28 and JH29.

89. JH87, called *View from the Portico, Pompeii.*

90. JH86, correctly identified.

91. JH88, called *Temple of Poseidon, Paestum*, the name by which this building traditionally has been known. This drawing was made from inside the Temple of Hera II looking north toward the Temple of Demeter, which appears in the background.

92. Denise Scott Brown, "A Worm's Eye View of History," *Architectural Record*, (February 1984): 73. Scott Brown could not have known the evidence contained in the travel drawings.

93. Scott Brown's claim, loc. cit., that Venturi introduced Kahn to ideas derived from mannerist architecture is buttressed by the lack of evidence of an interest in such architecture in Kahn's travel drawings, even those from 1950–51.

94. Kahn, Otterlo, 208.

95. For a discussion of the development of Kahn's manipulation of light, see Urs Büttiker, *Louis I. Kahn: Light and Space* (New York: Whitney Library of Design, 1994).

96. Two other drawings, JH97 and 99, show the same church.

97. The other renaissance/baroque structure he drew was Palladio's San Giorgio Maggiore in Venice, also capped by a prominent dome.

98. JH55 and 60, later incorporated in an oil painting, JH61.

99. *Kahn Archive*, vol. 2, 540.18, 540.20.1. They bear a remarkable resemblance to *Torre Saracena at Amalfi* (JH 48) and *Atrani from Torre Saracena.* (JH 49).

100. That Kahn remembered and reused structures and scenes he had drawn years earlier is hardly unique to him. For example, Giuliano Gresleri, "Viaggio e scoperta, descrizione e trascrizione," *Casabella*, 51 (January/February 1987): 8–17, demonstrates that clear relationships exist between drawings of buildings that Le Corbusier made in 1911 and buildings he designed as late as the 1950's.

101. Ibid., 540.179.

102. Ibid., 540.218.

103. Ibid., 540.219.

104. Eugene J. Johnson, "United States of America," in Warren Sanderson, ed., *International Handbook of Contemporary Developments in Architecture* (Westport, CT: Greenwood Press, 1981), 514–15. Kahn's interest in stepped streets, and the architectural progression they create, is clear from drawings such as JH56–59.

105. Kahn's successors for the next dozen years were a diverse and interesting lot. The Academy engaged some leading new architects of the period as well as some

who were more important as teachers than as designers. In 1951–52 the architect in residence was Frederick J. Woodbridge, in 1952–53 Jean Labatut of Princeton, and in 1953–54 Pietro Belluschi. In 1954–55 there was Ernesto Rogers, but during the next two years there was no architect in residence. Francis Comstock of Princeton appeared in 1957–58, Nathaniel Owings came in the fall of 1958, and in the spring of 1959 Labatut returned. In 1959–60 Edward Durrell Stone and Francis Comstock each appeared, and in January 1961 Max Abramovitz began a two-month residency. In 1961–62 there was Roy F. Larson, followed in 1962–63 by James N. Hunter, who was succeeded the following year by Edward Larabee Barnes and J. B. Bakema.

106. It was Kahn, in turn, who subsequently pushed for the appointment of Howe as chairman of architecture at Yale (B&D, 45).

107. "Mr. Philip Johnson has suggested your name to us as one who might possibly be interested in a Prix de Rome Fellowship." Mary T. Williams, executive secretary, American Academy in Rome, to LIK, 27 March 1947, "American Academy in Rome," LIK Box 61, Kahn Collection. Howe wrote to Kahn on March 31 urging him to apply (George Howe to LIK, 31 March 1947, "American Academy in Rome," LIK Box 61, Kahn Collction), and again on 10 April he urged Kahn with the following words: "I do think we can have fun together in Rome and as I am a member of the Jury of Selection, I ought to be able to cook up this dish to our mutual satisfaction." George Howe to LIK, 10 April 1947, "American Academy in Rome," LIK Box 61, Kahn collection.

108. Applications were due on 18 April. In "American Academy in Rome," LIK Box 61, Kahn Collection, there is a receipt for registered mail sent on 14 April 1947.

109. "The policy of the Academy is to award its Fellowships in Architecture to promising young men at the beginning of their architectural careers rather than to older members of the profession with a background of successful and distinguished practice.

"I am, therefore, sorry to advise you that in the light of this policy the Fine Arts Committee felt that your application and submissions for a Fellowship in Architecture could not be considered by the Architectural Jury at its recent meeting.

"By the appointment from time to time of Architects in Residence, the Academy provides an opportunity for architects of your age and distinction to visit Rome in the capacity that Mr. Howe intends to serve this coming year.

"It is unfortunate that our announcement did not make this policy sufficiently clear and I regret exceedingly that you should have had the inconvenience of sending us your exhibits without possible reward." Michael Rapuano, chairman, Fine Arts Committee, to LIK, 28 May 1947, "American Academy in Rome," LIK Box 61, Kahn Collection. The announcement of the fellowships in architecture at the Academy in no way suggested that the Academy had a policy of offering fellowships only to architects beginning their careers. A copy of the announcement is in "American Academy in Rome," LIK Box 61, Kahn Collection.

110. Two remarks by George Howe suggest that this was the case: "Your name was already placed on the list of competitors before the new proposal was advanced . . . ." George Howe to LIK, 10 June 1947, "American Academy in Rome," LIK Box 61, Kahn Collection; and "I don't know if you have been apprised of the fact that when Louis Kahn's name was brought up for consideration as a Fellow of the Academy the point of view of the committee as expressed by William Platt was that established architects of reputation were not proper candidates for Fellowship but should rather be considered for appointment as Resident Architects. His submission, therefore, was not considered at all at the judgment of the candidates for Fellowship. . . ." George Howe to Laurance Roberts, 18 June 1947, "American Academy in Rome," LIK Box 61, Kahn Collection. Howe, of course, had been present at the meeting during which Kahn's application was rejected outright.

111. Fikret K. Yegül, *Gentlemen of Taste and Breeding: Architecture at the American Academy in Rome 1894–1940* (New York/Oxford: Oxford University Press, 1991), 34–36 and 224, n. 5 and 6. Certainly the two men given fellowships did not have Jewish names.

112. George Howe to LIK, 10 June 1947, "American Academy in Rome," LIK Box 61, Kahn Collection. At the time, Howe was living in St. Louis, acting as professional advisor for the Jefferson National Expansion Memorial Competition.

113. LIK to George Howe, 13 June 1947, "American Academy in Rome," LIK Box 61, Kahn Collection.

114. George Howe to LIK, 18 June 1947, "American Academy in Rome," LIK Box 61, Kahn Collection.

115. George Howe to L. B. Roberts, director, American Academy in Rome, 18 June 1947, copy in "American Academy in Rome," LIK Box 61, Kahn Collection. Howe's disappointment at Kahn's rejection as a fellow lingered, as three postcards from Howe to Kahn reveal:

"Dear Lou—I wish you could have come to stay with me in Rome! Everything going well—I hope with you too. Best to all at Cube 12. GH." George Howe to LIK, date illegible, "Louis I. Kahn Personal Greeting Cards, Personal Letters" LIK Box 60, Kahn Collection.

"Dear Lou, Thanks for the wishes, sketch, and confidence. It was wonderful to see you again. Love to A. Tyng. Happy Year. GH. Amac. Rome 2.I.49" George Howe to LIK, 2 January 1949, "Louis I. Kahn Personal Greeting Cards, Personal Letters" LIK Box 60, Kahn Collection.

"Dear Louis. Terribly sorry to hear about your back! Hope it's all right again. I miss you a lot over here. We could have had fun. Best GH." George Howe to LIK, date illegible, "American Academy in Rome," LIK Box 61, Kahn Collection.

116. Mary T. Williams to LIK, 1 December 1949, LIK Box 61, Kahn Collection.

117. The envelope, with the application enclosed, was mailed to Kahn on 30 November 1949. The empty application still lies in the envelope. Fulbright Application for Academic Year 1950–51, "American Academy in Rome," LIK Box 61, Kahn Collection.

118. Mary T. Williams to LIK, 30 March 1950, and LIK to Mary T. Williams, 31 March 1950, "American Academy in Rome," LIK Box 61, Kahn Collection.

119. Laurance P. Roberts to LIK, February 17, 1950, "American Academy in Rome," LIK Box 61, Kahn Collection.

120. Mary T. Williams to LIK, 14 November 1950, "American Academy in Rome," LIK Box 61, Kahn Collection. By the fall of 1950 the Academy had a full house of 28 fellows, a situation that taxed the institution's capacity seriously. There were two second-year fellows in architecture, Spero P. Daltas and Henri V. Jova, and three first-year fellows, Joseph Amisano, Dale C. Byrd, and Thomas L. Dawson, Jr. Fellows in other disciplines included James S. Ackerman in art history, Otto J. Brendel in classical studies, and Lukas Foss in composition.

121. Invoice, Thos. Cook & Son to LIK, for ticket on TWA flight 954, leaving New York 30 November and arriving Rome 1 December. "American Academy in Rome," LIK Box 61, Kahn Collection.

122. Frank E. Brown, *Roman Architecture* (New York: George Braziller, 1961), 10.

123. B&D, 74, n. 11, see the appreciation of Kahn and Brown for Roman architecture as parallel, but there is little evidence that Kahn had actually looked carefully at Roman architecture or truly pondered its significance before his encounter with Brown at the Academy. Nor is there any written evidence for Kahn's quest for origins that predates his coming under the spell of Brown's incantations in front of the monuments themselves. Sarah Ksiazek, "Architectural Culture in the Fifties: Louis Kahn and the National Assembly Complex in Dhaka," *Journal of the Society of Architectural Historians* 52 (December 1993): 426, n. 38, notes that the word "institutions" does not appear in Kahn's written statements about his projects before 1958 but does appear consistently thereafter. People who knew Kahn at the time insist, she adds, that he had been using the word long before 1958. In Kahn, a late bloomer if ever there were one, ideas were often slow to mature.

124. Louis I. Kahn, "Spaces Order and Architecture," *The Royal Architectural Institute of Canada Journal*, 34, 10 (October 1957): 375–77. Reprinted in Latour, *Writings*, 75–80.

125. Brown, 30.

126. Louis I. Kahn, "Order in Architecture," *Perspecta 4: The Yale Architectural Journal* (1957): 58–65. reprinted in Latour, *Writings*, 72–75.

127. Brown, 30.

128. Kahn, "Order in Architecture."

129. JH331, called *Pompeii*. The drawing may not show Pompeii, but it was certainly made in that part of the world. I am very grateful for the help of Malcolm Bell, William MacDonald, and Miranda Marvin in trying to establish the subjects of these drawings.

130. JH332, Holman 54, as *Italian landscape*,

the words inscribed on the sketchbook mount.

131. JH333. The togate figure on a tall pedestal, seen against stumps of columns, is certainly reminiscent of the figures of Roman worthies who stand in the piazzale, surrounded by similar stumps of columns. What the forms behind the broken column may represent is still unclear.

132. JH334. As Hochstim rightly pointed out, there is a surreal quality to this drawing, accentuated by the hornlike shapes of the projecting masonry at the tops of two of the structures. Similar hornlike projections graced the Biblioteca Greca in Kahn's day (see Salvatore Aurigemma, *Villa Adriana* [Rome: Istituto Poligrafico dello Stato, 1961], figs. 43 and 49, which reproduce photographs taken before 1955), but they have subsequently disappeared. The dark "nose" at the right of the drawing seems to be Kahn's invention.

133. JH335. Everyone to whom I have shown this drawing thinks of Ostia, but as yet the location of the wall has not been established.

134. JH408, Holman 78, who gave it the erroneous title *Interior, Egypt*. Hochstim followed Holman by including the sketch in the section of his catalogue devoted to drawings Kahn made in Egypt, but the subject is certainly Roman. Everyone to whom I have shown this drawing thinks of the Baths of Caracalla, but the mosaic in the drawing is not to be found at the baths today. Moreover, the niches at Caracalla are all raised above the level of the pavement rather than at the level Kahn shows here.

135. JH409, Holman 74, erroneously titled *Interior, Egypt*. Again Hochstim followed Holman's identification. William MacDonald kindly identified the type of building this drawing shows. Hochstim suggests that both of these drawings may have been made after Kahn returned from Italy, a possibility that should not be discounted.

136. B&D, 50.

137. Daniel S. Friedman, "Salk Institute for Biological Studies," in B&D, 443.

138. B&D, 70.

139. JH337, correctly identified. The draftsman, Thomas Vreeland, recalled that "Kahn had often mused upon Hadrian's Villa in his attempt to conjure the essence of a 'place of the unmeasurable.'"

140. JH336, Holman 53, called *Rome, 1951*. Vincent Scully, "Introduction," in JH, 15, has argued that this drawing is a fantasy that incorporates structures from Mussolini's Foro Italico, although Scully concedes that "on the right . . . a façade remotely suggesting St. Peter's intrudes." He repeated this argument in a talk he gave at the Museum of Modern Art, Vincent Scully, "Louis I. Kahn and the Ruins of Rome," *The Members Quarterly of the Museum of Modern Art* (Spring 1992), 3, and in "Jehovah on Olympus, Louis Kahn and the End of Modernism," *A & V, Monografías de Arquitectura y Vivienda* 44 (1993): 100.) That façade suggests the façade of Saint Peter's because Bernini designed it to harmonize with the façade it flanks. Scully seems to have been misled by a desire to claim Kahn's work as a major source for the architecture of Aldo Rossi. Earlier Scully, Introduction, 17, had called the drawing "a pastiche after De Chirico." Holman got the place right but put Kahn at too low a vantage point and dated the drawing to the wrong year. See n. 120.

141. Postcard, LIK to Office of Louis I. Kahn Architect, undated, "Letters to L. I. Kahn," LIK Box 60, Kahn Collection. Because Kahn mentions that he is about to leave for Greece and Egypt and wishes the office staff a "merry new year," it must have been written around the first of January, 1951.

142. See n. 162.

143. Kahn Collection. The letter is written in pencil on letterhead of the American Academy in Rome. The letter has been excerpted by Reed, diss., 134, and in B&D, 50. Reed, diss., 133–38, is richly documented with material from the Kahn Archive that deals with Kahn in Rome.

144. Kahn, "Monumentality," 77–88. For Kahn and the issue of monumentality, see B&D, 42–44; Ksiazek, 417–20, and n. 4 for bibliography.

145. LIK to American Academy in Rome, 25 April 1947, "American Academy in Rome," LIK Box 61. The statement continues: "I believe that living in the environment [sic] of the great planning and building works of the past should stimulate better judgement [sic] in maturing these thoughts. My ultimate aim is to develope [sic] material for an illustrated treatise of my architectural and planning ideas."

146. Michael Graves, revised version of an interview with Kazumi Kawasaki, originally published in *A + U, Architecture and Urbanism*, November 1983, Extra Edition, in Latour, *l'uomo*, 165.

147. Robert A. M. Stern, *George Howe: Toward a Modern American Architecture* (New Haven: Yale University Press, 1975), 172–74.

148. George Howe, "Flowing Space: The Concept in Our Time," in Thomas H. Creighton, ed., *Buildings for Modern Man: A Symposium* (Princeton: Princeton University Press, 1949), 164–69. Quoted in Stern, 173.

149. Stern, 172.

150. Stern, 173–74. Howe may have been contemplating writing a book about his spatial theories. In 1949, when he accepted the job at Yale, Howe said that he had intended not to enter academia but to live in Europe and write a book. Ibid., 210, n. 50.

151. JH318–320, 324–329.

152. JH339 and JH338, Holman 55, which seems to have been the first of Kahn's Italian pastels to be published: Alison and Peter Smithson, "Louis Kahn," *Architects' Yearbook* 9 (1960): 103, fig. 1. That the Smithsons had requested a reproduction of the drawing in the fall of 1957 is clear from a letter Kahn wrote to Peter Smithson: "Dear Peter: I read your delightful letter and you certainly may look for the material you requested. I have had several color shots made of the Siena drawing and will send you them as soon as they are processed along with all the other things." LIK to Peter Smithson, 10 December 1957, "October 16, 1957–September, 1958," LIK Box 9, Kahn Collection. In reply to a query about how the Smithsons came to know of the Siena drawing and why they found it significant, Peter Smithson wrote: "One always believes there must be an architect somewhere in the United States, and this drawing seemed evidence of that there probably was. How did we know about it? Direct from K., perhaps?" Peter Smithson to author, 13 June 1995.

153. JH340, Holman 56.

154. JH341–347. JH345–347 are reproduced in their actual size in Wurman and Feldman as 11, 25, and 12, respectively. With the exception of JH346, the drawings are all on sheets of paper of the same size, which must have been contained in one sketch pad.

155. JH348, Pisa, and JH349–352, Venice. All of these drawings are the same size, and must have been in one sketch pad.

156. JH353. Holman 58, as *Venice. 1951*.

157. JH354, as *Ca'D'Oro, Venice, Italy*. Holman 57, as *Saint Mark's Cathedral, Venice*.

158. Kenneth Day to LIK, with copies to McAllister and Braik and Office of Louis I. Kahn, 12 December 1950, "Rome 1951," LIK Box 60, Kahn Collection.

159. Louis R. McAllister to LIK, 8 January 1951, "Rome 1951," LIK Box 60, Kahn Collection.

160. For Kahn and city planning see Peter S. Reed, "Philadelphia Urban Design," in B&D, 304–313. Reed, diss., provides the most extensive treatment of Kahn's urban planning that we have.

161. Reed, "Philadelphia Urban Design," fig. 412. Kahn also described his own design for the Penn Center project in Philadelphia as "an attempt to recreate Pisa." Stern, 226.

162. Reed, diss., 136, n. 85, records the memory of one of the Academy fellows, Joseph Amisano, of Kahn's fondness for De Chirico's images of Italian spaces.

163. Drawings that Kahn made in 1947–48 for the Triangle Area Redevelopment for the Philadelphia City Planning Commission show him thinking in almost purely Corbusian terms for a civic center marked by slab towers on pilotis. *Kahn Archive*, vol. 1, 270.40, 270.41, 270.43.

164. Ibid., 455.1. This is one of the extremely rare instances in which Kahn included a sketch of a building he had drawn in Europe on a sheet for one of his own projects.

165. Henry Hope Reed, "Rome: The Third Sack," *Architectural Review* 107 (February 1950): 91–110.

166. "Dear Lou, When I arrived back here I was surprised to find in my mail a copy of that February '50 Review on Rome from a book dealer, which I had been seeking at book stores for some months but had given up hope on. Therefore I can let you keep this one which I am sending under seperate [sic] cover, in case you should want it. I certainly enjoyed my visit. Sincerely, Bob" Robert Venturi to LIK, 11 September 1951, "Louis I. Kahn (Personal) No. 4 (1951) + 1952," Box 60, Kahn Collection.

167. Robert Venturi to LIK, 28 November 1951, "Louis I. Kahn (Personal) No. 4 (1951) + 1952," Box 60, Kahn Collection. Reed, diss., 144.

168. Reed, diss., 142. Reed points out that

Tunnard established the city planning program at Yale in 1950 and in 1952 organized a symposium on monumentality.

169. Between 1937 and 1940 the fellows at the American Academy had enjoyed similar opportunities for travel. See *American Academy in Rome, Annual Report*, "Report of Director," 1936/37 through 1939/40.

170. Laurance P. Roberts to Kahn, 31 July 1951, "American Academy in Rome," LIK Box 61, Kahn Collection. Years later Roberts repeated this comment in a thank-you note for the part Kahn had taken in gifts given to Roberts upon his retirement as director of the Academy: "You don't know with what pleasure I recall your stay at the Academy. It was a high point for that institution, and all its fellows." Laurance Roberts to LIK, 21 May 1960, "Letters—Personal to LIK 1959–1960," LIK Box 65, Kahn Collection.

171. *American Academy in Rome. Report 1943–1951*, 20.

172. Postcard, LIK to Office of Cronheim and Weger Louis I. Kahn, no date, "Letters to L. I. Kahn," LIK Box 60, Kahn Collection.

173. JH, 241, on the basis of an interview with William H. Sippel, the fellow who ended up in the hospital.

174. JH410, 413–421, 425. The last was not done on the spot, but it depends mightily on his having been there.

175. JH411–412.

176. JH410. Dashur is a site south of Saqqara with seven pyramids, of which six may be shown in this drawing.

177. For instance, Scully, interview with Alessandra Latour, 15 September 1982, in Latour, *l'uomo*, 147.

178. Anne Griswold Tyng, interview with Alessandra Latour, 2 May 1982, in Latour, *l'uomo*, 51.

179. JH400.

180. The Karnak drawings include JH399, called *Southeast Pylons, Temple of Ammon, Karnak*, which shows (left to right) the entrance gate and pylons of the Temple of Khonsu, Karnak. I am very grateful to Peter F. Dorman, field director of the Epigraphic Survey, the Oriental Institute, University of Chicago, for identifying the subject of this and several other Kahn drawings of Egypt, and to Rita Freed for her good offices in securing Dr. Dorman's assistance.

181. JH404.

182. JH394–398; the last three of these are very similar. JH394–397, charcoal drawings, were all in one sketchbook, which Kahn also used when he got to Greece (JH369–372 and 381). The sketchbook is now lost, but Hochstim was able to photograph it in 1972. He does not indicate the order of the drawings in the sketchbook. JH398 is a pastel.

183. JH403, identified as *Composition, Temple of Ammon, Luxor.* I am particularly grateful to Dorman for explaining the subject of this drawing: "The colossal column in the drawing is the only remaining column from the kiosk of Taharka that once stood in the middle of the court; the large statue at left is of an unnamed king that stands on the north side of the temple axis at the entrance of Pylon 2 (visible at far left); and the pylon behind the column is the back side of Pylon 1. The view is topographically impossible (the statue would normally be out of sight to the right, and facing in the opposite direction). . . ." Peter F. Dorman to author, 1 October 1995.

184. JH395, Wurman and Feldman 8. Hochstim identifies the drawing as the court of Rameses II, but the view is actually of the court of Amenhotep III, looking toward the west side, with the south side to the left. The break that shows in the Kahn drawing between the west and south sides exists in the court as it now stands.

185 JH401, identified as *Court, Temple of Khons, Karnak.* Holman 78, as *Temple Ruins, Egypt.* I am grateful to Peter F. Dorman for the identification of this drawing.

186. Hochstim, 241.

187. The Athenian drawings include JH369, left side, and JH371–380. JH369 shows the Acropolis from the northwest, with the Erechtheion to the left and the Propylaea to the right, not from the southeast as Hochstim would have it. To those drawings listed in Hochstim should be added that of the Nike Temple and Propylaea recently given to the Herbert F. Johnson Museum, Cornell University.

188. JH375, Holman 61, and JH376. Both are pastels made sufficiently late in the afternoon for the sun to tint the clouds with sunset hues. One shows the enormous columns of the Temple of Olympian Zeus in the left foreground, while the other eliminates those columns and concentrates on the Acropolis itself. On the postcard Kahn sent his office from Greece, both temples, in their entirety, are seen from the southeast. "Letters to L. I. Kahn," LIK Box 60, Kahn Collection. The text of the card reads in full: "outside of Athens and the incomparable Acropolis I have visited Corinth, Mycene [sic] and the Theatre of Epidaurus. The Fellows and I plan a trip to Delphi where much remains exist. In most cases we find the remains are down to rubble with only a few columns standing. But what is standing is enough to imagine the rest —the [?] are so magnificant [sic] and so glorious that imaginative reconstruction is relatively simple (with a few reconstruction maps) I now know that Greece and Egypt are musts. I am very anxious to tell you all about it."

189. JH378, called *Acropolis, Frankish walls*, a restatement of the title of Holman 59, who in turn got it from Wurman and Feldman 18. The walls are not Frankish but date from the fifth century B.C.

190. JH374, called *Acropolis* and bearing an inscription on the verso "Acropolis, Athens." Holman 60, as *Acropolis, Athens.* I am very grateful to Joan C. Malloy, who recognized the site from which this drawing was made and who made many valuable comments on Kahn's Athenian drawings.

191. Kahn made two drawings, JH371–372, from high in the western corner of the Theater of Herodias Atticus.

192. Curiously, Kahn does not seem to have drawn the Parthenon itself on angle, although that is the primary view of the building from the Propylaea.

193. JH379, now missing.

194. JH380, Holman 63.

195. JH373, as *Propylaea, Acropolis.* Holman 62, as *Propylaea, Parthenon (!), Acropolis, Athens.*

196. JH377.

197. JH382, Holman 66. I am very grateful to Charles Williams, director of the excavations at Corinth for many years, for his comments on the sketches Kahn made there, which form the basis for the present discussion of the Corinthian sketches.

198. JH381, where both drawings are shown in the same plate. Unfortunately, the sketches are now missing.

199. JH383, Holman 65.

200. He had already done the same thing with the sky in his pastel of the interior of the Parthenon, JH380.

201. JH384. Holman 64.

202. There is one pure landscape sketch clearly made from Delphi, JH357 and Holman 68, which is a view from the modern town looking southwest toward the sea.

203. JH363, 364, 365, called *The Oracle, Delphi.* It is not clear how much Kahn knew about the original purpose of the hole, nor is it clear who put the rather overblown title, *The Oracle*, on the drawings. Holman 67 titled JH365 *Delphi, Greece, 1951.* He incorrectly placed Kahn above the whole sanctuary. To make these drawings Kahn stood midway between spots from which he made other drawings of Delphi. Above and to the right of the hole in JH363 is the entablature of the round temple that dominates the foreground of JH368, a brilliant charcoal drawing unfortunately now lost that shows the lower sanctuary, a site called Marmaria, and in the background the upper sanctuary, whose temple and theater reappear in JH367. Kahn had not lost the habit he had developed in the 1920s of making a set of related drawings of the same site.

204. LIK in an interview with Jan Hochstim, December, 1972. JH, 27.

205. James S. Ackerman, letter to author, 25 April 1995.

206. Louis I. Kahn, "Order Is," *Perspecta 3: The Yale Architectural Journal* (1955): 59. Reprinted in Latour, *Writings*, 58–59.

207. JH367, called *Sanctuary of Apollo*, which is more accurate than the title *Delphi from Marmaria Greece* which the drawing was given in the exhibition catalogue at Max Protetch Gallery in 1981. Protetch, 16.

208. William Bell Dinsmore, *The Architecture of Ancient Greece* (New York: W.W. Norton, 1975; reprint of 3rd rev. ed., 1950), 339.

209. Dinsmore, 142, suggests that the extremely wide intercolumniations must have been spanned by a wooden entablature.

210. Kenneth Day to LIK, 18 January 1951, "Rome 1951," LIK Box 60. B&D, 426, date this project 1951–56, but there are letters from Day to Kahn dated December 1950 that mention the project, which seems to have been under way before Kahn left for Rome. Kenneth Day to LIK, 12 December 1950, 19 December 1950, 20 December 1950, "Rome 1951," LIK Box 60, Kahn Collection.

211. The second sketch is preserved inside the

pages of Day's letter of 18 January 1951. Kahn first drew in the rectangular shapes of the apartment blocks, then filled in their areas with ink hatching.

212. Kenneth Day to LIK, SS Isle [sic] de France, French Line, Sailing 27 February 1951, Le Havre, France, 21 February 1951, "Rome 1951," LIK Box 60, Kahn Collection. The letter reads, in part: "We are studying the balance of the plot plan in the light of the ideas suggested in the letter which you wrote the day after your return to Rome; the little odd-shaped courts attract me, and we hope to be able to develop forms which will provide both adequate density and commonsense use of the existing paving and utilities."

213. JH25, charcoal and white pastel; JH37, colored pencils and pastel; and JH207, pastel and watercolor.

214. Scully, Introduction, 13.

215. B&D, Fig. 12. For this period in Kahn's career, when he came strongly under the influence of European modernist ideas about architecture, see B&D, 24–28.

216. JH200, 204–208, 211.

217. Holman 53 gives the title of the drawing as *Rome. 1951.* based on the fact that Kahn had incribed the word "Rome" on the sketchbook mount. Holman erroneously believed, p. 41, that all Kahn's drawings from this trip date to the spring of 1951. JH336 follows Holman 53 in title and date. I would prefer to date the drawing to December 1950.

218. JH332 and 333 are on the same size paper, 19 x 22 cm, as that of the view of the Piazza San Pietro, and so they probably come from the same sketchbook. Stylistically, they seem earlier than most of the other pastels from this trip. Both of these drawings are signed and dated 1951. They may have been made during the first days of January, before Kahn left for Egypt and Greece. JH400, 410, and 419, all Egyptian scenes, are also described by Hochstim as being of generally the same dimensions, and so Kahn may have taken this sketchbook to Egypt with him.

219. Both Holman and Hochstim list the Greek before the Egyptian drawings, thus reversing the order in which they were actually made.

220. JH400.

221. Holman 72 notes that the drawing of the temple at Luxor is stylistically "reminiscent of the drawings of Siena."

222. JH405.

223. JH406.

224. JH407 as *Column capitals, no. 3, Karnak, Egypt*, Holman 76 as *Temple interior, Karnak, Egypt*. The drawing is inscribed "Karnak" on the verso.

225. JH413, 416–18, 420.

226. JH418, 421.

227. JH410.

228. JH417, 419, 420.

229. No pastels with architectural elements are known from Delphi, but there is one pastel landscape, JH357 and Holman 68. The inscription on the verso, "Delphi III," suggests that there were once at least two other pastels of Delphi, but these are not known.

230. JH354 says that this drawing "is in step with the abstract expressionism sweeping the American art world at that time."

231. See, for instance, Guston's *White Painting* of 1951, San Franciso Museum of Modern Art, Robert Storr, *Philip Guston* (New York: Abbeville Press, 1986), fig. 21. Kahn must have been aware of Guston as a painter, because Guston had been a fellow at the American Academy in 1948–49 and had won the Joseph Pennell Prize at the 45th Annual Philadelphia Watercolor and Print Exhibition, Pennsylvania Academy of the Fine Arts, 1947. Storr, 112, 120. But the works Kahn might have seen in Philadelphia or Rome would not have been close to Kahn's Venetian drawing in style. The calligraphic vigor of Kahn's drawing may have been inspired by a painter to whom Guston was very close and to whom Guston's mature style was deeply indebted: Bradley Walker Tomlin. Tomlin's abstract calligraphic oil paintings had been exhibited in the 142nd and 144th Annual Exhibitions of Painting and Sculpture, Pennsylvania Academy of the Fine Arts, in 1947 and 1949, and Kahn probably saw them there. Emily Lowe Gallery, Hofstra University, *Bradley Walker Tomlin: A Retrospective View* (Buffalo: Buffalo Fine Arts Academy, 1975), 158. It is also possible that Kahn could have made this pastel after his return to Philadelphia as a memory of his trip to Venice.

232. "Rome 1951," LIK Box 60, Kahn Collection.

233. For an account of Kahn's activities in the 1950s, see B&D, 54–73.

234. A. and P. Smithson, "Louis Kahn," *Architects' Yearbook* 9 (1960): 103.

235. Kahn had been invited by the Dutch architect J. B. Bakema, who organized the congress, in a letter of 15 June 1959, to which Kahn referred in a letter of 17 July to Bakema: "The letter you sent me June 15, has been answered by telegraph stating my acceptance to attend your conference September 7–15. I have no record of the telegraph and therefore I want to reassure you that I am looking forward to your meetings then. I note also that you will be in Washington University from October to January. I welcome you to Philadelphia." LIK to J. B. Bakema, July 17, 1959, "Master File April 1 thru October 30 '59," LIK Box 9, Kahn Collection.

236. According to Kahn's passport of those years, issued 25 April 1958, and renewed 28 January 1960, he landed at Orly on 4 September, departed from Le Bourget for Amsterdam on 10 September, returned to Le Bourget on 14 September, flew to Geneva on 15 September, returned to Orly on 19 September and was admitted to the United States at New York on 20 September. It is not clear if he visited Ronchamp before the CIAM meeting or if he traveled to Ronchamp through Switzerland after the meeting. Kahn Collection.

237. The influence of French neoclassical architects on Kahn's work seems to have been precipitated by the publication of Emil Kaufmann, *Three Revolutionary Architects: Boullée, Ledoux, and Lequeu* (Philadelphia: American Philosophical Society, 1952). See Marcello Angrisani, "Louis Kahn e la storia," *Edilizia Moderna* 86 (1965): 83–93, whose arguments are expanded by Kenneth Frampton, "Louis Kahn and the French Connection," *Oppositions* 22 (Fall 1980): 21–53.

238. Rudolf Wittkower, *Architectural Principles in the Age of Humanism, Studies of the Warburg Institute, vol. 19* (London: Warburg Institute, 1949; 2nd ed., London: Tiranti, 1952). For a general study of the impact of Wittkower's book on the architects of its day, see Henry Millon, "Rudolf Wittkower, *Architectural Principles in the Age of Humanism:* Its Influence on the Development and Interpretation of Modern Architecture," *Journal of the Society of Architectural Historians* 31 (1972): 83–91. Also Ksiazek, 420–21.

239. Frampton, 21–30, argues convincingly that Kahn must have been introduced to the ideas of French structural rationalism, particularly in the work of Viollet-le-Duc and De Baudot, while he was a student in Paul Cret's classes at the University of Pennsylvania. Thus he was intellectually prepared to understand the ideas that Tyng and Fuller presented to him.

240. B&D, fig. 83.

241. The conflict between the two geometries did not resolve itself in Kahn's work until the final version of the plan of Erdman Hall at Bryn Mawr College began to emerge in late 1961 and early 1962. See Michael J. Lewis, "Eleanor Donnelly Erdman Hall, Bryn Mawr College," in B&D, 352–57.

242. Kahn's entry into the competition for the Washington University Library of 1956 utilized the concept of the stepped pyramid. He had drawn the stepped pyramid of Zoser at Saqqara in 1951, JH411–412.

243. De Long, in B&D, 61, suggests that the relaxed planning may have resulted from the presence of Robert Venturi in Kahn's office in 1956.

244. For drawings that show Kahn worrying over the shape of these towers, see *Kahn Archive*, vol. 1, 490.9–490.27.

245. For a discussion of the history of the Richards design, see Alex Soojung-Kim Pang with Preston Thayer, "Alfred Newton Richards Medical Research Building, University of Pennsylvania," in B&D, 324–29.

246. *Kahn Archive*, vol. 1, lxvi, 490.31.

247. Frampton, 41.

248. B&D, 66, fig. 96, 99.

249. Ibid., fig. 102.

250. Kahn always claimed that he never read books; he just looked at the plates. In this case, however, he had talked with Colin Rowe, one of Wittkower's most important students, about the book in December 1955, and Rowe subsequently sent Kahn a new copy of it. Ibid., 79.

251. Newman, *CIAM*, 94–95.

252. Ibid., 90.

253. Ibid., 91.

254. The other, Wendell H. Lovett of Bellevue, Washington, had received a particularly nasty drubbing from Alison Smithson for what she saw as his lack of invention and methodological rigor. Ibid., 48–52.

255. Ibid., 214.

256. Ibid., 210.

257. Representatives of the church first contacted Kahn in April 1959. See Robin B.

Williams, "First Unitarian Church and School, Rochester," in B&D, 340–345.

258. Reed in B&D, 413.

259. Kahn, Otterlo, 208.

260. Ibid., 211.

261. Reed, in B&D, 313, n. 35, points out that in June 1950 Kahn had received an overdue notice from the Yale Library for William Douglas Simpson, *Castles from the Air* (London: Country Life; New York: Charles Scribner's Sons, 1949).

262. Scully, *Kahn*, 39.

263. LIK, "Toward a Plan for Midtown Philadelphia," *Perspecta 2: The Yale Architectural Journal* (1953): 10, reprinted in Latour, *Writings*, 28.

264. LIK, "Order in Architecture," *Perspecta 4: The Yale Architectural Journal* (1957): 59, reprinted in Latour, *Writings*, 73.

265. LIK, "Foreword," dated 26 August 1962, in Wurman and Feldman.

266. The book was exhibited at the Max Protetch Gallery in New York in 1981, and five of the sheets were illustrated in Protetch, pl. 6. The book consists of sixteen pages, of which three are blank. Because some of the drawings cover two facing pages, there are only twelve drawings in the book.

The Hochstim ordering of the drawings makes it difficult to understand their relationship. The first page contains JH437, followed by JH450, which occupies two pages. The next pair of pages contain JH438 on the left and JH452 on the right. Both of these are horizontal drawings; when one turns the book to right the drawings, JH438 becomes the bottom and JH452 the top. These drawings were all made while Kahn stood inside the walls of the barbican of the Château Comtal or on the bridge that leads to it. The bridge is visible in JH438 and JH437, and Kahn stood on it to draw JH450.

Next comes a pair of blank sheets, followed by JH456 on the left page and a blank page to the right. JH456 shows a detail of the Tour Saint Nazaire, which is across town from the Château Comtal, and so we seem to have a logical break in the sequence of drawings. JH456 is followed by JH443, which occupies two pages. Across the fold, Kahn drew the same Tour Saint Nazaire shown in a detail on the preceding page, and so these drawings are also related to each other in terms of location. On the next pair of pages, JH 451 occupies the left and JH464 the right. JH451 was drawn from about the same spot as JH443, only Kahn had turned to look in the opposite direction. JH464, however, was made at an entirely different location, the Tour Carrée de l'Evêque. At this point the seemingly logical sequence of drawings completely breaks down. On the next left hand page one finds JH466, upside down in relation to the rest of the drawings in the book and out of sequence as well, since it shows a view taken only a few paces to the left of where Kahn stood in front of the Château Comtal to make JH452. Opposite JH466 is JH454, right side up in terms of the rest of the book. Here we are back to the inner walls at the south angle of the city, of which JH451 is also a view, but from a different point on the walls. The last page contains an interior of the Tour Carrée de l'Evêque, the same tower of which we get a disorienting view in JH464. All of this suggests that Kahn started off using the first few pages of the book in sequence. Then he got distracted, turned the book around, and drew JH466 upside down. Then he moved across town and sketched in two other locations, around the Tour Saint Nazaire and the Tour Carrée de l'Evêque, opening the sketch book somewhat at random as he did so.

267. Hochstim's organization of the Carcassonne drawings obscures the relationships the drawings have among themselves in terms of location. Thanks to the intimate knowledge of Carcassonne possessed by Veronique Barthes, a guide to the fortifications, we can now identify almost all the drawings and organize them according to sites within the city.

Porte d'Aude: JH436, Porte d'Aude from the north; JH453, Battlements of Porte d'Aude, with Château Comtal in background; JH449, Porte d'Aude and Château Comtal.

Château Comtal: JH437–440, Towers, gate and bridge of Château Comtal from the barbican; JH448, Château Comtal, Tour Pinte, and western walls; JH450, Towers of Château Comtal, moat and barbican; JH452, Château Comtal, Tour de Saint Paul, Tour Pinte, and southern Tour de la Porte; JH466, Château Comtal, Cour du Midi, and Tour Pinte.

Tour Saint Nazaire and environs: JH443–445, Bell tower of the Church of Saint Nazaire, Tour Saint Nazaire, and towers of the inner wall (the tall, ghostly form is the late gothic tower of Church of Saint Nazaire); JH446–447, In the Lices, looking west past Tour and Porte St. Nazaire; JH451, Inner walls at southwest corner of city that surround Roman Theater; JH454 and 455, Inner wall at southwest angle of city (cf. 451); JH456 and 457, Tour Saint Nazaire and stairs that go up from Theater; JH460, Tour Saint Nazaire, detail, showing rusticated masonry.

Tour Carrée de l'Evêque: JH464, Interior of the Tour Carrée de l'Evêque; JH465, Room with wooden ceiling in the Tour Carrée de l'Evêque.

Looking out from city: JH458 and 459, Looking west across walls to tower of Church of Saint Vincent in lower city.

In the Lices: JH441, In the Lices, looking south from the Porte Narbonnaise.

Unidentified: JH433–434 are landscapes that have not been identified; JH461, 462, and 463 are hard to identify because they show such small details; JH442, Holman 88, is also difficult to identify; Veronique Barthes thinks it is not Carcassonne, but the drawing is inscribed "Carcassonne" in faint pencil on the lower right. Perhaps it is one of the "invented shapes"of which Kahn wrote in 1962.

268. LIK, "Order in Architecture," *Perspecta 4: The Yale Architectural Journal* (1957): 59, reprinted in Latour, *Writings*, 73.

269. One or more of these towers appears in JH437–440 and JH452.

270. JH438–440.

271. JH460.

272. JH474–475.

273. Pierre de Gorsse, *Albi Cordes* (Paris: Éditions Alpina, 1954), 8–9. "Loose Material Found Unfiled 1/2/86 (PSR)," LIK Box 68, Kahn Collection. The drawing is JH478.

274. These skeletal structures go back to Kahn's proposal for a large steel skeletal structure in Kahn, "Monumentality." Curiously, in his otherwise very thorough study of Kahn's relations to French architectural tradition, Frampton, 32–36, points out the relationship of Kahn's proposal to Beauvais cathedral and Choisy's diagram thereof, but he fails to consider the only drawings Kahn ever seems to have made of French buildings, those of Albi, Carcassonne, and Ronchamp.

275. JH467–471. Hochstim arranged the drawings in an order in which he suggests Kahn made them, but equally good arguments can be adduced for other sequences.

276. Eugene J. Johnson, "A Drawing of the Cathedral of Albi by Louis I. Kahn," GESTA 25 (1986): 164.

277. I am grateful to Ed Epping for suggesting this relationship between the spaces constructed in Kahn's drawings and the spaces constructed in his buildings.

278. LIK, "Foreword," in Wurman and Feldman.

279. Johnson, 161.

280. LIK, "Order in Architecture," *Perspecta 4: The Yale Architectural Journal* (1957): 59, reprinted in Latour, *Writings*, 73.

281. LIK, "Toward a Plan for Midtown Philadelphia," *Perspecta 2: The Yale Architectural Journal* (1953): 23, reprinted in Latour, *Writings*, 45.

282. In this respect it is interesting that Kahn's office did not supply Scully with an Albi or Carcassonne drawing for Scully's monograph of 1962, even though Scully, *Kahn*, 41, talks about Kahn's interest in Carcassonne, which he illustrates (pl. 127) with a bird's-eye view from Viollet-le-Duc. Indeed, in 1962 Scully seems not to have been informed of Kahn's sketching expedition to Carcassonne and Albi.

283. Le Corbusier et Pierre Jeanneret, *oeuvre complète 1910–1929* publiée par W. Boesiger et O. Stonorov (Zurich: Les Éditions d'Architecture, 1930).

284. B&D, 52.

285. Ibid.

286. Ibid., 58.

287. *Light Is the Theme: Louis I. Kahn and the Kimbell Art Museum* (Fort Worth: Kimbell Art Foundation, 1975).

288. He did, however, continue to collect images of buildings by buying slides, three of which, probably acquired while he was visiting vernacular structures in Britain in the company of the architect James Stirling in the early 1960s, are reproduced in Ksiazek, figs. 7, 9, 11.

IN THE FOOTPRINTS OF THE MASTER: The Photographic Campaign

Ralph Lieberman

1. Extensive restoration work on the palace was begun in the mid-nineteenth century and finished in 1909 (see *Comune di Piacenza. Gotico, Neogotico, Ipergotico: architettura e arti decorative a Piacenza, 1856–1915*, a cura di Marco Dezzi Bardeschi [Bologna: Grafis Edizioni, 1984], especially Marco Dezzi Bardeschi, "Il Palazzo Gotico," 114–29).
2. A photograph dating from the late 1880s shows the arcade in question still open (ibid., 124, fig. 17); the earliest photograph made after the restoration that we have been able to locate dates from 1932 and shows the arcade bricked up, with windows in each bay, as it appears today, but as there is no record of restoration work of this sort after 1909, it seems safe to assume that it was closed by then. Kahn could only have known it was once open from an old postcard view.
3. JH104.

SELECT BIBLIOGRAPHY

Angrisani, Marcello. "Louis Kahn e la storia." *Edilizia Moderna* 86 (1965): 83–93.

Brown, Jack Perry. *Louis I. Kahn: A Bibliography.* New York: Garland, 1987.

Brownlee, David B., and David G. De Long. *Louis I. Kahn: In the Realm of Architecture.* New York: Rizzoli, 1991. (n.b. This is now the standard work on Kahn, with extensive bibliography.)

Büttiker, Urs. *Louis I. Kahn: Light and Space.* New York: Whitney Library of Design, 1994.

Frampton, Kenneth. "Louis Kahn and the French Connection." *Oppositions* 22 (Fall 1980): 21–53.

Hochstim, Jan. *The Paintings and Sketches of Louis I. Kahn.* New York: Rizzoli, 1991.

Johnson, Eugene J. "A Drawing of the Cathedral of Albi by Louis I. Kahn." *GESTA* 25 (1986): 159–65.

Kahn, Louis I. *Louis I. Kahn, Writings, Lectures, Interviews.* Edited by Alessandra Latour. New York: Rizzoli, 1991.

———. "Monumentality." In *New Architecture and City Planning, A Symposium,* edited by Paul Zucker, 77–88. New York: Philosophical Library, 1944.

———. "Pencil Drawings," *Architecture* 58, 1 (January 1931): 15–17.

———. "The Value and Aim of Sketching." *T-Square Club Journal* 1, 6 (May 1931): 4, 19–21.

Kimbell Art Museum. *Light Is the Theme: Louis I. Kahn and the Kimbell Art Museum.* Fort Worth: Kimbell Art Foundation, 1975.

Ksiazek, Sarah. "Architectural Culture in the Fifties: Louis Kahn and the National Assembly Complex in Dhaka." *Journal of the Society of Architectural Historians* 52 (December 1993): 416–35.

Latour, Alessandra. *Louis I. Kahn, l'uomo, il maestro.* Rome: Edizioni Kappa, 1986.

Lobell, John. *Between Silence and Light: Spirit in the Architecture of Louis I. Kahn.* Boulder: Shambhala, 1979.

Loud, Patricia Cummings. *The Art Museums of Louis I. Kahn.* Durham, NC, and London: Duke University Press, 1989.

"Louis I. Kahn," *A & V, Monografías de Arquitectura y Vivienda* 44 (1993).

The Louis I. Kahn Archive. *Personal Drawings.* 7 vols. New York and London: Garland, 1987.

Max Protetch Gallery. *Louis I. Kahn: Drawings.* Los Angeles: Access Press, 1981.

Newman, Oscar. *New Frontiers in Architecture: CIAM '59 in Otterlo.* New York: Universe Books, 1961.

Pennsylvania Academy of the Fine Arts. *The Travel Sketches of Louis I. Kahn.* Introduction by Vincent J. Scully, catalogue by William G. Holman. Philadelphia: Pennsylvania Academy of the Fine Arts, 1978.

Reed, Peter Shedd. *Toward Form: Louis I. Kahn's Urban Designs for Philadelphia, 1939–1962.* Ph.D. dissertation. University of Pennsylvania, 1989.

Ronner, Heinz, and Sharad Jhaveri. *Louis I. Kahn: Complete Work, 1935–1974.* 2nd ed. Basel and Boston: Birkhäuser, 1987.

Scully, Vincent. *Louis I. Kahn.* New York: George Braziller, 1962.

———. "Louis I. Kahn and the Ruins of Rome,"*The Members Quarterly of the Museum of Modern Art* (Spring 1992): 1–13.

———. "Marvelous Fountainheads. Louis I. Kahn: Travel Drawings," *Lotus International* 68 (1991): 48–63. Reprint of Introduction to Pennsylvania Academy of the Fine Arts, *The Travel Sketches of Louis I. Kahn,* 1978.

Sekler, Eduard. "Public Institutions, Kahn, Louis I. Reading of Volume-0," *Journal of Architectural Education* 49 (September 1995): 10–21.

Smithson, Alison and Peter. "Louis Kahn." *Architects' Yearbook* 9 (1960): 102–118.

Tentori, Francesco. "Ordine e forma nell'opera di Louis Kahn." *Casabella* 241 (July 1960): 2–17.

Tyng, Alexandra. *Beginnings: Louis I. Kahn's Philosophy of Architecture.* New York: John Wiley & Sons, 1984.

Wurman, Richard Saul. *What Will Be Has Always Been: The Words of Louis I. Kahn.* New York: Access Press and Rizzoli, 1986.

Wurman, Richard Saul, and Eugene Feldman. *The Notebooks and Drawings of Louis I. Kahn.* Philadelphia: Falcon Press, 1962. Reprint. Cambridge, MA, and London: MIT Press, 1973.

CREDITS

Williams College Museum of Art

Exhibition and Catalogue Project Staff

Diane Hart Agee, *registrar*

Kristina Almquist, *catalogue designer*

Will Eikleberry, Silvina Fernandez-Duque, Katie Ganino, Vicki Hsueh, Susan Mun, Svetla Stoeva, *undergraduate assistants*

Fort Orange Press, Albany, New York, *catalogue printer*

Marion Goethals, *assistant director*

Scott Hayward, *preparator*

Stefanie Spray Jandl, *Andrew W. Mellon curatorial associate*

Eugene J. Johnson, *guest co-curator*

Mary La Ruffa, Isabel Taube, *graduate assistants*

Michael J. Lewis, *guest co-curator*

Ralph Lieberman, *site photographer*

Brenda Niemand, *editor*

Hideyo Okamura, Greg Smith, Gary Sojkowski, *art handlers*

Amy Reichert, *exhibition designer*

Deborah M. Rothschild, *project director*

Zelda Stern, *development*

Catalogue Photography

All art photographs by Michael Agee, except where otherwise credited

Museum Staff

Diane Hart Agee, *registrar*

Kenneth Blanchard, *security monitor*

Amber Chand, *museum shop manager*

Merritt Colaizzi, *education assistant*

Marion M. Goethals, *assistant director*

Ann Greenwood, *Prendergast associate*

Scott Hayward, *preparator*

Stefanie Spray Jandl, *Mellon curatorial associate*

Robert Kove, *security monitor*

Silvio J. Lamarre, *security monitor*

Dorothy Lewis, *senior accounting clerk*

Robert McDonough, *security officer*

Tina Maher, *shop assistant*

Nancy Mowll Mathews, *Eugénie Prendergast curator*

Brenda Niemand, *public relations assistant*

Hideyo Okamura, *art handler*

Amy Oliver, *American catalogue researcher*

Vivian Patterson, *associate curator, collections management*

Judith Raab, *assistant to the director*

Barbara Robertson, *director of education*

Deborah M. Rothschild, *curator of exhibitions*

Linda Shearer, *director*

Gary J. Sojkowski, *art handler*

Marilyn Superneau, *security officer*

Rachel Tassone, *catalogue assistant*

Amy Tatro, *museum secretary*

Elizabeth Thoresen, *secretary*

Theodore Wrona, *security supervisor*

Visiting Committee

John D. Coffin, *chair*

Michael S. Engl, *co-vice chair*

Stephen D. Paine, *co-vice chair*

Lucinda Barnes, Milo C. Beach, Nancy K. Breslin, Charles M. Collins, Michael A. Dively, Margaret Stone Drewyer, Romeyn Everdell, Michael Glier, Linda B. Goldstein, Elaine P. Kend, Katy Kline, Harvey R. Plonsker, Earl A. Powell III, Martha D. Tucker, David P. Tunick, James N. Wood, Stuart B. Young

Members Emeriti

S. Lane Faison, Jr., Whitney S. Stoddard

Advisory Members

Stephen R. Birrell, *vice president for Alumni Relations and Development, Williams College;* Charles Haxthausen, *director, Graduate Program in Art History, Williams College;* Robert L. Volz, *custodian, Chapin Library of Rare Books, Williams College;* Michael Conforti, *director, Clark Art Institute;* Gary C. Burger, *director, Williamstown Art Conservation Center*

Members Ex Officio

Harry C. Payne, *president, Williams College;* Carol J. Ockman, *art history*, and Barbara E. Takenaga, *studio art, co-chairs, Department of Art;* Keith C. Finan, *associate provost;* Linda Shearer, *director, Museum of Art*